POWER TOOLS

for Studio One 2

POWER TOOLS

for Studio One 2

Master PreSonus' Complete Creation and Production Software
Volume 1

INCLUDES DVD-ROM!

Larry the O

HAL LEONARD BOOKS
An Imprint of Hal Leonard Corporation

Published in 2012 by Hal Leonard Books
An Imprint of Hal Leonard Corporation
7777 West Bluemound Road
Milwaukee, WI 53213

Trade Book Division Editorial Offices
33 Plymouth St., Montclair, NJ 07042

Hammond D. Puppy photos by Angela Oppenheimer. Used with permission.

Printed in the United States of America

Book design by Kristina Rolander

Library of Congress Cataloging-in-Publication Data is available upon request.

ISBN 978-1-45840-226-4

www.halleonardbooks.com

Contents

Acknowledgments

I'll keep the list of thanks short, if well deserved: the long-suffering Bill Gibson, eminently reasonable John Cerullo, project editor Bernadette Malavarca, and old friend Brad Smith at Hal Leonard Publishing; Jonathan Hillman at PreSonus; my brother, Steve Oppenheimer, who supported me both as brother and as PR Manager for PreSonus (and got me started on doing a Studio One book in the first place); my wife, Angela; my puppy, Hammond; and the entire West Stockdale Accordion Orchestra and Catering Society for loaning me four dollars for a double cappuccino.

Okay now—back to work. All of you.

Larry the O
January 2012

Introduction

MEET THE NEW KID ON THE BLOCK

PreSonus Studio One 2 is the newest and one of the most interesting digital audio workstation (DAW) programs, and this book is your guide to getting started working with it. Created by PreSonus in partnership with the design and programming team that created Nuendo and parts of Cubase, Studio One 2 has quickly gained popularity since its release for its ease of use, workflow orientation, and great sound. One of the few major DAWs available for both Windows and Mac OS, Studio One 2 was recently released—the second major upgrade for the program in the few years it has been out. *Power Tools for Studio One 2* is not just the first major book to cover this fresh new program, but it also gives the first detailed look at the new features introduced in Studio One 2.

Flavors and Features

Studio One 2 comes in three flavors: Studio One 2 Artist, Studio One 2 Producer, and Studio One 2 Pro. Producer adds ReWire, AU/VST plug-ins, MP3 import and export, and more third-party content to Artist. Naturally, the step up to Pro brings a host of powerful features not found in either Producer or Artist. Make no mistake, though, Producer and Artist are more than capable tools, and they are available quite inexpensively. In fact, Studio One 2 Artist comes bundled with PreSonus interfaces and mixers. Of course, it is always possible to upgrade at any time, which you may want to do once you are familiar with Studio One 2 and want more.

Here are a few of the reasons Studio One 2 has garnered such quick acceptance since its release in 2009. Features available exclusively in Pro are indicated as such.

CROSS-PLATFORM COMPATIBILITY

- Compatible with ASIO or Windows Audio under Windows OS and Core Audio on the Mac.

HIGH AUDIO QUALITY

- **Brand-new audio engine.** Most of the major DAWs were created years ago and their code base has been updated, patched, and expanded since then. Well-structured software can always be grown over time, but, as a brand-new code base, Studio One 2 was built from the ground up to take advantage of technology like multiple processors, which didn't exist when the older DAW giants were born. This makes Studio One 2 very efficient and responsive.
- **64-bit operation (Pro only).** Here's another example of a new code base incorporating at its base new technology developments. Studio One 2 Pro provides both a full 64-bit audio path (including the bundled PreSonus plug-ins) for finer detail in the sound, and 64-bit memory addressing, to facilitate large track counts and other memory-hungry services. Studio One 2 Pro even switches to 32-bit processing on-the-fly to accommodate third-party 32-bit plug-ins.
- **Great bundled plug-ins.** Studio One 2's bundled plug-ins sound great and cover a lot of territory. The basic EQ and compression plugs are good enough to throw around like candy. The nice part about that is that you can save your gourmet plugs that have higher CPU requirements for the most critical applications.
- **Compatible with other formats.** Studio One 2 is compatible with VST 2, VST 3.1, and Audio Units plug-in formats, as well as ReWire (Producer and Pro).

UI AND WORKFLOW

- **Completely integrated recording, editing, mixing, and mastering** (mastering in Pro only). The mixing/mastering integration is unprecedented; it's very easy to open a mix for tweaking and then instantly update the mix in the mastering session.
- **Integrated workspace.** The Song window encompasses Arrange, Edit, Mix, and Browser views in a single window.
- **Drag-and-drop until you're blue in the face.** Drag a file, effect, or virtual instrument from the Browser and drop into a track or onto a channel strip to instantiate it. Or go the other way around and drag any of those things to the Browser. Clips can be dragged to the desktop as well.
- **Versions feature.** Instead of saving a new copy of a session document every half hour for safety, you can simply save a new version within the same document and restore it any time it is needed. Get started working this way, and you'll never go back to saving copies.
- **Unlimited Undo.** You know you'll need it.
- **Start page.** Provides convenient access to audio hardware setup, opening existing Songs and Projects or creating new ones, downloading updates, tutorials, and a PreSonus news feed.

- **Automatic time-stretching of imported audio** that contains tempo information to fit it to the Song's tempo.

AND OTHER COOL STUFF

- **Scoring to QuickTime video.** (Pro only)
- **Tight integration with PreSonus hardware.** Low-latency monitoring in PreSonus FireStudio-series interfaces shows up in Studio One 2. Studio One 2 also detects PreSonus interfaces and provides a selection of I/O configuration presets for them.
- **Unprecedented integration between recording/mixing and mastering.** Realize while mastering that your mix needs a tweak? Easy. Open your mix, make your tweak, and update the file on the mastering side with just a few keystrokes. Nothing else like it exists. (Pro only)
- **SoundCloud integration** (Pro only). Songs or Projects can be exported directly from Studio One 2 Pro to SoundCloud, making it a snap to post mixes to Facebook, a podcast, or elsewhere in "the cloud."
- **Integration with Celemony Melodyne.** The industry's leading pitch-manipulation software is now tightly intertwined with Studio One 2 in a way that no other program matches. Moving audio from a Studio One 2 track into Melodyne is fast and seamless.
- **Included content and instruments.** Gigabytes of loops and samples, plus great third-party instruments like Native Instruments Kore Player and Guitar Rig, and EZ Drummer.

Yeah. Right about now, you ought to be feeling really good that you bought Studio One 2!

ABOUT THIS BOOK

Power Tools for Studio One 2 will give you a solid introduction to Studio One 2 and show you how to get around it to record, edit, mix, and master your audio. It will also give you access to the hardcore, not-entirely-documented features of Studio One 2. *Power Tools for Studio One 2* is not just the first major book about the program, it is also the first and only place all of the new features and hidden power of Studio One 2 are revealed.

Mac and Win

Cross-platform software presents difficulties when writing. Does one give equal emphasis to both platforms? When software is well written, it looks and acts very similar on any platform, but there are always differences. How far do we go to accommodate that?

This book tries to strike a balance, and both Mac and Win machines running Studio One 2 were used in writing this book. However, because the differences between the Mac and Win versions were largely common Mac/Win differences discussed in many other places, it did not seem like time and space well spent to show exact equivalents and screen shots for every case.

Thus, I have not been scrupulously evenhanded. While I strove to strike a balance and do, in fact, give equivalents below and elsewhere, the orientation of the book is a bit more toward Mac, since that is what my primary production machine is. I do not believe it will make this work any less useful to Windows users.

When key shortcuts are given, they will show the Mac modifier keys, but the Windows equivalents will usually be shown in parentheses right next to it.

COMMON MAC-TO-WIN EQUIVALENTS

- Shift = Shift
- Ctrl = Ctrl
- Option = Alt
- Command/Cmd = Windows, Alt, or Ctrl
- Right-click/Ctrl-click = Right-click

What Is in This Book

There is a lot in Studio One 2, much of which has not been documented until now. There is so much, in fact, that *Power Tools for Studio One 2* is in two volumes. The one that is now before your eyes—volume 1— introduces Studio One 2 in detail and shows you how to record, play, and edit with it. While the book is first a guide to the program, it is written with applications very much in mind. This book gets your first track recorded, then steps you through everything from loop recording to drum replacement.

Power Tools for Studio One 2 is written to get you up and working as quickly as possible, then take you into further detail. There is important information in every chapter, even the early chapters that deal with the basics. Where Studio One 2 is unclear or confusing in its terminology, I have created my own terms and names and tried to use them as consistently as possible.

While other major DAWs are at version 5, 6, or 9, Studio One 2 has a sizable and sophisticated feature set that makes it an excellent production environment, especially for music. This book would have to be twice as long as it is to be comprehensive. Well, okay, *Power Tools for Studio One 2 is* twice as long as this book, but the approach taken in this book nevertheless is to go well beyond the fundamentals, but not worry about detail on every single feature.

Here are a few words about each chapter, so you can understand how the book is structured:

- Introduction: That's this chapter, and after this summary, it's over. Simple enough?

- Chapter 1, "On Your Mark": This initial chapter takes you from minimum system requirements for Studio One 2 through installation, getting your interfaces connected, taking your first look at Studio One 2, and all the way to getting some sound out of it. It is a big chapter that lays the foundation for your understanding of the program.
- Chapter 2, "Get Set to Record": Here's where we get everything set up for you to record your first track, including the metronome, input monitoring, and headphone mixes.
- Chapter 3, "Go! Recording with Studio One 2": Record, playback, and overdubbing. Learn how to punch, loop record, and use layers for different takes.
- Chapter 4, "Virtual Instruments and MIDI": This chapter is pretty self-explanatory and tells you about the bundled virtual instruments, gets you going with a drum groove, starts you recording MIDI Instrument tracks, and shows you how to freeze tracks to free up CPU resources.
- Chapter 5, "Basic Editing": Here, you are introduced to Studio One 2's editing tools and how to execute basic editing operations.
- Chapter 6, "Advanced Editing": This chapter takes you further into the big world of editing audio and MIDI, including fades, quantizing, meter and tempo changes, and time-stretching and compression.
- Index: Think it sounds boring? Wait until you're in midcreation and need to figure out how to do something. Nothing gets you back on the road faster than a decent index.
- About the Author: I don't know why. It's just that way.

Wait ... This Is Just Volume I?

Studio One 2 has so much in it that has never been documented that I couldn't get it all in one book. Consequently, *Power Tools for Studio One 2* is in two volumes. I have just finished describing what is in the first volume, which you have before you now. Here is a sneak peek at what will be in volume 2:

- **Working with Loops:** Play with loops much? Sure you do. Here's where you find out how to make loops fit into your Song, whether they are audio or MIDI loops. There is also coverage of PreSonus's proprietary Audioloop and Musicloop file formats.
- **Working with Video:** In Studio One 2 Pro, you can score to a QuickTime movie. Here's where you'll learn how that works.
- **Mixing:** This is a biggie. Studio One 2 has great mixing facilities. From the basics of the Mix view's channel strips to grouping, routing, plug-ins, and control surfaces, this chapter will orient you to mixing in Studio One 2.

- **Automation:** One of the most powerful tools for mixing is automation. Level, mute, effects settings, and virtual instrument parameters are only some of what Studio One 2 allows you to automate. This chapter will spell it all out.
- **Mastering:** This chapter is all about the Project side of Studio One 2, which is all about mastering. Studio One 2 stands out for the ease with which it is possible to go back and make an adjustment in the mix of a Song and then pop right back into mastering with the new mix.
- **Share Your Work:** All done? Great. Now all you have to do is get your music out to the world. Burn a CD directly from Studio One 2, create a disk image, publish for digital release . . . it's all in this chapter.
- **When Things Go Wrong:** Sometimes they do, especially when there's a computer in the picture. This book can't solve every problem for you, but if it helps you solve just one or two, you'll be a much happier person.

1

On Your Mark

GETTING TO KNOW YOUR COMPUTER

Before you begin working with PreSonus Studio One 2, you'll need to be familiar with your computer. Computers range from entry-level models to muscle machines with enough power to create dozens of tracks for simultaneous playback. So before we get too far, it is important to understand what your computer is capable of.

Studio One 2 comes in three versions: Artist, Producer, and Pro. Each version is available for both Mac OS X and Windows. Most of what we cover here are features that are found in all three versions. Where that is not true, it will be noted.

Minimum System Requirements for Studio One 2

MAC

- Operating Systems: Mac OS X 10.5.2 or higher
- Hardware:

  Minimum: PowerPC G4 1.25 GHz or Intel Core Solo 1.5 GHz processor, 1 GB RAM

  Recommended: PowerPC G5 or better or Intel Core Duo or Intel Xeon processor or better, 2 GB or more RAM

WINDOWS

- Operating Systems: Windows XP, Windows Vista, and Windows 7
- Hardware:

  Minimum: Intel Pentium 4 1.6 GHz processor or AMD Athlon 64 (Turin), 1 GB RAM

  Recommended: Intel Pentium 4 2.8 GHz EM64T or better or AMD Athlon 64 3000+ or better, 2 GB or more RAM

WINDOWS AND MACINTOSH SYSTEMS

- Internet connection
- DVD-ROM drive
- Monitor with resolution no lower than 1024 x 768 pixels
- QuickTime software for video features
- Audio interface (or use onboard audio). See the section "All About Interfaces," in this chapter.
- MIDI interface (if you will use external MIDI devices)

REQUIRED MEMORY

While Studio One 2 will run with the memory specification given above, your RAM needs may be considerably higher if you use a lot of virtual instruments (especially some of the really nice, big ones), convolution reverbs, and other plug-ins with high processor demands. Large virtual instruments (VIs) like Native Instruments Kontakt or Spectrasonics Omni need at least 2 GB of RAM to work with, and so it is easy to see how quickly RAM requirements can become an issue.

Buying lots of RAM is almost certainly your most effective solution, but an alternative approach is to make extensive use of bouncing, freezing, and track transformations to free up the resources consumed by some CPU hogs.

REQUIRED DISK SPACE

- Mac Application: 185 MB
- Windows Application: 150 MB
- Content (Optional): Artist: 6.76 GB; Pro: 12.47 GB

Depending on how you record, you can end up with a very large number of files, as well as files that are very large in size. Disk space is relatively cheap, so be sure to buy drives that are large as well as fast.

When you are figuring out how much disk space you need for your system, remember that you will need to back up your precious session data onto different disks. The old computer adage goes that "digital data does not exist unless it is in more than two places," and two copies (double redundant backup) is really the way to go. If, however, you cannot make that happen, be certain you have at the very least one large backup disk with enough space to make a copy of every file in your current projects.

SR/bit depth	pgm dur (min)	MB/min of disk space 1 trk	8 trks	16 trks	24 trks	32 trks
44.1/16	1.0	5.3	42.3	84.7	127.0	169.3
	5.0	26.5	211.7	423.4	635.0	846.7
	10.0	52.9	423.4	846.7	1270.1	1693.4
	60.0	317.5	2540.2	5080.3	7620.5	10160.6
44.1/24	1.0	7.9	63.5	127.0	190.6	254.1
	5.0	39.7	317.6	635.2	952.8	1270.4
	10.0	79.4	635.2	1270.4	1905.6	2540.8
	60.0	476.4	3811.2	7622.4	11433.6	15244.8
48/16	1.0	5.8	46.1	92.2	138.2	184.3
	5.0	28.8	230.4	460.8	691.2	921.6
	10.0	57.6	460.8	921.6	1382.4	1843.2
	60.0	345.6	2764.8	5529.6	8294.4	11059.2
48/24	1.0	8.6	69.1	138.2	207.4	276.5
	5.0	43.2	345.6	691.2	1036.8	1382.4
	10.0	86.4	691.2	1382.4	2073.6	2764.8
	60.0	518.4	4147.2	8294.4	12441.6	16588.8
88.2/24	1.0	15.9	127.0	254.1	381.1	508.2
	5.0	79.4	635.2	1270.4	1905.6	2540.8
	10.0	158.8	1270.4	2540.8	3811.2	5081.6
	60.0	952.8	7622.4	15244.8	22867.2	30489.6
96/24	1.0	17.3	138.2	276.5	414.7	553.0
	5.0	86.4	691.2	1382.4	2073.6	2764.8
	10.0	172.8	1382.4	2764.8	4147.2	5529.6
	60.0	1036.8	8294.4	16588.8	24883.2	33177.6
192/24	1.0	34.6	276.5	553.0	829.4	1105.9
	5.0	172.8	1382.4	2764.8	4147.2	5529.6
	10.0	345.6	2764.8	5529.6	8294.4	11059.2
	60.0	2073.6	16588.8	33177.6	49766.4	66355.2

Fig. 1-1: Disk space usage for a given sample rate and bit depth (resolution).

Hard Disks: USB or FireWire?

DAWs (digital audio workstations) record digital information onto a hard drive that is separate from the one on which the application is installed. Recording and playing audio can occupy much of a hard drive's time, so much so that the application itself and the audio being recorded end up competing against each other using a single disk. Not good.

You can add additional hard drives inside your computer, if there are any unused drive bays, or connect external drives to your computer's FireWire or USB buses. If you install an internal drive, check your computer's specifications to find the fastest drive you can use in your system.

There is much confusion about whether USB or FireWire is better for audio. Many people think that the speed of the bus is all that makes the difference. There are three versions of USB, each much faster than the last, and two of FireWire (with more coming), one at twice the speed of the other, but the bus speed specification is far from the whole story. The ways that the bus is structured and handled have a tremendous impact on actual performance.

For example, a casual comparison of USB 2 (480 Mbps bit rate) and FireWire 400 (400 Mbps) might make USB 2 look faster. The fact is that FireWire's design was more directly aimed at media streaming such as audio recording, so it is both more effective and more efficient at carrying audio. If you're really interested, the difference lies in eye-glazing terms like *isochronous streaming*, *bus clocking*, and *peer-to-peer communications*.

In short, if you choose to use one or more external drives, USB can serve admirably in simple applications like recording and playing back two tracks at a time, or in your backup system, but FireWire is preferable for recording, especially if you are recording multitrack. Many studios use external FireWire drives that spin at 7,200 rpm, connected through the Mac's FireWire 400 or 800 ports.

It is important to realize, however, that USB and FireWire—while the most common drive interfaces—are certainly not the only ones. Other interfaces like eSATA and the new emerging Thunderbolt technology have plenty of speed for audio work, and there are sophisticated drive configurations like RAIDs, SANs (storage area networks), and NAS (network attached storage) for larger setups. Consider your needs and do your homework before committing.

Additional Recommendations and Options

- **Expanded RAM.** Tracks and virtual instruments, among other things, get memory-hungry, so the more RAM you can put in your computer, the better. At least 2 GB of RAM for large virtual instruments is recommended.
- **A MIDI or USB musical keyboard controller for playing virtual instruments.** (Note: A MIDI keyboard also requires a MIDI interface for the computer.) If the controller has inputs for footswitches and pedals, so much the better.
- **A MIDI or FireWire control surface for tactile mixing.** Working with the mouse is the most precise way to mix, but control surfaces can be great for recording and automation moves.

Why does this information matter? Because Studio One 2 won't run properly unless its minimum requirements for the processor, operating system version, minimum amount of RAM, and hard-drive space are met. These are the factors that enable or limit your computer's ability to record, play virtual instruments, and use reverbs and other effects. The number of simultaneous audio tracks, virtual instruments, and convolution reverbs you can run are directly determined by these specs. A system meeting the minimum requirements will run Studio One 2 usefully, but the amount of real fun you can have will be limited. A beefy computer with lots of RAM and drive space will let you do a lot (run dozens of tracks, for instance) before you run out of computer power.

How to Find More Details About Your System

MAC

- Choose Apple > About This Mac: A window will open displaying the version of OS X currently running on your Mac, followed by the processor description and the amount of memory (RAM) installed.
- Click on the More Info button in the About This Mac window to start up the System Profiler. System Profiler provides a detailed list of every component of your system, broken out into Hardware, Network, and Software sections. The Hardware section tells you about installed drives, memory, PCI or other cards, USB devices, graphics cards, and more.
- **System Preferences > Hardware > Sound control panel:** Selects input and output devices and alert sounds
- **Applications > Utilities > Audio MIDI Setup utility:** A comprehensive utility for describing how your audio and MIDI systems are configured. This utility is the front end for Core Audio and Core MIDI, the audio and MIDI layers of the Mac OS.

Fig. 1-2: The About This Mac window, found under the Apple menu.

Exploring the System Profiler will make you more familiar with your machine. Knowing what's under the hood will save you many headaches, such as buying a software package you can't run, or trying to make a hardware device work with a machine that doesn't support it.

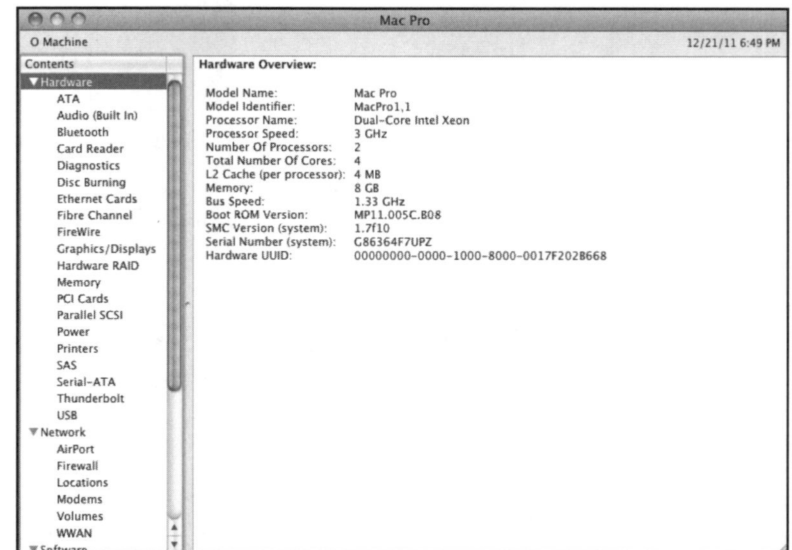

Fig. 1-3: Clicking the More Info button in the About This Mac window gives access to extensive details about your system.

WINDOWS:

WINDOWS XP

- Choose Control Panel from the Start menu. Open the System control panel from the window that appears.
- The General and Hardware tabs will probably be the most useful for an overview of your Windows machine.

- The Sounds and Audio Devices control panel is also worth a look, as that is where your audio system is defined for Windows.

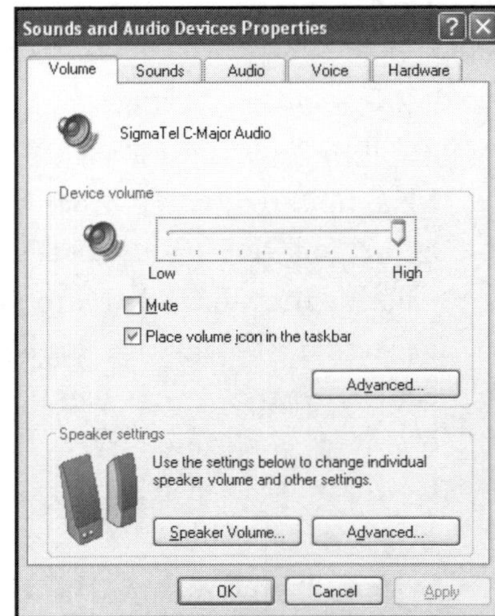

Fig. 1-4: The Windows XP Sounds and Audio Devices control panel has information about your computer's audio interface and facilities.

WINDOWS VISTA AND WINDOWS 7

One good place to get system information is System Information:

1. Click on the Start button and type "System Information" into the search box.
2. Click on "System Information" in the results that appear.
3. Click on the System Summary tab to get most information you will need.

Specific information on sound devices is in the Device Manager:

1. Click on the Start button.
2. Click on Control Panel to open the control panel window.
3. Click on the System and Security section.
4. Open the System control panel.
5. Click on the Device Manager tab. You'll find information on all of your computer's hardware devices in this tab, including audio interfaces.

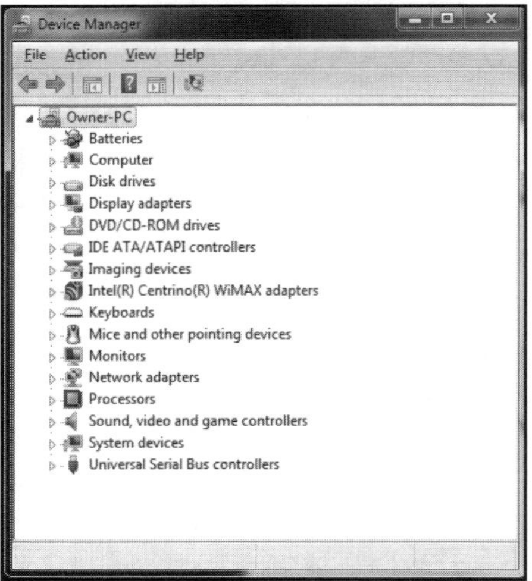

Fig. 1-5: In Windows 7, the Device Manager control panel is the place to find information about your computer's hardware functionality.

ALL ABOUT INTERFACES

Studio One 2 stores your sessions and audio on hard drives, but it uses audio and MIDI interfaces to communicate with the outside world.

MIDI Interface

If you will be using a MIDI keyboard or other controller, or have any external MIDI devices, you will need a MIDI interface for your computer. Since MIDI involves much less data than audio, a USB MIDI interface will work fine. You can find basic MIDI I/O on many audio interfaces as well.

On the MIDI side, the calculation for number of inputs and outputs is pretty easy: how many external MIDI devices will you be using? For many people, a single keyboard controller might be all they need to accommodate. You might have an outboard sound module or processor that you want to control through MIDI, or maybe you have a percussion controller as well as a keyboard. Count up the devices and that's pretty much what you'll need. If an extra device or so needs to be integrated into the system, it can sometimes be done just by daisy-chaining using a MIDI Thru port, but it is best to keep the number of daisy-chained devices down to one or two to avoid building up MIDI latency that can make instruments play out of time.

Audio Interface

Your most important decision will be choosing an audio interface. As with drives, there are interfaces that connect over USB and those that connect over FireWire. There are even some that connect to special plug-in cards.

The previous section took a look at the issue of choosing FireWire or USB for audio, and everything said there applies to audio interfaces as well as disk drives, even more so. Again, as with drives, FireWire interfaces are, on the whole, better choices. Beyond all the reasons discussed before, USB interfaces that are powered off of the USB bus (rather than plugging in to a wall outlet) often suffer from a soft but audible clock noise that gets into recordings. Unfortunately, FireWire has always worked more smoothly on Mac than in Windows. As usual, some research is recommended before making purchases.

Systems like MOTU's PCI-424 card, based on a plug-in card and proprietary interfaces, can provide greater speed and control, as they use a fully optimized interface (even though it uses the same connectors as FireWire). The compromise is that these systems cannot be used with a laptop computer or easily moved from one computer to another. If you are doing serious work involving high channel counts and high sample rates, these systems are well worth considering.

HOW MANY AUDIO INPUTS AND OUTPUTS DO YOU NEED?

This is an important question to ponder before deciding on an interface. If you will be recording a full drum kit at once, you will want an interface with eight inputs, not two. When your need outstrips the number of inputs you currently have, there are several strategies you can adopt:

- Overdub some instruments.
- Combine some inputs into one or more submixes before they are recorded. The downside of this is that those instruments cannot be treated separately later; you must get the sound you want as you record.
- It is often possible to connect multiple interfaces, though connecting interfaces from different manufacturers could be quirky in practice.
- Upgrade to a larger interface.

Any of these methods can be made to work, but it's best simply to have as many inputs available as you will usually need at one time.

Outputs involve different considerations. Of course you will need a master stereo output for monitoring, but you may need more outputs for headphone mixes or alternate destinations, such as a live stream. Got an awesome boutique analog compressor you like to use on your stereo mixes? Studio One 2 will make it easy on the software side, but you'll need both outputs (as sends) and inputs (as returns) to accommodate it.

If you are thinking of doing any surround work, you will want to have at least six outputs for 5.1 audio, and, quite possibly, more for things like a simultaneous stereo mix.

WHAT OTHER INTERFACE FEATURES SHOULD I BE THINKING ABOUT?

Some interfaces include microphone inputs with onboard mic preamps, while others have line inputs, or even instrument (guitar/bass/keyboard) inputs. Think about what you will be recording and choose an interface with the types of inputs you need.

Also consider that the quality of onboard interface mic preamps varies widely. If you have (or plan to get) other mic preamps (for example, outboard pres or those built into a mixer), you may not need to worry about having mic pres in your interface. If, on the other hand, you are doing field or live recording, mic pres in the interface could be important.

As mentioned above, some audio interfaces include MIDI connections. This can mean one less device to deal with.

Studio One 2 and PreSonus Interfaces

PreSonus has long made audio interfaces. As one might guess, the company integrates its interfaces quite tightly with Studio One 2. Studio One 2 includes a collection of setup templates for PreSonus interfaces that automatically configure the audio I/O for the interface and supplies a track setup with tracks prepared to record from all inputs.

All of PreSonus's interfaces to date connect over FireWire, except the AudioBox USB. The second-generation AudioBox VSL interfaces provide performance comparable to the FireWire interfaces.

The FireWire and AudioBox VSL interfaces contain DSP mixing and effects onboard for low-latency monitoring while recording, and this monitoring is used directly by Studio One 2. Were you to use another manufacturer's interface with onboard DSP mixing, you would have to run a separate application alongside Studio One 2 to manage it. This is not a lot to deal with, but low-latency monitoring being controlled invisibly from Studio One 2 is decidedly more elegant.

There are a few other notes to make about PreSonus interfaces. First, PreSonus is also a mic preamp manufacturer, so the preamps in the company's interfaces are quite good. Second, Studio One 2 Artist comes free when you purchase any of the interfaces. You might even have bought this book because you got Studio One 2 Artist this way!

Third, it is worth mentioning that PreSonus makes a range of digital mixers, StudioLive, that have FireWire output and can act as interfaces. This means you get a very nice mic preamp and great-sounding basic facilities (EQ, dynamics) on every channel, plus a multichannel interface that includes a stereo return from your computer to the StudioLive.

Install and Configure Your Interfaces

Install your interfaces according to the manufacturer's instructions. Also be sure to verify that they are working.

When you start up Studio One 2, experiment with changing the sample rate and see if the interface changes with it. If not, you will always have to be vigilant in ensuring that the interface is set to the same sample rate as the Song on which you're working. If the interface and the Song are at different rates, Studio One 2 will expend a great deal of processor power trying to resample the whole session in real time to accommodate the rate difference. That could cause some distressingly audible, if understandable, artifacts.

MEET STUDIO ONE 2

Install Studio One 2

Now that you have determined that your computer is adequate to run Studio One 2 and you have your interfaces in place, install Studio One 2 according to PreSonus's instructions. The installation process is simple and straightforward.

If you store loops, sound effects, and other content on a particular disk, you may want to install the third-party content that comes with Studio One 2 Pro on that drive. Should Studio One 2 ever lose track of this content, or you want to point the program toward additional content, define the target folder in Preferences > Options > Locations.

Starting Up Studio One 2

Double-click on the Studio One 2 application to open it. As Studio One 2 boots up, you will see messages scrolling by as it loads each of its components. If any problems are encountered, the program displays a message telling you what it was unable to do successfully.

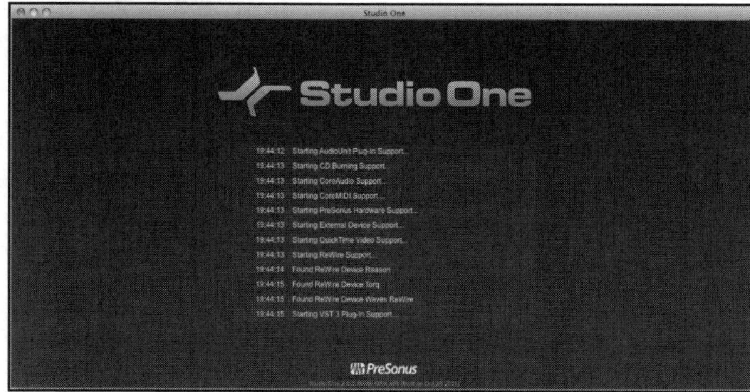

Fig. 1-6: As Studio One 2 boots, it lists each service it is starting up.

What's Where: Getting Started with Studio One 2

Your work in Studio One 2 will be done in its three main pages: Start, Song, and Project. *Songs* are the sessions in which you will create your music, while *Projects* are mastering sessions that can contain a number of Songs.

The Preferences (Options in Windows) dialog box is another place you will visit a lot, since it has a number of important configuration options. I'll get to those in this section, but mostly just to orient you to Studio One 2's user interface so that you know where things are and what you're looking at. I'll also help you make sure that Studio One 2 is set up to work.

More detail, information on how to actually work in Studio One 2, and explanations of menu commands that are not part of the graphic user interface will be discussed in the chapters to come.

The place to begin our tour is the Start page, at which you are looking right now.

THE START PAGE

The Start page is, naturally, a good point from which to dive into Studio One 2. On the Start page it is possible to create new Songs and Projects, open existing ones, configure your audio and MIDI systems, create basic metadata, and get news and tutorials about Studio One 2.

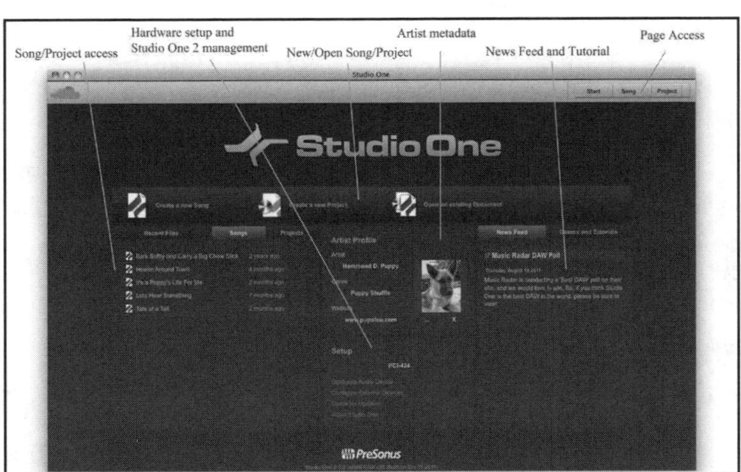

Fig. 1-7: The Start Page provides a good jumping-off spot to open an existing document or create a new one.

There is one more item of importance on the Start page, so subtle you could easily miss it. At the very bottom of the page, in extremely small type, is displayed the exact version of Studio One 2 that you have. This can be crucial information for any support needs you may have. This information is also available in the Studio One 2 > About Studio One dialog box.

THE SETUP SECTION: CONNECTING STUDIO ONE 2 TO YOUR AUDIO AND MIDI DEVICES

In the bottom center of the page is the Setup section. All of the audio and MIDI devices defined in Audio MIDI Setup on the Mac (Hardware and Sound control panel or Device Manager in Windows) are available in Studio One 2.

Defining Your Audio Interface

If your audio interface has been correctly installed and selected in:

- Audio MIDI Setup on the Mac
- Hardware and Sound control panel in Windows 7
- Sounds and Audio Devices control panel in Windows XP

... then you should see it named in the field just below the word "Setup," with the currently selected sample rate displayed just below that.

If the name of your audio interface is already displayed, you may not need to change anything, but you should know how setup works.

- To change your audio system setup, click on the Configure Audio Device... link. The Preferences > Audio Setup pane will open.

Fig. 1-8: The Preferences>Options>Audio Setup pane is where you configure Studio One 2's low-level audio functions.

The most important part of the Audio Setup pane is the Audio Device drop-down menu at the top. Every audio interface available in your system will show up in this menu. If your interface has its own configuration software, you can click on the Control Panel button next to the Audio Device field to open it.

Just below the Audio Device field is the Device Block Size field with its drop-down menu. This is the buffer size parameter mentioned often in discussions of DAWs. See the section "Understanding Buffer Size" in chapter 2, "Get Set to Record," for more information on this important parameter and how to set it. This is the only setting in the Audio Setup pane that you are likely to change on a regular basis.

Below the Device Block Size field is the Process Precision setting. This sets the accuracy of the math that is used in processing your audio. Switching this setting from the default 32 bits to 64 bits—if your system will allow it—can improve the sound of your mixes. If your computer seems to be struggling, leave it set to 32 bits.

Best not to touch the multiprocessor setting. If your computer is multiprocessor, the setting should already be selected, and unless you experience some kind of performance problem you should leave it as it is.

When we make a new Song, we will talk about the last step in connecting Studio One 2 to your interfaces, which is connecting the hardware I/O on your audio interface to Studio One 2's software I/O in the Audio I/O Setup pane. That discussion is in the "Song Setup View" section below.

Defining Your MIDI Devices and Control Surfaces

Studio One 2 lumps all varieties of MIDI devices and control surfaces into the category of External Devices. Once you have defined all of your external devices, they are always available in Studio One 2. There are three flavors of external device:

- **Keyboards.** Actually, this refers to any hardware MIDI device that is intended to be a musical controller, but the most common kind of controller is a keyboard, hence the name.
- **Instruments.** This refers to any MIDI device that can produce sound: sound modules, workstations, and so on.
- **Control Surfaces.** A control surface is a hardware device that is configured like a mixer or other audio controller, with faders, transport controls, and so forth. A control surface may or may not be a MIDI device. For example, Mackie Control Universal Pro communicates over MIDI but uses a proprietary software protocol. PreSonus's FaderPort is a USB device, not a device using MIDI hardware. Both of these fall into the category of Control Surfaces in Studio One 2.
- To change your MIDI system setup, click on the Configure External Devices... link. The Options > External Devices pane will open.

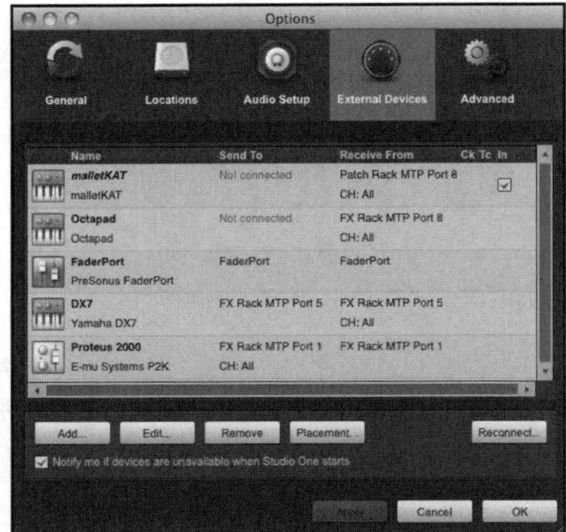

Fig. 1-9: External devices, including MIDI controllers and sound modules, are defined in the External Devices preferences pane.

The pane should show all of the devices defined or recognized in the MIDI window of Audio MIDI Setup.

- To add a new External Device, click on the Add button at the bottom of the pane.
- If you find your device in the list on the left side of the pane, click on it once to select it. If not, click on New Keyboard, New Instrument, or New Control Surface in the list once.
- If you found your device in the list, you will see its manufacturer, name, and model fields in the upper right section of the pane. If you selected one of the generic choices, you will need to fill in these fields yourself.

Now you need to configure the device in the lower right corner of the pane.

- The Receive From and Send To drop-down menus allow you to choose the ports used to communicate with the device. The ports in the list may be on your MIDI interface, or, in a case like the FaderPort, communications might use a different kind of interface. Fortunately, none of that need concern you; all entries in the drop-down list are the same from the user standpoint. These two are the only settings you need to make for a Control Surface.
- If you've selected a Keyboard or Instrument, there will be a row of boxes showing the MIDI channels to be used with the device. The All button selects all channels, or, if all channels are already selected, deselects them all.
- You can designate one of your Keyboard devices to be the default MIDI controller for virtual instruments by checking the Default Instrument Input box at the bottom. For Instruments, there are checkboxes that will enable MIDI clock, MIDI timecode, or MIDI Start messages to be passed on to the device. With the Split Channels box checked, a separate Instrument track is recorded for each MIDI channel of incoming data.
- If the device has knobs, sliders, wheels, or other hardware controllers you might want to use to control software parameters, you will want to create a Device Controller Map for the device. For more information on this, see the section "Using Hardware Controllers with Studio One 2: Control Link" in chapter 4, "Virtual Instruments and MIDI."

ARTIST PROFILE: DEFINING BASIC METADATA

Metadata is descriptive information about a file or other object, hence the common definition of "metadata" as being "data about data." Metadata can be contained in many kinds of audio files, and is read and displayed by most audio player applications. If you want people to know who they are listening to, you must include metadata. Much of that metadata, such as your name, will be the same for every file you create. Studio One 2 makes it easy to define this basic metadata right on the Start page. Once defined, that information will automatically be put into every file you create.

Studio One 2 lets you enter much more detailed metadata for each Song and Project you create, as we will discuss in the Meta Information discussion below.

In the Artist Profile section you can define your name, musical genre, and URL, and upload a picture that will be part of the metadata as well.

- To add Artist or Genre metadata to your profile, simply click in the field.
- To add a URL to your profile, double-click in the field. Once a URL is entered, clicking on it once will open a browser window and take you to the indicated page.
- To add a picture to your profile, click on the "…" button directly below the silhouette on the right side of the section.

- To remove a picture from your profile, click on the X button directly below the silhouette on the right side of the section.

NEWS FEED AND TUTORIALS

The last section of the Start page is on the right. The News Feed tab will show the latest Studio One 2 news from PreSonus about new versions, promotions and giveaways, educational materials, and other developments you might want to know about.

If you have properly installed Studio One 2, clicking on the Demos and Tutorials tab will show you a list of training materials that have been installed.

CREATING, OPENING, AND SWITCHING BETWEEN SONGS AND PROJECTS

You can create new Songs and Projects, or open existing ones, from the Start page, Song page, or main menus.

CREATING A NEW SONG OR PROJECT

- To create a new Song from anywhere in the program, press Cmd + N (Ctrl + N in Windows) or choose File > New Song from the main menu bar.
- To create a new Project from anywhere in the program, press Shift + Cmd + N (Shift + Ctrl + N in Windows) or choose File > New Project from the main menu bar.
- To create a new Song or Project from the Start page, click on the Create a new Project or Create a new Song link at the top of the page.
- To create a new Project from the Song page, only if no Project is already open, click on the Project page select button in the upper right of the Song page.

OPENING AN EXISTING SONG OR PROJECT

There are a number of ways to open an existing Song or Project listed below. The file access area on the left side of the Start page has three tabs: Recent Files, Songs, and Projects. Recent Files, as the name indicates, shows the last several files on which you worked, and how long it has been since Studio One 2 last modified them.

The Songs and Projects tabs display all Songs or Projects contained in the Studio One user data folder at the location defined in the User Data tab of Studio One's Preferences. For more information on this, see the "Preferences/Options" section in this chapter. Songs or Projects stored in other locations will not be displayed in the Songs or Projects tabs, but they will show up in the Recent Files tab if they were among the last few files worked on.

Use any of these techniques to open an existing Song or Project:

- To open an existing Song or Project from anywhere in the program, choose File > Open from the main menu bar.
- To open an existing Song or Project from the Start page, click on the Open An Existing Document button.

- Click on the name of the Song or Project you want to open if you see it under the Songs or Projects tab on the left of the page.
- Click on the name of the Song or Project you want to open if you see it under the Recent Files tab on the left of the page.

SWITCHING BETWEEN OPEN SONGS AND PROJECTS

- QuickSwitch is the fastest method of flipping freely between multiple open Song and Project documents (and the Start page). To access QuickSwitch, hold down the Ctrl key and press Tab. A list of open documents will pop up. While continuously holding down the Ctrl key, press the Tab key to step through the list. When the Ctrl key is released, the selected document will become active.
- To switch to an open Song or Project from anywhere in the program, choose the desired Song or Project from the list of open documents that appears in View > Songs or View > Projects.

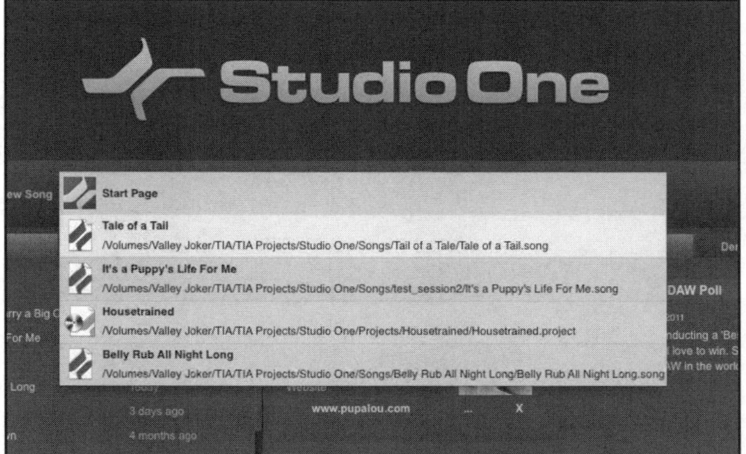

Fig. 1-10: QuickSwitch is a fast way of switching amongst all open Songs and Projects.

- To switch to an open Song or Project from the Song or Project page, click on the arrow next to the Song or Project page select buttons in the upper right of the current page, and choose the desired Song or Project from the list of open documents that appears.

THE SONG PAGE

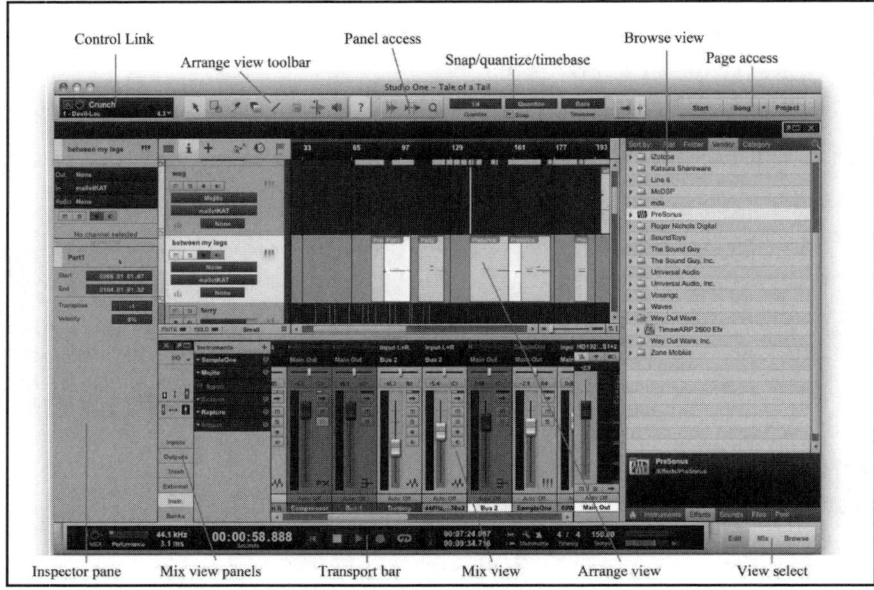

Fig. 1-11: The Song page, where most work is done in Studio One 2.

This is where you will spend most of your time. The Song page is Studio One 2's MIDI sequencing, audio recording, editing, and mixing environment. As one would expect, there is a lot going on here, so let's walk through it.

PAGE SELECT BUTTONS

In the upper right corner you will find the page select buttons. These switch your view between the Start, Song, and Project pages. Studio One 2 can have more than one Song open at a time; a drop-down menu next to the Song button lets you switch between the open songs.

SONG PAGE VIEWS

There are four views available on the Song page: Arrange, Edit, Mix, and Browse. We will discuss these in great detail as we go along, but here I will introduce you to these views and the way in which they work together.

The page is often divided vertically into two panes. The upper pane always shows the Arrange view. The lower pane can be switched between Edit and Mix views of the currently selected track in the Arrange view by using key shortcuts or by clicking on the view select buttons in the lower right corner. Either pane can be made larger (at the expense of the other, obviously). To resize the Edit and Mix view panes, do the following:

1. Place your cursor at the bottom of the scrollbar below the Arrange view. The cursor will change to a double-headed arrow with a line between the arrows.
2. Drag up or down to adjust the panes as desired.

The Arrange view contains tracks for everything that is playing: Audio, Instrument (MIDI), Automation, and Folder tracks. These tracks are populated with Events and Parts. The Arrange view also contains special tracks for markers and tempo changes, panels for time manipulation tools, and the automation display and editing.

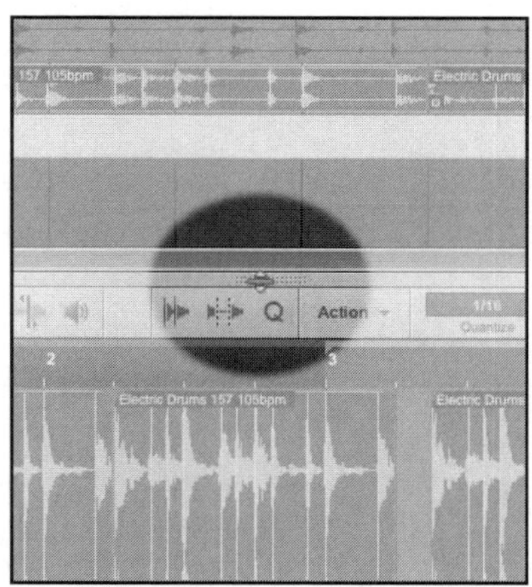

Fig. 1-12: The boundary between views can be dragged to resize them when the cursor turns to the double arrowhead.

The use of the terminology "Events" and "Parts" is not consistent in Studio One 2. For example, PreSonus uses "Events" as a generic term that encompasses both Audio Events and Instrument Parts, but then, in Studio One 2, Audio Parts were added. So the difference between Parts and Events is unclear, which can make things confusing to talk about. Since this book is intended to make Studio One 2 more understandable in all respects, the definitions are used consistently in this book and, as far as possible, conform to their use in Studio One 2. We define Events, Parts, and notes generically as "items." So, if I select two Events and a Part, I have three items.

An Audio Event is what is variously called a region or soundbite in other DAWs. It is a portion of an audio file, a little window into the file defined by a start and end point. If you use any Audio Event more than once in your Song, the program is not actually making a separate copy of the audio, just making note of each place where it is used. Thus, if you change something about that Event in one place, all the other places that Event is used will change the same way. It is possible, however, to tell Studio One 2 to make an entirely independent copy of an Event that you can treat differently than the others. We'll get to that when we talk about editing.

A Part is a collection of items that is treated as a single entity. Most often, you will work with Instrument Parts. When you edit an Instrument Part you find that it consists of individual notes, but you can have an Instrument Part that is a verse, for example, and then copy the Part around, rather than having to go to the Edit view, select all of the notes you want to copy, and doing it that more low-level way.

Studio One 2 introduced Audio Parts. These are similar to Instrument Parts, except that instead of containing notes they contain Audio Events. This enables you to construct a percussion loop, for instance, and then copy or move it around, maintaining the ability all along to edit (fades, start and end times, and so on) at the individual Event level and to quantize the Events. This is a more advanced version of the REX file, which contains small samples of audio collected into a single file but retaining their individuality.

Edit view shows the Audio Editor for audio tracks, and the Music Editor for Instrument tracks.

Mix view is, as one would expect, Studio One 2's mixing environment. It displays audio controls for everything you hear: audio files, virtual instrument returns, effects returns into aux buses, live inputs, submix masters, and, of course, the main master. The main mixer section uses the standard channel strip paradigm, but greatly enhanced by extensive drag-and-drop capabilities. There is also good flexibility in displaying quite a bit of information.

TIP: Note this important distinction:

Arrange view: What's being played. Audio, MIDI, and automation data.

Mix view: What's being heard. Audio tracks, VI returns, submix/group busses.

This means that, in Studio One 2, there is not always a mixer channel for every track, or vice versa; there is not a one-to-one correspondence between the two views. MIDI and automation tracks are playing control or performance information for a virtual instrument (VI), plug-in, or MIDI device of some sort. They don't actually contain any audio, so there is no need for mixer channels for them. You will, however, see mixer channels for every audio track in the Arrange window.

The Browse button causes Studio One 2's browsing environment to appear in a pane on the right side of the page.

SONG PAGE PANELS

Studio One features a number of sophisticated features for working with audio and MIDI. The Song page includes several panels that collect the numerous settings of some of these features for easier access.

There are currently four panels: Record, Quantize, Strip Silence, and Audio Bend. In addition, there is the Info panel (called "Info View" in the program, but it fits the description of a panel more than a view), which displays context-sensitive tips for the action you can take at any time. Each of these panels is discussed in detail in the sections that address their functions.

MIX VIEW PANELS

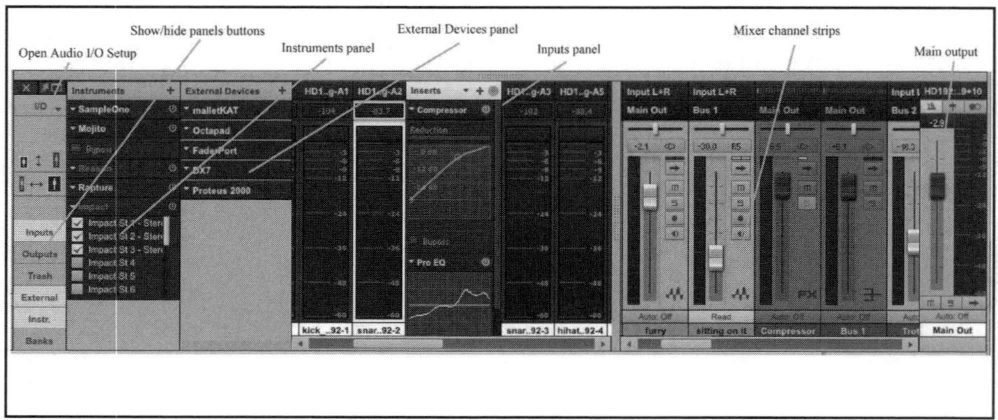

Fig. 1-13: The Mix view allows you to show or hide any of its several panels. Main Out is always visible, and regular mixer channels are visible unless hidden using the Arrange view Track List.

There are many items in the Mix view. To keep the screen from being any more cluttered than it absolutely needs to be, there are a number of panels that make visible different groups of Mix view items, such as Inputs or External Devices. With Mix view selected, a column of buttons along the left side makes these panels appear or disappear.

TRANSPORT BAR

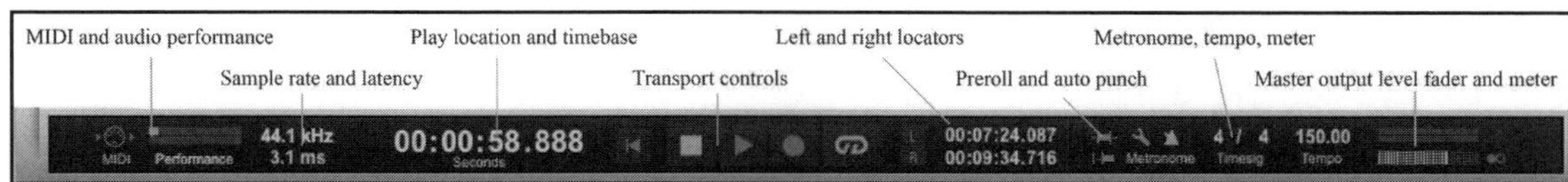

Fig. 1-14: The Transport bar provides access to a variety of information and configuration parameters well beyond basic transport control.

Running along the bottom of the Song page is the Transport bar, which holds basic transport, locator, and metronome controls, as well as a number of status displays, including play location and current tempo and time signature. Working from left to right in the Transport bar, here are the controls:

- The MIDI connector icon on the left end of the Transport bar shows when there is MIDI activity. Clicking on the icon brings up the MIDI Monitor window. For more about the MIDI Monitor, see the section "MIDI Monitor" in chapter 4, "Virtual Instruments and MIDI."
- The Performance meters to the right of the MIDI activity indicator show current CPU and disk usage. Clicking in this area opens the Performance Monitor window. For more on the Performance Monitor, see the section "Be an Efficiency Expert" in this chapter.
- The position counter shows the current play location in any of the four time bases: Seconds, Samples, Bars, or Frames. To enter a location, click in the counter and type the desired location. To change the time base, click-and-hold on the Timebase label and choose the desired format from the drop-down menu that appears. For information about time bases in Studio One 2, see the section "It's About Time Base" in this chapter.
- The transport buttons provide the most essential transport control. They are, from left to right: Return to Zero, Stop, Play, Record, and Loop Active.
- The Autopunch and Preroll buttons activate and display the status of those two recording functions.
- In the Metronome section, the Metronome Setup button opens a dialog box that lets you configure how the metronome will sound and operate. The button with the metronome icon enables and disables the metronome.

- The Timesig field shows the time signature at the current play location. You can set the time signature by clicking on the numerator or denominator and choosing the desired value, but doing so removes any time signature changes that may be in the song.
- The Tempo field shows the tempo at the current play location. You can change the tempo by placing the mouse cursor over this field and dragging, or clicking in the field and entering the desired value.
- The Master section has a meter on top that shows the main output level, and a master fader. These are the same as (and are linked to) the master fader in the mixer. You can change the fader by clicking at the desired level or dragging.

LARGE TIME DISPLAY

Perhaps you are sitting a little way back from your computer monitor because you are recording yourself. Maybe you are performing automation and it's very important to focus on where you are in the Song. There are many reasons for needing a larger time display than the one in the Transport bar, and that is the reason Studio One 2 has a large time display window.

- To open the large time display window, choose View > Time Display from the main menu bar.
- The large time display will show whatever units are currently selected for display in the Transport bar time display.

TOOLBAR

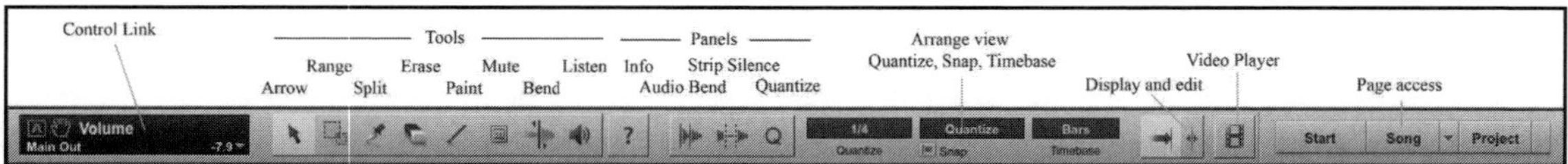

Fig. 1-15: The Arrange View toolbar.

At the top of the Song page is the toolbar. On the left is the value and control information of the currently selected Mix parameter. This display also shows what is happening if you are using a MIDI controller or control surface to operate the Studio One 2 mixer or a virtual instrument.

In the center of the toolbar is the tool array, which will be discussed in Chapter 5 "On the Cutting Room Floor: Basic Editing." To the right of the tool array are the buttons that open and close the Info, Audio Bend, Strip Silence, and Quantize panels. The same buttons (minus the Info panel button) are found in the Edit view toolbar. Moving toward the right side, the quantization and time base controls are next, with the quick access buttons (Start, Song, and Project) on the right edge.

INSPECTORS

Detailed data viewing and editing is available in different types of inspectors in the program. There are Track, Event, Part and Note inspectors, plus a small Edit view inspector. Inspectors provide important editing capabilities that are most easily, or, in some cases, exclusively available in an inspector. The Inspector pane contains all of the inspectors except the Note inspector.

- To open the Inspector pane: press F4 or click on the lowercase i button in the upper left corner of the Arrange view.

Fig. 1-16: The Inspector pane button in the Arrange view toolbar.

For more information on inspectors, see the section "Inspectors" in chapter 5, "On the Cutting Room Floor: Basic Editing."

BROWSER

When you first open the Song window, you may not see the Browser, but making it visible is easy:

- To make the Browser window visible, press the F5 key or click on the Browse button in the lower right corner next to the Transport bar.

There are six tabs at the bottom of the Browser that select what you are browsing:

- **Home:** The house icon takes you to the Browser Home page. Most of the Browser Home page simply duplicates what the tabs do, but there are also buttons for two utility functions.
- **Instruments:** Displays all of the virtual instruments Studio One 2 finds, including bundled instruments from PreSonus.
- **Effects:** Displays all of the signal processing plug-ins Studio One 2 finds, including bundled plug-ins and FX Chains.
- **Sounds:** Displays content in PreSonus Sound Set format found by Studio One 2.

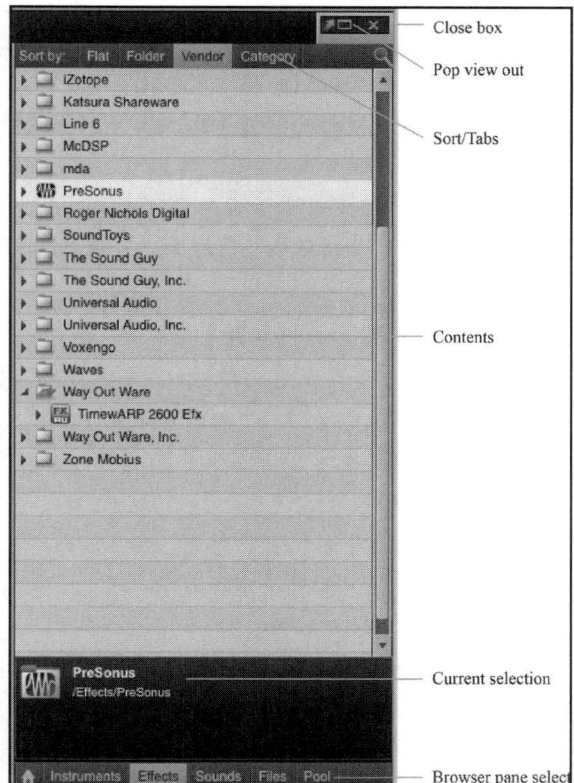

Fig. 1-17: The Browser.

- **Files:** This tab provides access to the file system on your computer. While many operations can be performed just as well directly in your computer's file system, there are some things that can only be done, or can be done better, using the Browser.

- **Pool:** This is a list of all of the audio files in the current Song, whether or not they are currently being used.

To sort the contents of the Instruments, Effects, or Pool panes, click on one of the Sort tabs at the top of the pane.

More information on Browser features can be found in the section "Let's Hear Something!" in this chapter, as well as wherever a Browser feature applies.

CONTEXTUAL MENUS

Much of Studio One 2's power is made conveniently accessible through contextual menus. These drop-down menus are invoked by right-clicking (or Ctrl-clicking on the Mac) on an item or location in the program. Right-clicking on a track header brings up the Track contextual menu, right-clicking on an Audio Event or Instrument Part brings up contextual menus for those, and so on.

In this book, when I describe how to access a command, I tend to cite its key shortcut first, contextual menu command second, and main menu command third. You will quickly find yourself right-clicking to execute commands as a matter of course. You likely will be right-clicking anywhere and everywhere in the program to discover all of the contextual menus!

For more on contextual menus, see the "Contextual Menus" section of chapter 5, "On the Cutting Room Floor: Basic Editing."

PREFERENCES/OPTIONS

There are many important settings in the Preferences dialog box (Options in Windows), and numerous ways to access them. We have already seen how to open the Audio Setup and External Devices panes from the Start page. We will note more of these alternate access methods as we work through the various parts of Studio One 2. The most obvious methods of opening Preferences are the following:

- To open the Preferences (Options) dialog box, press Cmd + , (comma), (Ctrl + , in Windows) or choose Studio One > Preferences (Studio One > Options in Windows).
- Individual sections of the Preferences dialog box can often be opened from areas in the program that deal with them.

Because there are many preference settings, there is a somewhat involved, though straightforward, structure to the Preferences dialog box. Unfortunately, there is also some very confusing use of terms, the first example being that the title bar reads "Options," the Windows name for the dialog box, even though it is called "Preferences" on Mac. Don't worry, though—we'll keep you straight by pointing out places where terminology is used confusingly.

There are two views: Options and Song Setup. The buttons in the lower left corner of the Preferences dialog box switches between these two views. Each view has several panes, and some (but not all) of the panes have tabs.

Let's walk through the Preferences dialog box and see what it can do for you.

OPTIONS VIEW

Yeah, it is a little confusing to have an Options view in a dialog box that already is called "Options" in Windows (Options > Options), but "Preferences" on Mac (Preferences > Options). If you ignore the awkward terminology, it's not hard to figure out what's going on.

The Options view has five panes: General, Locations, Audio Setup, External Devices, and Advanced.

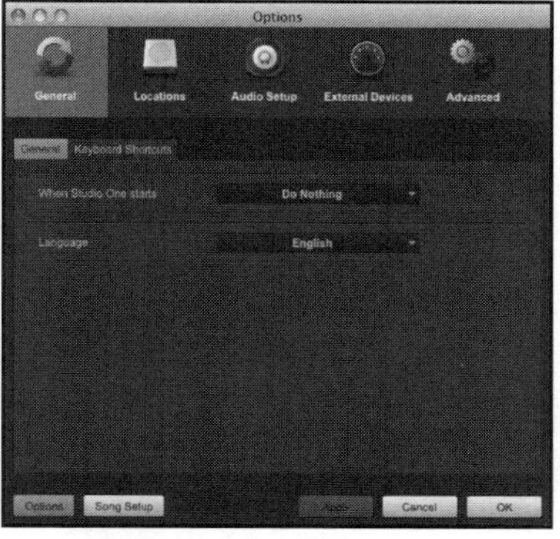

Fig. 1-18: There are only two settings in the Preferences>Options >General>General tab. (In Windows, this is Options>Options>General> General!)

General

The General tab of the General pane (try not to think about it too much) just has two simple settings that you will likely never touch once you set them up as you want.

Keyboard Shortcuts

On the other hand, the Keyboard Shortcuts tab is something you may visit often. Many important Studio One 2 commands do not have default key shortcuts assigned to them. In this book, we try always to cite the key shortcut as the first method of executing any command for which a default key shortcut exists. If no key shortcut is mentioned, it is almost certainly because there is no default. Get in the habit of assigning key shortcuts to any command you use with regularity.

To quickly view the full set of currently assigned Keyboard Shortcuts, do the following:

- Choose Help > Keyboard Shortcuts. Studio One 2 will create an HTML page of the current shortcuts and display them in your browser.

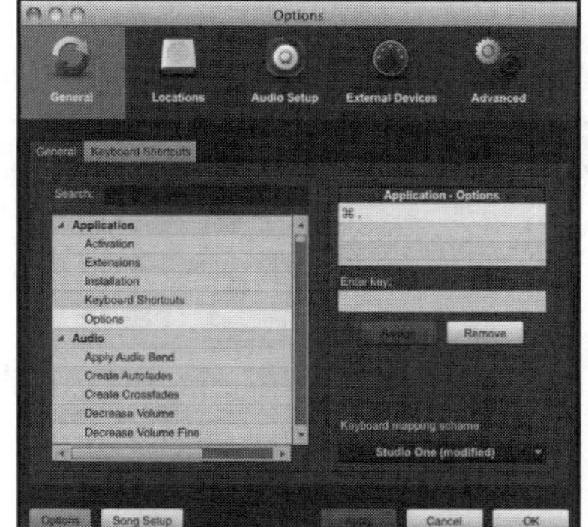

Fig. 1-19: In the Preferences> Options>General>Keyboard Shortcuts tab you can define shortcuts for nearly every function in Studio One 2.

On the left you will see a scrolling list that shows nearly every menu command and many of the functions of the program, with the currently assigned key shortcut to its right. Note that the Keyboard Shortcuts tab is the first item in the list. It will save you a lot of time to start out by assigning a key shortcut to it.

Assigning is easy:

1. Locate the command or function you want in the list.
2. Click on it to select it.

3. Click in the Enter key field on the right. (This has nothing to do with the Enter key, so just pretend it says something like "Type shortcut.")
4. Type the key shortcut you want to use.
5. Click on the Assign button. Ta-daa!

To remove a key shortcut, do the following:

1. Locate the command or function you want in the list.
2. Click on it to select it. The current shortcut will appear, selected, in the box above the Enter key field.
3. Click on the Remove button.

Note that it is possible to assign more than one shortcut to a command or function. You simply have to make sure that no existing shortcuts are selected in the box above the Enter key field when you click on the Assign button.

The list of commands and functions is long, and scrolling through it can be an inefficient means of finding one particular command or function. Using the Search field is much faster.

- To search the list for a desired command or function, type into the Search field above the list. As you type each letter, it narrows the search.

Fig. 1-20: The Search field narrows the list of shortcuts as you type. Note in the illustration that the search term "layer" also captures the "video player" command, as well as commands dealing with layers.

The Keyboard mapping scheme drop-down menu in the lower right corner will let you assign Pro Tools, Logic, or Cubase shortcuts to the same functions in Studio One 2.

This menu also allows you to import entire sets of keyboard shortcuts previously saved from Studio One 2, and export sets, either as XML files or as a text file.

Locations

In the Locations pane you tell Studio One 2 where to find items it needs and where to put items you create. It has five tabs.

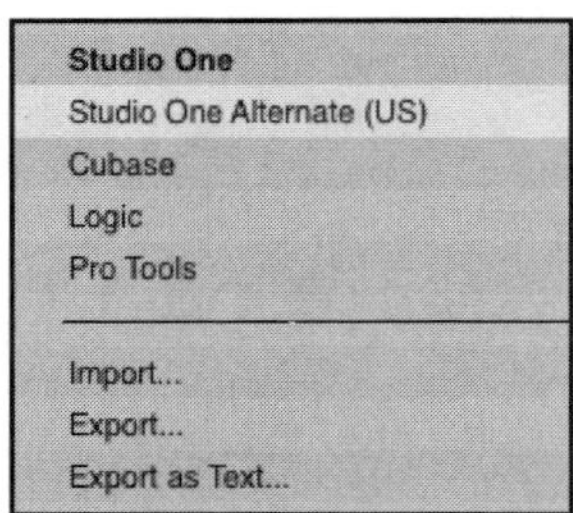

Fig. 1-21: If you are used to another DAW, the keyboard shortcut mapping drop-down can ease your transition to Studio One 2.

Adding and Removing Locations

- To add or remove an item in all tabs except User Data, click on the Add or Remove button at the bottom of the pane.
- To add a location, click on the appropriate tab, drag the folder you want to designate as a location, and drop it into an open area of the tab.

- To delete a File Type or a Sound Set, Instrument Library, or VST Plug-Ins location, click on the appropriate tab, next click on the item you want to delete, and then press the Delete key.

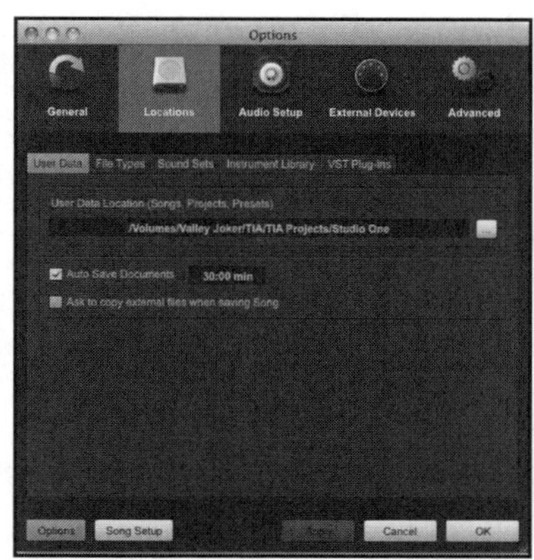

Fig. 1-22: The location defined in this tab is the default storage location for Songs, Projects, Presets, and other data. You may want to reference this location often.

User Data

The sole field in this tab, User Data Location, sets the default location for Songs and Projects you create, along with data related to them. Of course, you can always choose to put a Song or Project anywhere you like; this is just the location Studio One 2 will use if you simply click on OK in the New Song or New Project dialog box without specifying a location.

File Types

The File Types tab presents a scrolling list of all of the file types Studio One 2 will show in the Browser. You can add or remove file types with Add and Remove buttons at the bottom of the list. Be careful about removing file types; Studio One 2 cannot deal with file types that are not in the list. On the other hand, adding a new file type does not give Studio One 2 the ability to open a file type it does not already recognize.

Fig. 1-23: The File Types tab lists all of the file types recognized by Studio One 2.

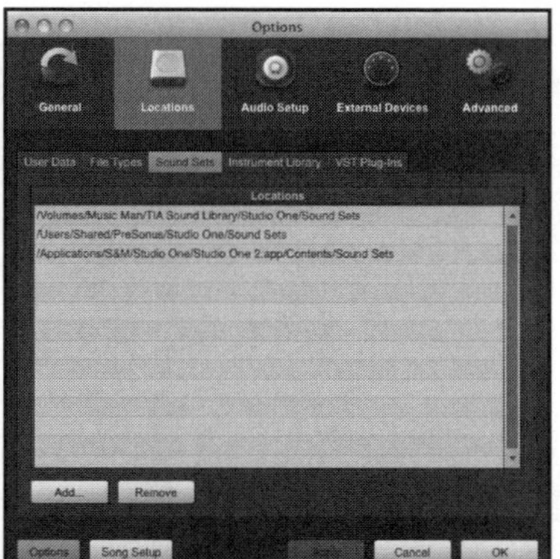

Fig. 1-24: Loops and samples bundled with Studio One 2 are stored in the locations listed in the Sound Sets tab.

Sound Sets

Samples for Studio One 2's included virtual instruments, as well as loops included with Studio One 2, are stored as Sound Sets. The Add and Remove buttons in the Sound Sets tab enable you to specify a list of places Studio One 2 should look to find this content.

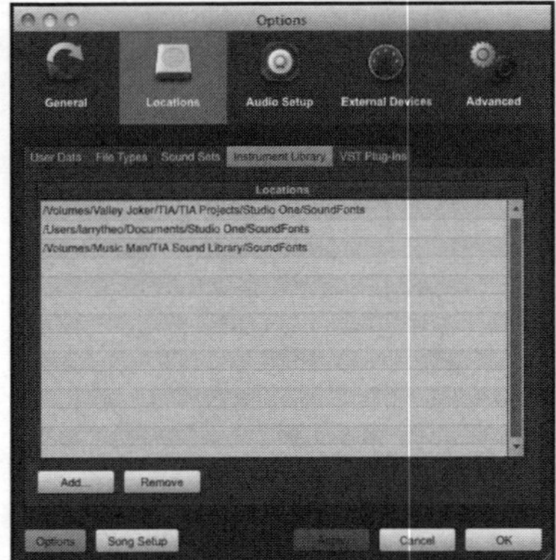

Fig. 1-25: The Instrument Library tab lists locations where SoundFonts, and SFZ files are stored. These files are usable by the PreSonus Presence virtual instrument bundled with Studio One 2.

Instrument Library

The Instrument Library tab is the same idea as the Sound Sets tab, only it specifies a list of locations Studio One 2 can check to find SoundFont files that can be loaded into the included Presence instrument.

SoundFonts are a file format created by Creative Labs' E-mu division. They hold (small) WAV files, along with key-mapping data used by samplers to define where on the keyboard each sound should play.

VST Plug-Ins

The VST Plug-Ins tab houses the list of locations in which Studio One 2 Pro can look to find VST plug-ins. Most of the time, Studio One 2 will simply find plug-ins without your having to do anything. AU, VST3, and ReWire-enabled plug-ins are always found automatically. However, if there are plug-ins that Studio One 2 is having trouble finding, use this tab to point Studio One 2 to the right location. It should then be able to find them when the program starts up.

If Studio One 2 is unable to load a plug-in, perhaps because it is not properly authorized, it places the plug-in on a "blacklist" and will not attempt to load it again. The Reset Blacklist button will cause Studio One 2 to scan all plug-ins the next time it starts up.

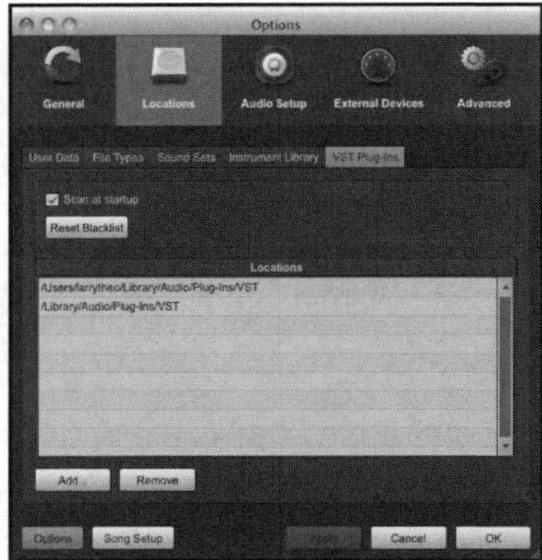

Fig. 1-26: Guess what is listed in the VST Plug-Ins locations tab? No listings are needed for Studio One 2 to find AU, VST3, or ReWire-enabled plug-ins.

Audio Setup

This pane was already discussed in the "Defining Your Audio Interface" section above. Feel free to go back and remind yourself of how it works.

External Devices

In this pane you maintain the list of MIDI devices and control surfaces you wish to use to control Studio One 2. For more information, go back to the discussion in the "Defining Your MIDI Devices and Control Surfaces" section above.

Advanced Options

The Advanced pane accesses a number of really tweaky settings. In fact, the Advanced settings are too esoteric for most users' needs and, as such, are beyond the scope of this book. The one exception is the MIDI advanced preferences, which are discussed in the section "Advanced MIDI Editing" in chapter 6, "Advanced Editing."

Appendix A lists the settings available in the Advanced pane for your reference. The Studio One 2 manual details these options, so take a look if you're curious, but be warned that some of the options in the Advanced pane can be risky to change unless you are sure you know what you're doing. That goes double for the Options > Advanced > Services tab.

Fig. 1-27: The Advanced Options pane contains many useful, if tweaky, settings. Be careful in this pane, most especially in the Services tab, or you may find Studio One 2 behaving in unexpected ways.

SONG SETUP VIEW

The Song Setup view has three panes containing information that apply only to the currently active Song. This view can also be accessed by choosing Song > Song Setup.

General

Obviously not the same as the General tab of the Options view, the General pane of the Song Setup view hosts some of the settings found on the Start page and more. You should already be familiar with what Sample Rate and Resolution are.

Frame Rate refers to the rate of SMPTE timecode, which is most often used when working to picture, but the labels in this drop-down menu are not quite correct.

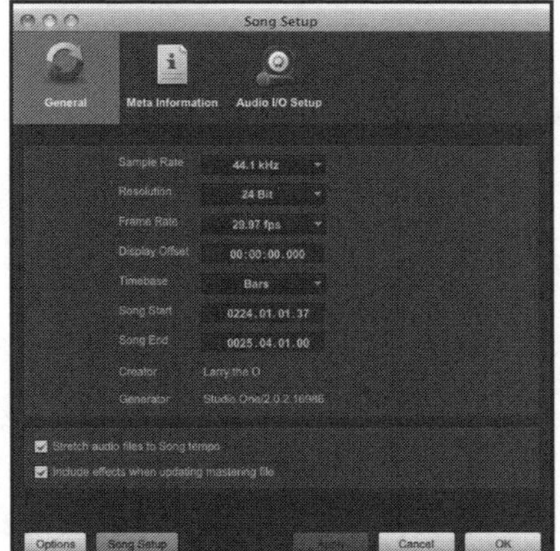

Fig. 1-28: Audio configuration parameters specific to the Song, such as sample rate and resolution, are set in the Song Setup>General pane.

TIP: While a full explanation of SMPTE timecode is beyond the scope of this book, I will just point out that the "29.97 dfps" value in the menu is correctly written as "29.97DF fps" (meaning 29.97 frames per second, drop-frame). "Dfps" would seem to mean "drop frames per second," which is not how drop-frame timecode works. You should also be very wary of using the "30 dfps" setting, as 30DF fps timecode is not a true SMPTE format, but rather a kludge devised to handle idiosyncratic problems arising in certain kinds of production.

Time base is simply the way that time is displayed in the Arrange view timeline (called the "time ruler" in Studio One 2), and can be changed at any time, either using the Timebase field here or at the top of the Arrange view. For more about time bases in Studio One 2, see the section "It's About Time Base," in this chapter.

- To set the Sample Rate, Resolution, Frame Rate, or Timebase, choose the desired value from the drop-down menus for the field.

TIP: Once any audio is recorded or imported into a Song, it is no longer possible to change the Sample Rate or Resolution of the Song. Be sure to set these values before you start work in your Song.

The Song Start and Song End fields are of limited use, as all they do is set the locations of the Song Start and Song End markers, which are more effectively set and changed, when necessary, in the Arrange view. The Song Start and End markers can be used in bouncing a file or when updating a Project during mastering.

When the Stretch Audio Files to Song Tempo checkbox at the bottom of the General pane is checked, the Tempo mode of new audio tracks will default to Timestretch. For more on Tempo mode and Automatic Time Stretching, see the section "Editing Audio" in chapter 6, "Advanced Editing."

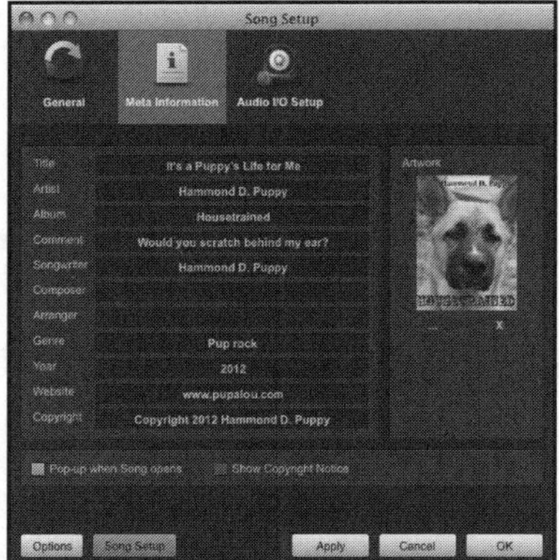

Fig. 1-29: The Meta Information pane contains metadata that can be stored with the final mix file of the Song.

Meta Information

The Meta Information pane contains metadata particular to the currently active Song. When a listener plays a digital file of this Song on a computer, the media player will display this information. Of course, it also serves as documentation for you.

- Click in any field and enter the desired information.
- When checked, the Pop-up When Song Opens checkbox causes the Song Information dialog box to be presented whenever that Song is opened in Studio One 2.
- The Song Information dialog box displays all of the Song metadata you have entered. Clicking on the Edit link at the top of the dialog box opens the Meta Information tab. This dialog box can also be opened by choosing Song > Song Information.
- When Pop-up When Song Opens is checked, the Show Copyright Notice checkbox becomes active. Checking it will cause a copyright notice to appear before the Song Information dialog box is displayed, to remind you, I guess, who owns the copyright for the song you are working on.

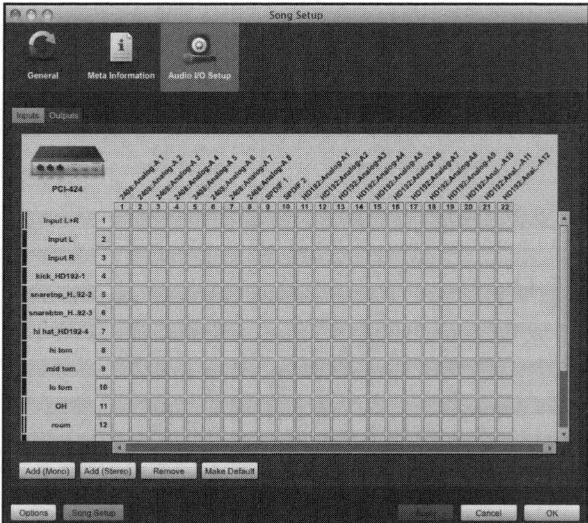

Fig. 1-30: The Audio I/O Setup pane is where physical interface inputs and outputs are mapped to Studio One 2's virtual inputs and outputs. Naming the virtual I/O can help sessions flow smoothly.

Audio I/O Setup

The Audio I/O Setup pane is one of the most important facilities in Studio One 2. Inputs and outputs in Studio One 2 are part of your Song and are separate from physical inputs and outputs on your interface. This pane is where you connect them. This separation (or, more correctly, "abstraction") of virtual I/O from physical I/O means that a Song can be opened on any computer with Studio One 2, or on the same computer with different interfaces, and all that needs to be done to make it play correctly or record into it is to remap the connections in this pane.

There are two tabs, unsurprisingly labeled "Inputs" and "Outputs." Both tabs work the same way: In the upper left corner you should see your interface identified. The row along the top will show the physical interface connections, while the column running down the left side will show the virtual inputs or outputs defined in the Song. You can name the virtual inputs any way you want, and doing so will make your Songs easier to work with.

For instance, if you regularly record drums (as I do), you probably have a pretty consistent setup that you use. Naming your inputs (for example, "Kick," "Snare Top," "Snare Bottom," "Rack Tom Hi,'" and so on) makes it a snap to ensure that everything is correctly configured and ready to record.

- To add a new virtual input or output, make sure that you have the correct tab selected, and click on the Add (Mono) or Add (Stereo) button at the bottom of the pane.
- To name a virtual input or output, double-click on the name to make editing active, and type in the name you want. Press Return or Enter to complete your entry.
- To connect a virtual input or output to a physical input or output, click in the box in the matrix where the row for the desired virtual input or output crosses the column for the physical input or output. Notice that as you move the cursor over any box, a pop-up tool tip tells you the connection clicking in that box will make.

Every Song has its own Audio I/O Setup, but if your workflow is at all consistent, you will find it beneficial to save your regular setup as a default that all new Songs will automatically use. Of course, you can change it any time, and those changes will be saved with the Song.

- To save a default Audio I/O Setup, configure the Inputs and Outputs tabs as desired and click on the Make Default button at the bottom of the pane.

The Audition Output

The Audition setting at the bottom of the Audio I/O Setup pane is very important. This is the output that will be used whenever you audition a file in Studio One 2's Browser. Note that this setting refers to the virtual outputs defined in your Song, not to physical interface outputs. If you move your Song to another machine or use a different interface, this output gets properly assigned as soon as you have remapped the interface inputs and outputs in the tabs above.

- To set the Audition output, choose the desired output from the drop-down menu in the Audition field.

EXTENSIONS

Studio One 2 has an extensions system that, like the extensions facility in your browser, allows new capabilities to be added to the program. Studio One 2's SoundCloud support comes in part from an extension, and more extensions are on the way. Extensions can be disabled if a problem occurs.

- To open the Extensions dialog box, choose Studio One > Studio One Extensions.
- To install a new extension, click on the Install button, locate and select the extension you wish to install, and click on the Open button to install it.
- To enable or disable an extension, select it in the list in the Extensions dialog box and click on the Enable or Disable button.
- To uninstall an extension, select it in the list in the Extensions dialog box and click on the Uninstall button.

THE PROJECT PAGE

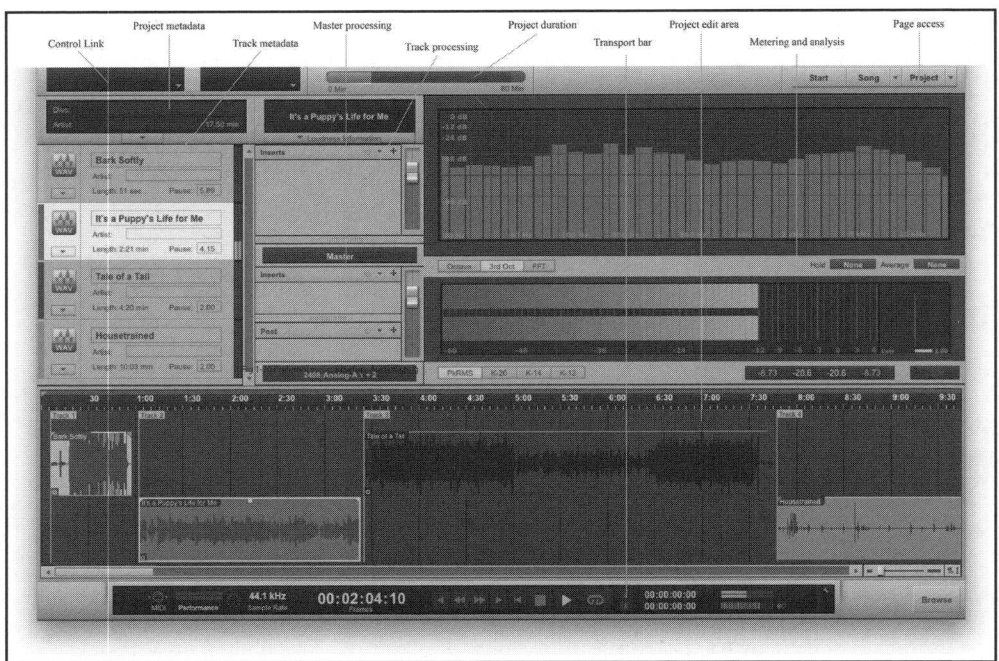

Fig. 1-31: The Project page.

The Project page is unique to Studio One 2; no other DAW has anything like it. Once you have created all the Songs for your album, the Project page lets you master and deliver them. Even if you plan to use a professional mastering engineer instead of doing it yourself, the Project page is invaluable in premastering the Songs for the greatest consistency across all of the mixes.

The real magic of the Project page is that you not only can bring your mixes in to it but you can also bring in the Songs themselves. The beauty of this is the ease with which you can decide while working on the Project page to adjust the mix of a single Song, open the Song, make the adjustment, and have the Project page automatically update to the new mix.

The Project page is discussed in the chapter about mastering in my upcoming book *Power Tools for Studio One 2*, volume 2.

It's About Time Base

Every sound or action that happens in Studio One 2 happens at a particular time, so how time is shown is very important. Studio One 2 gives you four ways to look at time, which are referred to as "time base formats." There are different time base settings for several areas of Studio One 2, but they all offer the same format choices.

Time base settings can affect more than simply how time is displayed. They can also affect quantization and Snap functions, insertion of new Events, tool and marker behavior, and so forth.

TIP: Since the Transport bar position counter is the only place that the play location is shown, the potential for confusion exists when the time base format of the Arrange or Edit view is different than that of the Transport bar time display. Be careful!

TIME BASE FORMATS

- **Seconds:** The units displayed in the timeline when this format is chosen vary with the zoom level. When zoomed way out, it shows minutes and seconds, or even hours, minutes, and seconds, if your Song is that long. As you zoom in it starts showing smaller subdivisions of time, until when zoomed in as far as possible, it shows seconds and milliseconds (thousandths of a second). In the Transport bar, the time is always shown in hours:minutes:seconds.milliseconds.
- **Samples:** Digital audio is constructed of streams of samples. Since the time between every sample is the same, the sample rate is effectively a clock using one sample as its unit of time. It is important to remember that the amount of time in seconds represented by a single sample changes with the sample rate. At a sample rate of 44.1 kHz, a sample is taken every 23 microseconds, while at 96 kHz a single sample represents only 10.4 microseconds. Thus, sample 44100 represents exactly one second if the sample rate is 44.1 kHz, but only 0.9 seconds if the sample rate is 48 kHz. The Samples format shows time as the number of audio sample intervals since the start of the Song. This is not a commonly used way of viewing time in a DAW, but there may be situations in which it could come in handy.
- **Bars:** As opposed to Samples, the system of bars and beats is one of the most popular ways of viewing time when making music. When time is represented in this way, there

are four divisions shown: bars at the left, then beats, then the beat subdivision, then hundredths of the beat subdivision. The beat subdivision is a little complicated. A beat subdivision is the equivalent of a 16th note, which can be a little confusing for some time signatures. Using a time signature of 4/4, there would be four subdivisions to each beat, but in 6/8, where the 8th note gets the pulse, there are only two subdivisions in each beat. What about 7/16 time, where the pulse is the 16th note, or even 11/32, where the 32nd note is the pulse? In those cases, the subdivision stays fixed at 1, and the hundredths become hundredths of a beat. Yeah, it's kind of a hinky system.

- **Frames:** If you are working to picture, you may need to look at time in terms of SMPTE timecode. Time is displayed as hours:minutes:seconds:frames. The number of frames in each second is determined by the frame rate setting in Preferences > Song Setup > General > Frame Rate. A reminder: first, the notation "dfps" that is used in Studio One 2 is incorrect, and second, 30DF fps is not an actual SMPTE timecode frame rate, so use that format with extreme caution.

TIME BASE SETTINGS

There are several places in Studio One 2 in which time bases are set. In most cases, they are independent of each other. Here they are:

Fig. 1-32: The Transport bar time base only affects time displays in the Transport bar, such as the play location and locators.

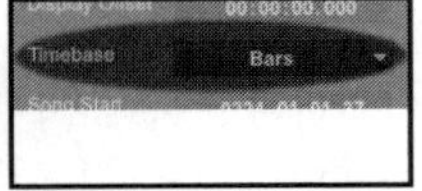

Fig. 1-33: The Arrange view time base determines the units used in the timeline.

- **Transport bar:** The time base format chosen from the drop-down menu below the play location in the Transport bar affects only the time displays in the Transport bar for the play location and the left and right locators.
- **Arrange view:** The format for the timeline in the Arrange view of the Song page is displayed in the Timebase field at the top of the page.
- There is a drop-down menu in the Preferences > Song Setup > General > Timebase field, which is connected with the Timebase field in the Arrange view. Changing either of these also changes the other.
- **Audio Editor:** The Timebase drop-down menu in the Edit view toolbar selects only the time base shown in that editor's timeline.

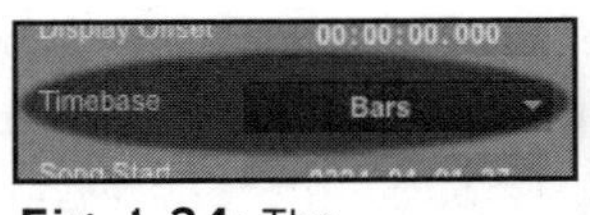

Fig. 1-34: The Preferences>Song Setup> General>Time base field is just another display of the Arrange view time base.

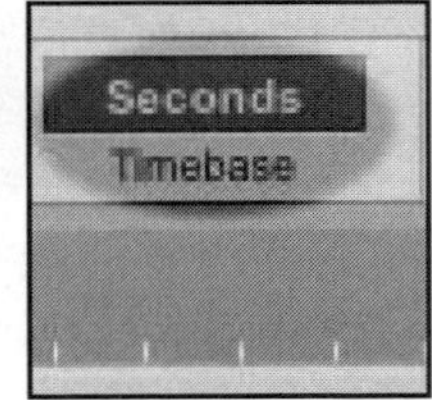

Fig. 1-35: The Edit view has its own time base, which is independent of the Arrange view time base. Shown here is the Audio Editor time base, which is also independent from the Music (Piano Roll) Editor time base.

- **Music Editor:** Studio One 2's piano-roll editor, called the "Music Editor," has its own time base format, which is chosen exactly as in the Audio editor: using the drop-down menu in the inspector on the left side of the editor.

Fig. 1-36: The Music (Piano Roll) Editor time base is separate from the Audio Editor time base, the Arrange view time base, and the Transport bar time base.

MARKER TRACK TIME BASE SETTING

When the Marker Track is visible, the button on the right of the Marker Track header is called a Timebase button, but its function actually has to do with locking the markers. When the Marker Track time base is set to Beats (not Bars), markers are locked to musical position, meaning that tempo changes will move them in time, while when set to Seconds, markers will maintain their locations in time regardless of tempo changes.

Be an Efficiency Expert

You want to spend your time being creative, and the more time and energy you spend fussing with the computer, the less you have for creating. There are several great techniques for working faster and customizing Studio One 2 to your style of working.

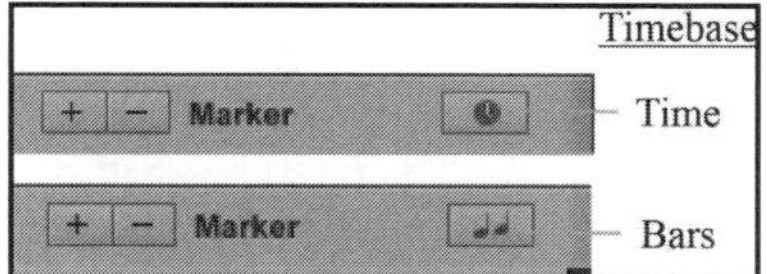

Fig. 1-37: The Marker Track time base is switched between seconds and bars by a button in the Marker Track header.

NAMING

Naming everything in your Song can be tedious, but I promise you that if you put out the effort to do it, you will thank yourself a

Fig. 1-38: The Song page with named and color-coded tracks.

thousand times over. Tracks, aux sends, submixes, even the inputs and outputs in Audio I/O Setup—name them all.

COLOR-CODING TRACKS AND CHANNELS

Color-coding can be used as another visual grouping indicator. People often do not bother with color-coding because it typically requires some time to walk through everything and assign colors, but if you work with any substantial number of tracks (say, more than 16 or so), you will come to realize that the few seconds spent here and there locating tracks or channels add up to more time than it takes to color-code them, especially if you color-code tracks or channels as you create them.

There are some obvious candidates for color-coding, like making all drum tracks one color, or coloring all the vocal tracks the same, but there are many other good cases for color-coding. Here are a few examples:

- Color all rhythm section tracks other than drums (bass, rhythm guitar, keys, and so on) the same. Solo or lead tracks are a different color.
- If you work with sampled orchestra sounds, try coloring each section.
- Using a single color for similar sounds from different sources. Perhaps you are combining string samples or sounds from several different virtual instruments, maybe even mixing them with some string tracks that you record yourself. Giving the same color to string tracks from all of these sources helps you see them as a section.
- Color assorted percussion the same.
- Make demo, rough, or work tracks a different color than final tracks.
- Color Instrument tracks differently than Audio tracks.

Mixer channels also can be easier to grasp when color-coded. When VIs have multiple audio outputs, their mixer channels may not match up with tracks on a one-to-one basis. In these cases, you might want to color-code the channels to match the tracks. Coloring buses being used as subgroup masters to match the channels feeding them is another good example, as is coloring effects return channels dedicated to a particular instrument to be the same as the instrument's channels. If you have snare top and snare bottom channels and then add a snare reverb, coloring them all the same makes it easy to check all your snare levels at a glance, just to give one example.

It is also possible to color Parts or Events individually in Studio One 2. This can be useful as well. For instance, you might assign all Parts or Events needing further editing work to have the same color. Zooming out then lets you see at one glance how much editing work is left to be done.

DEFAULT AUDIO I/O SETUP

Many people work in the same way consistently, with their systems configured the same most of the time. One way to save time when starting new Songs is to make and save a default Audio I/O Setup, as described in the "Audio I/O Setup" section above. Every time you create a new Song, your inputs and outputs will automatically be configured to your usual way of working.

TEMPLATES

If you tend to record in similar ways over and over again, as most people do, you can save a lot of time by using templates. Studio One 2 comes with a number of preconfigured Song templates. Most of them are designed for those using PreSonus interfaces, but there are a few that are more generic, application-oriented templates.

Fig. 1-39: The Rock Band template is a good illustration of the efficiency gained in using templates. Observe how the tracks are layed out and named.

It is most likely, however, that you will need to customize any existing template to your studio's setup, and quite possible that none of the existing templates will suit your needs. No worries—making your own template is easy, and while it takes some time to do, an investment in making good templates translates into significant time savings over the long run. What was just said about the benefits of naming goes double for templates.

To make your own customized template, do the following:

- Press Cmd + N (Ctrl + N in Windows) or choose File > New Song from the main menu bar.
- If you want to use one of the existing templates as a starting point, choose it, set the sample rate and other parameters as desired, and click on OK.
- Customize the template as desired.
- Choose File > Save as Template from the main menu bar, give it an appropriate name related to the application it is designed for, and click on OK.

At the most basic level, you will want to make sure that inputs and outputs are configured the way you usually use them. If you always bring the kick drum mic into input 1 of your interface and the snare into input 2, set up channels for them with those inputs.

Likewise, you'll want to set your master output to the interface outputs you usually use. If you have outboard gear you like to use, create channels for them and set them up for the interface inputs and outputs you usually use for that.

Submixes and groups are also great to set up in your template: for instance, drum and vocal submixes. If you have certain channel effects that you always use, say, a favorite vocal compressor plug-in, go ahead and set that up, too. You might even have a compressor preset you can load.

Templates take little space to store, so don't be shy about making versions that are slight variants of each other, if you'll use them regularly. The more presets you have, the more important a good file-naming scheme becomes for these, as well. As your templates evolve and you save the new versions as different files, be sure to get the old versions out of the way by archiving them to a different folder. That way, you can be certain you're always opening the latest version. Remember, if your templates are not well organized, they can't accomplish their purpose—that is, increasing your efficiency.

EFFECTS PRESETS

The same idea applies to effects presets, though not always to the same degree. Creative processing presets (like echo, reverb, and flanging) can work very well across a wide set of uses. Corrective processing, however, such as most EQ and compression, is very often particular to the source to which it is being applied and doesn't work as well for other things.

Even in that circumstance, presets can be worth making, especially if you have recurring needs. For example, if you always record vocals by the same person or always use the same vocal mic, you might be applying largely the same correction every time. Preset time!

As with templates, organization is fully half the battle. You want to be able to drop down a menu, skim down it, and know pretty quickly exactly which preset best fits what you're trying to do.

KEY SHORTCUTS

It is hard to overstate the efficiency gained by becoming proficient with key shortcuts. You have already seen that Studio One 2 allows you to assign key shortcuts to almost every function in the program, but there aren't enough key combinations possible to accommodate all of the functions, and most people use only a small set of commands for the bulk of their work anyway. The trick, then, is understanding which commands are most important to your workflow, and then giving them shortcuts that are easy for you.

Finding out which commands you really need shortcuts for involves simple observation: when you are working, take note of which commands you invoke repeatedly. A good rule of thumb is that the third time you use a command, you should consider making a shortcut for it. That means the ones you use the most will get shortcuts the fastest, the things you use less often will get them in time, and the things you never use will never get them.

What makes key shortcuts effective is having them "under your fingers," and there are two ways you can accomplish that: you can make them very intuitive (which is the best case), or they can be assimilated over many repetitions (which is the fallback when you run out of easy, intuitive key combinations).

Although consistency is, uh, key in setting up your key shortcuts, if you do several different kinds of work (albums, film, games), you can always have multiple sets of key shortcuts. Use similar key shortcuts in different sets for similar functions.

MACROS

Key shortcuts make a huge difference, but sometimes you will find sequences of commands you do repeatedly. For example, when recording you may often enable metronome, count-off, and Auto Punch, then go to the left Locator, and start recording. After you do the recording pass, you disable the metronome and count-off, go back to the left Locator, and play back to listen. Wouldn't life be simple if each of those sequences was a single key combination?

Macros can give you exactly that capability. Studio One 2 does not have a built-in capability to create macros of Studio One 2 commands . . . yet. But as of this writing, there is one under development, and it may even have been added to the program by the time you read this. The addition of an onboard macros feature will represent a tremendous step forward in expediting workflow!

When it arrives, Studio One 2's Macros feature will be enough to meet most people's needs, but you don't have to wait. Third-party automation software will let you create macro sequences right now, and if you have really heavy production demands, you will find functions in these programs that exceed anything you are likely to find in any Studio One macros feature. The most basic of the third-party programs can record mouse-clicks and keyboard input you perform and allow you to play them back using key combinations, but more advanced automation software goes far beyond that. Some macro programs can access system functions and offer conditional statements and other features normally associated with programming languages. In fact, these powerful programs do amount to scripting environments, but they are normally aimed at nonprogrammers.

On the Mac, QuicKeys has long provided these capabilities (http://startly.com/products/quickeys/mac/4). On Windows, there are several choices, including Workspace Macro Pro (www.tethyssolutions.com/macro-automation.htm).

Here comes organization again: if you're using macros, create a system for assigning key shortcuts that avoids conflict between the key combinations used to play back macros and those used for Studio One 2 shortcuts. This is especially important since many of your macros might just be sequences of Studio One 2 key shortcuts.

Macros can sometimes take a little fine-tuning before they work exactly the way you want, so expect to have to fiddle with them some until they're right. Once they work, however, they can enable you to take leaps forward while you work, making short work of long sequences that you execute time and time again.

MARKERS

Markers enable you to jump quickly to specific locations in your Song. For musical uses, like marking the beginning of a verse, marker times will generally be expressed in musical terms: bars and beats. For some tasks, especially working to video or in a game, it can be important to place a marker at a time location, instead of a musical one.

Studio One 2's marker facilities are basic but effective for many situations. For more information, see the section "Markers" in chapter 3, "Go! Recording with Studio One 2."

MINIMIZING REAL-TIME RESAMPLING

Studio One 2 is very smart about sampling rates. Most of the time, if it encounters a discrepancy somewhere, such as between the sample rate of the Song and that of the interface or an audio file being imported, it resamples on the fly instead of creating a new file at the proper sample rate. This is both powerful and useful, but also costly. Resampling multiple streams simultaneously definitely makes a processor break a sweat, which puts the brakes on using lots of VIs, convolution reverbs, and other processor-intensive tools. In addition to which, it simply makes for a more complex scenario, something more prone to problems.

Therefore, it is recommended that you take care to ensure that the audio interface and your Song are set to the same sample rate, and consider converting the sample rate of files with rates different from that of the Song. Studio One 2 is able to request PreSonus interfaces (and many from other manufacturers) to change to the Song's sample rate when the two rates differ, but there are some interfaces that do not accommodate this, so always double-check.

As for imported files, they can be converted in the Browser or with your favorite sample rate converter.

MONITORING PERFORMANCE

It can be very helpful to see how your computer is being taxed by your session. Both audio and MIDI activity can be viewed.

PERFORMANCE MONITOR

The Performance Monitor displays details about how much load audio is placing on your machine. Meters for the two most critical performance parameters—percentages of CPU and disk use—reside in the Transport bar to the right of the MIDI activity indicator.

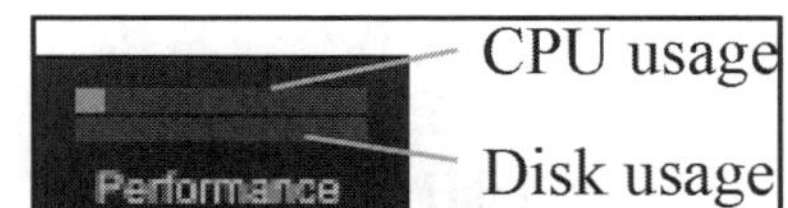

Fig. 1-40: The Performance meters in the Transport bar keep the CPU and disk usage in view at all times.

The Performance Monitor can be opened using either of these methods:

- Click on the performance meters in the Transport bar.
- Choose View > Performance Monitor from the main menu bar.

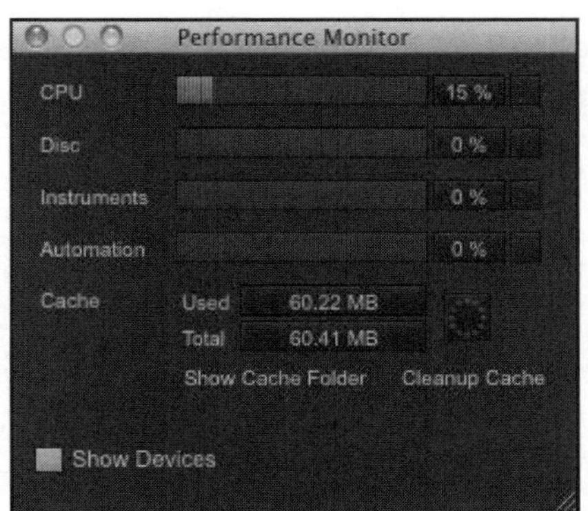

Fig. 1-41: The Performance Monitor window, which gives a more complete view of resource usage, can be reached simply by clicking on the Performance meters in the Transport bar.

The Performance Monitor window contains these displays:

- **CPU:** Thermometer and text displays showing the percentage of available CPU power being consumed by your Song.
- **Disc:** Thermometer and text displays showing the percentage of available disk access bandwidth being consumed by your Song.
- **Cache:** Used (amount of memory currently in use for caching), Total (available space for caching).
- **Cleanup Cache button:** Removes unneeded data from the cache.
- **Instruments:** Thermometer and text displays showing the percentage of available CPU power being consumed by the virtual instruments used in your Song
- **Automation:** Thermometer and text displays showing the percentage of available CPU power being consumed by automation used in your Song.
- **Show Devices checkbox:** When checked, this box opens a display that shows all VIs and plug-ins currently in use. For each one, it shows the percentage of CPU it is using with both a meter and a text readout, the device's name and an icon indicating its type, its path (location in the channel signal path), and the amount of latency through it.

MIDI MONITOR

MIDI Monitor enables you to see the MIDI messages coming into and going out from Studio One 2. This does not tell you anything about performance directly, but it can be helpful information. For more information on using MIDI Monitor, see the section "MIDI Monitor" in chapter 4, "Virtual Instruments and MIDI."

Orientation Graduation

Now you should have a pretty good idea how Studio One 2 is set up and where you will go to do different tasks. There's much more to Studio One 2, but the best way to move on at this point is to start using it!

LET'S HEAR SOMETHING!

Your system is set up, Studio One 2 is installed, and your interfaces are configured. We're ready to hear some music!

Make a New Song

- Go back to the Start page and click on the "Create a new Song" link. The New Song dialog box will open.
- Click in the Song Title field and name your song.
- If you want to store your Song somewhere other than the default location shown, click on the button beneath the right end of the Song Title field, navigate to the desired destination, and click on Open to select it.
- Set the Sample Rate to 44.1 kHz and the Resolution (bit depth) to 24-bit.

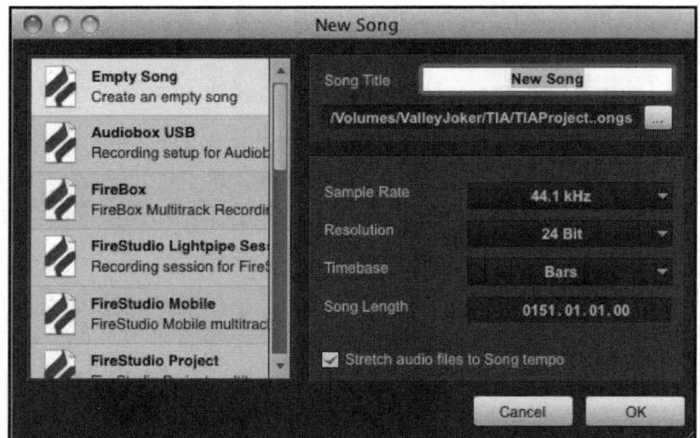

Fig. 1-42: The New Song dialog. Note the storage location below the Song Title field, and the list of templates on the left side.

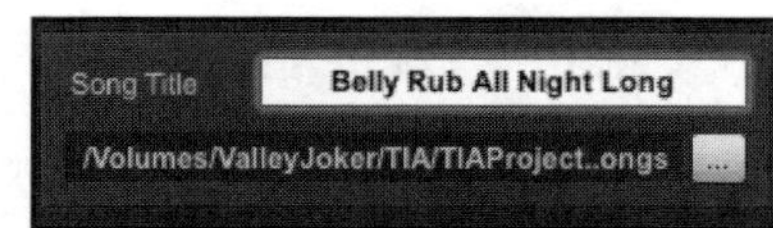

Fig. 1-43: Naming the new Song.

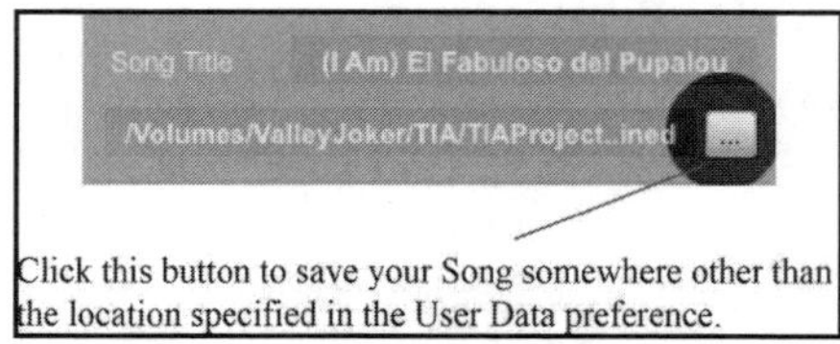

Fig. 1-44: Choosing a location for saving a Song.

- The Empty Song template should be selected by default in the template list on the right of the dialog box, but if it is not, click on it once to select it.
- Leave the rest of the options as they are for the moment and click on OK. A new, blank Song will appear.

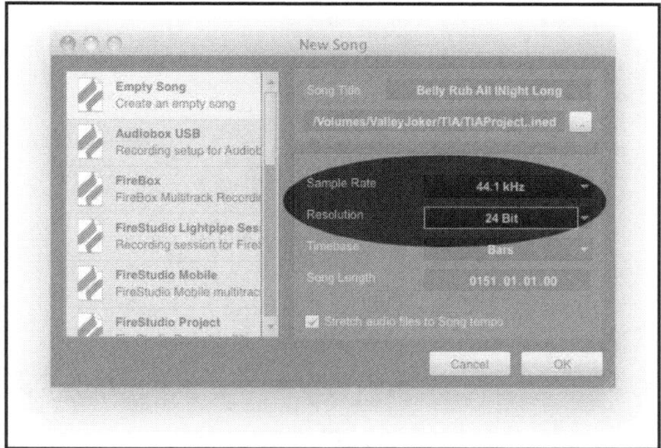

Fig. 1-45: Setting sample rate and resolution.

Be sure to double-check when you create a new Song that its sample rate agrees with your interface's. If it doesn't, change one or the other. Remember that you can usually open your interface's control software using the Control Panel button in Preferences > Options > Audio Setup. Of course, you can also simply open your interface's control software directly.

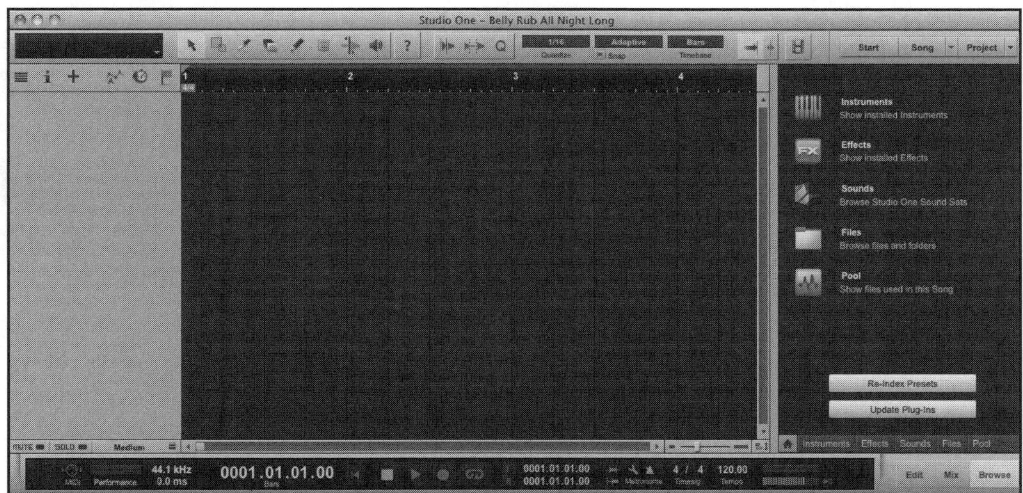

Fig. 1-46: A new, empty Song document.

Fill in the Song Metadata

Before we even bring in any audio, let's be organized and enter some metadata, at least for the title, artist, and songwriter. The Song metadata is located in Preferences > Song Setup > Meta Information. For more information, go back and look at Meta Information in the previous section.

Importing Audio

The fastest way to hear something in Studio One 2 is to import some existing audio and play it. There are two ways to do this:

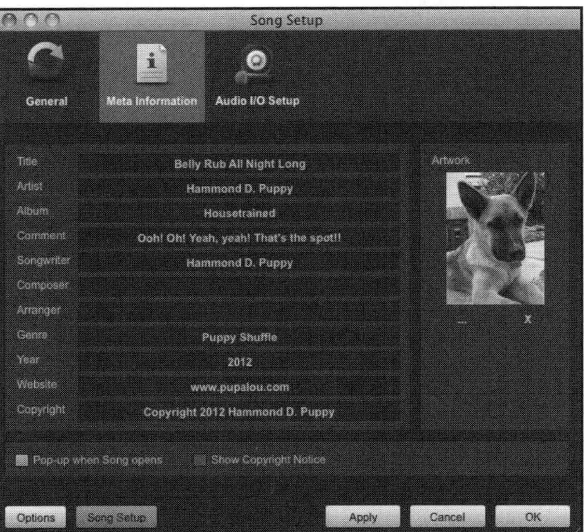

Fig. 1-47: Fill in the metadata for the Song as soon as possible after creating it.

- Drag audio files into Studio One 2 directly from the Mac Finder or Windows Explorer.
- Drag an MP3 file into Studio One 2, which will perform the required conversion to a new file with uncompressed data, and, if necessary, sample-rate convert the file to the sample rate of the Song at the same time. The new file it creates is put in the Song's Media folder.

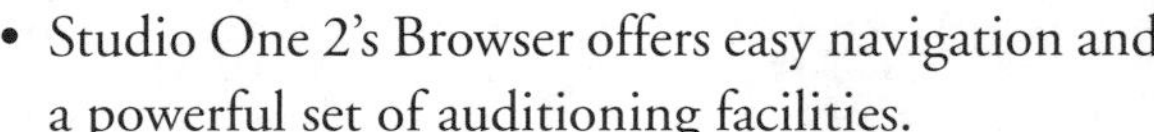

- Studio One 2's Browser offers easy navigation and a powerful set of auditioning facilities.

Let's take a look and see what the Browser can do.

- Click on the Browse button or press F5 (the default key shortcut) to open the Browser.
- Click on the Files button at the bottom of the Browser to show your file system.

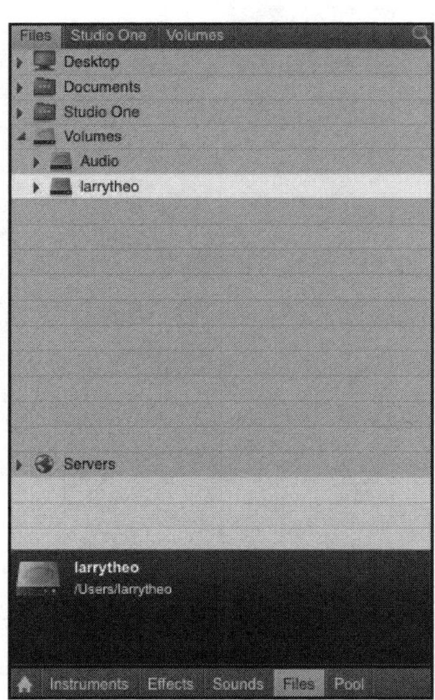

Fig. 1-48: The Files tab of the Browser.

When the Files pane opens, it defaults to showing you four folders:

- **Desktop:** Shows the folders on your computer's desktop.
- **Documents:** Shows the Documents folder on your computer.
- **Studio One:** Shows the folder indicated in Preferences > Options > Locations > User Data.
- **Volumes:** Shows all the mounted disks and volumes on your computer.

We're going to grab some tracks from "I'm Alright," one of the demo songs that was installed with Studio One 2. (If you didn't install the demo songs, you can locate some other WAV, AIFF, or MP3 file that is already on your computer somewhere.) You could just open the demo song, but how much fun is that compared with creating a new song and importing the audio yourself?

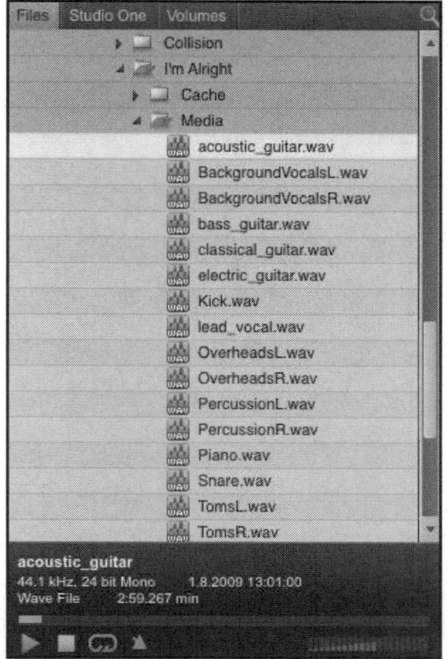

Fig. 1-49: The acoustic guitar example track in the Browser.

- Click on the Volumes folder to show its contents, and navigate to Documents/Studio One 2/Demos and Tutorials/Songs/I'm Alright/Media.
- Scroll down and find acoustic_guitar.wav.
- Drag acoustic_guitar.wav into the Arrange area. When the "ghost" outline of the file is at the start of the Song, let go of the mouse button to drop it there.

What happened? Studio One 2 automatically created a mono audio track in the Arrange view and a corresponding channel strip in the Mix view. If you look at the channel strip in the mixer, you will see that at the very top it says "Input L," and, just below that, "Main Out." This tells you that if you were to record into this track, the input would come from the virtual input Input L, and the channel's output would be routed to Main Out.

Fig. 1-50: When an audio file is dragged from the Browser and dropped in an empty area of the Arrange view, a new Audio track is created, as well as a new mixer channel.

TIP: In Studio One 2, there is not a one-to-one correspondence between tracks in the Arrange view and channels in the Mix view. Mix view shows only audio sources, while the Arrange view can have Instrument and Automation tracks as well as audio.

TIP: If you drag a mono audio file to an existing empty stereo audio track, it will automatically become a mono track. Conversely, if you drag a stereo file to an empty mono audio track, it will change to stereo. If you drag a mono or stereo file to a track that already has stereo or mono audio on it, the track will accept the audio but will retain its existing stereo or mono status. This means that you can drop a stereo file of mono audio (such as mono audio ripped from a CD) onto a mono track, and it will play in mono.

You're almost ready to hear this track. You just have one more thing to do: check that the Main Out is correctly mapped to your interface.

- Look at the top of the Main Out output strip at the far right of the mixer and observe the interface outputs named there.
- If the named outputs are not the interface outputs connected to your monitoring system, click on the name and choose the correct outputs from the drop-down menu.

Now the mix of your song will play out of the interface outputs you have chosen.

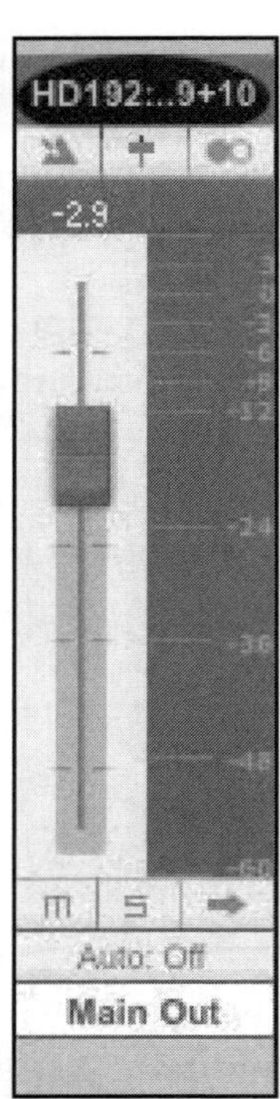

Fig. 1-51: Main Out strip with interface outputs highlighted.

Play, Baby!

Well, you have a new Song with some audio in it. Press the Spacebar and you should hear your music play!

Auditioning in the Browser with the Preview Player

You've seen how easy it is to import audio using the Browser, but it is often desirable to hear the audio before importing it—maybe to make sure it is the right file, or maybe to choose between several candidates. The Browser's Preview Player has excellent auditioning capabilities for that purpose. When you audition with the Preview Player (or directly from a list in the Browser), it will play through the Audition output, as described in the section "Meet Studio One 2" in this chapter. Let's import another file to our song, but this time we'll use the Preview Player to listen to it first.

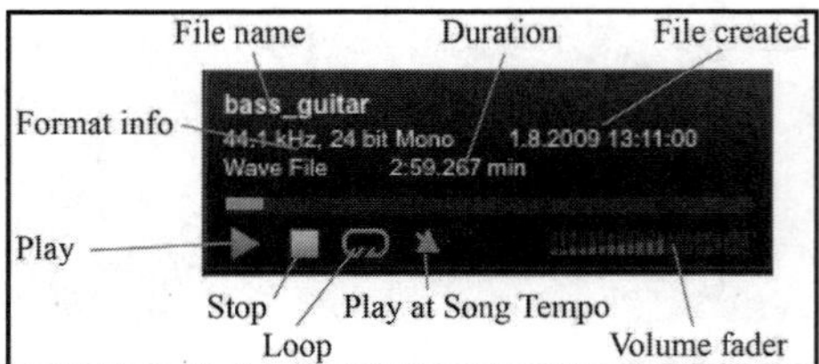

Fig. 1-52: The Preview Player in the Browser lets you audition files and loops directly from the Browser, even in tempo with the Song.

- The Browser should still be displaying the contents of Documents/Studio One 2/Demos and Tutorials/Songs/I'm Alright/Media. If it isn't, navigate back there again.
- Scroll down to the file bass_guitar.wav and click on it to select it.

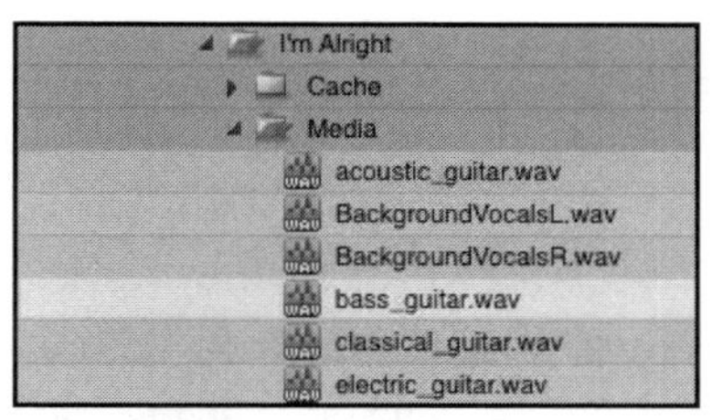

Fig. 1-53: The bass guitar example track in the Browser.

The action now shifts to the bottom of the Browser, where the Preview Player has appeared. The first thing you will notice is the information about the selected file that is being displayed: its name, sample rate, bit depth, duration, file type, and creation date. Now let's hear that file.

- To audition a file in the Browser, double-click on its name in the Files list, or click on the Play button.
- To stop playback, click on the Stop button.
- To start playback from the middle of the file, drag the Play Location bar to the desired location and click on the Play button.
- To loop playback of the file, click on the Loop button.
- To change the audition volume, click in the Audition Volume fader at the desired level, or drag the fader to that level.

AUDITIONING FILES IN SYNC WITH THE SONG

The Preview Player has one other great feature: letting you audition a file in tempo with the Song. This works only if there is tempo information stored in the audio file, as there is in many loops. Since you must start playback of the Song and the file separately, there is a bit of timing involved to start file playback on the right beat.

(If the file does not have a tempo stored in it, there are several ways to add one. For more information see the section "Audio File Tempos" in chapter 6, "Advanced Editing.")

To audition a file in tempo with the Song, do the following:

1. Select the file you want to audition in the Browser.
2. Click on the Play At Song Tempo button in the Preview Player.
3. Start playing the Song.
4. At the point in the Song where you want to hear the file, click on the Play button in the Preview Player. The file will play in sync with the Song.

More About the Browser

While you are in the Browser, it's a good time to get familiar with the rest of its file-handling capabilities in the Files and Pool panes. We will explore the rest of the Browser panes as we get to the topics to which they relate, but we'll start here with a brief overview.

The Browser is a very powerful environment for accessing content libraries and the content used in the Song. It is constituted of five panes devoted to different sorts of content, plus a home page for easy access to the panes. The contents of each pane are searchable, sortable, and customizable. A flexible player for auditioning loops and audio files is integrated, and can even be synced to Song playback.

The five panes are the following:

- **Instruments:** Lists all of the virtual instruments, both included and third-party, currently available.
- **Effects:** Provides access to all audio plug-in processors and stored chains of effects (FX Chains).
- **Sounds:** Gives access to loops, beats, and other audio content.
- **Files:** This is how you navigate to any file in your computer's file system. All mounted volumes are shown and accessible. Studio One 2 presets and Songs are also available from the Files tab.
- **Pool:** The Pool is all of the audio files actually being used in the Song, whether they reside somewhere in your file system or were created by Studio One 2.

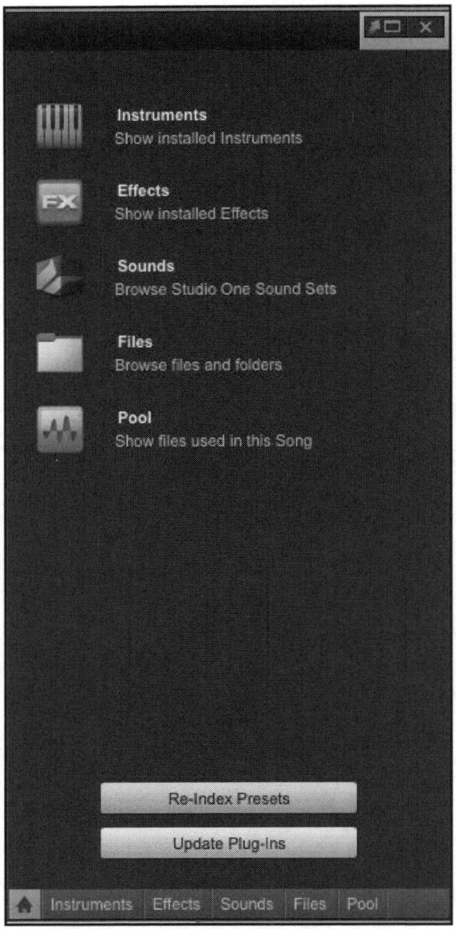

Fig. 1-54: The Browser home page. The buttons duplicate the functions of the tabs at the bottom.

THE BROWSER HOME PAGE

The Browser home page is really quite simple: it has one button for each of the five panes, plus two plug-in-related utilities. The buttons duplicate the functionality of the tabs at the top of the Browser.

- To access a pane from the home page, click on its name or icon.
- To tell Studio One 2 to scan and organize your presets, click on the Re-Index Presets button.
- To check for the latest versions of PreSonus plug-ins, click on the Update Plug-Ins button.

TABS AND FOLDERS

The Files pane opens a view onto a tremendous number of files, essentially all that are available on your computer system. When you are working on a project, you will usually want to deal with a smaller set of files that is likely to reside in an enclosing folder. Perhaps you would like able to look only at the files used in the project you are working on, or you might want to only look at your library of drum loops.

The Browser allows you to add a tab at the top for any folder in the file system. You can add as many tabs as you want and name them whatever you like. Tabs you create are global: they will show up in every Song and Project.

The Browser lets you manage folders and files as well. Tab, folder, and file-management functions are accessed by right-clicking (or Ctrl-clicking on the Mac).

- To manage files in the Files pane of the Browser, right-click on the file and choose the desired function. You can rename, delete, or show files in the Finder (Explorer in Windows). You can also import a file to the Pool.
- To manage folders in the Files pane of the Browser, right-click on the folder and choose the desired function. You can rename, delete, or show the folder in the Finder (Explorer in Windows), or create a new folder inside the selected one.
- To manage tabs in the Files pane of the Browser, you can right-click on a tab, folder, or file and choose the desired function. The functions are slightly different in each of these cases.
- In all cases, you can choose Rename Tab, Close Tab (which removes it), Up, or New Root Tab. The Root Tab is the folder that is at the top of tab. Up redefines the tab to move up one level in the folder hierarchy. New Root Tab duplicates the Files tab. Why would you want to do that? Because it is one way to create a new tab for a folder. Read on . . .
- If you have right-clicked on a folder, you can choose Set as Root. This makes the selected folder be the root of that tab. This is often the second step of a process that starts with making a new root tab.
- Another way to create a new tab with a selected folder as the root is to choose New Tab From Here when right-clicking on the folder you want to be the root.

SORTING THE DISPLAY

To sort the files in the Instrument, Effects, and Pool tabs, click on one of the buttons at the top of the Browser.

- **Flat** sorts alphabetically.
- **Folder** (Instruments and Effects tabs) sorts by the actual folder organization of the files.

- **Vendor** (Instruments and Effects tabs) sorts by the manufacturer of the plug-in or VI.
- **Category** (Instruments and Effects tabs) sorts by plug-in format (VST2, VST3, AudioUnit, PreSonus).
- **Track** (The Pool) lists each track and shows every file used on it.
- **Type** (The Pool) sorts by file type (Audio or Sound).
- **Location** (The Pool) groups files by the source folder.
- **Record Take** (The Pool) sorts audio files by the order in which they were recorded, and reports the time and date they were recorded and the file names. Files that were imported instead of being recorded are sorted as "Not Recorded."

TIP: If you add or rename a track, Track sorting of the Pool may not update automatically. Simply right-click (or Ctrl-click on the Mac) anywhere in the Pool and choose Refresh to force it to update. Switching to another kind of sorting or another view and then back will also cause it to update.

SEARCHING IN THE BROWSER

- To access Browser Search in the Instruments, Effects, Sounds, and Files tabs, click on the magnifying glass icon in the upper right of the pane, and type in the search phrase. The feature is a live search, so it will find as you type.

COLLAPSING DIRECTORIES IN THE BROWSER

- To collapse all directories in the Browser and go back to the top level, press Option + Up Arrow.

FILES TAB CONVERSION UTILITIES

Among other handy capabilities, the Files tab has a few very useful commands for converting selected files. PreSonus has introduced a few new file types of their own, notably the Musicloop and Audioloop formats, which are briefly described in the section "Musicloop and Audioloop File Formats" in chapter 3, "Go! Recording with Studio One 2." For more about Musicloop and Audioloop files, see the chapter "Working with Loops" in my upcoming book *Power Tools for Studio One 2*, volume 2.

- A selected stereo file can be split to a pair of mono files by right-clicking on it in the Browser, and choosing Split to Mono in the contextual drop-down menu that appears.
- A selected pair of mono files in the Browser can be combined into a single stereo file by right-clicking on it in the Browser and choosing Merge to Stereo in the contextual drop-down menu that appears.
- A selected audio file can be sent to a new instance of the Sample One sampler by right-clicking on it in the Browser and choosing Send to New Sample One in the contextual drop-down menu that appears. A new instance of Sample One will be created and the sound loaded into it.

THE POOL

The Pool button at the bottom of the Browser opens the Pool pane, which shows all of the files in your Song. There are two kinds of files: audio and Sounds. So what the heck is "Sound" supposed to mean? In PreSonus-speak, a "Sound" is included content, be it a sample, loop, or virtual instrument preset, stored in the Soundset file format.

The Pool lets you see a waveform display for each audio file ("Sound" files are empty), sort the files in a number of different ways, audition files exactly as in the Files pane, and, of course, drag them into the Song.

TIP: There is nowhere in Studio One 2 that lists Events (regions) in a Song, only files.

VERTICAL ZOOM OF THE WAVEFORM DISPLAY

- To enlarge the waveform displays of files in the Pool, click-and-drag on the magnifying glass icon in the upper right corner. Note that on other tabs, this icon instead brings up Browser search.

FILE MANAGEMENT IN THE POOL

As in the Files pane, right-clicking in the Pool brings up a host of management options.

Right-clicking on a file in the Pool brings up these options:

- **Rename File:** Renames source file on disk.
- **Locate File:** The difference between Locate File and Locate Missing Files is subtle. Both commands are used to reconnect Studio One 2 with one or more files it has lost track of, perhaps because a file or Song got moved. Locate File is somewhat more, um, forceful (for lack of a better word), in that it forces Studio One 2 to associate the file you point to with the file you clicked in the Pool, even if it is an entirely different file than was associated with that file in the Pool before.
- **Show in Finder:** Reveals the file in the file system.
- **Select on Track:** Choosing this command selects all Events used on tracks that are based on the file.
- **Remove from Pool:** Removes the file from the Song, but not from the disk.
- **Delete File Permanently:** Removes the file from your disk. USE WITH CARE!
- **Convert Files:** Converts the sample rate, bit depth, and/or file format of the selected file or files. This is most often used to convert files that do not match the sample rate or bit depth of the Song to match them. Available file formats include WAV, AIFF, FLAC, and Ogg Vorbis.
- **Refresh:** Forces an update to show all changes to the Pool.
- **Locate Missing Files:** Almost the same thing as Locate File, except that it is intended for finding multiple files and wants exactly the files it was associated with before.
- **Remove Unused Files:** A cleanup function that removes from the Pool (but not the disk) any files that are not currently used in the Song. This is an excellent thing to do

when the Song is done and you are archiving it, or when you are sending the song to someone else to mix.

- **Copy External Files:** Often, your Song will use files or loops from various places on your computer. Aside from being generally confusing and posing a risk if any of those files get moved, this also makes it impossible to move your Song to another computer. Copy External Files finds all files used by the Song that are not already in the Song's Media folder and copies them there.
- **Show Media Folder in Finder:** The Media folder is the Song's default storage place for all of the files it uses. This command takes you to the folder.

If you right-click in the Pool but not on any file, you get a subset of the above options that apply only to multiple files.

FILE CONVERSION: SRC AND FILE FORMATS

The Convert Files command mentioned above deserves a little extra attention because the ability to perform sample rate or file format conversion is an important one. Use of Convert Files is intuitive—in fact, downright obvious (as well it should be)—but significant enough to justify calling out the procedure. Convert Files works only on files that are in The Pool.

Files can be converted to WAV, AIFF, FLAC, and Ogg Vorbis formats. Available resolutions are 8-bit, 16-bit, 24-bit (all fixed point), or 32-bit floating point.

Available sample rates (in kHz) are 11.025, 22.05, 32, 44.1, 48, 88.2, 96, and 192.

To convert the sample rate, resolution (bit depth), or file format for one or more files in the Pool, do the following:

1. Right-click on the file you wish to convert. To convert multiple files simultaneously to the same settings, select all of them using standard selection techniques, then right-click on any of them.
2. Choose Convert Files from the contextual drop-down menu that appears. The Convert Files dialog box will then appear.
3. Set one or more of the available parameters to the desired values.

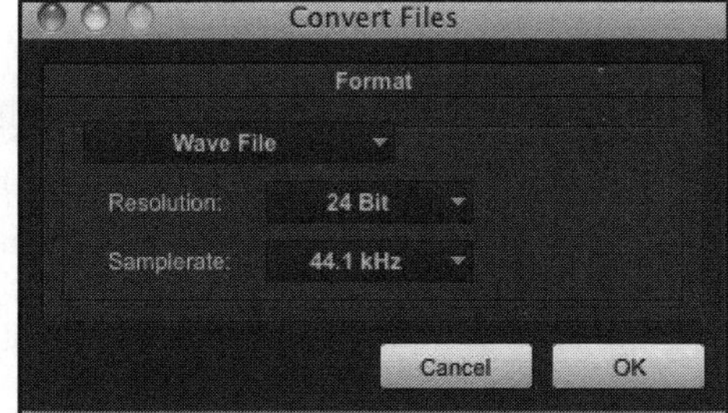

Fig. 1-55: The Convert Files dialog is reached by right-clicking in the Browser.

4. If you choose FLAC as the file format, set the Compression Level slider that appears to the desired amount of compression. Note that only 16-bit and 24-bit resolutions are available.
5. If you choose Ogg Vorbis as the file format, you must either click on the Variable bit-rate button and set the Quality slider that appears to the desired quality level, or click on the Managed bit-rate button and enter values in the Maximum, Average, and Minimum bit-rate fields that appear. Note that you do not set resolution for an Ogg Vorbis file.

CHOOSING AND USING MICROPHONES

To record anything other than synthesizers and samplers, you will usually need a microphone. Which microphone you choose is one of the biggest factors in determining how good your recordings will sound. Microphones are precision devices; truly outstanding ones can cost serious money and are well worth it, if you have the dollars to spend. Fortunately, there are a great many low-cost microphones available nowadays that do a more than credible job. There are many manufacturers making good, low-cost microphones, including familiar names like Rode and Shure, but many manufacturers who once made only high-end microphones, such as DPA, now have more affordable offerings. I have not had the pleasure of trying DPA's lower-cost options, but the absolute clearest, most uncolored, affordable mics I've found are from Earthworks, and I use my Earthworks mics more than any others for acoustic instruments and as my go-to drum overhead mics.

The many small, boutique mic manufacturers have some excellent offerings as well, but not everything that looks gourmet tastes gourmet, so do your research and, whenever possible, try before you buy. Personal taste plays a huge role in mic selection, so the best mic for you might be horrible in someone else's judgment, and vice versa.

Understanding a little about the different kinds of microphones and what they are good for will go a long way in helping you choose the right one(s) for your needs. Professionals usually amass a collection of microphones over the course of years, just to have the right one for anything they need to do.

MICROPHONE TYPES

A microphone is a kind of transducer—a transducer being a device that converts energy from one form to another. In the case of microphones, acoustical energy is transduced into mechanical and then electrical energy. Transduction is a difficult task, and is impossible to achieve without some degree of compromise or imperfection. Sometimes these imperfections are a problem, and other times the imperfections can impart desirable qualities.

There are three types of microphones commonly used in recording: condenser, dynamic (also called "moving coil"), and ribbon. Each of these types employs a different method of transducing sound, but all of them use a diaphragm that is moved by the sound you are trying to capture and record into Studio One 2.

Whatever type it is, every microphone responds to sound from some area around it, which is called its "pickup pattern." The sound heard from a microphone also depends greatly on how it is placed relative to the instrument being recorded. It is also very important to note that the microphone preamplifier has a tremendous impact on how a microphone sounds. The same microphone can sound very different plugged into different preamps, so finding the correct combination of mic and preamp is crucial. It is common to find one particular combination of mic and preamp that seems just right, so experimenting with combinations is very worthwhile.

Let's take a closer look at these considerations, starting with mic types.

Condenser Microphones

Condenser microphones are probably the most common type found in recording because of the wide range of frequencies they can capture and their clarity and crispness of sound. "Condenser" is the British word for the electrical component known in the United States as a "capacitor," and the capsules of condenser microphones (the part that actually captures sound vibrations from the air) work on the principle of *capacitance*.

A capacitor is actually an energy storage element, kind of like a small water tank. A capacitor consists of two conductive plates placed very close to each other, and the amount of energy it can store is determined by the size of the plates and how close together they are.

In a condenser microphone capsule, one of those plates is the diaphragm that is moved by the sound you are recording. As it moves closer to and farther from the other plate (called the "backplate"), its storage capacity changes, creating a small electrical signal. That signal is so small that the microphone itself has to contain a small preamplifier just to make the signal large and strong enough to get to your recorder. The onboard preamp also serves the purpose of converting the very high output impedance of the capsule to a lower impedance that can carry the signal across a mic cable. (Sorry, explaining the electronics is more than we can do in this book, but you will benefit from gaining more understanding of these topics elsewhere.) Thus, condenser microphones always require some amount of power. See the section "Powering Condenser Microphones" in this chapter for more information on this.

The diaphragm in a condenser microphone is very light in weight and moves easily. This is how the condenser microphone is able to capture such a wide range of frequencies and provide excellent transient response. There are large-diaphragm condensers, which are better at picking up low frequencies, and small-diaphragm condensers, which can have more extended high-frequency response; however, both kinds handle very wide frequency ranges.

Condenser microphones are the best all-around choice for recording vocals and acoustic instruments. They are also often used for drum overheads. If you can afford only one microphone, you will probably want a condenser.

POWERING CONDENSER MICROPHONES

In order to generate its signal, the backplate of a condenser microphone's capsule must have an electrical charge. There are two main ways this is accomplished. One relatively inexpensive way to do it is to put a "permanent" charge on the backplate (it actually wears off after a number of years). Microphones that use this technique are called "electret condensers," and these require power only for the onboard preamplifier, which is usually supplied by a regular flashlight or photographic battery in the microphone.

Tube condenser microphones usually come with a dedicated power supply that provides the much higher power required by tubes, as well as charging the plates of the microphone capsule.

Professional solid-state microphones use a system called "phantom power," in which power for both the backplate and the onboard preamp is supplied by the mic preamp into which it is plugged. Most phantom power supplies provide +48V of DC power, though many condenser microphones can also work with other voltages. If you buy a condenser, make sure you have a preamp that can supply phantom power for it.

Microphones that do not need phantom power are generally not bothered by its presence (which is good, because many small mixers supply phantom power to some or all of their inputs at once, but cannot send it just to one input). However, there are a few microphones, notably older ribbon mics, that can be destroyed by phantom power. Be sure you know whether your noncondenser mics can handle phantom power before you switch it on at the preamp or mixer.

TUBE VERSUS SOLID-STATE

Tube condenser microphones and microphone preamps carry a lot of mystique. Are they really better? It depends.

The earliest days of condenser microphones predated transistors (which are solid-state devices), so all condenser mics were tubes. When transistors began to be used in microphones, they sounded different than tubes. Put into a broad generality, people felt that tube condenser mics had a "warmer" and "rounder" sound, while solid-state condensers were more "precise" and "uncolored."

It's not really that simple, though, because there are bad tube condensers that sound dull and boxy, and bad solid-state condensers that sound shrill and flat. A condenser microphone is not inherently better or worse because it has a tube or an FET or some other device inside.

Having said that, good tube condensers get their warmth largely from the kind of distortion they generate, which is rich in even harmonics. Furthermore, the amount and distribution of these harmonics will vary with the level of the sound being recorded, so the effect is dynamic. The trade-off for gaining this quality is that a tube condenser consumes more power than a solid-state condenser. It is supplied by a dedicated power supply, and more than a little of the power consumed gets thrown off as heat. Because of the physics of tubes, tube condenser mics need some time to warm up (generally 45 minutes to an hour or so) before they reach their best sound. If left on for many hours, the sound can start to change again, and the components can become more stressed. Thus, there is a window within which tube condensers will sound their best. This also means that a vocal recorded at the beginning of a session with a tube condenser can sound a bit different than the same vocalist recorded later the same day.

Solid-state condensers are more stable in this regard, and do not run hot as tube condensers do. Good solid-state condensers can also have a clarity and crispness that is better for some sources.

Dynamic or Moving Coil Microphones

Dynamic microphones rely on electromagnetic induction to transduce sound into an electrical signal, a different operating principle than condenser microphones. In a dynamic microphone, the diaphragm is attached to a coil of wire mounted in the middle of a ring-shaped magnet. As the diaphragm is moved by the sound, the coil of wire is moving back and forth through the magnetic field. When a wire is moved through a magnetic field, a signal is electromagnetically induced, generating the signal you will record. No power is needed for dynamic microphones, as they have neither backplates that need powering nor onboard preamps.

The moving-coil mechanism is much sturdier than the capacitive mechanism in condenser mics, making dynamic mics very popular in live performance. In the studio, they are often used for drums or electric guitars, but their heavier mechanism is less responsive than that of condensers, making them generally less suitable for vocals and acoustic instruments. As always, this is a generalization; there are exceptions.

Ribbon Microphones

Ribbon microphones use electromagnetism, as dynamic mics do—moving a wire back and forth through the field of a magnet. In the ribbon mic, however, there is no coil of wire attached to the diaphragm. Instead, the diaphragm is itself a very thin, corrugated ribbon of electrically conductive metal foil mounted in the gap of a magnet, thus fulfilling the role of the coil of wire. In older ribbon mics this diaphragm was very fragile, and putting a ribbon mic too close to a drum or a loud amplifier could destroy it. Modern ribbon mics are much more robust, but it is still wise to take care in using them on extremely loud sounds or placing them right up against a loud source.

The sound of ribbon mics is distinguished by two things: a slow, smooth tailing off of high frequencies, and a bidirectional pickup pattern. (We'll discuss pickup patterns in just a moment.) The silky quality of ribbon mics makes them popular for vocals, especially those that are softer, rather than screaming rockers (think Sinatra or Norah Jones). They are also sometimes used (carefully) for guitar amps or brass instruments. Ribbon mics are nowhere near as versatile as condenser mics, but they have a particular sound quality that can't be beat for some uses.

Like condenser microphones, the output of the ribbon microphone capsule is extremely low, but ribbon mics traditionally did not include onboard mic preamps. This placed greater demands on the mic preamp into which it is plugged, requiring from it a lot of gain, very low noise, and high input impedance. Many otherwise excellent preamps are not up to the task of amplifying ribbon mics, and there are mic preamps created specifically for this purpose.

Ribbon mics have experienced a real renaissance in the past several years, and some of the newest models do, in fact, incorporate onboard mic preamps, sometimes powered via phantom power.

If you use a ribbon microphone, make sure that you understand the model you have and treat it right. With proper care and feeding, a ribbon mic can give you results you can't get with any other kind of mic.

Boundary Microphones

While the physics behind boundary microphones have long been known, commercial products exploiting them date back only to the mid-1980s, when Crown International released boundary microphones under the trademarked name PZM (for pressure zone microphone). Boundary microphones use condenser microphone elements housed in a very specific way, in which the microphone element is placed very close to a plate (the "boundary"). This results in a few very useful pickup characteristics that we will discuss in a moment. Boundary microphones can be relatively inexpensive and can provide performance for some applications that no other kind of mic can.

Clip-On Microphones

Clip-on microphones are condenser microphone elements with little or no housing, but a convenient mounting system. The fact that they have no housing makes them very small, which is helpful in several situations.

The original clip-on mic was the lavalier, which is clipped onto a person's clothing. You see these on TV talk shows all the time, clipped onto a shirt or lapel. Lavaliers see virtually no use in music recording.

There are, however, clip-on microphones made for attaching to drums or guitar amplifiers, and these can be very useful for music. The small diaphragm size limits the low-frequency response of clip-on microphones, but their close proximity to the source being recorded can make up for this.

Other variations on the clip-on idea include microphone elements on long, thin stems, or on headsets. While headset mics are most valuable in live performance, mics on stems, like clip-ons, can be great for getting into tight spaces.

For years, lavaliers and other clip-on mics had poor response in comparison with, say, a nice professional condenser. In more recent years, precision manufacturing has hugely improved the fidelity of these "micro-mics," and they are far better suited to recording than in the past.

PICKUP PATTERNS

The type of microphone, the construction of its housing, and, in some cases, electrical manipulation, determine the area from which it picks up sound. Understanding these patterns is critical to making a good recording. Some microphones, especially condensers, allow you to choose between two or more different patterns, and some even allow continuous variation between them.

There are three basic pickup patterns: omnidirectional, bidirectional, and unidirectional. There are several varieties of unidirectional pattern, and this is the kind most often used in many kinds of recording.

Omnidirectional

Since "omni" means "all," you might correctly guess that an omnidirectional microphone picks up sound from all directions, from the back just as well as from the front. This can be good and bad. On the plus side, omnidirectional microphones tend to have the purest, least colored tonal quality. (Note that it is very often the case that a microphone is chosen for a task because of the particular tonal coloration it does impose!) For recording an acoustic guitar and violin duo, for example, omnidirectional mics could be a great choice.

The other good thing about omnidirectional mics can also be a bad thing, and that is that, since they pick up sound from all around, they capture room reverberation as well as the source you are recording. If you are in a nice-sounding space, maybe a small theater or recital hall, an omnidirectional mic will capture the lovely ambience as well as the instruments. If, however, you are in a poor-sounding space or there are other sound sources nearby you do not want captured by this mic (such as other instruments), the ambient sound the omni mic picks up, called "bleed," will be undesirable. In these situations, an omnidirectional mic is a poor choice.

Bidirectional

Again, the name is satisfyingly descriptive. "Bi" indicates "two," so it comes as no surprise that bidirectional mics pick up sound from the front and the back of the microphone equally (well, very close to equally), while ignoring sound coming from its sides. Bidirectional pickup patterns are also called "figure-8" patterns, since that is how they look when you graph them.

There are several useful applications for a bidirectional pickup pattern. For a start, a bidirectional mic can capture some room reverberation, though less than an omnidirectional mic.

Another situation in which bidirectional mics are useful is if you want to record two vocalists at the same time onto a single track, such as for backup vocals. The vocalists can stand on opposite sides of a bidirectional mic and sing into it while looking at each other. The Beatles did this often.

Note, however, that both voices are being mixed acoustically while you are recording them, and you will not be able to change their balance or tone independently later. Move the vocalists closer or further from the mic to get the balance you need before you start recording.

Bidirectional pickup can be useful when you want to record several musicians sitting in a semicircle or a circle. A bidirectional mic could be good for recording a drum circle, for example. (Depending on how the drummers are sitting, an omni might work as well or better.)

Bidirectional mics can be just as useful for what they don't pick up as for what they do: if you orient a bidirectional mic sideways to an unwanted sound, that sound is pretty effectively rejected. This can gain you some isolation without having to use physical means like baffles. However, never forget that a bidirectional mic picks up as well behind it as in front, meaning that it offers no rejection of unwanted sound behind it.

Two bidirectional mics placed at right angles to each other provide omnidirectional pickup, but in stereo. Bidirectional mics are also used in M-S stereo miking, described below.

Ribbon microphones are inherently bidirectional in their pickup, and many variable-pattern condensers can be set to bidirectional patterns. It is exceedingly rare to find a bidirectional dynamic microphone, though they have been made before.

Unidirectional

Unidirectional mics are more sensitive to sound coming from in front of them than from any other direction, but the width of the area that is picked up is different for the several unidirectional patterns found in various microphones. The most accurate pickup comes directly in front of the mic, or "on-axis" to it. As you move toward the side of the mic, the frequency balance changes and coloration is introduced, the specifics varying from mic to mic. Unidirectional mics also often exhibit a high-frequency boost, which can be very useful for emphasizing the presence range of frequencies. Of course, there are times when this is not desirable, but it is helpful in getting a sound to cut through a mix.

The most common pattern is called a "cardioid" pattern, so called because it resembles a valentine heart shape. A mic with a cardioid pattern is sensitive to sound coming from in front of it, falling off toward the sides. It is least sensitive to sound coming from directly behind it.

The supercardioid pattern is similar to the cardioid, but with a narrower pickup pattern. This is good when an unwanted source is located nearby—for example, when miking rack toms in a drum kit. Using supercardioid mics on the toms can help get better isolation on each one. (I use Shure Beta 87 mics for this.) This narrowing in the front, however, is counterbalanced by a slight widening of the pickup pattern in the rear (called a "lobe").

Thus, while a supercardioid mic picks up a narrower space in front, it captures a bit more sound from the rear than a mic with a cardioid pattern.

The hypercardioid pattern takes the supercardioid idea further: an even narrower front pickup pattern and an even larger rear lobe.

Shotgun microphones take the idea of directionality to the extreme. In a shotgun mic, the mic capsule is built with a long tube on the end. This tube narrows the pickup pattern to the point that the microphone picks up only what is directly on-axis, and rejects sound that is even a little to the side. This is great for picking up sounds at a distance or in very noisy situations. The trade-off, however, is that what little off-axis sound does get captured is extremely colored.

The Special Case of Boundary Microphones

Boundary microphones are made by placing a mic element in the pressure zone that occurs right at the surface of a boundary. There are a few very distinctive characteristics that arise from this:

- **Hemispherical pickup pattern:** A boundary mic picks up half of what an omnidirectional mic does. If an omni's pickup pattern is a sphere, cut that sphere in half and you have the pattern of a boundary mic.
- **Extreme rejection:** If a boundary mic picks up everything in the hemisphere in front of it, it picks up virtually nothing behind it. The degree of rejection is extremely high, meaning that you could aim a boundary mic at an ensemble at a live performance and pick up almost none of the audience and room reverberation behind it.
- **Constant direct-to-reverberant ratio:** If you stand in an auditorium when a musician is playing, the farther you get from the musician, the more room reverberation and the less of the direct sound of the musician you hear, until, at a certain distance, the ratio becomes constant. Most microphones work this way, too, but boundary microphones, because of the action of the pressure zone, exhibit much less of this differentiation. If a musician is miked with a boundary microphone, taking several steps back or to the side will make much less difference than using any other kind of mic.
- Low-frequency pickup depends on the boundary size: the lowest frequency picked up by a boundary mic is determined by the size of the boundary. If mounting a boundary mic on a two-foot-by-two-foot sheet of Plexiglass extends the low-frequency pickup considerably, you can imagine what mounting it on a wall does! This makes boundary mics very useful as room mics when recording drums (assuming the room has good-sounding acoustics).

MICROPHONE PLACEMENT

Once you've picked the right mic for the job, the way it is placed relative to the instrument you are recording makes a tremendous difference to the sound. Sometimes moving a mic less than an inch can make a noticeable change in the sound, so experiment with placement to find the best sound before you hit Record in Studio One 2.

The distance from the mic to the source and the orientation of the mic relative to the source are two of the biggest considerations. Distance changes the sound in two big ways: first, as we've already noted, the farther you get from the source, the more reverb, room ambience, and sound from other sources you will pick up. Second, distance changes the tone you will get.

As you get farther from the source, you will lose more and more high frequencies. With a very bright source like a trumpet, this could be a good thing, but with an acoustic guitar it might get too dark. If you put the mic very close to the source, you will get less reverb and other sources, and more high frequencies. With many unidirectional mics, you will hear the low frequencies increase as you get very close; the closer you are, the more low-frequency emphasis. This is called the "proximity effect," and can be very useful for getting warmth out of vocals and low-end body out of toms in a drum kit, especially when using clip-on mics. However, it can be a drag if you get lots of low-frequency thumping by miking that acoustic guitar too close.

Close-miking also places more emphasis on the sound right in front of the mic, which might mean more squeaks from the player's fingers on the strings of a guitar, or key noise from a saxophone. We generally hear acoustic instruments from several feet away, giving time for the acoustical contributions of the various parts of the instrument to blend into a balanced sound. Close-miking distorts that balance, often requiring equalization later in the process to compensate. Sometimes multiple microphones may be placed on an instrument to accomplish the same thing, but this carries its own dangers, since adding two microphone outputs together can result in frequency cancellations caused by phase differences in the sound arrivals at the microphones.

As I've already said, bidirectional and unidirectional microphones pick up sound differently depending on the direction from which the sound comes. This fact can be used to your advantage in a few ways. One way is to orient the mic so that unwanted sounds come from the direction in which it is least sensitive. Another way is to use the change in tone as the source is further off-axis. For example, if you have a cardioid mic placed near where the neck of an acoustic guitar meets the body, you can point the mic more toward where the guitar is being picked in order to get a bit less of the string squeaks and more of the finger-picking sound. Similarly, if a vocalist is producing a lot of plosives (the puffs of air from *p* and *b* sounds) or sibilance (harshness on *s* sounds), angling the mic slightly to put the vocalist a little off-axis can be just the ticket.

Mic placement is an art, and a difference of a fraction of an inch in placement can make an astonishing difference to the sound. It is always better to get the best sound by using the right mic properly placed than it is to try and fix a poor recording later, so don't be afraid to spend a little time doing tests to get it right the first time.

PROTECT YOUR MICROPHONES!

Microphones are precision instruments, so treat them with care. When a vocalist sings into a microphone, it can be subject to a few kinds of abuse. One such abuse comes from plosives, which don't sound good and, over time, are bad for the mic. Even more, the breath contains a great deal of moisture, which collects on the diaphragm over time, increasing the accumulation of dust and other particles in the air (including smoke) onto the diaphragm. Over the course of use, this collected moisture and dust will degrade the sound of your mic, and there is no easy or inexpensive way to restore it.

You can protect against these and other issues by using a pop screen when recording vocals. A pop screen is simply a very light screen mounted on the mic stand and positioned a couple of inches in front of the mic itself. You can buy pop screens at any music or audio store, or make one yourself from an embroidery hoop, a wire clothes hanger, and a nylon stocking.

Pop screens provide the additional benefit of making the vocalist sing at least a little distance from the mic, since many vocalists are unsure how close to be.

Keeping your microphone in a case when it's not in use is another good way to preserve your investment. Expensive mics usually come with well-built, hard-side cases, but even a vinyl bag provides some degree of protection. Shock can damage a microphone in a second, so take great care not to drop microphones or leave them where they can get knocked to the floor, and avoid bumping them into hard surfaces.

Finally, microphones are sensitive to temperature change and extreme temperatures. Besides avoiding recording in midday desert sun or in subzero temperatures, you should also cover microphones that need to stay mounted but not used for any length of time, such as when leaving a setup overnight. (When possible, it's better to take the mics down and put them away overnight, even if you leave the stands and cables in place.)

Many microphones come with a soft bag of some sort that you can place over them. In a pinch, you can use a vinyl bag or even an old sock, as long as it is very clean and does not tend to generate a lot of static electricity (which some socks certainly can). Putting a dirty old sock over your nice tube condenser is not doing anything to help you or your mic.

DIRECT BOXES (DIs)

Electric and electronic instruments can be recorded without the use of microphones; however, they usually require an interface to match the impedance, signal level, and signal balancing between the source and the recorder. This is most commonly done with a simple device called a "direct box" (short for "direct injection box," leading to the abbreviation "DI").

There are two basic approaches to making a DI: passive, which uses a transformer to do the hard work, and active, which uses circuitry and requires power. Most active DIs can be powered with batteries, but active DIs also can be powered by phantom power, just as can condenser microphones. The active circuitry is most often solid-state, but tube DIs are certainly to be found.

There are good and bad models of passive and active DI. The quality of design and parts (especially the transformer in a passive DI) can result in very different sounds for the same applications. Ultimately, you will choose the one you think sounds the best. It also may be that no one DI sounds great for everything you do. While a DI is not a transducer, DIs can have that same sense of having different "flavors," and you choose the flavors that please your palate.

One other note on DIs: they should be built like tanks. Even in the studio, DIs sometimes get stepped on, knocked down, or wedged in somewhere. Most are made to be quite strong, but the issue is worth a mention.

PREAMPS, COMPRESSORS, AND CHANNEL STRIPS

A microphone cannot be recorded directly. It requires, at the very least, preamplification. Often, it is also useful to use compression to even out the difference between the loudest and softest levels. Some people like to adjust tone with an equalizer while they are recording. All of these functions are best done in the analog world, before the signal from your mic gets to your interface and goes into the computer. A signal that unexpectedly gets loud enough to overload the interface must be controlled before it gets there.

The choice of preamplifier is critical. Mics can need a lot of amplification, and that's a hard thing to do cleanly. That makes the mic preamp one of the first areas in which mixer manufacturers make compromises, because it is expensive to put a high-quality mic preamp on every channel. This is why outboard mic preamplifiers are popular and worth considering, if you can manage the expense. Having said that, mixer preamps are, on the whole, much better than they used to be and, in cases like PreSonus's StudioLive mixers, can be very good choices for those that can't afford fancier wares. Remember that because a mic preamp is outboard does not mean it is great. Look around at what people say, and, if possible, borrow a model and try it out before you buy it to make sure it sounds good.

Tube mic preamps are very popular because of the warmth they can impart, but there is no guarantee that a preamp will sound good just because it has a tube. Indeed, there are manufacturers who make a cheap design, stick a tube in it, and then try to put it forth as a "gourmet" mic pre. I say again—do your research. It is worth noting that there are many engineers who will not use a tube mic pre with a tube condenser, presumably to avoid "overdosing" on that "tube sound."

There are compressors and equalizers available at all prices. You will usually, but not always, get what you pay for, so do your homework before plunking down your hard-earned cash.

The idea of a channel strip is, essentially, to provide all of the functions of one channel of a good mixing console in an independent rackmount package. Channel strips typically combine a mic preamp, equalizer, compressor, and, often a limiter as well. These can be very convenient devices to have and can really get a session going faster, since they eliminate a lot of patching.

Affordable channel strips are available from PreSonus (my favorite of these, but, in the spirit of full disclosure, I do have a close relationship with PreSonus), Focusrite, dbx and others. There are a great many boutique, high-end channel strips as well, including Universal Audio, Avalon, Grace Designs, Millenia, GML, and Empirical Labs, just to name a few. These may be pricey, but they can sound absolutely amazing.

A channel strip is a good place to splurge, if you can. Microphones and mic pres are the biggest factors in determining how good your recorded tracks sound, and there is no amount of fixing bad tracks that can sound as good as tracks that were well-recorded in the first place. Plus, good mics can last for decades and don't become obsolete. Mics and mic pres/channel strips are good investments.

Whatever signal path you use, connect the output of it to an input of your interface, and you are ready to start recording in Studio One 2!

ABOUT USB MICS

USB mics are a whole new family of mic products that have appeared in recent years. Heavily used by podcasters and broadcasters for their convenience, USB mics are usable in a studio situation but are frequently not the best option. This is because you have no choice in preamplification and processing, and because many of them are not made with music recording in mind. If you have a USB mic available to you, there is little to lose by experimenting with it, but if you are going to buy a microphone for recording, I would not suggest a USB mic be at the top of your list.

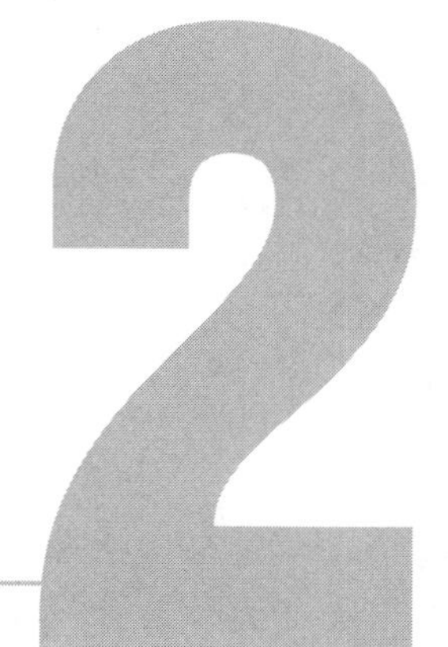

Get Set to Record

Your computer is ready, your mic is set up. Now it's time to record into Studio One 2. First, you'll configure the session for recording and import a drum loop to play over. Then, you'll make sure that the input level and monitoring are good. Once those are done, there's nothing left to do but have fun!

Fig. 2-1: The Add Tracks dialog.

SET UP THE SONG

Make a New Audio Track

1. Create a new Song, as you did in chapter 1, "On Your Mark." Set the Song to 44.1 kHz sample rate and 24-bit resolution. Check that your interface has the same settings. Name the song and store it on the disk to which you are recording. (Not the system disk, remember?)
2. Press T or choose Add Tracks from the Tracks menu in the main menu bar to bring up the Add Tracks dialog box. Let's make a single mono track for now.
3. Type your track name into the Name field in the dialog box.
4. Type "1" into the Count field.
5. Be sure that Mono is selected in the Format field (the other choices are Stereo, Instrument, Automation, and Folder).
6. The Preset menu has a drop-down list of channel presets for guitar, vocal, and lots of other instruments. These presets configure the new channel with processing suitable for the indicated source. Take a look and if you see something that looks good, select it.

Fig. 2-2: A new mono track in the Arrange view and mono channel in Mix view.

7. Click on OK. You will now see a new track in the Arrange view and a corresponding new channel in the Mix view. Wow. (If you don't see the mixer, press F3 or click on the Mix button at the bottom of the Song window.)

The Track

Your source material, be it audio or MIDI, is contained on the tracks in Studio One 2's Arrange view. We introduced the Arrange view in chapter 1, "On Your Mark"; here, we will simply point out the important features so that you have a coherent picture of the environment. More detail on each feature is discussed in the applicable spots later in the book. Check the Contents or Index to find these discussions. For information on sizing tracks, see the section "Zooming" in chapter 5, "On the Cutting Room Floor: Basic Editing."

THE TIMELINE

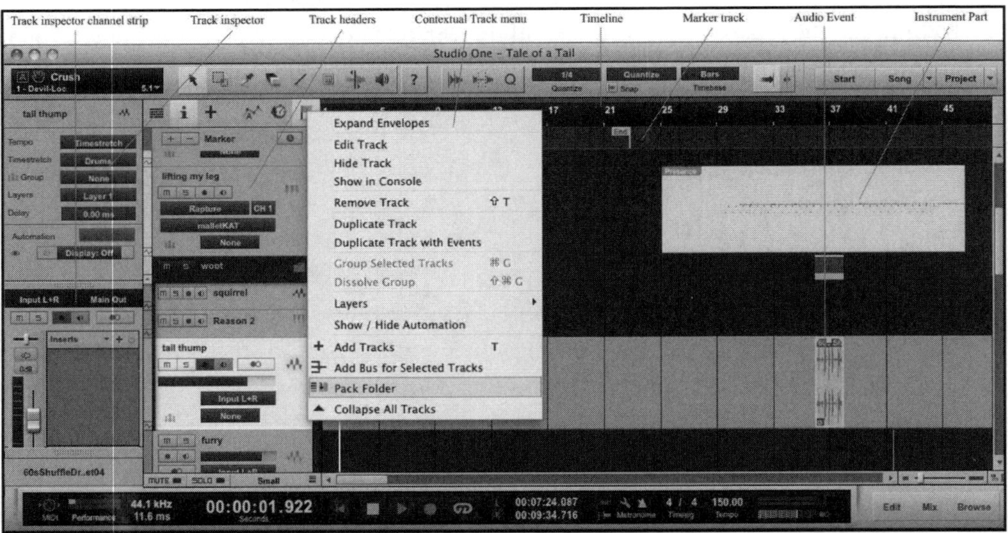

Fig. 2-3: Arrange view track features.

At the top of the Arrange view is the timeline, the units for which are selected by any of these methods:

- Click in the Timebase field at the top of the Song window and select the desired time base from the drop-down menu that appears.
- Right-click (or Ctrl-click on the Mac) in the timeline, move the cursor to the Timebase entry, and choose the desired units from the submenu in the contextual menu that drops down.
- Click in the Timebase field in Preferences > Song Setup > General and choose the desired format from the drop-down menu that appears.

The timeline hosts three other important features that I want to mention here: the left and right locators (which designate the loop start and end points), the Marker track, and the Tempo track. I will talk more about the locators when I discuss loop playback and recording in chapter 3, "Go! Recording with Studio One 2."

Fig. 2-4: The Marker track button in the Arrange view toolbar.

- To open or close the Marker track, click on the button with the flag icon above the track headers.
- To open or close the Tempo track, click on the button with the clock icon above the track headers.

Fig. 2-5: The Tempo track button in the Arrange view toolbar.

TRACK TYPES

- Audio tracks contain audio data as Audio Events or Audio Parts, plus automation information for the track. An Audio track can be mono or stereo; the Channel Mode selector in the track's header switches the track between the two.

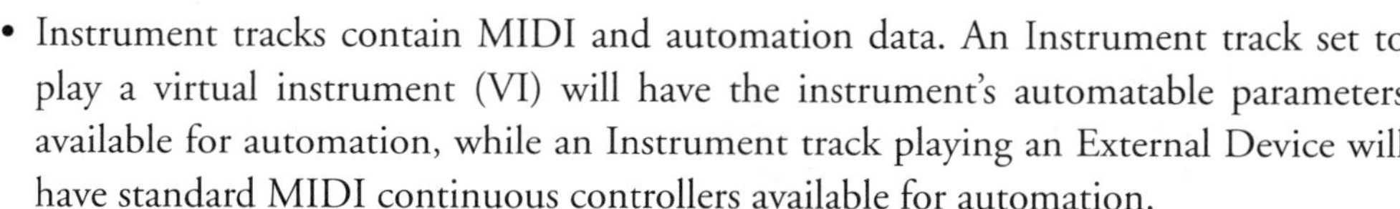

- Instrument tracks contain MIDI and automation data. An Instrument track set to play a virtual instrument (VI) will have the instrument's automatable parameters available for automation, while an Instrument track playing an External Device will have standard MIDI continuous controllers available for automation.
- Automation tracks contain only automation data, but a single Automation track can contain automation for parameters of different devices. For example, one Automation track could hold volume automation for every virtual instrument in the Song.
- Folder tracks are a way of grouping other tracks. For instance, you might put all of your drum tracks together in a folder track.

THE TRACK HEADER

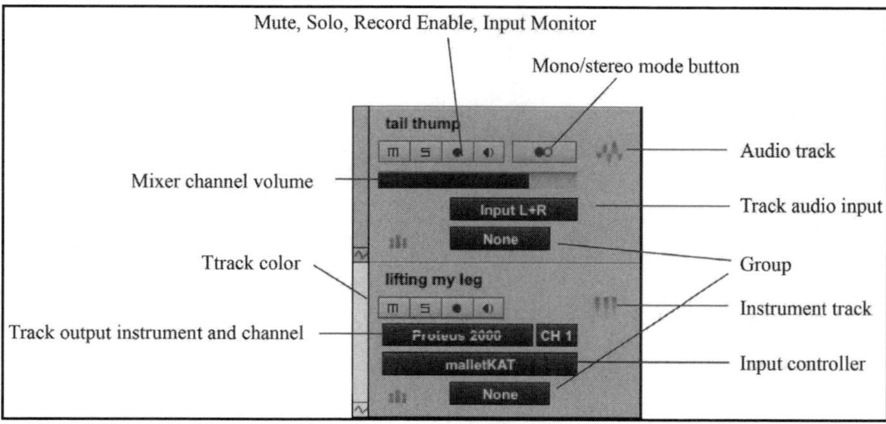

Fig. 2-6: Headers for Audio and Instrument tracks.

To the left of the main Track area, each track has a header. For Audio and Instrument tracks, it contains these functions:

- Mute button
- Solo button
- Record Enable button
- Input Monitor button
- Channel Mode (Mono/Stereo) button (Audio tracks)
- Volume bar (Audio tracks)
- Record Input field (Audio tracks)
- Instrument Output field (Instrument tracks)
- Instrument Input field (Instrument tracks)
- Instrument Editor button (Instrument tracks)
- Edit Group field

Automation View

Audio and Instrument tracks have an alternate view that displays and allows editing of automation data. Automation tracks always show an automation view. For more about automation, see my upcoming book *Power Tools for Studio One 2*, volume 2.

To access Automation view on all Audio and Instrument tracks use any of these methods:

- Press the A key.
- Click on the Show Automation button (with the letter A and zigzag line icon) above the track headers.
- Choose Track > Show Automation from the main menu bar.
- To access Automation view on a single track, right-click on the track and choose Show/Hide Automation from the contextual drop-down menu that appears.

THE TRACK INSPECTOR

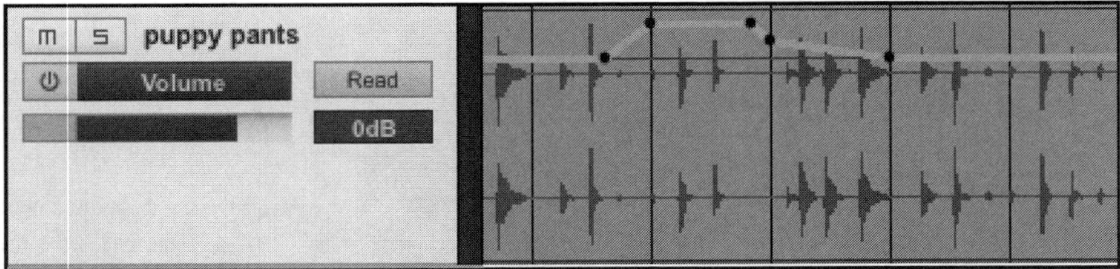

Fig. 2-7: When in Automation view, a track shows the selected automation parameter in place of Events or Parts.

The Track inspector provides access to important track-level editing and automation functions, listed here. For more about the Track inspector, see the section "Inspectors" in chapter 5, "On the Cutting Room Floor: Basic Editing." (Also look in the upcoming Power *Tools for Studio One 2*, volume 2, for details of automation.)

- Tempo field (Audio tracks)
- Timestretch field (Audio tracks)

- Group field
- Layers field
- Delay field
- Automation Mode field
- Automation Parameter field
- Automation Enable/Disable button
- Automation Parameter Color Select
- Timebase field (Instrument tracks)
- Transpose field (Instrument tracks)
- Velocity field (Instrument tracks)
- Input Filter checkbox (Instrument tracks)
- Instrument Editor button (Instrument tracks)
- Device display (Automation tracks)
- Automation Parameter Value field (Automation tracks)
- Automation Parameter Value bar (Automation tracks)
- Track List (Folder tracks)

Fig. 2-8: Inspectors for Audio and Instrument tracks.

TRACK INSPECTOR CHANNEL STRIP

It is common to need access to mixer facilities for a track while you are working on it in the Arrange view. When an Audio track or Instrument track with a virtual instrument inserted is selected, the Track inspector shows a channel strip for it similar to those in the Mix view. Because mixer channel strips are covered in *Power Tools for Studio One 2*, volume 2, I will give only a brief description of each control here.

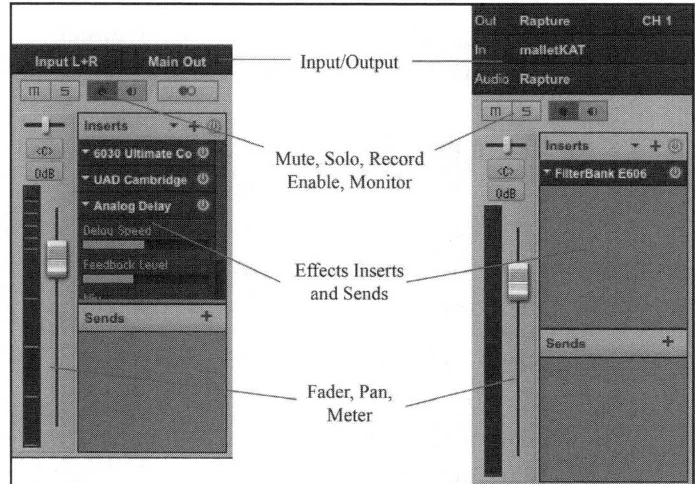

Fig. 2-9: Track inspector channel strips for Audio and Instrument tracks.

Input/Output Select

- To select an audio input for a selected Audio track, click in the Channel Input field at the top of the channel strip and select the desired audio input from the drop-down menu that appears.
- To select an audio output for a selected Audio track, click in the Channel Output field at the top of the channel strip and select the desired bus or audio output from the drop-down menu that appears.
- To select an Instrument (MIDI) input for a selected Instrument track, click in the Instrument Input field at the top of the channel strip and select the desired external

controller or ReWire MIDI input from the drop-down menu that appears. The Configure selection opens Preferences > Options > External Devices so that you can add or edit external devices to your MIDI setup.

- To select an Instrument (MIDI) output for a selected Instrument track, click in the Instrument Output field at the top of the channel strip and select the desired virtual instrument or external devices from the drop-down menu that appears.
- To select an Instrument audio output for a selected Instrument track, click in the Audio Output field at the top of the channel strip and select from the audio outputs available for the instrument.

TIP: Think of channel strip Instrument audio outputs as the output jacks of an instrument or ReWire application. These virtual output jacks are routed in software into Studio One 2's mixer channels. But audio from external devices comes from physical output jacks that must be connected to audio interface inputs, so they cannot be patched as virtual outputs. Thus, you cannot select an Instrument audio output for an external device from the channel strip.

Mute/Solo/Record/Monitor Functions

For Audio tracks, toggling any of these functions in the Track inspector channel strip causes the corresponding function in the Mix view channel strip to toggle as well. For Instrument tracks, only the Solo function also toggles in the Mix view channel strip named in the Instrument Audio Output field.

- To mute a selected Audio or Instrument track, press the M key or click on the Mute button on the channel strip.
- To solo a selected Audio or Instrument track, press the S key or click on the Solo button on the channel strip.
- To enable a selected Audio or Instrument track for recording, press the R key or click on the Record Enable button on the channel strip. Note that the Monitor button is enabled and disabled with Record Enable.
- To toggle input monitoring for a selected Audio or Instrument track, press the U key or click on the Monitor button on the channel strip. Note that this toggles monitoring independently of the Record Enable status.

Level and Pan

The level and pan controls in the Track inspector channel strip correspond to the same controls in the Mix view channel strip. For an Instrument track, this means that the Track inspector channel strip is controlling the audio return from the instrument, not sending MIDI volume and pan data to control the instrument itself.

- To set the level for a selected Audio or Instrument track, click on or drag the fader to the desired level, or click in the Level field and type in the desired value.
- To set the panning for a selected Audio or Instrument track, click on or drag the Pan slider to the desired position, or click in the Pan field and type in the desired value.

Inserts and Sends

As in any standard mixer, the Track inspector channel strip includes effects inserts and aux/effects sends. As with the level and pan controls, inserts and sends on Instrument channels apply not to the instrument itself, but to the mixer channels through which the audio outputs of the virtual instrument or ReWire application are returned.

Signal flows from top to bottom in the Inserts section.

For more information on inserts and sends, see the "Mixing" chapter in *Power Tools for Studio One 2*, volume 2.

- To add an insert effect, drag it from the list of effects in the Effects tab of the Browser to the Inserts area, or click on the + (plus sign) button at the top of the Inserts area and choose an effect from the drop-down list that appears.
- To add a preset effects chain as an insert, click on the arrow at the top of the Inserts area and choose an FX Chain from the drop-down list that appears. To open a folder in the list, hover the cursor over it. To close a folder in the list, click on the folder name.
- To enable or disable all insert effects, click on the Insert Activate button at the top of the Inserts area.
- To route the channel to an output, bus, aux channel, or effect sidechain, click on the + (plus sign) button at the top of the Sends area and choose a destination from the drop-down list that appears. To add a send to a sidechain, hover the cursor over the Sidechains label and choose a sidechain from the drop-down list that appears.
- To create a new bus or FX channel and route the channel to it, click on the + (plus sign) button at the top of the Sends area and choose the Add Bus Channel or Add FX Channel command at the bottom of the drop-down list that appears.

Other Functions

- To open the Instrument editor for an Instrument track from the Track inspector channel strip, click on the keyboard icon next to the track name at the top of the channel strip.
- To change an Audio track between mono and stereo, click on the Channel Mode button just above the Inserts section of the channel strip.

COLOR-CODING TRACKS

- To color-code a track from the Track inspector, click on the color bar to the left of the track header in the Arrange view, the color bar to the left of the track name at the top of the channel strip, or the color bar at the bottom of the corresponding channel strip in the Mix view, and choose a color from the drop-down color palette that appears. The chosen color will appear in all three locations.

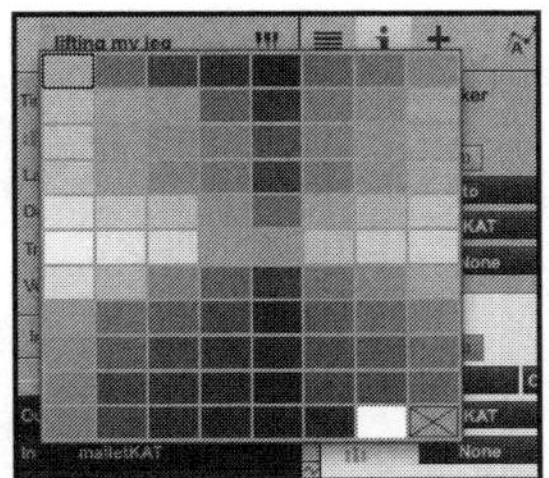

Fig. 2-10: The Track inspector color select palette.

Configure the Input and Output

Assuming that you have connected your mic signal to an interface input, you need to check and, if necessary, configure four things, in order to set up the basic recording path:

1. Interface input to virtual input
2. Virtual input to channel input
3. Channel output to Main Out
4. Main Out to interface output

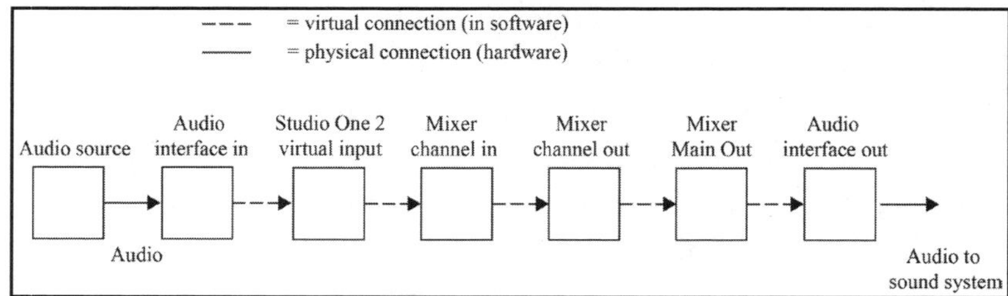

Fig. 2-11: The signal path when recording into Studio One 2.

Here's how:

1. Taking note of which interface input the mic signal is feeding, click the I/O button on the left of the Mix view to open the Audio I/O Setup Preference pane.
2. If there are no virtual inputs on the left side, click on the Add Mono button to add one. Name it "Mic In 1." If there are existing virtual inputs, double-click on one and give it that name.
3. Click in the box at the intersection of the row for the virtual input you've named and the column for the interface input you are using. An M will appear in the box.
4. Close the Preferences dialog box and return to the Mix view.
5. Click at the top of the newly created mixer channel to drop down the menu of virtual inputs. Choose the Mic In 1 input. The mic is now routed to the record channel.

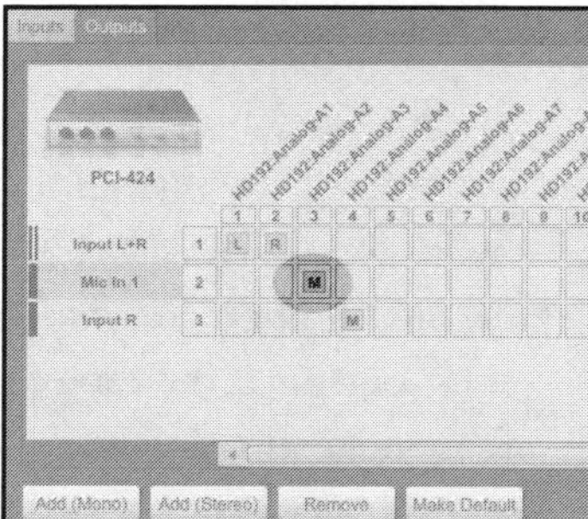

Fig. 2-12: An audio interface input mapped to a virtual input in the Audio I/O Setup preference pane.

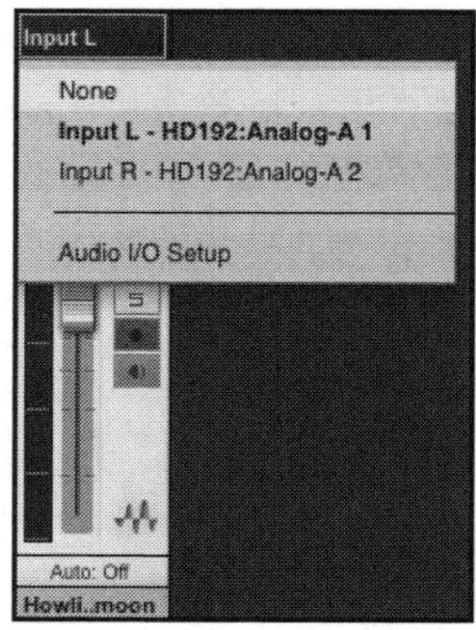

Fig. 2-13: Selecting a virtual input for a mixer channel.

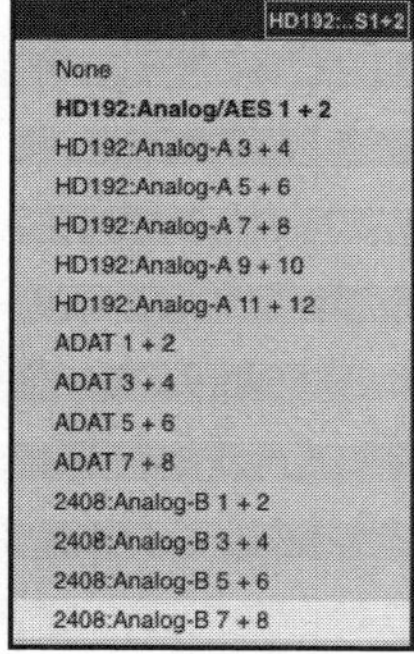

Fig. 2-14: Selecting an interface output for Main Out.

6. The channel's output setting is immediately below the input selection. If it does not say "Main Out," click on it to drop the menu down, and choose Main Out.
7. Look at the top of the Main Out channel on the right of the mixer. If the interface output there is not the one you use for monitoring, click on the name to drop down the menu and select the correct interface output.

The basic signal path is now configured: the mic feeds the interface, the interface is mapped to a virtual input, the virtual input is routed to the channel, the channel is routed to the main output, and Main Out is assigned to the monitoring output of your interface. Yeah!

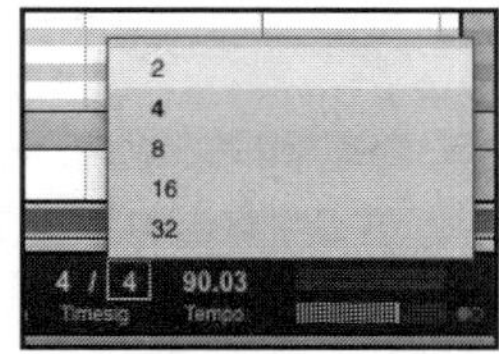

Fig. 2-16: The time signature field in the Transport Bar, shown with the pop-up menu for the denominator displayed. The numerator pop-up allows selection of 1 to 16 beats for each bar.

Set the Time Signature and Tempo

The default settings for time signature and tempo are 4/4 and 120 bpm, respectively. Not the settings you want? No problem.

- To set the time signature, click on the numerator of the time signature shown in the Transport bar (Timesig field) and choose the desired number of beats per measure from the drop-down menu that appears. Then click on the denominator to choose the desired pulse value from its drop-down menu. You can also open the Edit Timesignature dialog box by double-clicking on the small time signature marker in the timeline at the beginning of the song.
- To set the tempo, click in the Tempo field in the Transport bar and type in the desired tempo.

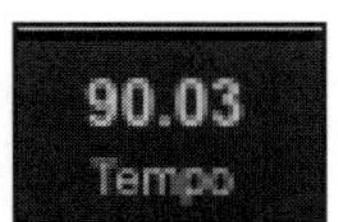

Fig. 2-17: Tempo field in the Transport Bar.

Metronome and Count-off

People often like to record while listening to a click, especially when laying drum tracks. Studio One 2 has a versatile metronome for this purpose. For a start, the metronome can be enabled or disabled and its level set independently for each output channel in the mixer. (Output channels are discussed in the chapter on mixing in volume 2 of *Power Tools for Studio One 2*.) The metronome can use separate sounds for accented and unaccented beats, play custom sounds if none of the included ones suit you, and even play at double-time for greater playing precision.

SET UP THE METRONOME

- To globally enable or disable the metronome, click on the button with the metronome icon next to the time signature in the Transport bar, or press the C key on the keyboard.
- To enable or disable the metronome for Main Out or another output channel, click on the button with the metronome icon above the meter in the channel strip.

- To set the volume for the metronome for Main Out or another output channel, click-and-hold the button with the fader icon to the right of the metronome button on the channel strip and drag the fader to the desired level. Note that the metronome is enabled by default.

Fig. 2-18: The Metronome area in the Transport Bar. The metronome enable/disable is on the right (shown enabled), while the metronome setup button is on the left with the wrench icon.

The Metronome Setup dialog box contains the rest of the settings for the metronome and count-off.

- To open the Metronome Setup dialog box, click on the button with the tuning fork icon next to the metronome button in the Transport bar.

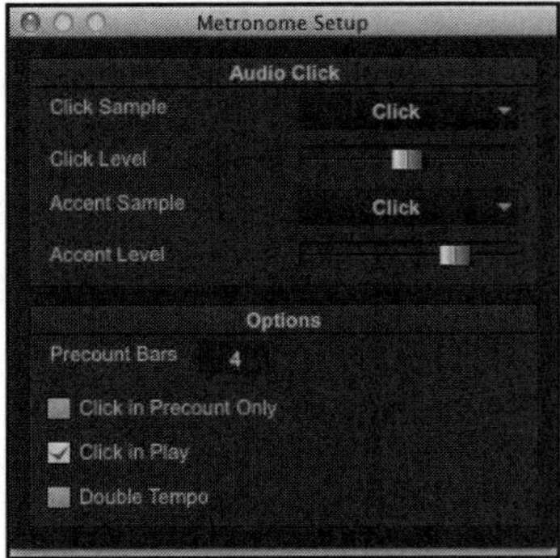

Fig. 2-19: The Metronome Setup dialog.

The Audio Click pane in the top half of the Metronome Setup dialog box is where the sound and level for the accented and unaccented clicks are set. The accented sound plays on the downbeat of each measure; the unaccented sound plays on all other beats in the measure. Generally, the accented sound is played louder than the unaccented sound, but you are free to set the levels differently, if, for example, you use different sounds to indicate accented and unaccented beats and want the levels to sound the same.

- To select a sound for the unaccented click, click in the Click Sample field and choose the desired sound from the drop-down menu that appears.
- To set the level for the unaccented click, drag the Click Level fader to the desired level.
- To select a sound for the accented click, click in the Accent Sample field and choose the desired sound from the drop-down menu that appears.
- To set the level for the unaccented click, drag the Accent Level fader to the desired level.

You can use any WAV, AIFF, or MP3 file as a click sound. Short sounds with sharp attacks generally make the best metronomes.

To add a custom click sound on a Windows machine, do the following:

- Locate the folder containing the Studio One 2 application. The default location will be in Program Files.
- Copy the audio file of your custom sound to the Clicks folder inside the Studio One 2 folder.

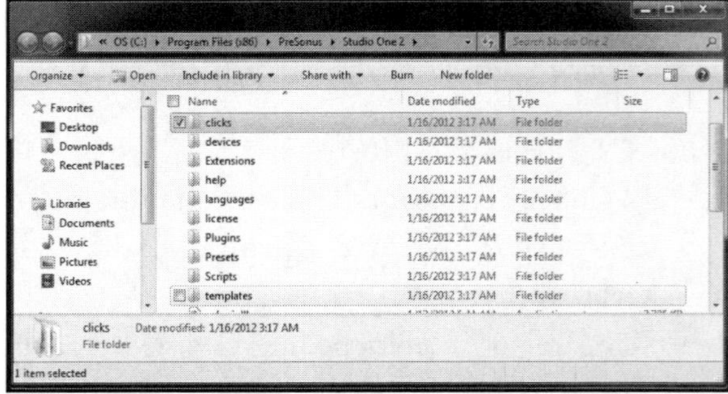

Fig. 2-19: In Windows, custom click sounds are stored in the PreSonus>clicks folder.

To add a custom click sound on a Mac, do the following:

- Right-click (or Ctrl-click on Mac) on the Studio One 2 application icon in the Finder. Choose Show Package Contents from the drop-down menu that appears.
- Open the Contents folder in the window that opens.
- Copy the audio file of your custom sound to the clicks folder.

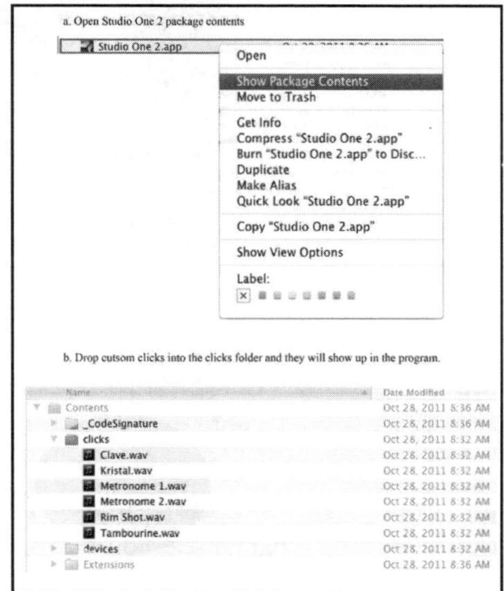

Fig. 2-20: Adding a custom click for the metronome in Studio One 2 for Mac.

Your custom sound will now show up in the Click and Accent Sample drop-down menus.

The Options pane at the bottom of the dialog box has settings for metronome behavior and count-off length. The metronome behavior controls are a bit strange. It looks as though there are two checkboxes, but, in fact, you can click in only one and it acts like a toggle.

- To set the metronome to click only during the count-off, check the Click in Precount Only box.
- To set the metronome to click whenever the transport is in motion, click on the Click in Precount Only box to uncheck it. When you do this, the Click in Play box will become checked.
- To set the metronome to click twice for each beat, click on the Double Tempo box. Note that this does NOT double the tempo of the song, only the rate of the click.

SET UP THE COUNT-OFF

Studio One 2's count-off feature is a bit unusual. It is called "Precount," which is an unusual but accurate term, as this feature combines a count-off with a preroll feature. Count-off and preroll are actually two different functions that both relate to what is heard before recording starts, but in Studio One 2 the two are intertwined.

Import a Drum Loop

Rather than playing to nothing but a click, it's often more fun to record over a drum loop. Let's import a loop, and then you can have the choice of using the loop and the click together or disabling one and just using the other.

1. If the Browser is not visible, press F5 to show it.
2. Click on the Sounds button at the bottom of the Browser to show all of the content included with Studio One 2 Pro. If you don't have Studio One 2 Pro, find a drum loop from any other collection you may have.
3. Audition drum loops in the Browser until you find one that you like. For our example, we'll use Studio One 2 Loops vol 1/Icebox/105bpm/Electric Drums 157 105bpm.wav.

Fig. 2-21: Files of all types can be dragged from the Browser into the Arrange view. Note that this drum loop is locating precisely on the beat because Snap is engaged.

4. Drag-and-drop the drum loop into the Arrange view. A new track will be created for it and assigned to Main Out.
5. Be sure that the drum loop's Audio Event in the Arrange view is selected. If it is not, click on it once to select it.
6. Press the D key on the keyboard or choose Edit > Duplicate from the main menu bar. A second copy of the Event will be pasted next to the first. Repeat this as many times as you wish until the loop extends over at least as much time as you intend to record.

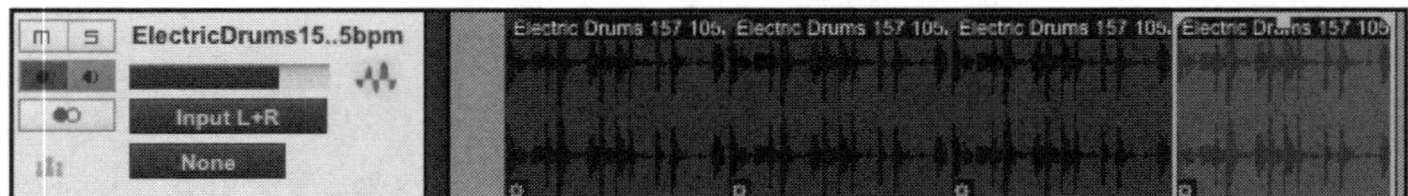

Fig. 2-22: Using the Duplicate command to do a repeat paste. When Snap is active (which it is not in this example), the pastes occur at grid lines, instead of placing the Events back to back, as in this figure.

7. Play the Song and check that you are hearing the loop (and the metronome, if you have it enabled.)

FINAL PREPARATIONS

You're almost ready to roll. All that's left is to make sure that you can hear everything you want to and have checked that the record level is optimal.

Record Enable the Track

The signal path is all set up, so now you need only arm the track for recording.

- To arm a track for recording, click on the Record Enable button on the channel strip in either the Mix view or the Track inspector, or on the track in the Arrange view. The Record Enable button will turn red to show that the track is armed.
- Another way to arm a track is to click on it in either the Mix or Arrange view to select it and press the R key.
- Additional tracks can be armed simply by clicking on their Record Enable buttons.

- To arm multiple tracks at once, Shift-click on each track header in the Mix or Arrange view to select the tracks, then press the R key or click on the Record Enable button on any of them.

Monitoring

Hearing what you're playing is plainly crucial to recording, but so is hearing any existing tracks you're playing along with, or other players recording at the same time.

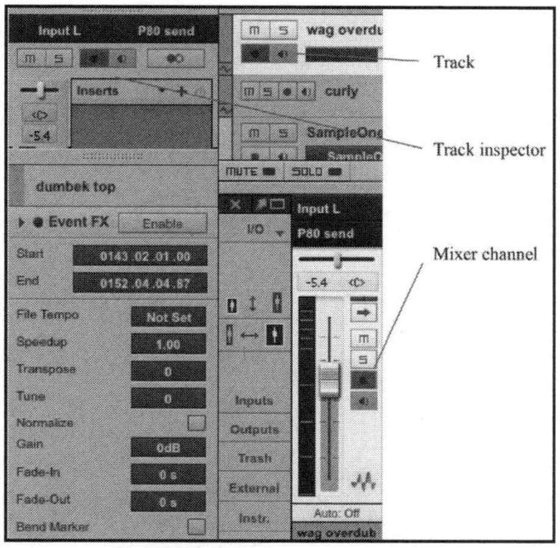

Fig. 2-23: Record-enable buttons are found on Mix view channels (bottom), Arrange view track headers (upper right), and in the Track inspector (upper left). Note the blue input monitor buttons, which, by default, get enabled when a track or channel is record-enabled.

ENABLING INPUT MONITORING

When you arm a track for recording, you should see the Monitor button next to the Record Enable button on the track (and the corresponding channel in the Mix view) turn blue. This means that the channel/track is now monitoring its input through Studio One 2.

Latency is an issue with input monitoring on a DAW like Studio One 2. For more information, see the upcoming sections "Understanding Buffer Size" and "Low-Latency Monitoring" in this chapter.

MAKING CUE MIXES

Any time you are recording with a microphone, you are very likely to be monitoring over headphones. If you are recording several musicians at once, you may even need to supply them with separate mixes so that each can hear things in the proportions they need. Mixes for monitoring over headphones while recording are called "Cue mixes." It is easy to set up Cue mixes in Studio One 2.

The hard part turns out to be having enough clean, loud headphone amplifiers and headphones to supply everyone. This remains true whether you are creating one mix or several. There are plenty of inexpensive headphone amplifiers to be had, but be careful: when a cheap amplifier distorts the Cue mix, musicians can't hear with clarity. Often, this inability to hear leads to a request to turn up the volume in the phones, which does nothing but create more distortion.

If you are recording alone, it may be simplest for you just to monitor Main Out over headphones. But if you are recording with others who want their own Cue mixes, or if you simply prefer for some reason to have a mix separate from Main Out, you can create as many Cue outputs as you have spare interface outputs. Each Cue output can carry a separate Cue mix, which, depending on your headphone amplifier situation, can be sent to one or several musicians. You can also set Main Out to be a Cue output, if you like.

To create a Cue output, do the following:

1. Open Preferences > Song Setup > Audio I/O Setup and click on the Outputs tab.
2. Click on the Add (Stereo) button to make a new stereo output channel.

3. Double-click on the name of the new output channel and give it an appropriate name.
4. Click on the Cue mix checkbox next to the name of the new output channel.
5. Click on OK to close the dialog box.
6. The Cue output channel strip will appear at the right of the mixer. Each Cue channel has its own level, mute, solo, metronome controls, and inserts.

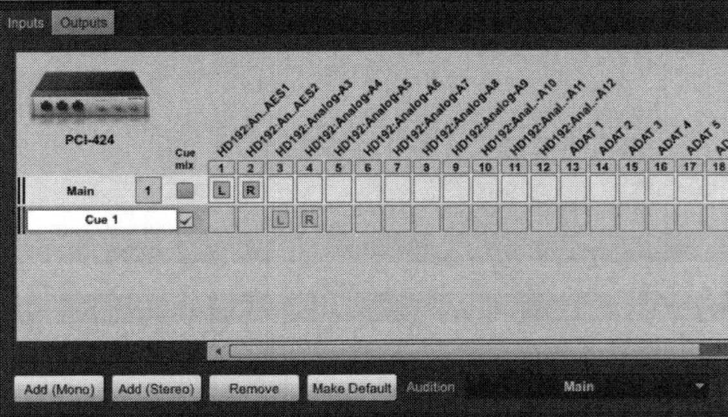

Fig. 2-24: Naming a new Cue output after creating it. Note that the Cue box to the right of the name is checked.

Set the output at the top of the channel strip to the desired interface output.

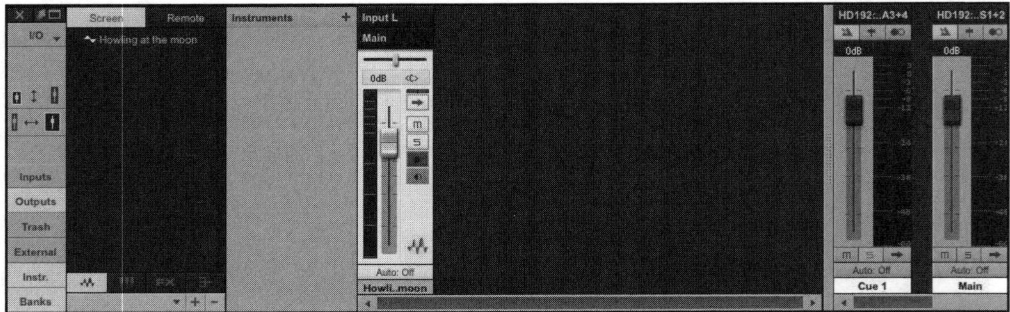

Fig. 2-25: The Mix view with a new Cue output channel on the right side. Clicking the Outputs panel show/hide button on the left would hide this output from view, but not the Main Out, which is always visible.

When you create a Cue output, a special prefader send is created for it on each input channel. Take a look.

1. Click on the arrow next to the Pan slider on any input channel.
2. A panel labeled "Cue mix" will appear to the right.

There are four controls in each Cue mix send: mute, lock, level, and pan.

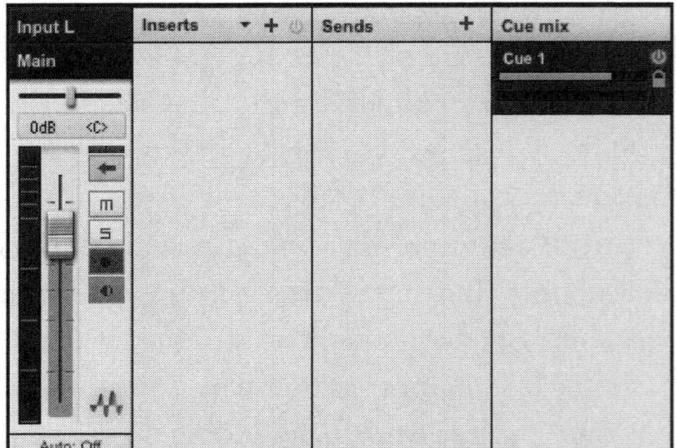

Fig. 2-26: A mixer channel strip, showing a Cue send on the right side.

- To remove the channel from a Cue mix, click on the blue button in the upper right corner of the Cue send to mute the send from that channel to the Cue mix. (Everyone does not always want to hear every channel.)
- To set the level and pan from the channel to the Cue mix separately from the level and pan of the channel in the main mix, click on the blue button with the lock icon to the right of the level fader in the Cue send. Unlocking the Cue send level and pan from the main mix level and pan is how you create Cue mixes with different balances than the main mix. Usually, each musician will want to hear what he or she is playing at a higher level than the rest of the mix. ("More me!" is the cry.)
- To set the level of the channel being sent to the Cue mix (assuming the Cue send is unlocked from the channel as described above), drag the fader below the Cue mix's name to the desired level.
- To set the pan of the channel being sent to the Cue mix (assuming the Cue send is unlocked from the channel as described above), drag the pan slider below the Cue mix's level fader to the desired position.

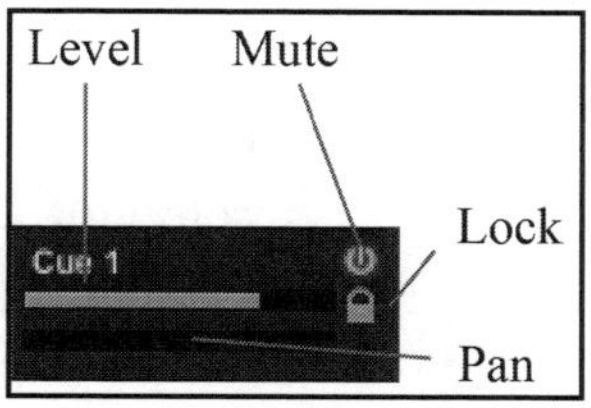

Fig. 2-27: Cue send controls.

It can take a while to get each Cue mix adjusted, but a good Cue mix can make a major difference in a musician's performance. Many musicians like to have effects in their Cue mixes, as well. When we get to effects in the chapter about mixing in volume 2 of *Power Tools for Studio One 2*, we'll show you how to add them to Cue mixes.

UNDERSTANDING BUFFER SIZE

Before you record, you will want to set Studio One 2's buffer size. Buffer size is an important and not terribly difficult concept that has somehow gathered an outsize mystique. A buffer is simply a small amount of memory set aside for very short-term storage, and a piece of software might use buffers for a variety of purposes. However, in DAWs, buffer size usually refers to the size of the track buffer, where samples are stored before being played. Choosing a track buffer size involves trading off a few different parameters, and understanding these trade-offs is the key to setting the size correctly.

Think of it like this: when you record into Studio One 2 (or any other DAW, for that matter), it's as though you are scooping water out of a bucket that is simultaneously being filled at a constant rate and pouring it into a pipe. If the bucket is small, it will be all you can do to scoop it out fast enough to keep it from overflowing, but if the bucket is large, you have a little more time before it fills up, which could even allow you to fit in another task before you have to scoop more. However, this means that it takes longer for the water to get from the bucket to the pipe.

In essence, Studio One 2's buffers (used for recording and playing each channel) correspond to how much slack the processor has: when the buffer is large, there's lots of slack for the processor to keep several different jobs going, but when the buffer is small (which yields the low latency that is desirable for recording), the processor has to work much faster and harder to keep up with the incoming data stream, and so can't do as many other things.

So what are the noticeable effects of different buffer sizes? Well, a larger buffer means more storage space that holds a larger number of samples. Since every sample represents a tiny slice of time, more samples in the buffer means more delay before any given sample is taken back out of the buffer.

Fig. 2-28: Small buffer sizes are needed when recording to keep monitoring latency low, but larger buffer sizes are useful in mixing to leave more processor power for plug-ins and other processor-intensive tasks.

This isn't really a problem when mixing, as long as the delay is the same for every track, but when recording, that delay shows up in the playback of any existing tracks, as well as in the signal you are recording. So, if you are recording the very first track, this latency (another word for "delay") shows up as a short but disorienting delay in hearing what you are playing, but if you are overdubbing to some existing tracks that are playing back with delay, things get really messy.

When recording—especially when overdubbing—it is better to set a smaller buffer size to keep the latency low. But that means the processor has to work harder, which is a lot of pressure if there are virtual instruments, convolution reverbs, lots of tracks, or other processor-hungry tasks going on.

The trick is to figure out just how short a buffer your computer can handle, which really depends on how fast and beefy a machine it is. The only way to find out for sure is through good old trial-and-error.

1. Open Preferences > Options > Audio Setup.
2. Select either 128 or 256 from the drop-down list in the Device Block Size field. Notice that the Input Latency and Output Latency displays change when you select a new buffer size.
3. Click on OK to close the dialog box.

Fig. 2-29: The Device Block Size setting in Preferences>Options>Audio Setup.

LOW-LATENCY MONITORING

Even with the help of the shorter buffer, the round-trip time for a signal to travel from a microphone, through the computer, and back to the artist's headphones can be long enough to be disconcerting to the artist. To deal with this, many modern interfaces include what is called "low-latency monitoring" (sometimes erroneously called "no-latency" or "zero-latency" monitoring), which is provided courtesy of a digital signal processing chip built into the interface itself. What latency there is in these systems is so tiny as to be undetectable to humans. If you are recording Martians, you may still have problems, but latency in their monitors will be the least of your worries.

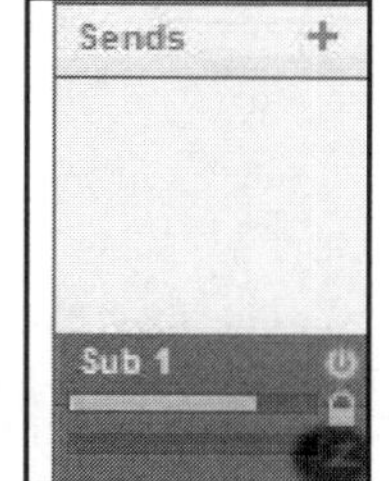

Fig. 2-30: When using Studio One 2 with a PreSonus interface having onboard DSP, Cue sends display a "Z" to indicate the availability of low-latency monitoring.

When your interface is from the same manufacturer as the DAW you are using, low-latency monitoring is usually invisibly integrated into the software. You don't see anything different, but it's there nonetheless.

PreSonus's FireStudio and AudioBox VSL interfaces supply this capability to Studio One 2. In this situation, low-latency monitoring is available for each Cue send on each channel.

- To engage low-latency monitoring when using Studio One 2 with a PreSonus FireStudio interface, click on the ZL (for "zero latency") button in the desired Cue send on the desired channel.

If you are using an interface from another manufacturer that has low-latency monitoring, there is probably utility software that came with the interface that allows you to configure the monitoring. For instance, MOTU interfaces come with CueMix software for this purpose. Studio One 2 plays nicely with CueMix, though it is understandably not as graceful an experience as the integration of a FireStudio interface with StudioOne, for two reasons.

First, the CueMix software (or equivalent for another manufacturer's interface) has to run in parallel with Studio One 2. Second, you must balance the mix of existing tracks coming out of Studio One 2's Cue output against the artist's live performance coming through the interface's low-latency monitoring. Even if it takes a little while to figure this out the first time, it is worth doing if your interface offers low-latency monitoring.

Fig. 2-31: MOTU's Cue Mix software, which controls low-latency monitoring in their audio interfaces, can be used in conjunction with Studio One 2.

There is a way to achieve true zero-latency monitoring, and that is to monitor through an analog console. Electrons moving at lightspeed produce no latency!

1. Create a mix of tracks to be monitored while recording and route it to an interface output (or, more likely, a stereo pair of outputs). Connect the interface outputs carrying this mix to inputs on the analog console.
2. Make sure the input signal is routed through the analog console *before* it reaches the interface input.
3. With the playback tracks and input signal both in the analog console, set up a mix in a prefader aux send and feed it to the headphone amplifier.

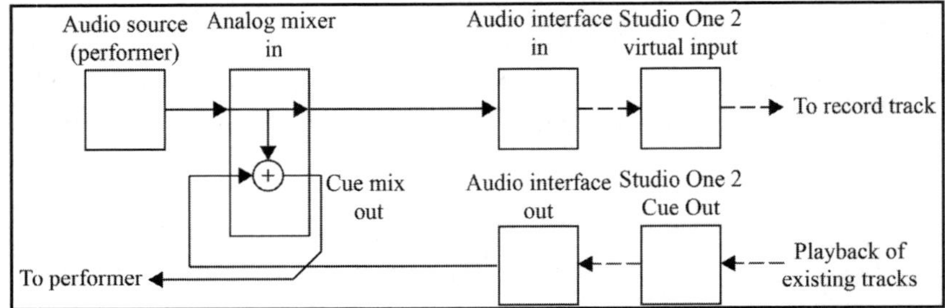

Fig. 2-32: With an analog console, performers can truly have zero latency in monitoring while recording because they hear their signal before it enters the computer. If a large buffer size is used, the performer will not hear any monitoring delay, but it may be necessary to slip the Audio Event after recording to bring it in sync with the rest of the tracks.

Check the Input Level

The last step is to double-check that the signal is actually getting into Studio One 2 and that the recording level is good.

First, make sure that you have sound going into the interface. Sing or play into the microphone. Take a glance at your audio interface. There is usually some sort of level indicator on an interface, and you should see some signal from your singing or playing. If you don't, then Studio One 2 has nothing to record. You'll have to troubleshoot your analog signal path.

Second, make sure you see signal getting into Studio One 2.

- Click on the Record Enable button on the record track in the Arrange view or on the corresponding channel strip in the Mix view. You can also select the track or channel and press the R key on the keyboard.
- To record-enable several tracks at once, select them all and record-enable any one of them.
- To record-enable one track while record disabling all of the rest, hold down the Option (Alt in Windows) key and click on the Record Enable button on the track.

You should now see signal on the channel meter in Studio One 2.

The last step is to set the record level. You cannot do this in Studio One 2. The channel fader has no effect on the record level. You must do this in the analog signal chain before the signal reaches the interface.

- Take a look at your analog signal chain (mic pre, compressor, maybe equalizer) and make sure you don't see any red lights or indications of overload when the performer (which could be you!) sings or plays.
- Now look at the channel meter in Studio One 2 while the performer sings or plays and make sure there is a healthy signal that goes at least halfway up the meter on average. It is not uncommon for the meters on your interface and those in Studio One 2 to show different levels. It takes some experimentation to find the best level, but the biggest concern is that neither show overload.
- The last gain control in the analog signal path is usually the best place to increase or decrease the signal going into the interface. However, if that control is set to one or the other extreme, you will need to adjust earlier gain controls until things look good all the way down the line.

When you see a good level in Studio One 2 and don't see any slammed meters or lit clip indicators elsewhere, you are ready to roll!

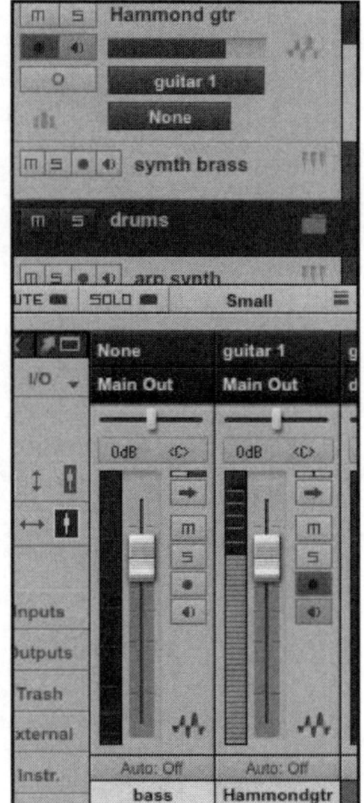

Fig. 2-33: With a correct signal path and a record-enabled track, input signal will show up on both the track and mixer channel meters.

Go! Recording with Studio One 2

Your recording system is working and ready to capture some hot tracks. Let's give it some. Lay down a track you can add things to later.

RECORD A TRACK

Since your track is already armed, to start recording you need only do the following:

- Press the * (star) key on your number pad, or simply click on the Record button in the Transport bar.
- If count-off and metronome are enabled and configured, you should hear the count-off.
- Now play some music!
- Press the Spacebar to stop recording, or press the * (star) key again to exit record without stopping playback. You can drop in and out of record manually through successive presses of the star key.

Fig. 3-1: The Record button in the Transport Bar.

Your track should now contain a new block with a waveform in it. In Studio One 2 this is called an Audio Event, appropriately, since your first recording into Studio One 2 is, most certainly, an event!

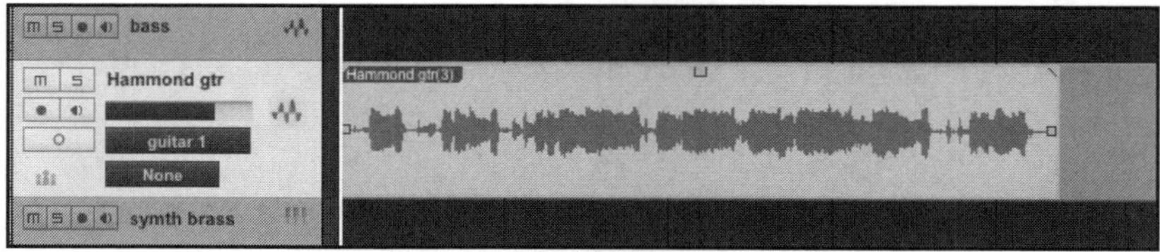

Fig. 3-2: After recording, the track will contain an new Audio Event.

To start recording from any point in the song, do the following:

1. Click in the timeline to set the play location to the place where you want to begin recording.
2. Press the * (star) key on your number pad, or simply click on the Record button in the Transport bar to start recording.
3. If a count-off is enabled, playback will begin during the count-off, and Studio One 2 will enter record when it reaches the location at which you clicked.
4. If count-off is disabled, recording will begin from the position at which you clicked the moment you put the transport into record.
5. Press the Spacebar to stop recording.

SAVE YOUR WORK!

As soon as you have done something you would be upset to lose, it's time to save. You can save manually using the commands in the File menu, or use Auto Save.

Auto Save

Auto Save relieves you of the burden of having to remember to save in the middle of an intense session. However, many people prefer to use Auto Save more as a backup, saving every half-hour or hour, and saving manually when needed in between, rather than relying on Studio One 2 to save every few minutes.

Studio One 2 can be set to Auto Save at any duration between 30 seconds and one hour.

To configure Auto Save, do the following:

1. Open Preferences > Options > Locations > User Data
2. Move the cursor over the Auto Save Documents field and drag up or down to the desired duration, or click in the field and enter the value. Be sure to enter the units as well, for example "55 seconds" or "15:30 minutes."

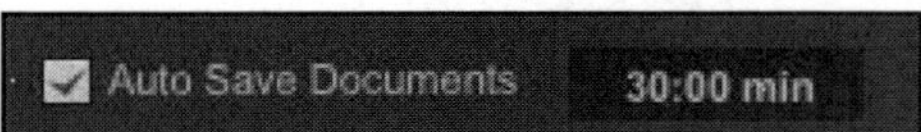

Fig. 3-3: The Auto Save setting from Preferences>Options>Locations.

PLAYBACK

- To hear what you just recorded, press the . (period) key on the number pad of your keyboard or choose Transport > Return to Zero from the main menu bar to set the play location back to the beginning of the song, or locate to wherever you started recording.
- To set Studio One 2 to automatically return to the beginning of the Song when the transport is stopped, choose Transport > Return to Start on Stop from the main menu bar.

- To start playback from any other point in the song instead, click in the timeline at the desired location, then press the Spacebar or Enter key to start playback. If preroll is enabled, playback will start earlier than the clicked point by the duration of the preroll.

You should hear what you just played. Press the Spacebar again to stop. Sounds awesome, eh?

Switching Audio Tracks Between Mono and Stereo

The Channel Mode button in the header of an Audio track switches the track between mono and stereo. If a mono audio file is dragged into an empty stereo Audio track, the Channel Mode will automatically switch to mono, and vice versa (dragging a stereo file to a mono track makes it stereo). However, the Channel Mode button can also act as a playback channel mode selector that yields more flexibility.

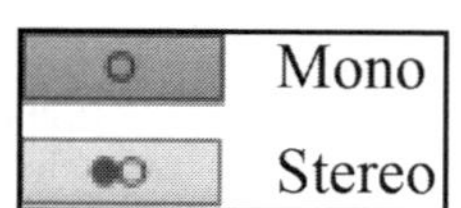

Fig. 3-4: The Channel Mode button in both its mono and stereo states. Note that the stereo example is from a track that is currently selected.

For example, if you have a stereo organ recording that you decide does not need to be stereo in the mix, simply change the Channel Mode to mono and the two channels will be summed to mono on playback. You also can have both mono and stereo files on one track and choose whether it plays in mono or stereo. Of course, a mono file played in stereo will sound no different than a mono file on a mono track that feeds a stereo output—either way, both channels play the same material—but the ability to have "dual mono" and stereo files on the same track can be convenient. Switching the Channel Mode only affects playback; it does not modify the original file.

Display Scrolling

- To enable or disable automatic scrolling of the display during playback to follow the play location, press F to toggle scrolling, click on the Autoscroll button in the Arrange view toolbar, or choose Options > Cursor Follows Edit Position from the main menu bar. Note that Autoscroll is enabled by default.

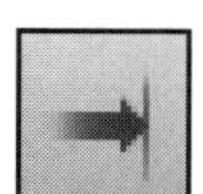

Fig. 3-5: The Autoscroll button from the Arrange view toolbar.

Loop Playback

You might hear a spot where you missed a note, but you can easily fix that by punching in. Before you do that, however, you probably want to rehearse the part. Loop playback is the tool for this. Setting up loop playback is easy; simply set the left and right locators in the Arrange view of the Song window to the loop start and end points, and enable looping.

THE LEFT AND RIGHT LOCATORS (LOOP START/END)

The locators mark start and end points for several tasks, including looping, Auto Punch, and designating the source for a bounce (mix to disk). Because of this, Studio One 2 talks about them as Loop Start/End markers in some places, and locators in others.

You can set the left and right locators using any of the following methods:

- Move the cursor to the top of the timeline until it turns into a pencil shape, and then drag in the timeline from where you want the loop to start to where you want it to stop. When you release the mouse, you will see the selected loop range.

Fig. 3-6: At the top of the timeline, the arrow cursor turns to a pencil to indicate that dragging will set the locators to the start and stop points of the drag.

- Move the cursor to the timeline and press Cmd-click (Ctrl-click in Windows) to place the left locator. Press Option-click (Alt-click in Windows) to place the right locator.
- Drag either locator in the timeline.
- Drag in the Arrange view with the Range tool to make a selection, and then press P on the keyboard to set the locators.
- Click on the Loop Start or Loop End display in the Transport bar and enter the desired value.

Fig. 3-7: The blue bar shows the active loop area in a Song.

To capture the current play location into a locator, do the following:

- Open Preferences > Options > General > Keyboard Shortcuts and assign key shortcuts to Set Loop Start and Set Loop End.
- Use the key shortcuts during playback to place the locators at the desired locations.

MORE LOOP EDITING COMMANDS

A number of loop editing commands do not appear anywhere in the user interface. They can be assigned shortcut keys, but they have no default shortcuts assigned to them. They are there and are helpful, so it is worth knowing about them. In order to use them, you'll have to assign—and remember—some shortcuts for them in Preferences > Options > General > Keyboard Shortcuts.

- **Set Loop Start/End.** These commands set the loop start or end point to the current play location position. This is ideal for grabbing loop points on the fly.
- **Go to Loop Start/End.** These commands make it easy to jump to the beginning or end of the loop.
- **Play from Loop Start.** A most useful function: jump to the start of the loop and play.
- **Shift Loop.** This slides the loop later in time by one loop length. That is, the start and end of a 5-second loop would each get moved by 5 seconds. Very helpful when putting automation in place, because you can work on one small area until you get all of your automation done for it, then slide the loop later and automate the next stretch.
- **Shift Loop Backwards.** This does the same thing as Shift Loop, only it moves the loop earlier in time.

You can enable looping using any of these methods:

- Press the / (forward slash) key on the keyboard.
- Click on the Loop button in the Transport bar.
- While dragging in the timeline to set the locators (as described above), press and hold down the Option key. When you let go of the mouse button, the locators will be set and looping enabled. Note that you must press the Option key *after* clicking the mouse button in the timeline and starting to drag.

Fig. 3-8: This loop is inactive, as indicated by the gray color.

Studio One 2 will perform loop playback for as long as it is enabled. If you move the locators, it will simply loop the new selected loop range.

LOCATING

Studio One 2 offers many commands for positioning the play location to a desired point in the Song. Note that positioning the play location may not cause the display to scroll there.

For information on locating to markers other than loop markers, see the following section, "Markers."

- To position the play location to the mouse cursor, press Cmd + Spacebar. This very nifty command places the play location at the time at which the mouse is pointing. That means you can move the mouse to a point of interest and instantly play from there.

TIP: On the Mac, Cmd + Spacebar is the default key combination for bringing up Spotlight. However, the Locate Playback to Mouse Cursor command shortcut can be reset in Options > General > Keyboard Shortcuts to something that will not conflict, such as Option + Spacebar (Alt + Spacebar in Windows).

- To return the play location to time 00:00:00.000 (bar 1, beat 1), press , (the comma key) or choose Transport > Return to Zero from the main menu bar.
- To locate to a specific time location, press Cmd + T or choose Transport > Goto Time from the main menu bar.
- To locate to the start or end of the loop, press Option (Alt in Windows) + [(left bracket) or Option (Alt in Windows) +] (right bracket), respectively, or choose Transport > Goto Loop Start or Goto Loop End from the main menu bar.
- To locate to the start of the selection, press L or choose Transport > Locate to Selection from the main menu bar.
- To locate to the end of the selection, choose Transport > Locate to Selection End from the main menu bar. There is no default key shortcut for this, but one can be assigned.
- To locate to the next or previous Event or Part, press Option + Shift + N (Alt + Shift + N in Windows) or Option + Shift + B (Alt + Shift + B in Windows) (respectively), or choose Transport > Goto Next Event or Goto Previous Event from the main menu bar.
- To enable locating to any empty spot at which you click, check the Locate When Clicked in Empty Space box in Options > Advanced > Editing > Tools.

Markers

Markers are extremely powerful tools that are useful in overdubbing, playback, editing, mixing, and mastering. They can be dropped at any location where work needs to be done:

- Locations where punch-ins or additional recording should be performed.
- To lay out the structure of a Song (verses, choruses, and so on).
- Locations where edits are to be performed.
- Locations where mix automation or adjustments are to be created.

- Locations from which to start playback and auditioning, for example, to facilitate comparisons between two or more spots in a Song.
- Starting and ending locations for operations like bouncing.
- Hit points for working to picture (that is, moments where there is visual action that needs to be highlighted by sound).

You will use markers differently depending on their purpose. In the case of punch-in or edit locations, markers may be placed for temporary use and then deleted, while song structure markers may be placed early in work on the Song and stay there from that time until the Song is done.

The left and right locators and Song Start and End markers are specialized markers that have different procedures for use. The locators are discussed in the Loop Playback section above, while the Song Start and End markers are discussed in the chapter "Mixing" in the upcoming volume 2 of *Power Tools for Studio One 2*.

The Marker Track

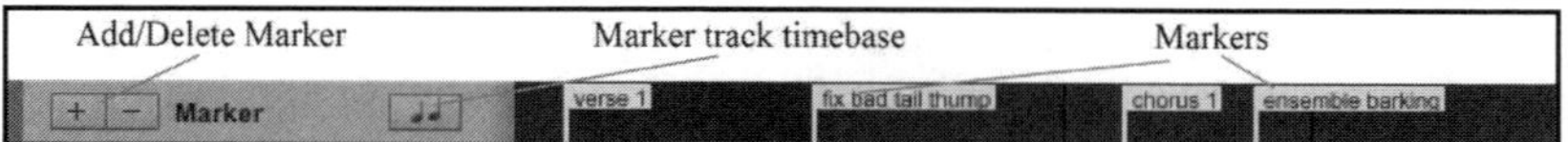

Fig. 3-9: The Marker track, set to Bars time base, with several markers.

Markers are viewed and edited in the Marker track. The Marker track can be set to lock the markers to one of two time bases: bars and beats (a location related to the Song's structure) or absolute time locations. The difference is this: when locked to a structural (bars and beats) location, such as the beginning of a chorus, markers will get moved in time if the tempo is changed in order to maintain their structural location. Markers locked to absolute time locations do not get moved when tempo changes, making them the usual choice when working to picture.

As of this writing, Studio One 2's marker implementation is effective, but rudimentary. For example, there is no marker list or inspector for viewing and editing a list of markers or editing a single marker's location value directly. As well, all markers use the same time base at all times. If you switch time bases on the Marker track from seconds to beats, and then change the tempo, all markers will move to hold their bars and beats position. You could not, for instance, have some hit points that are always locked to an absolute time location, and other markers that move with tempo. They all either move with the tempo or not.

Fig. 3-10: The Marker track button in the Arrange view toolbar.

- To open the Marker track, click on the Marker track button at the top of the track headers in the Arrange view.

CREATING, DELETING, AND EDITING MARKERS

- To insert a marker, press the Y or Insert keys, or click on the + (Add Marker) button in the Marker track header. Any of these can be done whether Studio One 2 is recording, playing, or stopped. By default, new markers are assigned successive numbers for their names.
- Pressing Shift + Y or Shift + Insert will insert a marker and bring up a dialog in which you can enter a name. Names can also be added and edited any time after insertion.

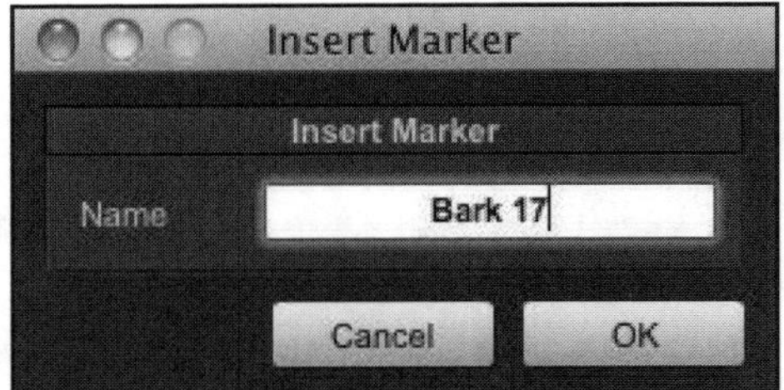

Fig. 3-11: Though labeled "Insert Marker," this dialog is for naming markers.

- To delete a marker, locate to it or click on it to select it and press the Backspace key. You can also click on the – (Delete Marker) button in the Marker track header. You may delete multiple markers by dragging over them in the Marker track to select them and pressing Backspace.

TIP: If you delete or move a marker, Studio One 2 will renumber the remaining markers that have default names. This is usually a problem because the usefulness of markers lies in the association of a marker number with a location, a relationship that renumbering changes. For example, say that marker 4 got dropped at the beginning of verse 2. Every time you locate to marker 4 you go to verse 2. Now you decide to delete marker 3 for some reason. In order to locate to verse 2, you now have to go to marker 3, since marker 4 got renumbered. Confusing, eh? Unfortunately, this behavior is not altered if the marker has a name instead of default numbering. It simply has to be accommodated when you delete or move markers.

- To rename an existing marker, double-click on it in the Marker track at any time and enter the desired name.
- To move a marker, drag it in the Marker track. Marker dragging is affected by Snap, if it is enabled.

LOCATING TO MARKERS

- To locate to the next marker, press Shift + N on the keyboard.
- To locate to the previous marker, press Shift + B on the keyboard.
- To locate to a specific marker, right-click (or Ctrl-click on Mac) in the timeline and choose the desired marker from the drop-down list that appears.
- To locate to any of the first seven markers, press (marker number + 2) on the number pad of your keyboard. To locate to marker 4, for instance, press the 6 key on the number pad. If dealing with this is way too much of a distraction to you, or you are using a keyboard lacking a number pad, such as a laptop, reassign the key shortcuts

in the Preferences dialog box, as described in the "Meet Studio One 2" section of chapter 1, "On Your Mark." One possibility is to create combinations of a number and a modifier key, for instance, the shortcut for marker 4 might be Option + 4 (Alt + 4 in Windows).

LOCKING MARKERS TO THE TIME BASE

- To set markers to be locked to bars and beats (structural) locations, be sure that the Timebase button in the Marker track header is displaying a musical notes icon. If it shows the clock icon, click on it to change it to the notes icon.
- To set markers to be locked to absolute time locations, be sure the Timebase button in the Marker track header is displaying a clock icon. If it shows the musical notes icon, click on it to change it to the clock icon.

Time	Bars

Fig. 3-12: The Marker track time base can be set to Time, in which case markers are locked to absolute time locations, or Bars, in which markers are marked to musical locations, meaning that they will move in time if the tempo is changed.

OVERDUBBING

The child of multitrack recording is surely overdubbing. The ability to record one or more tracks in a specified time slot in a song while listening to everything else that has been recorded is the foundation on which most of modern recording is based. Studio One 2 has a full set of overdubbing facilities, including manual and auto punch in/out, plus loop recording.

When recording MIDI to an Instrument track, there are two record modes: Overdub and Replace. The difference is simple: recording in Overdub combines the new part you play with the existing part, which you will also hear while recording. Replace, as you might guess, replaces existing material in the area that is recorded. Read more about Instrument track recording modes in chapter 4, "Virtual Instruments and MIDI."

MANUAL PUNCH-IN

- Check that you have armed the track(s) on which you wish to record and your levels are set correctly.
- Begin playback anywhere you like.
- To manually punch into record, simply press the * (star) key on your number pad or click on the Record button in the Transport bar to punch in, as usual.
- To exit record, press the * (star) key on your number pad or click on the Record button in the Transport bar again. Studio One 2 will exit record but continue playback until you stop it.

AUTO PUNCH

Auto Punch automates the punch-in process. Punch-in and punch-out locations are set, playback is started some time before the punch-in point, and record-enabled tracks drop into record automatically when the punch-in point is reached. Recording continues to the punch-out point, when record is exited.

There are many reasons to use automated punch in/out—in fact, some people hardly work any other way. For example, it lets you execute punches whose timing is too tight to do accurately manually. Auto Punch is also great when you are playing or singing while you record. You are well served by being fast and smooth with setting Auto Punch In and Out points.

Working with Auto Punch is typically done using preroll to start playback before the punch-in point.

To use Auto Punch, do the following:

- Check that you have armed the track(s) on which you wish to record and your levels are set correctly.
- Enable preroll by pressing O on the keyboard or clicking on the Preroll button in the Transport bar. Preroll length is set in the Metronome Setup dialog box. Note that preroll length can be set only in musical bars, not in minutes or seconds.
- The punch-in and punch-out points are marked by the left and right locators, respectively. Drag in the timeline to set them, or use any other method described in the "Loop Playback" section above.
- Press I to turn Auto Punch on.
- Locate to any point in the Song before the punch-in point.
- Start playback. You will hear the track and can play along with it. Studio One 2 will automatically drop into record when it reaches the punch-in point and exit record at the punch-out point.

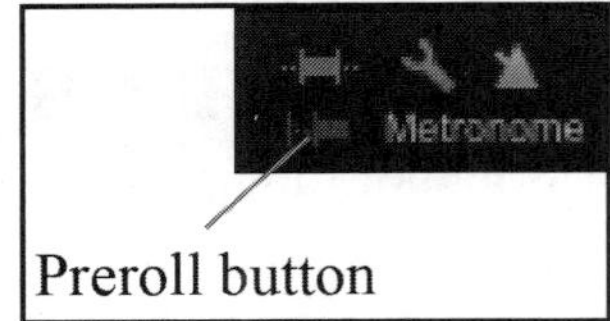

Fig. 3-13: The Preroll button in the Transport bar, shown enabled.

Fig. 3-14: The Auto Punch button in the Transport bar, shown enabled.

Don't worry if your punch is tightly fit into the middle of the existing material in the track, because Studio One 2 automatically creates very small (10 ms) crossfades at the punch-in and punch-out points to prevent clicks or pops from occurring. These crossfades can be manually edited. I'll show you how to do that in chapter 5, "On the Cutting Room Floor: Basic Editing."

Hey, you're on your way to recording your masterpiece!

TRY A PUNCH-IN

Let's put all of this powerful new information into practice by adding a new track to part of the one you recorded before. For this example, we will assume that you are adding a guitar track by running your guitar into a DI and then straight into your interface. We'll use Studio One 2's amplifier emulation and other guitar processing to get a good sound.

For now, we're just going to grab a preset, but we'll explore plug-ins more in the chapter on mixing in *Power Tools for Studio One 2*, vol. 2.

1. Press the F5 key or click on the Browse button to open the Browser.
2. Click on the Effects tab to show the list of Studio One 2's effects.
3. If the Sort By area above the list is not set to Flat, click on the Flat button.
4. At the top of the list you will see a folder called FX Chains. Click on it to reveal its contents.
5. Click on the Guitar folder to reveal its contents.
6. Find the effects chain preset called S1 Guitar Channel, drag it to an open area in the Arrange view, and drop it there. Studio One 2 will create a new audio track with a rack of guitar processing already in place. Pretty dope.
7. The default for this preset is a stereo input. Your input is probably mono, so click on the Channel Mode (mono/stereo) button in the track header in the Arrange view. Now you have a mono input!
8. Configure the input and output selections at the top of the channel strip in the Mix view for the appropriate interface input and outputs. If you don't see what you expect in the drop-down input and output lists, open Preferences > Song Setup > Audio I/O Setup and make sure it is correctly configured.
9. To minimize any delay between when you play something and when you hear it, make sure that the buffer size (Preferences > Options > Audio Setup > Device Block Size) is set to the smallest size that allows recording and playback without glitching or other artifacts. For more about

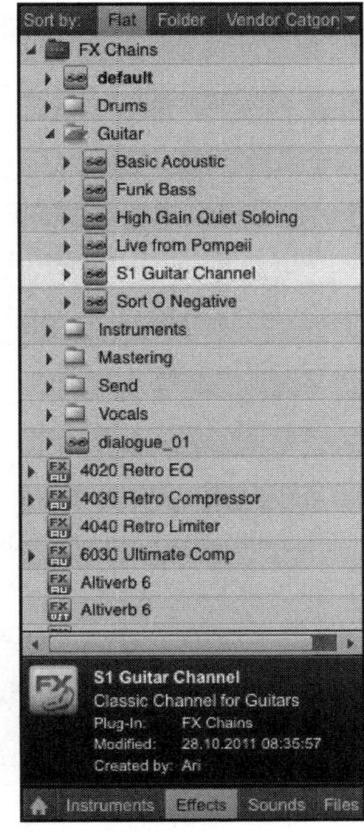

Fig. 3-15: The Browser list of FX Chains for guitars that is included with Studio One 2.

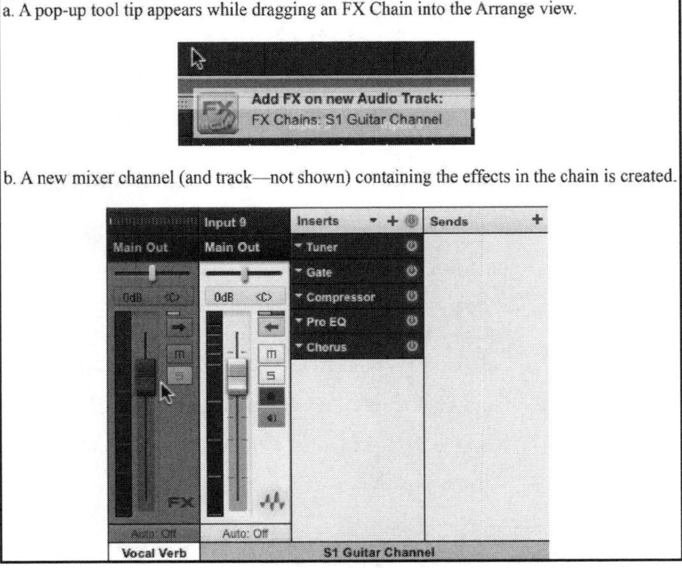

Fig. 3-16: A new track and mixer channel containing an entire recording chain can be created simply by dragging it from the Browser to the Arrange view.

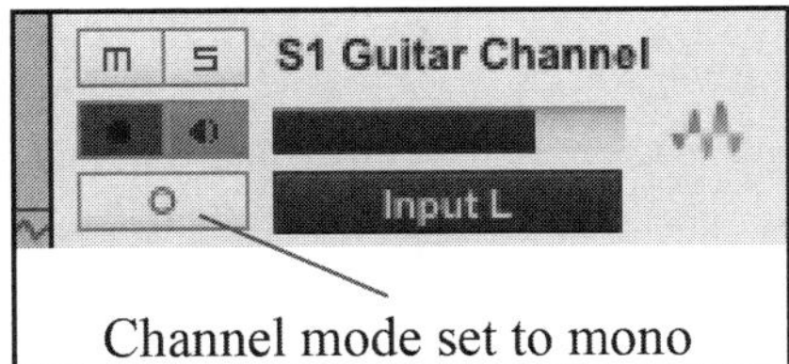

Fig. 3-17: The channel mode of a stereo track can be set to mono, which will sum the two channels to a mono output.

buffer size, see the section "Understanding Buffer Size" in chapter 2, "Get Set to Record."

Fig. 3-18: When recording, it is good to set the Device Block Size setting as small as your computer will allow.

10. Arm the track for recording. If you have a PreSonus interface with low-latency monitoring, click the ZL button on each track to use it. If you have another interface with low-latency monitoring, you will monitor through it instead of through Studio One 2. Click the monitor button on each track to disable monitoring through Studio One 2.
11. Play a little of the Song and play along with it to be sure you hear both the existing track and your new signal.
12. Set the Auto Punch In and Out points as described above to the area where you want to add the new part.
13. Enable Auto Punch.
14. Configure and enable the metronome and count-off if you want them.
15. Press * (star) to start playback with Auto Punch.
16. Listen to or play along with the music until you come to the punch-in location. Studio One 2 will drop into Record and you can play the new part.
17. Press the Spacebar to stop any time after Studio One 2 exits Record at the punch-out location.
18. Now play back what you just recorded. Voila!

LOOP RECORDING

Loop recording is a handy technique in which Studio One 2 loops as described in the "Loop Playback" section above, but records a new take each time through the loop. By default, loop recording writes the new take sequentially into the same audio file. When you are done, there is a single file containing each take in order of recording time. In the track in the Arrange view, the loop recording appears as a single Audio Event with an indicator (in the lower left corner) that there are multiple takes.

To loop record, do the following:

1. Set up for loop playback as described in the "Loop Playback" section above.
2. Record-enable the track(s) on which you wish to record.
3. Record as described above, using the manual, Auto Punch, or Preroll method.
4. When you have done as many passes as you want, stop Studio One 2 to exit Record.

Working with Takes

Files containing multiple takes can be used in several ways: selecting a single take to use, editing between takes to create a "comp" (composite) take, splitting takes to separate layers on a track, or splitting takes to separate tracks.

- To select one take and use it, right-click (or Ctrl-click on Mac) on the Audio Event in the track and select the desired take from the contextual drop-down menu that appears.
- To split takes into layers, making use of existing layers, right-click (or Ctrl-click on Mac) on the Event with the takes and choose Unpack Takes > Unpack Takes to Existing Layers from the contextual drop-down menu that appears. Takes will be unpacked into the existing layers, starting with the first layer below the track and moving down. If there is material already in the existing layers, the takes will be put on top of them in the track. If there are more takes than existing layers, new layers will be created as needed. The take and layer that were active on the track before unpacking will remain so.

woofwoof(5)
File Tempo 114.00 Speedup 1.00
Transpose 0 Tune 0
Bend Marker Threshold 0%
Select Take
Take 1
Take 2
Take 3
Take 4
Unpack Takes
Cut ⌘X
Copy ⌘C
Delete Del
Duplicate D

Fig. 3-19: Takes for an Audio Event are accessed from the Event contextual drop-down menu.

- To split takes into new layers, right-click (Ctrl-click on Mac) on the Event with the takes and choose Unpack Takes > Unpack Takes to New Layers from the contextual drop-down menu that appears. Any existing layers will be left untouched, while a new layer will be created for each take.
- To split the takes into separate tracks, each containing one take, right-click (Ctrl-click on Mac) on the Audio Event in the track and choose Unpack Takes to Tracks from the contextual drop-down menu that appears.

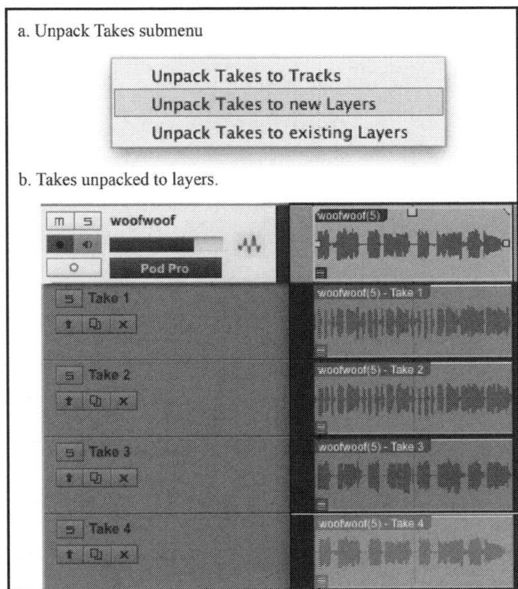

Fig. 3-20: Unpack Takes.

Musicloop and Audioloop File Formats

Musicloop and Audioloop are proprietary file formats created by PreSonus to facilitate the use of loops in Studio One 2. For more information on using these formats, see the chapter "Working with Loops" in *Power Tools for Studio One 2*, vol. 2. All I will do here is give a quick description of them.

The Musicloop format stores a VI preset, FLAC audio data, multichannel preset chains, and a file of MIDI notes. It's an entire loop performance in a single file.

The Audioloop format tags an Audio Part with a tempo and applies lossless compression to it. For more information on Audio Parts, see the section "Editing Audio" of chapter 6, "Advanced Editing."

USING LAYERS

Each track in the Arrange view can contain a stack of playlists, sort of like a layer cake. Each playlist layer can be entirely separate from the others, sharing only a "playback vessel," which is the track. In Studio One 2, you can listen to only one layer on a given track, but it is easy to duplicate, edit separately, and cut/copy/paste between layers.

This makes layers extremely useful in editing, but they are just as useful in recording. Layers are the most convenient way of recording multiple takes of an instrument in separate passes (when you are not loop recording). (Editing applications of layers are described in chapter 6, "Advanced Editing.") Combining the recording and editing applications of layers makes them a great tool for punch-ins. If you make layers your friends, you will be rewarded with many benefits. Whether that makes you friends with benefits is not for me to say.

Layer operations are performed in the Layers control field in the Track inspector.

- To access the Layers control field: click on the lowercase i button above the Arrange view or press the F4 key to open the inspector for the currently selected track.
- To make a new layer: Choose Add Layer from the drop-down menu in the Layers field.
- To duplicate a layer: Choose Duplicate Layer from the drop-down menu in the Layers field.
- To delete a layer: Choose Remove Layer from the drop-down menu in the Layers field. If there is only one layer in the Track, this choice will be grayed out.

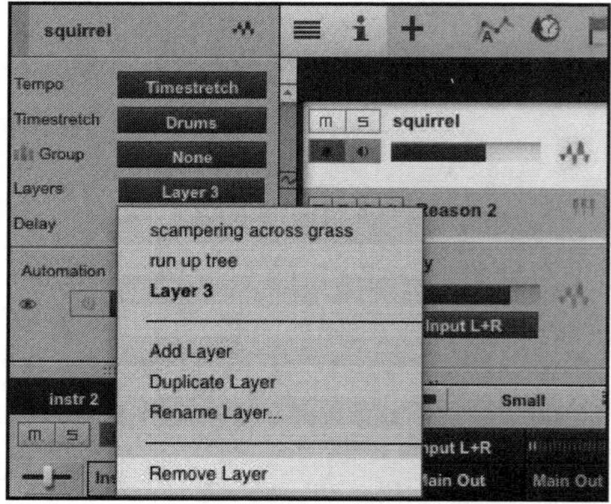

Fig. 3-21: The Layers field provides selection and management functions for layers in a track.

Layers and Punch-Ins

When you record a part, you can always punch in directly to the original recording, but what if you want to try recording a few different alternatives in one section and then compare them? Layers are valuable in overdubbing because you can punch in on copies of a take. As an example, here's how you could try the comparison just mentioned:

1. Select the track on which you want to experiment and click on the lowercase i button or press the F4 key to open its inspector.
2. Choose Duplicate Layer from the Layers drop-down menu. Repeat as many times as experiments you want to try. You now have several copies of the original recording.
3. Choose the first copy from the Layers drop-down menu.
4. Set up a loop of the spot where you want to experiment as described. You'll probably want to set up some preroll, as well.
5. Play the loop and try one of your new ideas.
6. When you feel as though you have something you want to record, stop playback and enable Auto Punch.
7. Record your new idea.
8. Choose a different layer copy from the Layers drop-down menu and record your next idea. Repeat as often as desired.

Fig. 3-22: The Inspector pane button in the Arrange view toolbar.

Another way of using layers for punch-in recording is to duplicate the current layer every time you complete a section of overdubbing, and then continue work on the copy. For example, you might make a duplicate after doing punch-in spot fixes of all the verses of the Song, and then continue work on the copy, making the spot fixes of choruses. This makes it simple to "peel back the onion" to earlier stages in the track recording.

PRINTING EFFECTS WHILE RECORDING

Many people like to record sounds without effects and add them later, but there are times when the effect is so integral to the sound that you might want to record the sound with the effects on it. This is easily achieved in Studio One 2 simply by inserting the effects on the input channel. It is important to remember that, once recorded, effects cannot be removed except by using the Undo function or history.

To print effects while recording, do the following:

1. Click on the Inputs button at the left of the Mix view. The input channels are now displayed.
2. Double-click on the input channel on which you wish to add the effects, and the Inserts section will appear.

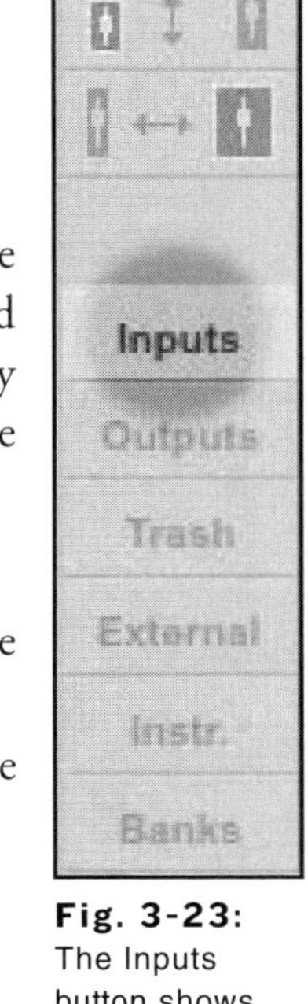

Fig. 3-23: The Inputs button shows or hides input channels in the mixer.

3. Click on the + (plus) sign at the top of the Insert section and choose an effect from the drop-down menu that appears, or click on the triangle at the top of the Inserts section and choose an effects chain from the drop-down menu that appears.
4. Adjust the effect as desired.
5. Double-click in the Inserts section to collapse it back into the input channel strip.

The signal with effects will now be recorded. Plug-in latency is automatically compensated for.

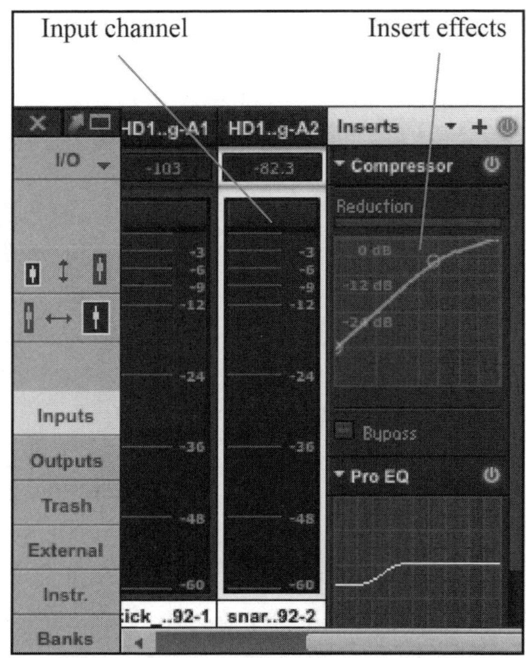

Fig. 3-24: To record with effects, the effects must be inserted on the input channel.

Virtual Instruments and MIDI

4

Studio One 2 does more than record, edit, and play back audio. It also is a MIDI sequencer and a host for virtual instruments. (A virtual instrument, or "VI," is one that is entirely software based.) Virtual instruments and hardware MIDI devices have two signal paths: the MIDI performance information that plays them, and the audio outputs they generate. Because some VIs can send signals out of multiple audio outputs in response to a single MIDI input stream, there are situations in which there is not a one-to-one correspondence between Instrument tracks in the Arrange view and Instrument channel strips in the Mix view. This will become clearer in the upcoming section "Multitimbral and Multichannel Instruments."

ABOUT MIDI

MIDI is a protocol (a scheme that devices use to communicate with each other) for carrying musical performance information: what note was played, how hard, whether a sustain footpedal was pressed, and so forth. MIDI does not carry sound data, only information describing how sounds should be played. It's a little like a player piano roll, which is just a music score that makes no sound until it is mounted on a player piano and played.

Originally, MIDI was used largely to play multiple keyboard synthesizers from a single controller, and it is still useful in controlling outboard synthesizers and equipment. But in today's studio, MIDI is most often used as the means by which keyboard or other controller information is entered into Studio One 2, and by which Studio One 2 plays virtual instruments like software samplers and synthesizers.

Strictly speaking, Studio One 2's internal communications with VIs use a proprietary protocol that is much higher resolution than MIDI. What difference does this make to you? It means that controller automation can have sample-accurate resolution, which is much higher than MIDI's resolution. It is also the basis for Studio One 2's Control Link system, which enables control of software parameters from hardware controllers. The last effect of Studio One 2's proprietary internal system is that automation in Studio One 2 uses a value range of –100 to +100, instead of MIDI's –128 to +127. This can be a little disorienting if you are used to working in another DAW, as other DAWs generally use the MIDI values, but it's not a difficult adjustment, since most people are familiar with percentages, too. Of course, data received from or sent to your MIDI interface is still in the form of MIDI messages.

If you plan to use virtual instruments or any other MIDI devices with Studio One 2, you will probably want a MIDI keyboard or some other kind of controller to play them. MIDI also enables Studio One 2 to be controlled by control surfaces such as Mackie's HUI family of control surfaces or PreSonus's FaderPort. Control surfaces like these are popular for mixing and editing plug-in and VI parameters.

THE DIFFERENCE BETWEEN VIRTUAL INSTRUMENTS AND AUDIO EVENTS

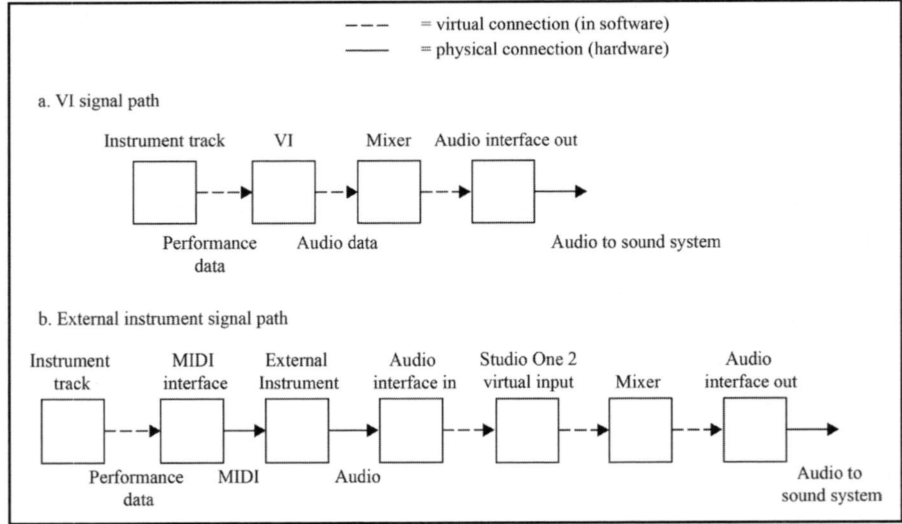

Fig. 4-1: There are important differences in the signal paths used by virtual instruments versus external instruments. External instruments have more connections, especially physical ones.

There are a few important points to understand about virtual instruments. One is that when you hear one, the audio it produces is being generated in real time, not played back from a recording. That takes processor power and other resources—and for sophisticated VIs, an appreciable amount of it. Thus, depending on how powerful your computer is and what else you are doing with it at the time, there can be a limit as to how many VIs you can run. If, for example, you are already playing back 22 audio tracks and running two convolution reverbs (which also require a healthy amount of processor power), your computer is working pretty hard. Now and then, you may reach the point where you are not able to run as many VIs and plug-ins as you would like.

One way of dealing with this problem is by freezing tracks. Most every DAW that can host VIs, including Studio One 2, offers a freeze feature, but they don't all work the same way. The general idea is that freezing an Instrument track records the audio output of the VI as it is played by the track(s). Once the audio is captured in a recording, the instrument itself can be disabled, freeing up all the resources it consumes. Of course, you can always reenable the instrument, make changes, and then freeze it again. The method by which tracks are frozen and unfrozen is one of the areas in which DAWs differ. Later in this chapter I will tell you about freezing tracks in Studio One 2.

By contrast, if you are using hardware MIDI devices, their audio outputs must be physically cabled into your interface and brought into Studio One 2 using regular Audio or Aux channels in the mixer, not Instrument channels. This means that the outputs of these devices are not captured by freezing, but by regular audio recording methods.

INSTRUMENT TRACKS AND SETTING UP VIRTUAL INSTRUMENTS

To use a virtual instrument in Studio One 2 you need to have four things set up:

- A properly installed virtual instrument.
- A properly installed MIDI controller. (A controller is not technically required, but it is usually the way VIs are played.)
- A properly configured Instrument track.
- A properly configured mixer channel to return the Instrument's audio output.

Installing Virtual Instruments and MIDI Controllers

Studio One 2 comes with four virtual instruments and also supports the many third-party instruments available in VST (Mac and Win) and AudioUnits (Mac) formats. Studio One 2 also supports ReWire, a protocol that allows applications like Studio One 2 to send MIDI or other control information to a separate but simultaneously running application (usually a VI or VI environment like Propellerhead Reason), and then receive the digital audio output of that VI for monitoring and recording. All of this takes place entirely in software; no hardware is involved.

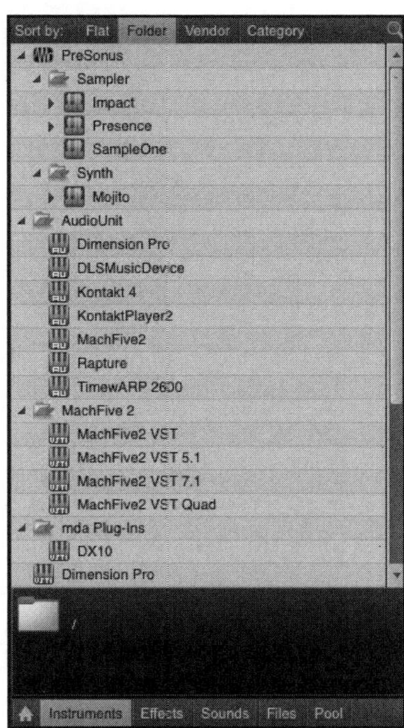

Fig. 4-2: The Browser Instrument pane shows all virtual instruments recognized by Studio One 2.

- To see a list of currently installed virtual instruments, click on the Instruments tab at the bottom of the Browser. You will always see at least the four PreSonus VIs in the list.
- To see the list of virtual instruments currently being used in a Song, click on the Instr button on the left of the Mix view to reveal the Instruments pane.
- To install a third-party VI, follow the manufacturer's installation instructions, and make sure that the location of the VI application is listed in the VST Plug-Ins tab of Preferences > Options > Locations so that Studio One 2 can find it. In most cases, you'll find VST plug-ins here:
- Windows VST VIs and plug-ins are installed into Program Files > vstplugins.
- Mac VST VIs and plug-ins are installed into ~/Library/Audio/Plug-Ins/VST or /VST3.

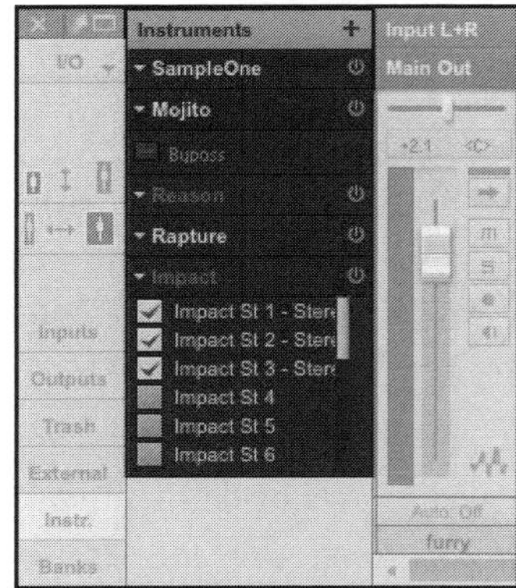

Fig. 4-3: The Mix view Instruments pane shows all virtual instruments being used in the Song and allows configuration of functions like enabling and disabling audio outputs (for instruments having multiple audio outputs) and accessing controller maps.

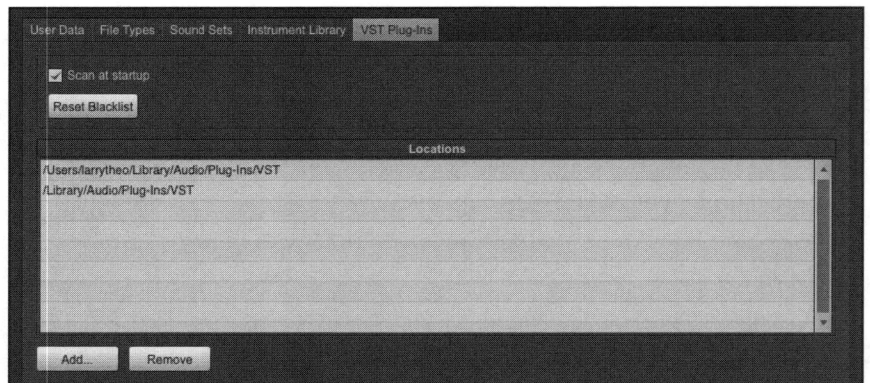

Fig. 4-4: The VST Plug-Ins tab of Preferences>Options>Locations defines where Studio One 2 should look for VST-format instruments and plug-ins.

- If a VI is installed elsewhere, click on the Add button and add the location to the list. Once added to the list, the VI should show up in the Browser.
- MIDI controllers must be configured in Preferences > Options > External Devices. For more information, see the "Meet Studio One 2" section of chapter 1, "On Your Mark." Note that the External Devices pane can be opened directly from an existing Instrument track by choosing Configure… from the drop-down menu in the Instrument Input field of the track.

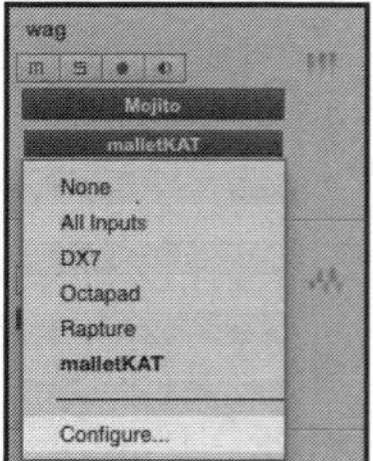

Fig. 4-5: The Instrument track input field selects a MIDI controller from which to record performance data into the track.

Instrument Tracks

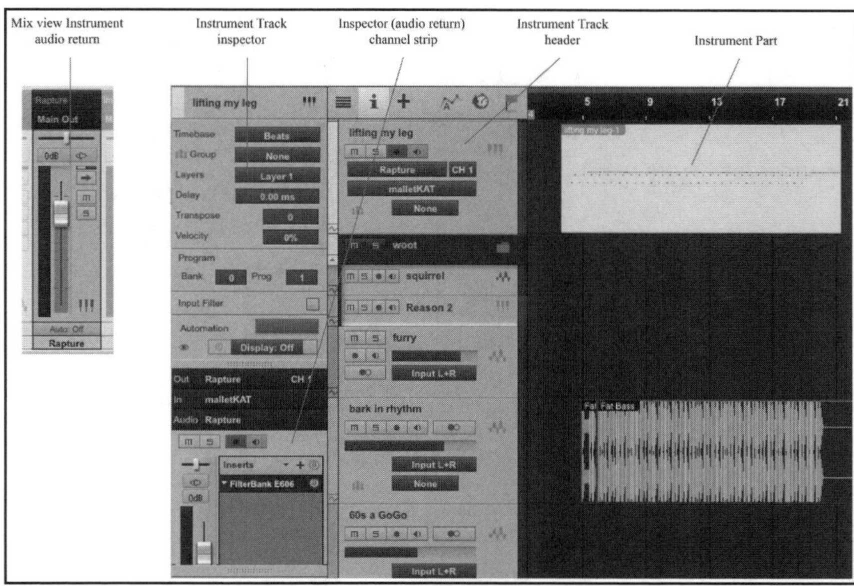

Fig. 4-6: The primary areas for working with Instrument tracks. Note that the mixer channel is named for the instrument ("Rapture"), not for the track. This is because several tracks could be simultaneously playing a multitimbral, multichannel instrument like Cakewalk Rapture.

Instrument tracks contain performance data only, no audio. Notes and continuous controller data generally constitute the bulk of the data in an Instrument track. Instrument tracks accept as input any controller that is set up as an External Device, and an Instrument track output can be routed to any VI or MIDI interface output. This means that Instrument tracks can play not only VIs, but external MIDI devices as well. The output can be changed at any time, making it a piece of cake to audition an Instrument track with different instruments, virtual or physical.

There are two ways to create an Instrument track:

1. An Instrument track is automatically created when you instantiate a VI, as described below. The output will be automatically configured as well.
2. Add an Instrument track by either choosing Track > Add Instrument Track or clicking on the Add Track button in the Arrange view. (Don't forget to set the track format to Instrument.) If you add an Instrument track, you will need to configure both its input and its output.
3. To configure the input of an Instrument track, click on the Instrument Input field of the track and choose a controller from the drop-down menu that appears. Note that None and All Inputs (that is, the track will record and monitor input from any controller) options are also available in the menu. See Fig. 4-5.

Configuring the output of an Instrument track means assigning it to the instrument that it will play. You can do this in either of the following two ways:

- Click on the Instrument Output field of the track and choose an instrument from the drop-down menu that appears.
- Drag an instrument from the Browser and drop it onto an existing Instrument track. The new instrument replaces the old one as the track output destination.

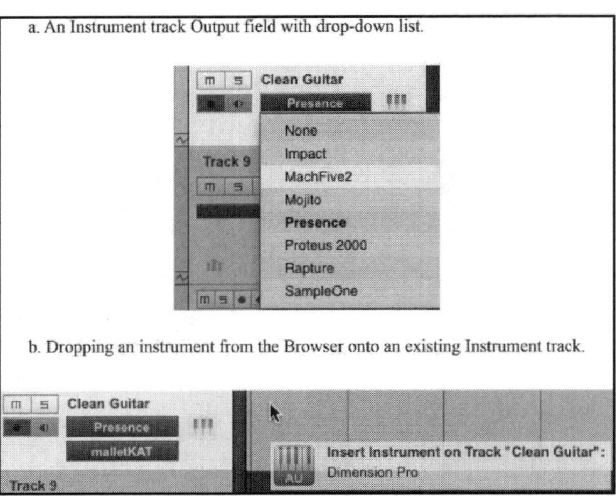

Fig. 4-7: Two ways to change an Instrument assignment.

Adding a Virtual Instrument to a Song

Either of these methods will add a VI to a Song:

- Drag an instrument from the Browser and drop it into an open area of the Arrange view. This will create a new Instrument track, with the dropped instrument as the track output and a mixer channel strip with the audio output of the instrument as its input. Presets for included PreSonus instruments are listed in the Browser under the instrument's name. If, instead of dragging the instrument's name, you drag one of the presets listed under the instrument's name, that preset will get loaded into the instrument as the Instrument track is created.
- Drag an instrument from the Browser and drop it into the Instruments pane of the Mix view. This will only add the instrument to the Song; it will not create a track or mixer channel. You can add an Instrument track and assign its output to the new instrument, or reconfigure an existing Instrument track to play the new instrument.

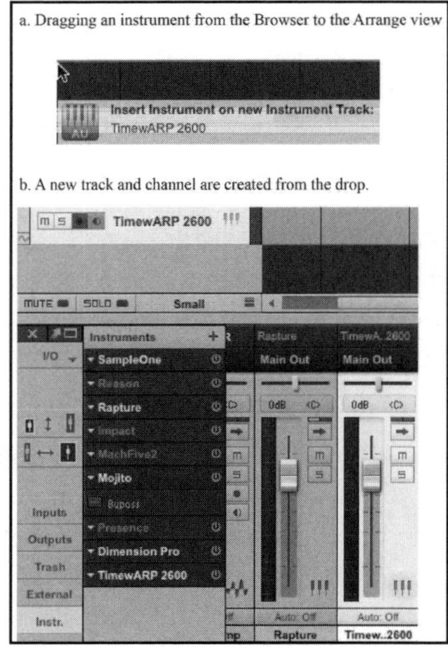

Fig. 4-8: Dragging a VI or VI preset and dropping it into an empty area of the Arrange view creates a new track and channel for the instrument.

Multitimbral and Multichannel Instruments

Virtual instruments have become sophisticated and powerful. One key aspect of this fact is that many VIs are multitimbral: that is, they accept multiple MIDI channels, each of which plays a different sound. If you think of this as several VIs in one package, it is easy to see that you will need to create and configure a separate Instrument track for each channel of MIDI data you want to send to the instrument.

Quite a few multitimbral instruments also can assign each of their sounds to play out of a different audio output (remembering that this is all in software; there are no physical outputs). This is called "multichannel capability." A drum machine might use six output channels: kick, snare, stereo tom mix, and stereo cymbal mix. This provides excellent flexibility in mixing. For example, giving the snare its own output enables the use of a different reverb for the snare than for the rest of the kit. Multichannel outputs are also useful with software samplers for the same reason: different sounds can be treated independently in the mix.

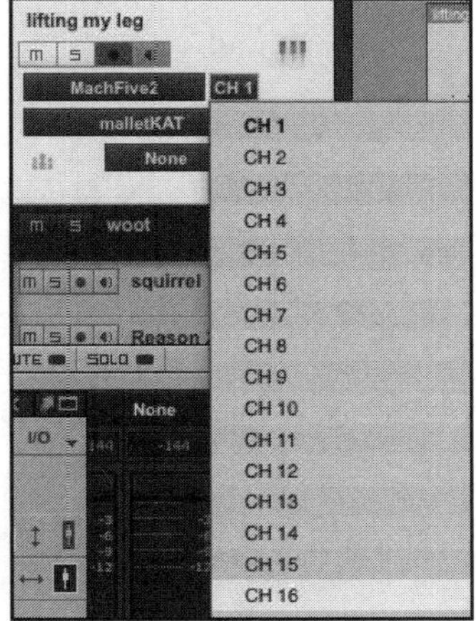

Fig. 4-9: The MIDI channel field, which selects the channel over which the track will play, only appears for instruments that are defined as multitimbral.

Studio One 2 accommodates both of these capabilities.

- If an instrument is multitimbral, a MIDI channel field will appear next to the instrument's name in the Instrument track header. Click in the field and choose the desired channel from the drop-down menu.

To access the outputs of a multichannel instrument, do the following:

1. Click on the instrument's name in the Instrument pane of the Mix view. A list of available outputs will appear. By default, the first output (mono or stereo) is enabled.
2. To enable an output, check the box next to its name in the output list for the instrument. An Instrument channel is created in the mixer for each enabled output. Disabling the output deletes its channel in the mixer.

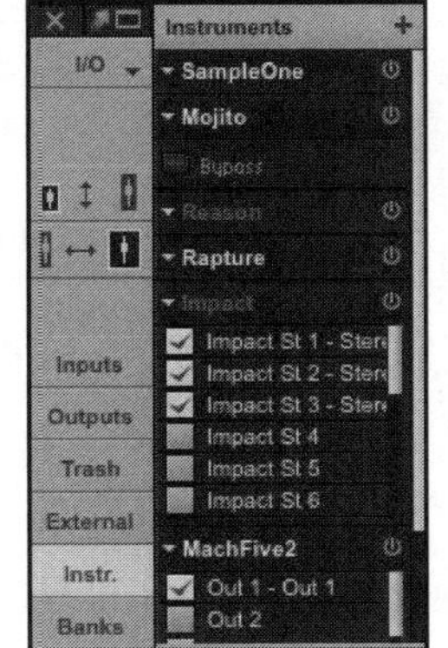

Fig. 4-10: Some VIs are multichannel, that is, they have multiple virtual audio outputs. These can be individually enabled or disabled in the Mix view Instruments pane. In this figure, Impact and MOTU MachFive 2 are both multichannel.

The Device (Instrument) Editor Header

At the top of each Instrument editor resides a host of controls for the instrument. These controls are the same whether the instrument is an included PreSonus VI or a third-party VI. Many third-party VIs have their own preset schemes, however. This means that the header's Preset Select field may not be able to access the presets of third-party VIs. In this case, presets must be accessed from the preset management features in the VI itself.

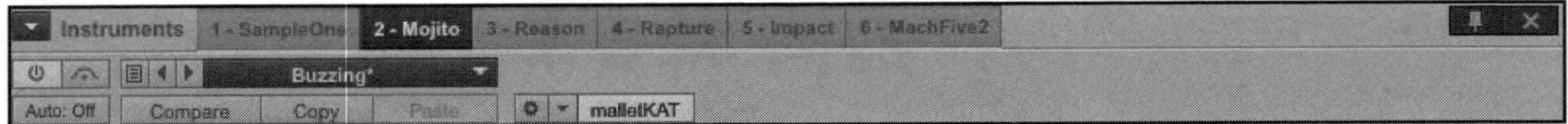

Fig. 4-11: VIs and plug-ins both have the Instrument editor header shown here in their editor windows.

Since the header in audio plug-in editors is the same as for Instrument editors, Studio One 2 refers to instruments and plug-ins collectively as "devices," making this the "Device editor header." For much more about the Device editor header, see "The Device (Plug-In and Instrument) Editor Header" section in chapter 5, "On the Cutting Room Floor: Basic Editing."

Using ReWire Applications with Instrument Tracks

Studio One 2 Pro supports Propellerhead ReWire protocol, which allows MIDI and digital audio to be passed between applications that support it. That means you can run programs like Propellerhead Reason in parallel and send their audio outputs to Studio One 2. Studio One 2 is also able to send MIDI to these applications.

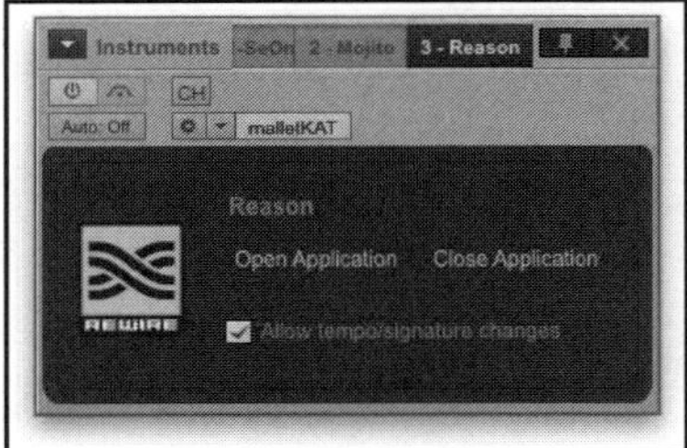

Fig. 4-12: The ReWire object window.

ReWire-enabled applications will usually just show up in the Instruments tab of the Browser, and they are added to a Song in the same way: drag the instrument to the Arrange view.

At that point, however, you will see something a little different: Studio One 2's ReWire object window. The header for this window is essentially the same as for other instruments. In the body of the window, however, are these functions:

- The Open Application button allows you to open many ReWire-enabled applications without having to leave Studio One 2. However, not all ReWire-enabled applications can respond to an external Open command, in which case you must manually open the application. It should open in ReWire slave mode.
- Similarly, the Close Application button will close many, but not all, ReWire-enabled applications. Note that closing the application will not remove either the Instrument track(s) being used for it or its mixer channel(s).
- The Allow Tempo/Time Signature Changes checkbox lets a ReWire-enabled application make changes to tempos and time signatures within Studio One 2. This box is checked by default; uncheck it to disable this service.

Using External Devices with Instrument Tracks

Instrument tracks are not limited to use with VIs; they are equally useful for playing any devices you may have that are identified to Studio One 2 as Instruments in the External Devices list (that is, they can produce sound, as opposed to a controller). In order to use an external MIDI device with Studio One 2, you must make the following connections:

1. Have a MIDI cable connected from a MIDI interface output to MIDI In on the external device, so that an Instrument track can play the device.
2. Connect the signal from the external device's audio outputs to your audio interface's inputs. It makes no difference whether they are connected directly or through an external mixing console, as long as the audio signal can get from the instrument to the interface.
4. To change the program running on the external device, enter bank and program number values into the Bank and Prog fields in the Program area of the Track inspector. The program change message is sent to the external device when you press the Return key to confirm the values.

Once physical cabling to and from the instrument is in place, the rest is easy:

1. Assign the output of an Instrument track to the MIDI interface output connected to the instrument.
2. Create an audio channel in the Mix view to receive the instrument's audio output and choose the appropriate audio interface input as the channel input.
3. For multitimbral or multichannel operation, create more Instrument tracks and audio channels as needed and configure appropriately.

MIDI Monitor

The MIDI Monitor window enables you to view MIDI messages coming into and going out of Studio One 2. A collection of filters enable thinning the message stream, making it easier to see only the data you want.

- To open the MIDI Monitor window, click on the MIDI connector icon on the far left of the Transport bar, or choose View > MIDI Monitor from the main menu bar.

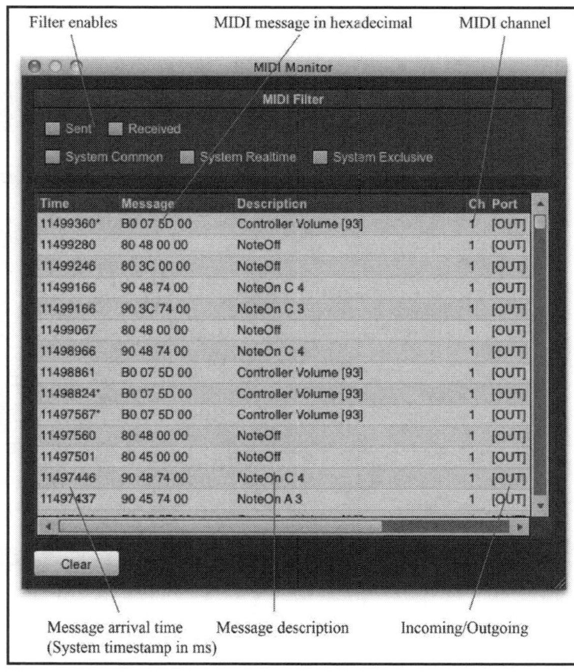

Fig. 4-13: The MIDI Monitor shows all MIDI messages coming and going to and from Studio One 2. Filters enable thinning of the data stream for easier reading.

THE MIDI MONITOR DISPLAY

In the MIDI Monitor window you will see the following information displayed in real time as messages arrive:

- **Time:** The system time stamp at the message's arrival, given in milliseconds.
- **Message:** The MIDI message displayed as hexadecimal values.
- **Description:** Identifies in text the type of message and its value.
- **Channel:** The MIDI channel from which the message was received.
- **Port:** The port from which the message was received, as described in your system MIDI setup (for example, Audio MIDI Setup on the Mac).

MIDI MONITOR FILTERS

At the top of the MIDI Monitor window are five checkboxes. Each of these activates a filter that removes the indicated messages. Remember: check the box to hide messages; uncheck it to view them.

The most common class of MIDI messages is Channel Voice messages, which carry note on, note off, and continuous controller messages. These messages cannot be filtered in MIDI Monitor; they are always visible.

- **Sent:** When checked, this box hides all MIDI messages being sent from Studio One 2, so that only incoming messages are seen.
- **Received:** When checked, this box hides all MIDI messages received by Studio One 2, so that only outgoing messages are seen.
- **System Common:** This is a class of MIDI message intended for all devices in a system. In practice today, System Common messages are, well, not that common.
- **System Real-Time:** This class of messages is used to synchronize all of the devices in a system. System Real-Time messages are still used sometimes, but you're not likely to see many of them.
- **System Exclusive:** This class of messages was originally intended as a "trap door" that would allow manufacturers to send and receive data specific to their devices. That purpose is and has been served by System Exclusive messages, but it has also been put to other uses, such as Universal System Exclusive messages that serve some of the same needs as System Real-Time or System Common messages, but with greater flexibility than either of those classes allow.

USING HARDWARE CONTROLLERS WITH STUDIO ONE 2: CONTROL LINK

Control Link is Studio One 2's system for enabling hardware controllers to change software parameters. These controllers could be the pitch bend and modulation wheels on a keyboard, the faders and buttons on a mixing control surface, or even the front-panel knobs of a sound module.

Control Link can be used to change nearly any parameter in the program, from the mixer to plug-in processors to VIs, and it is pretty simple to operate. The basic process goes like this:

1. For each external device, create a map of the hardware controllers on it that you want to use.
2. Configure the map to have the desired types of controllers (sliders, buttons, and so on).
3. Create a link between a hardware controller and a software parameter.

Making Device Controller Maps

You can make a controller map for any MIDI device that can transmit movements of its hardware controllers. However, the device must be defined as an External Device in Studio One 2, as described in the "Meet Studio One 2" section of chapter 1, "On Your Mark." If the device was chosen from the list of presets when it was created in Preferences > Options > External Devices, all of its controllers will already be defined and it is ready to link to parameters.

To make a device controller map for an External Device not chosen from the preset list, you must open a Controller Map window for the device and move each hardware control to create a software representation of it (an "avatar" for the hardware, more or less).

THE DEVICE CONTROLLER MAP WINDOW

To open a Device Controller Map window, do the following:

1. In the Mix view, click on the External button on the left side to show the External Devices currently defined in Studio One 2.
2. Double-click on the name in the list of the device for which you want to map controllers. The Controller Map window opens.
3. It is also possible to open the Controller Map directly from a plug-in or Instrument editor window by opening the Edit Mapping panel and clicking on the name of the current controller, if one is showing, or selecting a controller from the drop-down menu in the Control area if no controller is already being displayed.

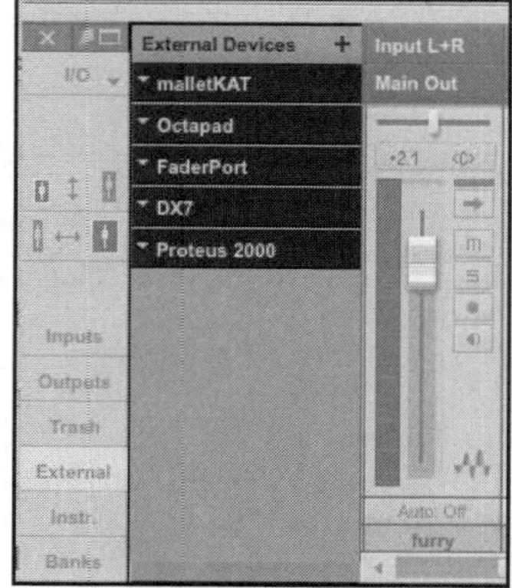

Fig. 4-14: The External pane in Mix view shows all external devices, including controllers and sound modules.

- To switch between External Devices for controlling parameters, click on the tab for the desired device at the top of the Device Controller Map window, or click on the arrow in the top left corner of the Map window and choose the desired device from the drop-down menu that appears.
- To edit the device's setup in Preferences > Options > External Devices, click on the arrow in the top left corner of the Map window, and choose Setup… from the drop-down menu that appears.

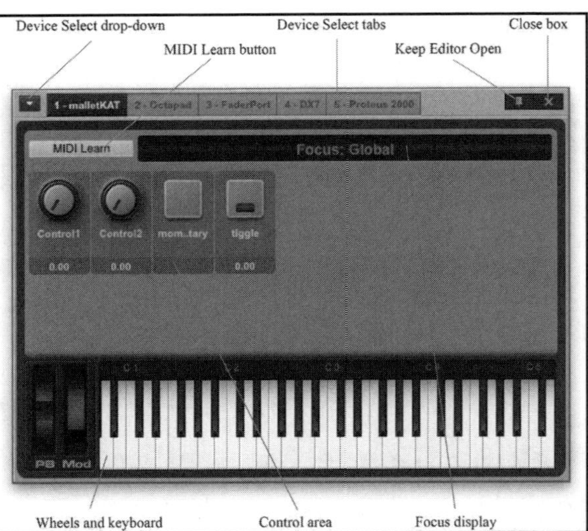

Fig. 4-15: The Device Controller Map links software controls to external hardware. In this figure, hardware controllers are linked to software controls that can be used to control or automate parameters.

- To remove the device from Studio One 2, click on the arrow in the top left corner of the Map window and choose Remove from the drop-down menu that appears.
- The MIDI Learn button is used to create and configure hardware controls, as described below.
- The Focus display shows whether the parameter has a global or local focus, as described in the "Global and Focus Mapping" section of this chapter.
- The Control area is where the software knobs, faders, and buttons representing hardware controls are displayed and configured.
- The pitch and modulation wheels respond to standard MIDI Pitch Change and CC 1 messages, respectively. These controls do not need to be added.

TIP: If you happen to move your modulation wheel while the map is in MIDI Learn, it will add a knob for CC 1, but disconnect the mod wheel in the window. If you find this useful, more power to you. If you find it annoying, you can delete the control as described below and the onscreen mod wheel will respond once again.

You can click on the onscreen keyboard with the mouse to play a note. It will also highlight to show notes played directly on the hardware controller.

CREATING AND CONFIGURING ONSCREEN CONTROLS FOR THE HARDWARE

1. Click on the MIDI Learn button. It will turn blue to show it is active.

2. Move each hardware control (slider, knob, button) you want to use, one at a time. Each time you move a different controller, a knob will appear for it in the map.
3. Double-click on the name immediately under a knob and rename it, if you wish.
4. To change the type of onscreen control from a knob (the default) to a fader or button, right-click on the knob and choose Fader or Button from the contextual drop-down menu that appears.
5. To delete an onscreen control, right-click (or Ctrl-click on Mac) on it and choose Remove from the contextual drop-down menu that appears.
6. When all controls have been created and configured, click on the MIDI Learn function to disable it.

About Button Behavior

Button behavior can get a bit tricky. Some hardware buttons or switches are momentary action: they turn on when the button is pressed and off as soon as it is released. The rest are toggle action: each time you press the button it changes state—for example, the first press turns it on, the second turns it off. Software buttons and switches are much more often toggle action than momentary.

What happens if you use a momentary hardware button with a toggle software function? Most of the time, everything works fine. In fact, it often does not matter which kind of hardware button action you use with a software toggle. But it could.

What's more, a toggle button in a Device Controller Map appears lit up when it is turned on, but that indication may not always work intuitively with the parameter to which it is mapped. For example, if a toggle button is mapped to a channel mute, you have to remember that when the button is "on," it is saying that the mute is on, meaning that the channel is off! Also, some combinations will take an extra button press at the beginning before the action starts working as expected. Or you might find that a toggle button used with a toggle software function might take two button presses each time to change the state.

MIDI Monitor can be helpful in determining the action of your hardware switches, but an empirical approach, that is, good old trial and error, is really the best method of ensuring that your controls will behave as desired and expected.

Linking Controls to Parameters

There are three ways to link hardware controls to software parameters and two places you can go to make the connections.

EDIT MAPPING PANEL AND SONG PAGE PARAMETER DISPLAY

Every plug-in, whether an effects processor or a VI, uses Studio One 2's plug-in header, including the preset architecture, bypass button, and so forth. The Edit Mapping panel is another of these standard resources to which every plug-in has access, and it is here that hardware controls finally get linked to parameters.

For those cases in which the parameter you want to control is not part of a plug-in, linking can be done using the Song window parameter display, which is essentially half of the Edit Mapping panel.

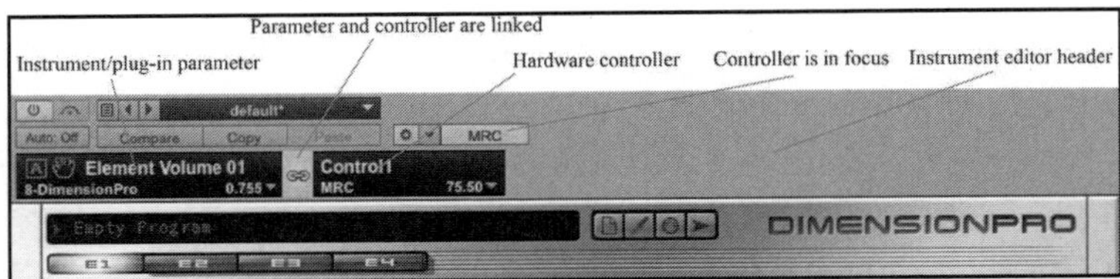

Fig. 4-16: The Edit Mapping Panel, shown here in the editor header for the Cakewalk Dimension Pro VI. The hardware controller is also displayed in the upper left of the Song window.

- To open the Edit Mapping panel, open the Instrument or plug-in editor and click on the Edit Mapping button. The panel will open beneath the button.

The panel consists of the parameter to be controlled on the left, the control to be used on the right, and the Link button in between. (The A button on the left is for automation editing, which is discussed in the chapter "Automation" in *Power Tools for Studio One 2*, vol. 2.) The parameter display changes in real time to reflect the current value of the parameter, whether it is changed through a hardware control or by moving an onscreen control. Clicking on the small arrow in the lower right corner of the Parameter area drops down a list of recently used parameters for quick access.

Fig. 4-17: The Recent Parameters list (here showed in the header of the MOTU MachFive 2 sampler) provides quick access to the last few parameters that were altered in the Song.

The Song page parameter display is nothing more than the parameter portion of the Edit Mapping display.

MAKING THE CONNECTION

To link a control to a parameter by moving both items, do the following:

1. With the mouse, move the onscreen control for the parameter you want to control from hardware. You will see the parameter and device appear in the parameter display of the Edit Mapping panel.
2. Move the hardware control. You will see it show up in the controller display of the Edit Mapping panel.
3. Click on the Link button or press Option + M (Alt + M in Windows). The control and parameter are now linked.

To link a control to a parameter by dragging, do the following:

1. Open the Device Controller Map for the hardware device.
2. Move the onscreen "avatar" for the hardware control. You will see the control in the controller display of the Edit Mapping panel.
3. Drag the hand icon at the top of the Edit Mapping panel and drop it on the onscreen control for the parameter you want controlled by hardware. The control and parameter are now linked.

To link a control to a parameter using a contextual menu command, do the following:

1. Move the hardware control. You will see it show up in the controller display of the Edit Mapping panel.
2. Right-click on the onscreen control for the parameter you want controlled by hardware, and choose Assign <parameter> to <controller> from the contextual drop-down menu that appears.

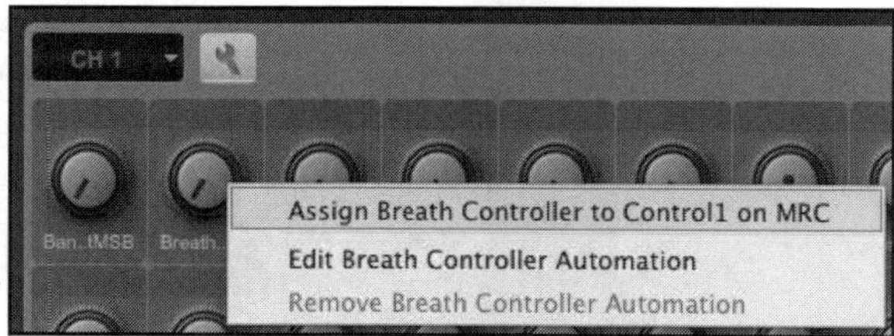

Fig. 4-18: The Device Controller Map links software controls to external hardware. In this figure, hardware controllers are linked to software controls that can be used to control or automate parameters.

Global and Focus Mapping

The link between a hardware control and a parameter can be constant once set up, or it can apply only in a particular context. As an example of the first, termed a Global mapping in Studio One 2, you might want the level of the vocal submix channel to always be under the control of the same fader on your controller, no matter what screen is showing. The function of that fader never changes.

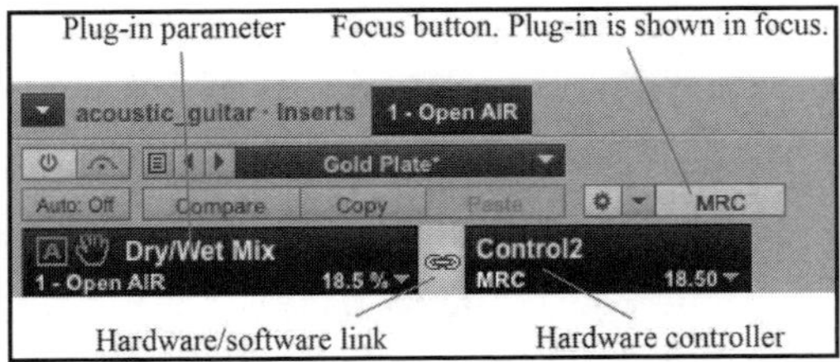

Fig. 4-19: In this example, Control 2 of a Lexicon MRC controller has been linked to control the Dry/Wet Mix of PreSonus's Open AIR convolution reverb. Since the Focus button is active, Control 2 will only affect this parameter, even when another plug-in or VI editor is open.

An example of the second would be if you had separate reverbs on each of the individual vocal tracks and wanted the same knob to control reverb decay time on whichever track you were working on. That would require a separate link for each vocal mixer channel. In this case, the function of the knob changes depending on the channel. Each of those links is called a Focus mapping.

For a Focus mapping to become active (either to create a link or to use it), not only does the plug-in window that uses the mapping need to be open and in front, but the Focus button also needs to be engaged. If you adjust the reverb decay of the first vocal, bring the reverb plug-in window for the second vocal to the front and start editing, you will change the decay time on the second vocal only if you click on the Focus button to bring it into focus. Otherwise you will still be changing the decay time on the first vocal.

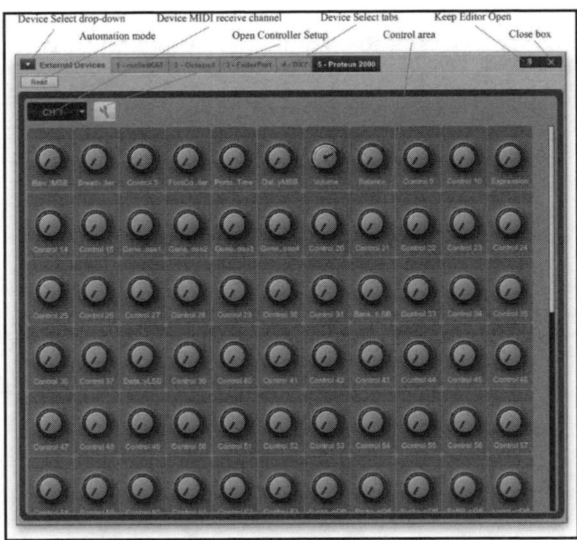

Fig. 4-20: This Device Controller Map is for an external sound module: an E-mu Proteus 2000. When one of the knobs is moved, the corresponding MIDI continuous controller message is sent to the Proteus 2000. An external controller can be mapped to this knob so that moving the controller causes the messages to be sent. The Proteus 2000 happens to have hardware knobs whose value can be sent as MIDI messages to Studio One 2. Thus, this particular sound module can both receive messages from the Device Controller Map and act as a controller for knobs on the map.

There are a fairly small number of basic functions that cannot be focus-mapped, most especially channel strip functions like track fader, track pan, and mute.

On the whole, Global mappings are useful for performance-like mixing, while Focus mappings are great for plug-in or VI editing.

- To make a Global mapping of a control to a parameter, check that the Focus button is not engaged, then follow the procedure given above for linking a control to a parameter.

- To make a Focus mapping of a control to a parameter, check that the Focus button is engaged, then follow the procedure given above for linking a control to a parameter.

Using Control Link with External Instruments

Control Link functions a little differently when used with external sound modules and other devices, but not a whole lot. The first difference is obvious as soon as you open the Device Controller Map. Unless you chose one of the devices from the External Devices list, what you will see is knobs for each of the standard MIDI continuous controllers.

The second difference is the Channel field in the upper left corner of the map. Only the channels defined for the device in Preferences > Options > External Devices will show up in the drop-down menu in the field.

Fig. 4-21: The wrench button in the Device Controller Map opens the Controller Setup window.

The third difference is the button with the wrench icon, which opens the Controller Setup dialog box. Each MIDI controller can be enabled or disabled separately in this dialog box, so that unneeded knobs can be removed. Typically, you won't need more than about a half dozen knobs for any particular plug-in or VI, but the rest are always available, in case you do need more.

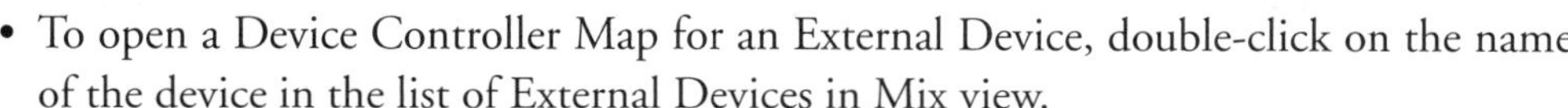

- To open a Device Controller Map for an External Device, double-click on the name of the device in the list of External Devices in Mix view.

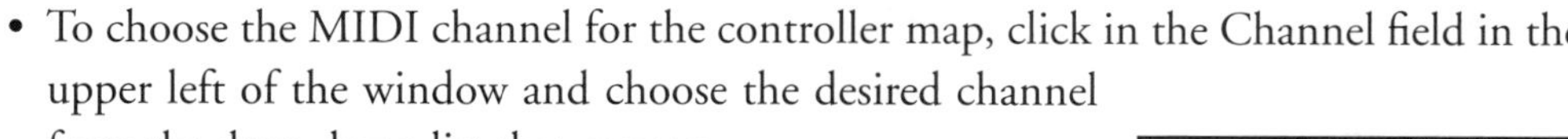

- To choose the MIDI channel for the controller map, click in the Channel field in the upper left of the window and choose the desired channel from the drop-down list that appears.
- A separate map can be set up for each channel. Maps for all channels will share control names, but different channels can have different values for the same control.
- To open the Controller Setup dialog box, click on the button with the wrench icon at the top of the window.
- To show the control for a MIDI controller, be sure that the box next to its name is checked.
- To hide the control for a MIDI controller, uncheck the box next to its name.
- To uncheck the boxes for all controllers, click on the Select None button at the bottom of the window.
- To check the boxes for all controllers, click on the Select all button at the bottom of the window.

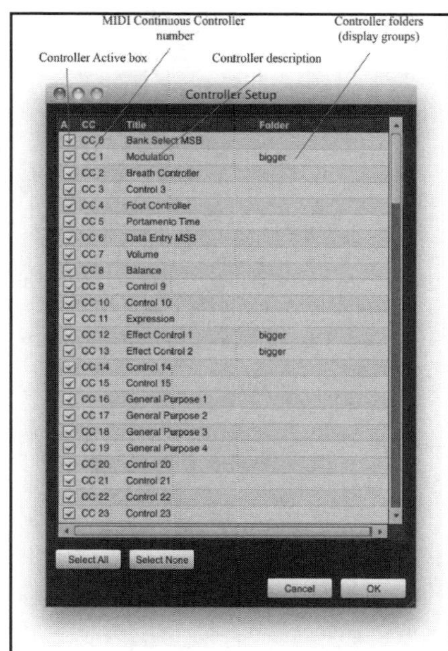

Fig. 4-22: The Controller Setup dialog is used with external sound modules that receive MIDI CC messages. The dialog can show or hide knobs for each CC number, but it also can group them using folders.

TRANSMITTING MIDI FROM A CONTROL

Any control on a controller map for a Keyboard device can be set to transmit its changes over MIDI. To send MIDI from a controller map control, do the following:

- In MIDI Learn mode, right-click on the control and choose Transmit MIDI from the contextual menu that drops down. Operation of the onscreen control will generate MIDI messages for its actions.

VISUALLY GROUPING CONTROLS IN THE MAP

- To visually group a number of controls together in the Controller Map, click in the Folder field next to the control's name in the Controller Setup dialog box and enter a folder name. Do the same for each control you want to appear grouped with others.
- There is no drop-down menu or place that folder names are stored, so be very careful to enter exactly the same folder name for each control in the group.
- This grouping is visual only; the functions of the controls are not connected in any way.

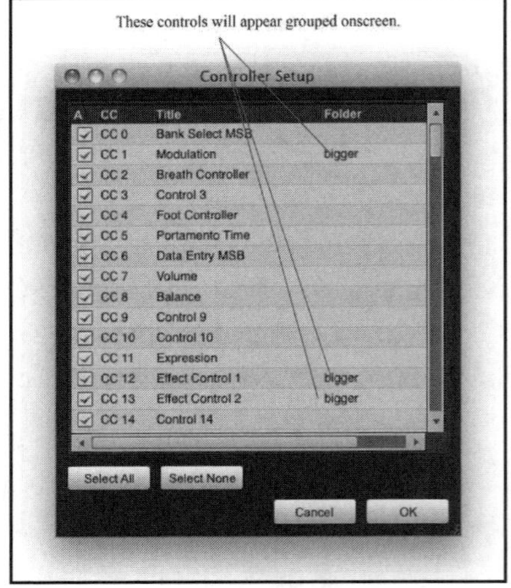

Fig. 4-23: All that needs to be done to group controls is to enter the same folder name next to each controller to be included in the group. It is all done with manual entry, so be very careful to watch for typos!

Of course, one of the most popular reasons for mapping hardware controls to software parameters is for automation, and control grouping is very useful in this context. This usage is described in the chapter "Mixing" in *Power Tools for Studio One 2*, vol. 2.

RECORDING ON INSTRUMENT TRACKS

Recording on Instrument tracks is nearly identical to recording on Audio tracks. The difference is that you are recording performance data rather than audio, so monitoring and recording audio are accomplished separately from the Instrument track.

The Record panel conveniently consolidates access to most Instrument track recording functions in one place.

Confirming That Your MIDI Controller Is Working

When recording audio it is necessary to confirm that the audio signal path is working and audio is reaching Studio One 2 before you can record. The same holds true when recording from a MIDI controller, except that it is MIDI data you need to see.

- To confirm that your MIDI signal path is working correctly, play on your MIDI controller and watch the MIDI indicator in the Transport bar for activity. If you see activity when you play and none when you stop, then MIDI data is reaching Studio One 2 from the controller.

- If you want to make a more detailed verification that everything is as it should be, open MIDI Monitor (simply clicking on the MIDI indicator opens MIDI Monitor) and watch it as you play to see what messages are being received.

Ah, but computers have a way of not working even when they are indicating that all is well. If you have confirmed MIDI activity is reaching Studio One 2 but the device being controlled is not responding or there is no audio from an Instrument when it is played, there is a problem in your MIDI or audio routing. Here are a few things to check:

- If you see activity on mixer channel meters but hear nothing, the problem is somewhere in your audio signal path.
- If there is no activity on any audio meters, it may still be an audio problem: a gain somewhere in the device may be turned down or an output muted or unassigned.
- A lack of activity on audio meters could also indicate a MIDI routing problem. Perhaps the controller is not selected as the track input, or maybe there is a discrepancy between the MIDI channel on which the controller is transmitting and the channel on which a multitimbral Instrument should be receiving.
- If the Instrument is assigned to play only over a specified note range, make sure that you are not playing outside that range. It could even be a transposition that is active in the controller itself.

Monitoring Instruments

When an Instrument track is armed for recording, by default, the Monitor button will also be enabled. This means that the input data from the controller will be passed to whatever VI or External Device has been assigned as the track's output destination. If this is off, you will hear nothing when you record, even assuming that all audio is properly configured. Since External Devices use regular audio channels in the mixer, you must enable input monitoring on its audio channels, as well, to hear its sound.

If a track is properly configured and armed with monitoring, and the Instrument channels of the VI or Audio channels for an External Device are similarly correctly set up, you should hear your instrument sound when you play on the controller.

- To make input monitoring change to whichever Instrument track or channel is selected, choose the Track > Instrument Input Follows Selection command from the main menu bar. One more reminder: if the audio channels are muted, you will hear nothing.

BUFFER SIZE AGAIN

Buffer size does not have much impact when recording performance data, because performance data is much less dense than audio data. It does, however, still affect monitoring the audio from the instrument, as well as the audio from tracks playing back, so everything discussed in the "Understanding Buffer Size" section of chapter 2, "Get Set to Record," still applies. Set your buffer size to be as small as possible when recording, but make it larger again when you are done.

The Record Panel

The Record panel collects many functions related to recording in a single panel.

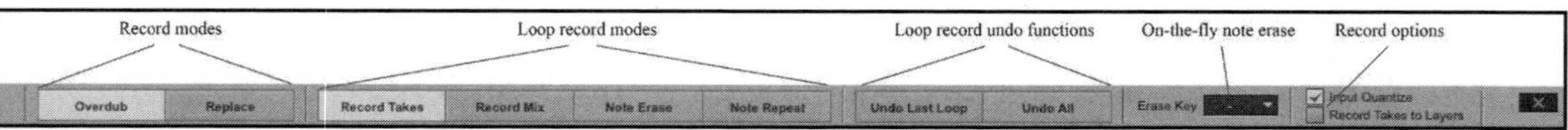

Fig. 4-24: The Record panel.

- To open the Record panel, press Option (Alt) + Shift + R or choose View > Record Panel from the main menu bar.

Here is a list of the Record panel's functions; explanations of each one appear in the appropriate places in the text.

- Overdub mode button
- Replace mode button
- Loop Record Takes mode button
- Loop Record Mix mode button
- Loop Note Erase mode button
- Loop Note Repeat mode button
- Undo Last Loop button
- Undo All button
- Erase Key field
- Input Quantize box
- Record Takes to Layers box

Instrument Track Record Modes

OVERDUB

In audio recording, "overdubbing" usually means to add an additional track of sound to an existing recording. In Studio One 2, Overdub mode is not the MIDI version of audio overdubbing, but rather the MIDI equivalent of sound-on-sound recording: each time through the loop, the new material you play gets combined with the existing material in that section, while you hear both the existing and new material.

This lets you build up a composite performance one piece at a time. Perhaps you simply want to double a melody or add a harmony. Maybe you want to build up a drum track by recording kick on the first pass, snare on the second, and hi-hat on the third (the old-school drum machine approach). Or perhaps you're writing and just want to experiment with layering new parts on top of a simple idea.

The result of recording MIDI in Overdub mode is all of the data mixed into a single Part, rather than keeping each pass separate, as in audio overdubbing.

- To select Overdub mode for recording Instrument tracks, be sure that the track(s) are armed for recording and that monitoring is correctly configured, then click on the Overdub button in the Record panel or choose Options > Record Mode Overdub from the main menu bar.

REPLACE

Replace mode is the MIDI equivalent of punching in, and is nondestructive. Whatever you play replaces what was there before, but the previous material is not erased. To get it back, you need only resize the Part with the old material to extend through the replaced portion. (You may need to bring the original Part to the front with the Event > Send to Front command. For more on front-to-back arranging, see chapter 6, "Advanced Editing.")

- To select Replace mode for recording Instrument tracks, be sure that the track(s) are armed for recording and that monitoring is correctly configured, then click on the Replace button in the Record panel or choose Options > Record Mode Replace from the main menu bar.

Loop Recording on Instrument Tracks

Studio One 2 offers two kinds of loop recording for Instrument tracks: Loop Record Mix and Loop Record Takes. These are the looping versions of Overdub and Replace modes.

Loop Record Mix merges data from the current record pass with existing data on the track. Loop Record Takes works the same with MIDI as loop recording audio does: successive passes are appended within a single file, but can be accessed individually in context. When you stop recording, the Part will have one take for each record pass through the loop, and you can choose which take you want to hear at any time. You can even edit between takes to create a composite, or "comp," take. More about comping can be found in chapter 6, "Advanced Editing."

LOOP RECORD MIX

- To select Loop Record Mix mode for recording Instrument tracks, be sure that the track(s) are armed for recording and that monitoring is correctly configured, then click on the Record Mix button in the Record panel or choose Options > Loop Record Mix in the main menu bar.

LOOP RECORD TAKES

Loop Record Takes writes the new material of each pass sequentially into the same file. When you are done, there is a single file containing each take in order of recording time.

- To select Loop Record Takes mode for recording Instrument tracks, be sure that the track(s) are armed for recording and that monitoring is correctly configured, then click on the Record Takes button in the Record panel or choose Options > Loop Record Takes from the main menu bar.

RECORD TAKES TO LAYERS

The Record Takes to Layers feature provides an alternative to Loop Record Takes. The difference is that each record pass through the loop becomes a different layer on the track, instead of a different take in the file.

- To record each take to a layer when loop recording, check the Record Takes to Layers box in the Record panel or choose Options > Record Takes to Layers in the main menu bar.

NOTE ERASE

This mode harks back to an earlier age. In old-school hardware drum machines, you erased drum notes from a loop you were building by pressing and holding the pad for the drum sound you wanted to erase during the time you wanted notes erased. In other words, when Note Erase is active, pressing a key will erase the drum sound on that note instead of recording it. Want to erase the hi-hat in every other bar? Make Note Erase active and, on every other bar, hold down the hi-hat key for the entire bar.

NOTE REPEAT

This is another old-school technique. In Note Repeat mode, holding down a note while recording causes that note to be inserted repeatedly at intervals of the Quantize duration for as long as the note is held down.

UNDO LAST LOOP

When loop recording, clicking on this button will undo only the last pass through the loop. Earlier passes through the loop are retained.

UNDO ALL

Yeah, it's just what you think: clicking on this button when loop recording undoes all passes through the loop from the time you started recording.

ERASE KEY

The note designated as the Erase Key momentarily enables Note Erase mode (though the Note Erase button doesn't visibly change state), making it easy to pop in and out of erasing on the fly. When loop recording, hold down the note set as the Erase Key and the note you want to erase. Release the Erase Key, and you're back to recording.

Input Quantizing

If you know that you are going to want a MIDI performance quantized, quantizing while you record makes perfect sense. What's more, input quantization is nondestructive; you can use Restore Timing to undo it later, if you need to.

To quantize MIDI input while recording, do the following:

1. Choose the desired quantize duration from the drop-down menu in the Quantize field in either the Arrange or Edit view.
2. Check the Input Quantize box in the Record panel or choose Options > Input Quantize from the main menu bar.

TIP: It is not necessary to check the Quantize or Snap box to activate input quantization.

Roll 'Em!

Just for review, here's a checklist of everything you should have set up for recording:

- MIDI data has been routed from your controller to the Instrument track.
- The Instrument track's output has been set to the VI or MIDI device you want to play.
- Audio returns from the VI or MIDI device are routed to Instrument or Audio channels in the mixer, as appropriate.
- The Instrument track is armed.
- Monitoring is enabled on the Instrument track, and, for a MIDI device, on its Audio channels as well.
- Record mode has been set to your preference of Replace or Overdub.
- Preroll/count-off and metronome have been set up and enabled as desired.

All these are done? You're ready to go! Just enter Record as described in the previous chapter. Everything described in chapter 3, "Go! Recording with Studio One 2" applies to recording Instrument tracks, including preroll/count-off, metronome, punching in and out, and loop recording. If you have questions about any of this, go back and take a look.

EXPORTING INSTRUMENT PARTS AS A STANDARD MIDI FILE

One or more selected Instrument Parts can be exported as a Type 1 (multitrack) Standard MIDI File. To export selected Instrument Parts, use either of these methods:

- Option (Alt in Windows)-drag the selected Part(s) to a desired location in the Files tab of the Browser. A .mid file will be generated and appear in the list.
- Right-click (or Ctrl-click on Mac) on one of the selected Parts and choose Instrument Parts > Export Parts as MIDI File from the contextual menu that drops down, or Event > Export Parts as MIDI File from the main menu bar.

TRACK TRANSFORM (FREEZING TRACKS)

Virtual instruments, convolution reverbs, and other processor-heavy plug-ins can put a hurt on your computer's power. The notion of "freezing" tracks arose in response to this limitation. The meaning of "freezing" varies somewhat from DAW to DAW, but it generally means capturing the audio from a VI to a track, and then disabling the power-hungry VI.

(The Transform to Rendered Audio/Transform to Real-Time Audio commands perform a similar function for Audio tracks. For more on these commands, see the chapter "Mixing," in *Power Tools for Studio One 2*, vol. 2.)

Studio One 2 takes a slightly different approach that offers some very useful traits. In many DAWs, if you want to make any changes after freezing the track, you "unfreeze" it (delete the audio and reactivate the VI), make the desired changes to the MIDI track playing the VI, and then freeze again.

In Studio One 2, however, once the audio is captured, you still see "ghostly" MIDI notes behind the audio. If you cut the audio and move it around, the MIDI notes travel with it. If you decide you want to change the sound or make other edits to the performance data, you can still turn the edited audio back into an Instrument track. It's fresh.

Transforming an Instrument Track into an Audio Track

When the Transform to Audio Track command is chosen, it replaces an Instrument track in the Song with an Audio track containing the captured audio, appropriately routed. The VI is disabled or removed altogether, depending on the settings in the Transform to Audio Track dialog box. The Transform to Audio Track dialog box features several options:

- **Render Inserts box:** When checked, the audio captured from an instrument includes any insert effects on its mixer channel strip. Note that this does not unload the effects on the VI's audio channel(s), which will still consume processor power.
- **Preserve Instrument Track State:** Checking this box makes Studio One 2 remember how the Instrument track is set up (in addition to remembering how the instrument itself is set up) so that the track can be transformed back to the exact state it was in at the time of capture.

- **Remove Instrument box:** When checked, this box causes the Instrument being browsed to be deleted from the Song after its audio has been captured.
- **Tail field:** Shows the amount of time added to the end of the selected data so that note decays, reverberation tails, and other lingering sounds are not cut off.
- **Channel field:** For instruments that have multiple audio outputs (such as Impact), this field allows selection of the output channel that will be used for the transformation.

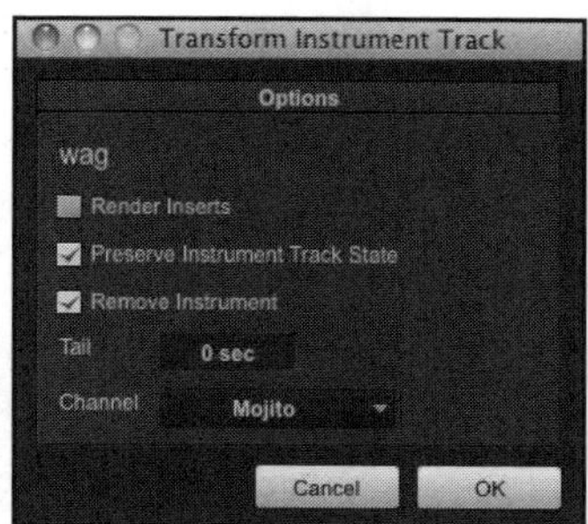

Fig. 4-25: The Transform Instrument Track dialog is displayed when the Transform to Audio Track command is invoked.

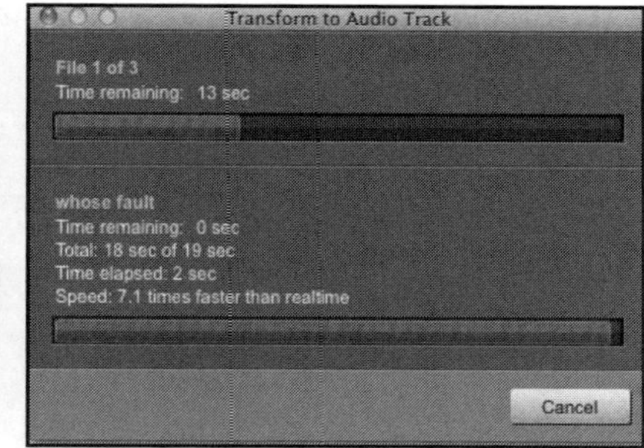

Fig. 4-26: The Transform to Audio Track dialog is shown while Studio One 2 is actually freezing an Instrument track into an Audio track.

To transform an Instrument track into an Audio track, do the following:

1. Right-click (or Ctrl-click on Mac) in the track header of the track you want to transform, then choose Transform to Audio Track from the contextual menu that drops down, or choose Track > Transform > Transform to Audio Track from the main menu bar. The Transform Instrument dialog box will appear.
2. Configure the options as desired.
3. Click on OK to execute the transformation.

Transforming an Audio Track into an Instrument Track

Note that this works only on audio tracks that were created from Instrument tracks.

- Right-click in the track header of the Audio track you want to transform, then choose Transform to Instrument Track from the contextual menu that drops down, or choose Track > Transform > Transform to Instrument Track from the main menu bar. The transformation is executed.

INCLUDED VIRTUAL INSTRUMENTS

PreSonus bundles four of its own virtual instruments with Studio One 2: Sample One, Presence, Impact, and Mojito. Nearly every parameter in these instruments can be externally controlled using Control Link and/or automated. As was said before, automation is discussed in the chapter "Automation," in *Power Tools for Studio One 2*, vol. 2.

SampleOne

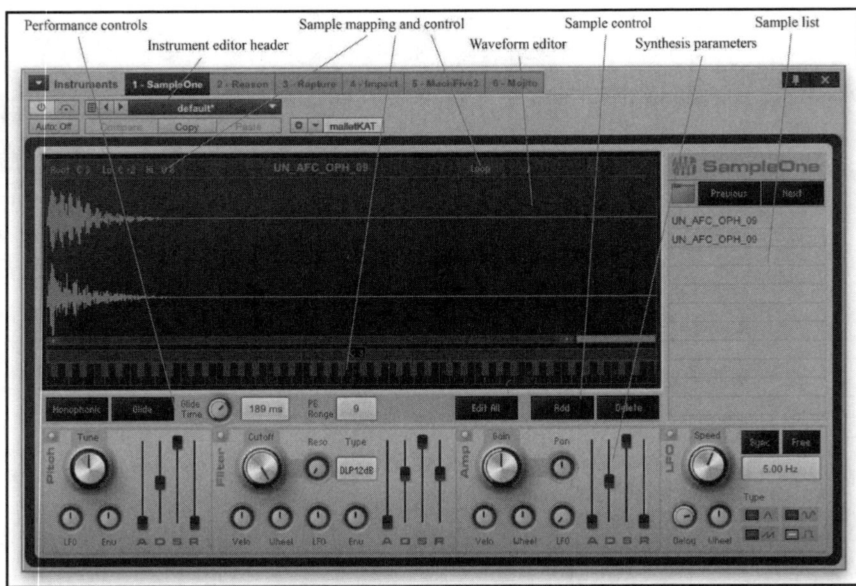

Fig. 4-28: The SampleOne user interface.

SampleOne is not a full-fledged sample player like Native Instruments Kontakt or MOTU MachFive, but it is adequate for many applications, is quick and easy to use, and consumes much less memory and processor power then more powerful samplers.

Up to 96 samples can be loaded into a single instance of SampleOne and mapped across the keyboard; up to 32 samples can play at a time. Filter, amplifier, and LFO settings are separate for each sample.

A few things you will not find in Sample One are the following:

- **Velocity response range for each sample.** This means there is no velocity crossfading or switching.
- **Positional crossfading.** When a sample reaches the end of its range, it simply no longer plays; it is not possible to set up crossfades across the keyboard.
- **Multitimbral or multichannel operation.** Each instance of SampleOne responds to only one MIDI channel and sends all of its audio out of one stereo pair of audio outputs.
- **Dynamic sample start time.** You can set the sample play start and end times, but they cannot be controlled dynamically by velocity or an envelope.

ADDING SAMPLES TO SAMPLEONE

There are five ways to add samples to an instance of SampleOne:

- Drag one or more samples from the Browser to the sample list in SampleOne.
- Drag an Audio Event from the Arrange view into the sample list in SampleOne.
- Select a range of Audio Events in the Arrange view and drag them into the sample list in SampleOne. Studio One 2 will bounce the selected range to a new audio file, which then gets added to the sample list.
- Right-click (or Ctrl-click on Mac) on any audio file in the Files or Sounds tabs of the Browser and choose the Send to New SampleOne command. Rather than adding the file to an existing instance of SampleOne, this creates a new instance and loads the file into it.
- Click on the Add button in the SampleOne window. A standard file open dialog box will be presented to you. Navigate to the desired file and click on the Open button to load it.

REX AND AUDIOLOOP FILES IN SAMPLEONE

You can import REX and Audioloop files into SampleOne. Just drag a REX or Audioloop file into the sample list and each slice of the file will be automatically placed onto a separate note of the keymap, starting with C3.

REPLACING A SAMPLE

1. Click on the sample you wish to replace in the sample list to select it.
2. Drag the new sample from the Browser (or Audio Event or range from the Arrange view) into the waveform display of SampleOne and drop it there. The old sample will be replaced.

DELETING A SAMPLE

1. Click on the sample you wish to delete in the sample list to select it.
2. Click on the Delete button in the SampleOne window to delete the sample.

SAMPLE PARAMETERS

Here are the programmable parameters for each sample and how to set them:

SELECT THE SAMPLE

You can select any sample to use directly, or by stepping through the samples in a given folder while you play them. Select a sample using either of these methods:

- Click on the sample you wish to adjust in the sample list to select it.
- Click on the Previous or Next buttons at the top of the sample list to step up or down through the list.

ROOT KEY

The root key is the key that will play the sample at its original pitch. The default value is C3. To set this, use either of these methods:

- Drag the root key handle just above the keyboard in the middle of the Sample One window to the desired note.
- Click on the Root field in the top left of the window and type in the desired note value.

KEY RANGE

The key range extends from the highest to the lowest note value that will play the sample. The default range is C2 to G8. To set the high or low note limits, use either of these methods:

- Move the cursor to the left end of the keymap range bar (the blue bar that the root key handle sits on) until it changes to the icon of a hand with a pointing finger, than drag to the right to change the low key. Do the same from the right end (but dragging left) of the keymap range to change the high key.
- Click on the Lo or Hi field next to the Root field and enter the desired note value.

SAMPLE PLAY START/END

SampleOne can play an entire sample or only a designated portion of it. The portion of the sample that will play (the play range) is determined by the Start and End parameters. To set the Start and End parameters, do the following:

- Move the cursor to the left end of the waveform display until it changes to the icon of a hand with a pointing finger, than drag to the right to change the Start point. Do the same from the right end of the waveform display (but dragging left) to change the End point.

LOOP

This function determines whether the sample will loop when played or simply play as a one-shot. Loop a selected sample using either of these methods:

- Click on the Loop button above the waveform display to activate it. The button will turn blue, and a blue bar showing the loop range will appear above the waveform display. Click-and-drag either end of the blue bar to change the Loop Start or End point.
- Click on the Start or End field and enter the desired Start or End point. Note that the Start and End points are shown as sample values.

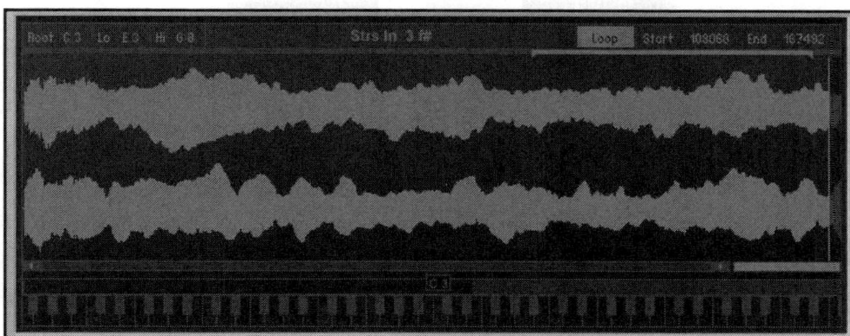

Fig. 4-29: A looped sample in SampleOne. The blue bar at the top indicates the looped area.

PITCH

A fixed pitch offset can be specified, and pitch modulation from an envelope or LFO can be added. To change the pitch, do the following:

1. By default, the Pitch section is active, as shown by the blue indicator above the Pitch legend. If the indicator is not blue, click on it to activate the Pitch section.
2. Drag the Tune knob clockwise to increase the pitch or counterclockwise to decrease it.
3. Drag the Env or LFO knobs clockwise or counterclockwise to add positive or negative modulation (respectively) as desired.
4. If using envelope modulation, set the ADSR sliders as desired.

FILTER

Each sample can be filtered by one of six models of analog synthesizer filters or three regular digital filters. The filter can be modulated by velocity, envelope, LFO, or the modulation wheel controller (MIDI CC 1).

1. By default, the Filter section is active, as shown by the blue indicator above the Filter legend. If the indicator is not blue, click on it to activate the Filter section.
2. Click on the Type field and choose the desired filter type from the drop-down menu. There are nine types available: modeled analog highpass, lowpass, and bandpass filters, each with a choice of 12 dB/octave or 24 dB/octave rolloff slopes, plus regular digital highpass, bandpass, and lowpass filters.
3. By default, the filter cutoff is set to 20 kHz. Drag the Cutoff knob counterclockwise to decrease the cutoff filter or clockwise to increase it. The Cutoff value is not shown in SampleOne. To see it, look at the Parameter area in the top left corner of the Song window.
4. Drag the Reso knob to the desired resonance value.
5. Drag the Velo, Wheel, LFO, and Env knobs clockwise or counterclockwise to add positive or negative modulation (respectively) from each of these sources as desired.
6. If using envelope modulation, set the ADSR sliders as desired.

AMPLILFIER

A fixed gain value can be specified, and amplitude modulation from velocity, modulation wheel, an envelope, or an LFO can be added.

1. By default, the Amplifier section is active, as shown by the blue indicator above the Amp legend. If the indicator is not blue, click on it to activate the Amplifier section.
2. Drag the Vol knob clockwise to increase the gain or counterclockwise to decrease it.
3. Envelope modulation is always active at full strength in the Amplifier. There is no knob for setting the modulation amount, so just set the ADSR sliders as desired.
4. Drag the Pan knob to pan to the left or right as desired.
5. Drag the Velo, Wheel, or LFO knob clockwise or counterclockwise to add positive or negative modulation (respectively) as desired.

LFO

Each sample has one LFO that can be used to modulate the pitch, filter cutoff, or amplifier gain. The LFO has no effect until the LFO knob in one of those sections has been set to some value other than zero.

1. By default, the LFO section is active, as shown by the blue indicator above the Amp legend. If the indicator is not blue, click on it to activate the LFO section.
2. Click on the button for the desired LFO waveform from the four options in the Type section.
3. Set the triggering option using the Sync and Free buttons. See the LFO Triggering section below for more details.
4. Drag the Speed knob or click in the Rate field (to the right of the Speed knob) and type in a value to set the LFO rate.
5. The LFO rate can be modulated using the modulation wheel (MIDI continuous controller 1). Drag the Wheel knob clockwise or counterclockwise to add positive or negative modulation (respectively) as desired.

LFO Triggering

There are three different triggering modes available for the LFO, which are set using the Sync and Free buttons. Clicking on either button toggles its state. The modes are the following:

- **Both buttons unselected:** This is the default mode. The LFO is triggered by the onset of a note. The Delay knob sets the amount of time over which LFO modulation fades in after the note begins. The Delay value is shown in a tool pop-up menu that appears and in the Parameter area in the top left corner of the Song window.
- **Sync button selected:** The LFO's cycle is locked to the tempo. The rate (Speed) is expressed as a note value.
- **Free button selected:** The LFO is free-running.

GLOBAL PARAMETERS

Between the waveform display and the sample parameters is a row of global parameters affecting all samples.

- **Monophonic:** Only one note will be played at any given time, but that note may consist of up to 32 stacked samples. When Monophonic is not enabled, up to 32 voices can be used to play different notes of the sample (assuming that no other sample is playing; 32 is the total number of voices that SampleOne can play at any time).
- **Glide:** Also known as "portamento," glide causes the pitch to glide from one played note to the next, instead of jumping to it. Drag the Glide knob or click in the Glide Time field to its right and type in a value to set the amount of time it takes for the pitch to glide from one note to the next.
- **Pitch Bend (PB) range:** Drag the PB Range knob to set the maximum pitch bend (in semitones) that can be produced using a pitch bend wheel or lever (MIDI Pitch Wheel message).
- **Edit All:** When the Edit All button is active, changing any sample parameter will alter that parameter for all loaded samples. It is turned off by default.
- **Add and Delete:** As already discussed, these buttons allow you to add a new sample to the sample list or delete the selected sample in the list.

Presence

Fig. 4-30: The Presence user interface.

Like SampleOne, Presence is a sample player, but the resemblance pretty well ends there. Rather than letting you drag audio files into the instrument and make your own keymaps, Presence loads Sound Sets, a proprietary format that contains presets for various instruments. You can also load SoundFont files into Presence, about which I will say more shortly. Presence offers considerably more than SampleOne in the way of modulation facilities, and also includes effects.

A collection of Sound Sets is installed as part of the Studio One 2 Pro installation. Occasionally, new Sound Sets become available for download from the PreSonus website. When that happens, you will see an announcement of it in the News Feed on the Start page. Finally, the Sound Set Maker utility from PreSonus allows you to create your own Sound Sets.

In short, Presence is more powerful, but uses prepackaged presets rather than letting you roll your own during your session.

It is not possible to access samples in Presence presets individually and adjust their parameters, so, in a sense, all of Presence's parameters are global. To be more precise, however, the filter, amp, and modulation parameter controls scale the values for each sample in the preset. Because these parameters are scaling (multiplication) factors rather than absolute values, the values of those controls are shown as percentages. The downside of this is that there is no way to know any value exactly.

The Amplifier includes its own envelope generator, but envelope modulation for all other sections offering it is performed by the Mod section envelope.

VOICE AND OUTPUT LEVEL INDICATORS

Presence can play up to 96 voices at a time. When a stereo sample is used in a preset, it uses two voices. The number of voices currently being used is displayed in the upper right corner of the Master area.

The Master area also contains a stereo output level meter. Under some circumstances, Presence can generate high output levels. The output level meter will tell you if you are clipping the output.

LOADING PRESETS

- To load a preset, click on the Browse Presets field and select the desired preset from the drop-down menu that appears. If you don't see any presets in the menu, check that the location where the Sound Sets are stored is listed in Preferences > Options > Locations > Sound Sets. The current preset name appears in the Master area at the top of the Presence window.

USING SOUNDFONTS

SoundFont is the brand name for a file format created by E-mu Systems (part of Creative Labs). A SoundFont file stores a set of (usually small) samples, along with basic performance information, such as a keymap, loop markers, and settings for velocity control of volume.

For Presence to load SoundFonts, it must be pointed to where they are stored. As part of the Studio One 2 installation process, a SoundFonts folder is created in ~/Users/<user name>/Documents/Studio One 2/SoundFonts/ on Mac, and C:\Documents and Settings\<user name>\My Documents\My Music\SoundFonts\ under Windows (in this case, XP). The path is also automatically added to Studio One 2. If you want to use this folder, simply deposit your SoundFonts into it and they should show up in Presence's Presets menu. If you prefer to store your SoundFonts elsewhere, you need only add the path to the folder to the Locations preferences.

TO ADD A SOUNDFONT PATH

1. Determine where you want to store your SoundFonts and create a folder in that location.
2. Open Preferences > Options > Locations > Instrument Library.
3. Click on the Add button. A standard file open dialog box will appear.
4. Navigate to the folder you created and select it. Once you see the path in the Instrument Library locations list, all SoundFonts in that folder will be available to Presence.

If you have SoundFonts stored in multiple locations, add the path to each location to the Instrument Library locations list.

SFZ SUPPORT

Presence also supports the SFZ file format developed by Cakewalk (formerly Twelve Tone Systems, now part of Roland Corp.). The SFZ format is another take on the same idea as SoundFont: audio samples and a bunch of metadata describing how they should be mapped and played. There are, however, a few important differences. For one, while SoundFonts encase both audio and metadata in a single file, SFZ files are actually two files—one containing audio, the other with metadata and pointers to the appropriate audio in the other file. For another, SFZ supports compressed audio for the samples.

While SFZ is a sophisticated format with quite a few options, it is stored as a text file, making it easy for anyone to edit if they have the format specification, which is available from Cakewalk. If "editing presets" by creating a file of specifications is a little much for you, you can look around for a dedicated SFZ file editor, but they are hard to find. SfZed is a free editor you can look for. Of course, you can always just use SFZ files you purchase and not worry about creating your own.

FILTER

Presence has a standard filter, and a high-quality filter mode that offers a choice of one of six models of analog synthesizer filters or three regular digital filters. The filter can be modulated by velocity, envelope, or the LFO.

1. By default, the Filter section is active, as shown by the blue indicator above the Filter legend. If the indicator is not blue, click on it to activate the Filter section.
2. By default, the High-Quality button is unselected and the standard filter is in use.
3. If you prefer to use a high-quality filter, click on the High-Quality button to select it, then click on the Type field and choose the desired filter type from the drop-down menu. There are nine types available: modeled analog highpass, lowpass, and bandpass filters, each with a choice of 12 dB/octave or 24 dB/octave rolloff slopes, plus regular digital highpass, bandpass, and lowpass filters.
4. By default, the filter cutoff is set to 0%, which means that Presence will use the original values for each filter as stored in the preset. To change the cutoff frequencies, drag the Cutoff knob counterclockwise to decrease them or clockwise to increase them. The Cutoff value is not shown in the Presence window. To see it, look at the Parameter area in the top left corner of the Song window.
5. Drag the Reso knob to the desired resonance value.
6. Drag the Velo, LFO, and Env knobs clockwise or counterclockwise to positively or negatively (respectively) scale the modulation from each of these sources as desired.
7. If using envelope modulation, set the ADSR sliders in the Mod section as desired.

AMPLIFIER

A fixed gain value can be specified for the amplifier, which can then be modulated by velocity, an envelope, or an LFO. The Amplifier section is always active.

1. By default, the gain knob (labeled "Vol") is set to 0%. Drag the Vol knob clockwise to increase the gain or counterclockwise to decrease it.
2. Envelope modulation is always active at full strength in the Amplifier. There is no knob for setting the modulation amount, so just set the ADSR sliders as desired.
3. Drag the Pan knob counterclockwise to negatively scale or clockwise to positively scale the panning.
4. Drag the Velo or LFO knob clockwise or counterclockwise to positively or negatively scale the modulation as desired.

MOD

The Modulation section has an envelope generator and a sine wave LFO that can be used to modulate various parameters. The LFO and envelope have no effect until the modulation amount at the target is set to some value other than 0% by moving the LFO or Env knob.

1. To use envelope modulation, set the ADSR sliders as desired and be sure that the Env knob is set at the target to a value other than 0%.
2. Set the triggering option using the Sync and Free buttons. See the LFO Triggering section below for more details.
3. Drag the Speed knob or click in the Rate field (below the Sync and Free buttons) and type in a percentage to scale the LFO rate.

LFO TRIGGERING

There are three different triggering modes available for the LFO, which are set using the Sync and Free buttons. Clicking on either button toggles its state. The modes are the following:

- **Both buttons unselected:** This is the default mode. The LFO is triggered by the onset of a note. The Delay knob sets the amount of time between when the note begins and when the LFO starts affecting parameters. The Delay value is shown in the Parameter area in the top left corner of the Song window.
- **Sync button selected:** The LFO's cycle is locked to the tempo. The rate (Speed) is expressed as a note value.
- **Free button selected:** The LFO is free-running.

PITCH

A fixed pitch offset for tuning can be specified, and pitch modulation from an envelope or LFO can be added. To change the pitch, do the following:

1. Drag the Tune knob clockwise to scale the pitch higher or counterclockwise to scale it lower.
2. Drag the Env or LFO knobs clockwise or counter-clockwise to positively or negatively (respectively) scale pitch modulation as desired.
3. If using envelope modulation, set the Mod section ADSR sliders as desired.

VIBRATO

The vibrato provides pitch modulation using its own LFO, separate from the Mod section LFO. To change the vibrato, do the following:

1. The Delay knob sets the amount of time between the note on and when vibrato starts to be heard. The Delay value is shown in the Parameter area in the top left corner of the Song window. Drag the Delay knob clockwise to positively scale the vibrato delay or counterclockwise to negatively scale it.
2. Drag the Speed knob clockwise or counterclockwise to positively or negatively (respectively) scale the vibrato rate as desired.
3. Drag the Depth knob clockwise or counterclockwise to positively or negatively (respectively) scale the vibrato depth as desired.

GLOBAL PARAMETERS

Between the waveform display and the sample parameters is a row of global parameters affecting all samples.

- **Monophonic:** Only one voice will be played at any given time. Click on the Monophonic button to enable monophonic operation. When Monophonic is not enabled, up to the full 96 available voices can be used to play different notes of the sample, assuming that no other sample is using any voices.
- **Glide:** Also known as "portamento," this causes the pitch to glide from one played note to the next, instead of jumping to it. Drag the Glide knob to scale the amount of time it takes for the pitch to glide from one note to the next.
- **Pitch Bend (PB) range:** Click in the PB Range field and enter the maximum pitch bend (in semitones) that can be produced using the onscreen pitch bend wheel.
- **Master Gain:** The Master Gain knob at the top right of the Presence window gives from +24 dB to –80 dB of gain to the overall output of the instrument. Drag the knob to the desired output level.

PITCH BEND AND MOD WHEEL

Presence includes onscreen pitch bend and modulation wheels. The pitch bend wheel is "hardwired" to pitch only. The modulation wheel is wired to control modulation depth. The exact targets of the mod wheel vary with the preset. Either wheel can be operated from an external controller using Control Link. See the "Control Link" section for more details.

EFFECTS

Presence incorporates seven different effects processors.

GLOBAL EFFECTS CONTROLS

The following controls affect all effects:

- **FX Mix:** The FX Mix knob is the master wet/dry control. It defaults to 100%, which is all wet (effects). Drag the knob to obtain the desired mix.
- **Bypass:** To bypass all effects, click on the Bypass button to the right of the Master area.
- **Enable or bypass an individual effect:** To enable or bypass an individual effect, click on the appropriate button in the row of buttons at the bottom of the Master area. You can also use the enable/disable button for the effect in the Effect Edit view, described below. Note that the Master area button for the Modulation effect is labeled with the currently selected effect type, rather than being labeled "Mod."
- **Keep FX:** Each preset contains its own effects settings that load with the preset. If you have set up effects that you like and want to use with whatever preset you select, the

Keep FX button, when active, will cause Presence to ignore the effects settings in the new preset when loading it and keep the current effects settings. Click on the Keep FX button to activate it.

- **Edit FX:** Click on the Edit FX button to open the Effect Edit view and edit individual effects parameters as described below.

MODULATION FX

The Mod section offers you a choice of flanging, chorusing, or phasing.

- To enable the Mod effects section, click on the Enable button next to the Mod legend or click on the first button in the Master area.
- Click in the Type field and choose the Mod effect you want from the drop-down menu that appears. Each effect has its own set of parameters.
- **Chorus parameters: Delay, Rate (Speed), Width, Depth.** Drag the appropriate knob to the desired value. For Delay and Rate you can also click in the field next to the knob and enter a value. The values of the Width and Depth settings are displayed not in the Presence window, but in the Parameter area at the top left corner of the Song window.
- **Flanger parameters: Delay, Feedback (FB), Rate, Width, Depth.** Drag the appropriate knob to the desired value. For Delay and Rate you can also click in the field next to the knob and enter a value. The Sync checkbox next to the Rate control, when active, causes the modulation to be locked to the tempo. In this case, the Rate control is labeled "Beats" and the rate is expressed as a note value. When not active, the Rate control is labeled "Speed" and expressed in hertz. Click on the Sync button to make it active. The values of the Feedback, Width, and Depth settings are displayed not in the Presence window, but in the Parameter area in the top left corner of the Song window.
- **Phaser parameters: Phase Speed, Feedback (FB), Rate, Mod Width, Depth.** Drag the appropriate knob to the desired value. For Phase Speed and Rate you can also click in the field next to the knob and enter a value. A major difference between the Phase Speed and Rate parameters is that Rate can be locked to the Song tempo by checking the Sync box next it. In this case, the Rate control is labeled "Beats" and the rate is expressed as a note value. When not active, the Rate control is labeled "Speed" and expressed in hertz. Click on the Sync button to make it active. The values of the Feedback, Mod Width, and Depth settings are displayed not in the Presence window, but in the Parameter area in the top left corner of the Song window.

EQ

The EQ is a seven-band graphic-style equalizer with a choice of two sets of center frequencies.

1. To enable the EQ effects section, click on the Enable button next to the EQ legend or click on the EQ button in the Master area.
2. Click on the Lead or Bass button to choose the set of center frequencies you want to use. The Bass set has bands that go both lower and higher than the Lead set.
3. Drag the sliders to the level desired for each band. The values for the sliders are displayed not in the Presence window, but in the Parameter area in the top left corner of the Song window.

DISTORTION

Presence offers a choice of eight kinds of distortion.

1. To enable the Distortion effects section, click on the Enable button next to the Distortion legend or click on the Dist button in the Master area.
2. Click in the Type field and choose the desired distortion type from the drop-down menu that appears.
3. Drag the Drive knob until the desired amount of distortion is heard.

PAN

The Pan section offers auto-panning using its own sine LFO.

1. To enable the Pan effects section, click on the Enable button next to the Pan legend or click on the Pan button in the Master area.
2. Set the auto-pan rate. The Sync checkbox next to the Rate control, when active, causes the modulation to be locked to the tempo. In this case, the Rate control is labeled "Beats" and the rate is expressed as a note value. When not active, the Rate control is labeled "Speed" and expressed in hertz. Click on the Sync button to make it active.
3. Drag the Rate (Speed/Beats) knob to the desired auto-pan rate or click in the Rate field next to the knob and type in the desired value.
4. Drag the Depth knob to the amount desired. The value is displayed not in the Presence window, but in the Parameter area in the top left corner of the Song window.

GATE

Presence includes a 16-step pattern gate. A pattern gate opens and closes according to a defined pattern that is locked to the Song's tempo. It works best on sustained sounds but can, of course, be used with anything. To set up a pattern gate you must set the length of the entire pattern, then set on which steps the gate opens and on which it closes. There is a short fade when the gate opens and closes to avoid clicks. The pattern can be made stereo, which allows you to define a separate pattern for each channel. A collection of preset patterns is included, but you can edit the pattern to be whatever you want.

- To enable the Gate effects section, click on the Enable button next to the Gate legend or click on the Gate button in the Master area.

- Set the pattern length. Click in the Beats field and select the desired pattern length from the drop-down menu that appears. The entire 16-step pattern will play in the duration selected.
- To select a preset pattern, click on the Pattern field and choose from the drop-down menu that appears.
- To edit the pattern, just click on a box to toggle between gate on (the box is filled) and gate off (the box is empty).
- To make a pattern stereo, click on the Stereo button. The display will change to show two rows of boxes. The top row is the left channel and the bottom row the right channel.
- To change a stereo pattern to mono, click on the Stereo button to deselect it. The left channel pattern will become the new pattern; the right channel pattern is discarded.
- Drag the Depth knob to the amount desired. The value is displayed not in the Presence window, but in the Parameter area at the top left corner of the Song window. When the value is less than 100%, the gate allows some signal through when it is closed. This can be used to create a rhythmic tremolo effect.

DELAY

Presence includes a tempo-locked delay that can act like either an insert effect (in-line with other effects), or a send effect (fed by dry signal before any effects have been added). The Delay section includes its own Mix control, which is independent of the master FX Mix.

- To enable the Delay effects section, click on the Enable button next to the Delay legend or click on the Delay button in the Master area.
- Click on the Send button to configure the Delay as a send effect. When the Send button is disabled, the Delay is an insert effect.
- Set the delay time value. Click in the Beats field and choose the desired note value from the drop-down menu that appears.
- Drag the Feedback (FB) knob to get the desired amount of feedback. The value is displayed not in the Presence window, but in the Parameter area at the top left corner of the Song window.
- Drag the Low Cut (LC) and/or High Cut (HC) filter knobs to obtain the desired amounts of frequency rolloff. The values are displayed not in the Presence window, but in the Parameter area in the top left corner of the Song window. The filters affect only the delayed sound. The filters are inside the feedback loop, so if there is feedback the filtering will become more intense with each repeat.
- Drag the Mix knob to the desired value. The value is displayed not in the Presence window, but in the Parameter area in the top left corner of the Song window. Note that Mix goes from 0% to 50%. It is not possible to get more delayed sound than undelayed in the mix.

REVERB

A generic, plate-ish reverb is included in Presence. It includes its own wet/dry mix control, independent of the master FX Mix.

- To enable the Reverb effects section, click on the Enable button next to the Reverb legend or click on the Reverb button in the Master area.
- Drag the Predelay (Pre) knob to the desired value. The value is displayed not in the Presence window, but in the Parameter area in the top left corner of the Song window.
- Drag the Size knob to get the desired decay time for the reverb. The value is displayed not in the Presence window, but in the Parameter area at the top left corner of the Song window.
- Drag the Damp knob to get the desired amount of high-frequency damping in the reverb. The value is displayed not in the Presence window, but in the Parameter area in the top left corner of the Song window.
- Drag the Mix knob to the desired value. The value is displayed not in the Presence window, but in the Parameter area at the top left corner of the Song window. Note that Mix goes from 0% to 50%. It is not possible to get more reverb than dry sound.

AUDITIONING SOUNDS WITH THE KEYBOARD

Presence includes an onscreen keyboard that is very handy for auditioning sounds as you tweak their parameters. Simply click on any key to play that note. Of course, you can always use an external controller to play Presence, as well.

Impact

Impact is a sample player designed to look and act like a hardware drum machine. The interface is based around a 4-by-4 matrix of "pads," each of which has its own pitch, filter, and amplifier settings, and its own output assignment. It is also possible to create velocity layering on each pad.

Note that you are not limited to loading only drum or percussion sounds into Impact's pads—you can load any sound you want. However, when a pad is triggered, the entire sample is always played.

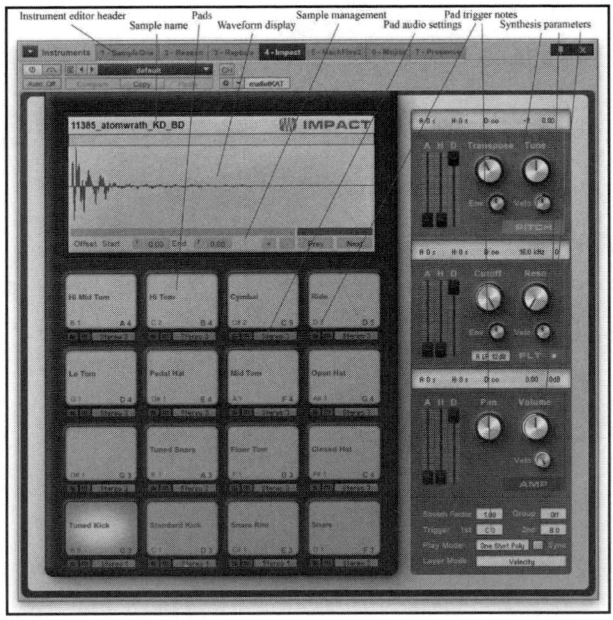

Fig. 4-31: The Impact user interface.

Further, if you trigger a pad while it is still playing a sample, it will start playing another copy of the sample on top of the first one. If you load a pad with long files and then trigger the pad a few times, you can quickly get a lot of sound going on at once!

A pad can be played by clicking on it or playing the note assigned to the pad from an external controller or a track.

Replace Sample...
Add Sample...
Rename Pad
Select in Pool
Clear Pad
✓ Play One Shot Poly
Play One Shot Mono
Play Toggle
Play Note On/Off
Play Synced

Fig. 4-32: The Impact pad contextual menu.

PAD BASICS: NOTE, RENAME, SOLO, MUTE

There are 16 pads in Impact. Right-clicking (or Ctrl-clicking on Mac) on a pad brings up a contextual menu of pad options:

There are two note assignments for each pad, which are shown in the lower corners of the pad.

- To set the note assignments for a pad, click on the pad to select it, click in the Trigger 1st or Trigger 2nd field at the bottom right of Impact, and either play a note on your controller, or simply enter the desired note value.
- To rename a pad, right-click (or Ctrl-click on Mac) on the pad and choose Rename Pad from the drop-down menu that appears. Enter the new name in the dialog box that appears after the command is selected.
- To solo a pad, click on the Solo (S) button below the pad. All other pads will be muted and only the soloed pad will sound.
- To mute a pad, click on the Mute (M) button below the pad. A mute pad will not sound when its note is played.

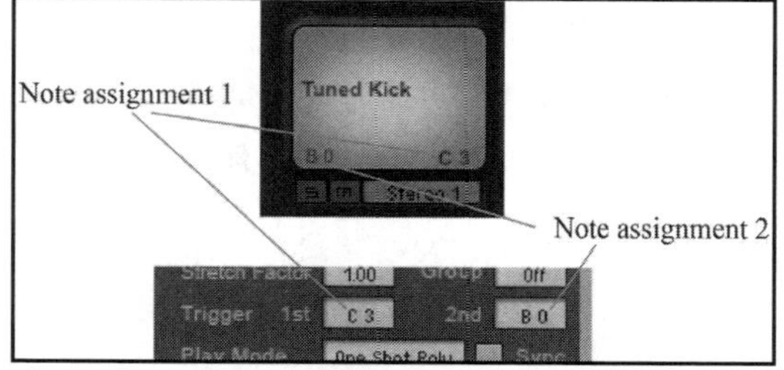

Fig. 4-33: Trigger note assignments for an Impact pad are displayed at the bottom of the pad, but they are set in the Trigger fields of the play parameter edit section in the lower right of the Impact window.

Unfortunately, it is not possible to use an external controller to solo or mute a pad.

PLAY MODE

There are several schemes a pad can use for playback when it is triggered. The Play Mode setting in the Playback Parameter section in the lower right corner of the Impact UI is where the desired scheme is chosen. While there are four choices listed in the Play Mode drop-down menu, there are actually five options available:

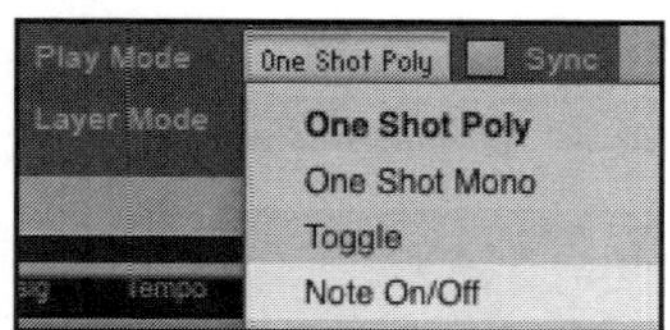

Fig. 4-34: There are four playback options in the Play Mode drop-down menu, plus the Sync box to it's right.

- **One-shot Poly:** Once triggered, a sample plays in its entirety. Each trigger that comes in starts playback of the sample, even if it is already playing. Thus, multiple copies of the sample can be playing at once.

- **One-shot Mono:** As with One-shot Poly, once triggered, a sample plays in its entirety. The difference is that if a trigger comes in while the sample is playing, playback from the first trigger is stopped when playback from the second trigger begins.
- **Toggle:** When set to Toggle, if the sample is still playing back when a second trigger arrives, the second trigger acts like a Sample Stop command—it halts playback, but does not trigger any new sample to play.
- **Note On/Off:** In MIDI, each note has a Note On message that starts it playing, and a Note Off message that marks the end of the note (though there might be a decay time on the sound that continues). This is often not a necessary structure with drum samplers, since the sounds are usually very short. In this context, a trigger to start playback is frequently all that is needed. Note On/Off mode, however, does use this structure: a Note On message triggers playback to start, and a Note Off message stops playback. Obviously, this is not a mode you will need for typical, short drum sounds, but rather for longer samples (for example, a complete sentence from a speech sample), it can be quite useful.
- **Sync:** When checked, this box to the right of the Play Mode field will delay triggering of sample playback until the next grid line as defined by the current Arrange view Quantize Value. So, if Quantize Value is set to 1/16th, a triggered sample will not play until the next 16th note after the trigger arrives.

ADDING AND DELETING SAMPLES

There are five ways to add samples to a pad:

- Drop one or more samples/audio files from the Browser onto the pad into which you want to load it.
- Drop an Audio Event from the Arrange view to the pad.
- Select a range of Audio Events in the Arrange view and drop them on the pad. Studio One 2 will bounce the selected range to a new audio file and add that file to the pad.
- Right-click (or Ctrl-click on Mac) on the pad and choose Add Sample… from the drop-down menu that appears. A standard file open dialog box will be presented. Navigate to the desired file and click on the Open button to load it.
- Click on the + (Add) button in the lower left corner of the waveform display. A standard file open dialog box will appear. Navigate to the desired file and click on the Open button to load it.
- If you drag a sample to a pad that already has a sample, the new sample will replace the old one.

You can delete a sample from a pad in either of two ways. You can also clear all samples from a pad by doing the following:

- Right-click (or Ctrl-click on Mac) on the pad and choose Delete Sample... from the drop-down menu that appears.
- Be sure that the pad from which you wish to delete a sample is selected. If it is not, click on it to select it, then click on the – (Delete) button in the lower left corner of the waveform display.
- To clear all samples from a pad, right-click (or Ctrl-click on Mac) on the pad and choose Clear Pad from the drop-down menu that appears.

LAYERING SAMPLES

Up to six samples can be assigned to a single pad in Impact. So what determines which of these samples will play? There are three layer modes available in the Layer Mode field located in the Playback Parameter section in the lower right corner of Impact's user interface.

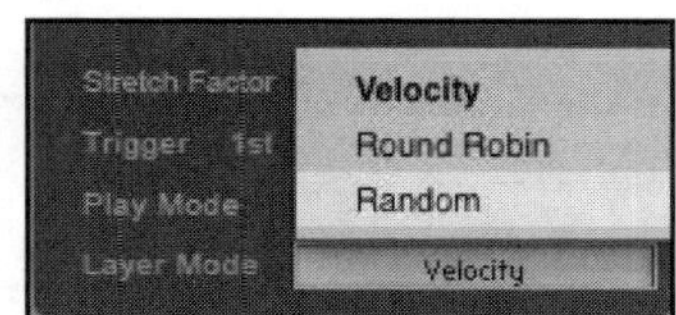

Fig. 4-35: Each pad can be assigned to one of Impact's virtual outputs by right-clicking on the output field below the pad and choosing the desired output from this menu.

VELOCITY LAYERING

One common technique for getting more realistic sounds is velocity layering. In velocity layering, each sample is assigned a range of velocity values to which it will respond. For example, you might assign a soft snare hit to respond to velocity values of 0–60, a medium hit to play with velocities from 61–90, a loud hit from 91–112, and a very loud hit with a rim shot from 113–128. Impact allows you to stack up to eight samples on each pad and divide the velocity range between them. Velocity ranges cannot overlap and there is no crossfading between layers.

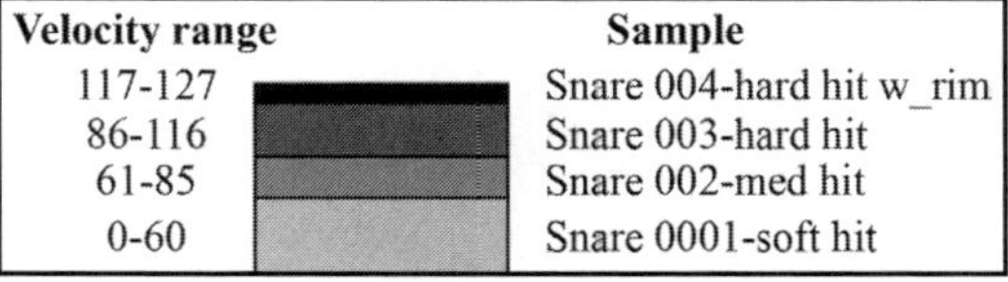

Velocity range	Sample
117-127	Snare 004-hard hit w_rim
86-116	Snare 003-hard hit
61-85	Snare 002-med hit
0-60	Snare 0001-soft hit

Fig. 4-36: Velocity layering, in which the velocity of a played note determines the sample that gets played, adds realism and life to parts played using sampled instruments.

To load samples for velocity layering on a pad, do the following:

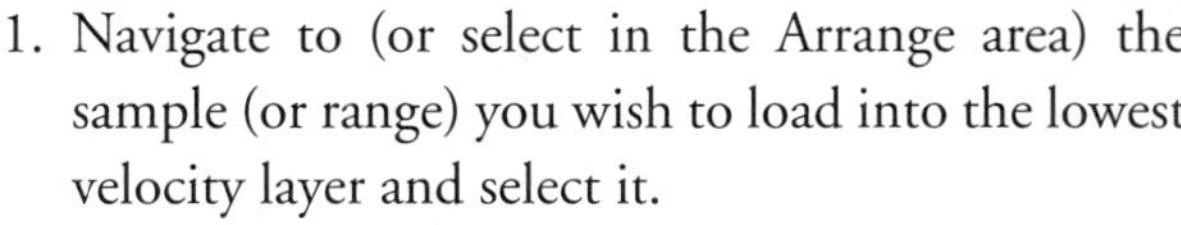

1. Navigate to (or select in the Arrange area) the sample (or range) you wish to load into the lowest velocity layer and select it.
2. Drag the sample to the pad you wish to load it into.
3. Navigate to the sample you wish to load into the next highest velocity layer and select it.
4. With the sample selected, hold down the Shift key and drag it to the pad. After you drop it on the pad, you will notice that the velocity range bar above the waveform display now has two sections.
5. Repeat with up to six more samples. Each sample dropped will become the highest velocity layer, pushing the others down. Note that you cannot rearrange the order afterward, so be sure to drag them in the ascending order you want to have.

To adjust the velocity range for a sample, simply drag the range boundary in the velocity range bar.

There are two ways to access a velocity-layered sample for editing or auditioning:

- Click in the section of the velocity range bar that you wish to access to select it.
- Click on the sample name at the bottom of the waveform display and choose the sample you wish to access from the drop-down menu that appears.
- Clicking on a velocity-layered pad will always play the currently selected sample. Of course, you can always use an external controller to hear how the layering works when you actually play.

To delete a velocity-layered sample, do the following:

1. Be sure that the sample you wish to delete is selected. If it is not, select it as described above.
2. Once it is selected, click on the – (Delete) button in the lower left corner of the waveform display.

ROUND ROBIN

Round robin very simply steps through the samples assigned to a pad; each time the pad is triggered Impact plays the next sample, cycling through the collection of samples on the pad.

RANDOM

The name says it all: each time the pad is triggered, one sample is chosen at random from the pool of samples assigned to the pad. This means that samples may be repeated on successive strikes—in fact, the fewer the samples assigned to the pad, the more likely this is to happen.

ASSIGNING A PAD TO AN OUTPUT

Impact has eight mono outputs and eight stereo outputs. Each pad can be assigned to one of those outputs.

To assign a pad to an output, do the following:

- Click in the Output Assignment field below the pad and choose the desired output from the drop-down menu that appears. If no mixer channel exists for the selected output, one is created for it.
- When multiple pads are assigned to an output, the desired balance of the pads must be achieved by adjusting the Amplifier gains for each of the pads.

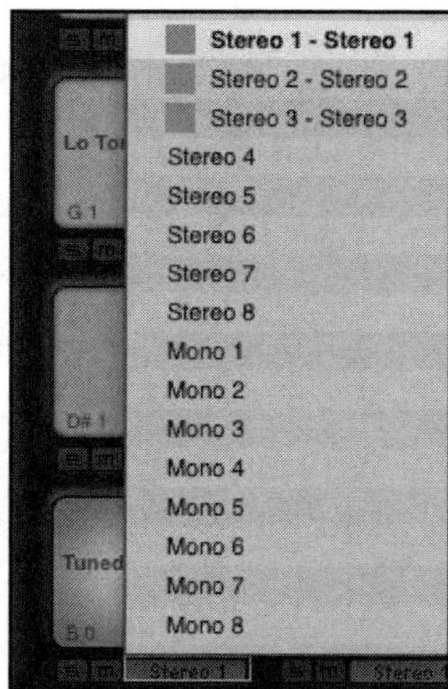

Fig. 4-37: Each pad can be assigned to one of Impact's virtual outputs by right-clicking on the output field below the pad and choosing the desired output from this menu.

GROUPS

Impact has four exclusive triggering groups. In these groups, triggering any pad in the group causes playback of all the other pads in the group to be silenced. This is useful for instruments like hi-hat, when it is desirable for a foot-close sound to cut off the ring of an earlier open hat hit.

To assign a pad to a triggering group, do the following:

1. Click on the pad you want to add to a group to select it.
2. Click on the Group (Grp) field in the lower right corner of the waveform display and choose the desired group number from the drop-down menu that appears.

PITCH

Each pad can be transposed or tuned, and the pitch can be modulated by a simple envelope generator or note velocity. Transpose and Tune are essentially coarse and fine tuning controls, respectively.

TRANSPOSE AND TUNE

- Drag the Transpose knob clockwise or counterclockwise to increase or decrease (respectively) the pitch in semitone steps. The Transpose knob has a range of +/–1 octave.
- Drag the Tune knob clockwise or counterclockwise to increase or decrease (respectively) the pitch by cents (100ths of a semitone). The Tune knob has a range of +/–100 cents.

The values for these controls are shown in the parameter bar above the Pitch section.

Fig. 4-38: Sample tuning is done with the Transpose and Tune controls in Impact's Pitch section.

PITCH MODULATION

- If you want envelope modulation of the pitch, set the Attack, Hold, and Decay time sliders as desired. The Hold value is the amount of time the envelope will stay at its full level between completion of the Attack and before beginning the Decay. The values for these controls are shown in the parameter bar above the Pitch section.
- Drag the Env knob clockwise or counterclockwise to add positive or negative (respectively) envelope modulation of the pitch. The value is shown in a tool pop-up as you turn the knob. The modulation amount can be set to shift the pitch over a range of +/–1200 cents (two octaves total).
- Drag the Velo knob clockwise or counterclockwise to add positive or negative (respectively) velocity modulation of the pitch. The value is shown in a tool pop-up as you turn the knob. The modulation amount can be set to shift the pitch over a range of +/–1200 cents (two octaves total).

FILTER

Each pad has a resonant filter that can be modulated by an envelope or velocity. There is a choice of six models of analog synthesizer filters or three regular digital filters. The filter can be modulated by velocity, envelope, or the LFO.

- The FLT section must be enabled for any filtering to be heard. When the indicator to the right of the FLT legend is blue, the filter is enabled. If it is not enabled, click on the indicator to enable the filter.
- Click in the Type field to the left of the FLT legend and choose the desired filter type from the drop-down menu. There are nine types available: modeled analog highpass, lowpass, and bandpass filters, each with a choice of 12 dB/octave or 24 dB/octave rolloff slopes, plus regular digital highpass, bandpass, and lowpass filters.
- By default, the filter cutoff is set fully open. To change the cutoff frequency, drag the Cutoff knob counterclockwise to decrease it or clockwise to increase it. The value for this control is shown in the parameter bar above the Filter section.
- Drag the Reso knob to the desired resonance value. The value for this control is shown in the parameter bar above the Filter section.
- Drag the Velo, LFO, and Env knobs clockwise or counterclockwise to positively or negatively (respectively) scale the modulation from each of these sources as desired.

If using envelope modulation, set the ADSR sliders in the Mod section as desired.

FILTER CUTOFF MODULATION

- If you want envelope modulation of the cutoff frequency, set the Attack, Hold, and Decay time sliders as desired. The Hold value is the amount of time the envelope will stay at its full level between completion of the Attack and before beginning the Decay. The values for these controls are shown in the parameter bar above the Filter section.
- Drag the Env knob clockwise or counterclockwise to add positive or negative (respectively) envelope modulation of the filter cutoff frequency. The value is shown in a tool pop-up as you turn the knob. The modulation amount can be set to change the cutoff over a range of +/–10 octaves.
- Drag the Velo knob clockwise or counterclockwise to add positive or negative (respectively) velocity modulation of the filter cutoff frequency. The value is shown in a tool pop-up as you turn the knob. The modulation amount can be set to the cutoff over a range of +/–10 octaves.

AMP

A fixed gain value can be specified, and amplitude modulation from an envelope generator or velocity can be added.

1. By default, the Gain knob is set to 0 dB. Drag the Gain knob clockwise to increase the gain or counterclockwise to decrease it. The value for this control is shown in the parameter bar above the Amplifier section.
2. Envelope modulation is always active at full strength in the Amplifier. There is no knob for setting the modulation amount, so just set the Attack, Hold, and Decay time sliders as desired. The Hold value is the amount of time the envelope will stay at its full level between completion of the Attack and before beginning the Decay. The values for these controls are shown in the parameter bar above the Amplifier section.
3. Drag the Pan knob to pan the signal to the left or right as desired. The value for this control is shown in the parameter bar above the Amplifier section.
4. By default, the velocity modulation amount (Velo) knob is set full clockwise (0 dB). Drag the Velo knob to the desired modulation value. The value is shown in a tool pop-up as you turn the knob.

STRETCH FACTOR

Stretch Factor is a time-stretching function built into each pad of Impact. The value in this field is a scaling factor for playback time, so a value of 1.0 plays the sample at its original speed, a value of 2.0 plays it twice as fast, and a value of 0.5 plays it at half speed. Pitch is not affected. Stretch Factor can be set anywhere in the range of 0.10 to 10.0.

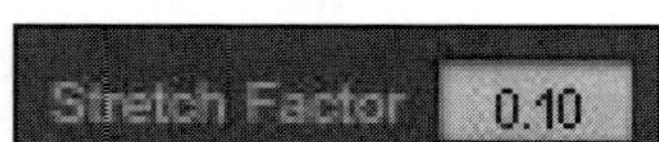

Fig. 4-39: Stretch Factor enables each pad to time-stretch samples on playback.

Mojito

Fig. 4-40: The Mojito user interface.

Mojito is a simple subtractive synthesizer intended to mimic a single oscillator analog synthesizer. It is especially effective for bass sounds, but is capable of many other useful sounds as well. Only the LFO speed is displayed in the Mojito window. All other parameter values can be viewed in the Parameter area in the top left corner of the Song window.

OSCILLATOR

Mojito's oscillator generates pulse and sawtooth waveforms and allows crossfading between the two. The oscillator includes its own LFO for modulating its parameters. Only the LFO Speed parameters are displayed in the Mojito window. All other parameter values can be viewed in the Parameter area in the top left corner of the Song window.

- Drag the Pitch knob to the desired tuning offset, up to a maximum of +/–1 octave.
- Drag the Wave knob to the desired mix of sawtooth and pulse waves. A displayed value of 0 is all sawtooth, while a displayed value of 1 is all pulse wave.
- Drag the Width control to set the desired pulse width for the pulse wave. This will have no effect if the Wave knob is set fully to the sawtooth wave. A displayed value of 50% means the oscillator is generating a square wave.

PORTAMENTO (GLIDE)

While called portamento, this feature is more than simply glide. In fact, the Portamento field (Porta) has little to do with portamento at all; it is a setting that manages retriggering when a new note is played while the previous note is still playing. When this happens, velocity is not applied to the new note. To set up glide and retriggering, do the following:

- Click in the Portamento field (Porta) and choose the desired retriggering mode.
- When set to Off, if a new note is played before the previous one is released, the old note is silenced and the Amplifier envelope is retriggered to play the new note. No pitch glide is applied, and the Time knob is inactive.
- When set to Legato, the envelope is not retriggered when a new note is played before the previous one is released, but the pitch will glide from the old note to the new one. This produces a smooth, legato effect with glide.
- When set to Trigger, the envelope is retriggered when a new note overlaps an old one, but the envelope does not start from zero. Instead, it starts from the value it had when retriggered. The pitch glides from the old pitch to the new one.
- Drag the Time knob to set the desired glide time for the pitch.

OSCILLATOR MODULATION

All three oscillator parameters (pitch, waveshape, pulse width) can be modulated with the Oscillator section's LFO. The LFO can be tempo-locked or free-running.

1. When the Tempo button in the LFO Speed area is disabled, the LFO is tempo-locked and the LFO rate is displayed as a note value. When the Tempo button is enabled, the LFO is free-running and the value is displayed in hertz. Click on the Tempo button to toggle between these two modes.
2. Drag the Tempo button to the desired rate, or type the desired rate into the rate field.

3. Drag the small knobs beneath the Pitch, Wave, and Width knobs to introduce LFO modulation of the parameter. Drag clockwise to introduce positive modulation or counterclockwise to introduce negative modulation.

FILTER

Mojito's filter emulates a 24 dB/octave analog synthesizer filter.

- Drag the big Cutoff knob to set the filter's initial cutoff frequency.
- Drag the Resonance (Reso) knob to the desired value. At very high settings, the filter will oscillate, which can result in an extremely hot output signal, so be careful!

FILTER MODULATION

Mojito's filter cutoff can be modulated from any combination of four sources.

- When the Tempo button in the LFO Speed area is disabled, the LFO is tempo-locked and the LFO Speed is displayed as a note value. When the Tempo button is enabled, the LFO is free-running and the LFO Speed is displayed in hertz. Click on the Tempo button to toggle between these two modes.
- Drag the Tempo button to the desired rate, or type the desired rate into the LFO Speed field.
- Drag the LFO knob to set the amount of LFO modulation applied to the cutoff. Drag clockwise for positive modulation and counterclockwise for negative modulation. When the knob is centered, there is no modulation. Modulation amount is expressed in cents and octaves.
- Drag the Key knob to set the amount that the cutoff frequency tracks as notes are played across the keyboard. In the fully clockwise position, an octave played on the keyboard causes an octave change in the cutoff frequency. In the fully counterclockwise position, the cutoff will not track the keyboard at all.
- Drag the Velocity knob to set the amount of effect that velocity will have on the cutoff. Drag clockwise to introduce positive modulation and counterclockwise for negative modulation.
- The Amplifier envelope generator is also used for envelope modulation of the filter cutoff. Drag the Envelope knob clockwise for positive modulation and counterclockwise for negative modulation. When the knob is centered, there is no modulation. Modulation amount is expressed in cents and octaves.

AMP

A fixed gain value can be specified, and amplitude modulation from an envelope generator or velocity can be added.

1. Drag the Gain knob counterclockwise to decrease gain or clockwise to increase it.

2. Envelope modulation is always active at full strength in the Amplifier. There is no knob for setting the modulation amount, so just set the ADSR sliders as desired.
3. Drag the Velo knob clockwise or counterclockwise to positively or negatively (respectively) scale velocity modulation as desired.

EFFECTS

Mojito includes a time-based modulation processor capable of flanging and chorusing effects, plus a soft overdrive function. While the FX section has its own sine LFO, it runs at the rate set for the filter LFO.

- Drag the Depth control to obtain the desired amount of modulation.
- The Color control is more or less a delay time control. When turned fully counterclockwise, the effect uses a longer delay and gives a chorus effect. In full clockwise position it uses a shorter time and is closer to a flanger, though without feedback.
- The Drive knob is not a heavy distortion effect, but something closer to an overdriven tube preamp sound. Drag the knob to get the desired level of punch and edge.

LET'S MAKE MORE MUSIC: GET A DRUM GROOVE GOING

Just to exercise your chops with virtual instruments, let's use Impact to make a drum groove.

1. Open the PreSonus folder in the Instruments list of the Browser.
2. Drag Impact from the list and drop it onto the Arrange area, or click on it to reveal its presets and then drag one of them to the Arrange area. Notice that Studio One 2 has created an Instrument track in the Arrange view for the MIDI information that will play Impact, and a new mixer channel with the default name "Stereo 1," the default output through which Impact's sound will flow. Impact itself will open right in front.
3. If you did not drag a preset already, pull down the menu in the upper left of Impact's window, just underneath the instrument's name (it probably says "default") and choose a drum kit.
4. Click on a few pads and make sure that you are hearing the kit. If not, check that the mixer channel is assigned to the Main Out.
5. If you have a MIDI controller connected, try playing Impact from it. The note name for each drum is shown on the pad. Find a few of the notes on your MIDI controller—for example, the kick and snare.

6. You'll notice that the Impact track is already armed for recording. Press the . (period) key on the number pad to return to the beginning of the tune, then set up the metronome and count-off (if they are not already).
7. Ready? Press Record button in the Transport bar (or hit the * (asterisk) key on the number pad) and lay down a little kick and snare groove.

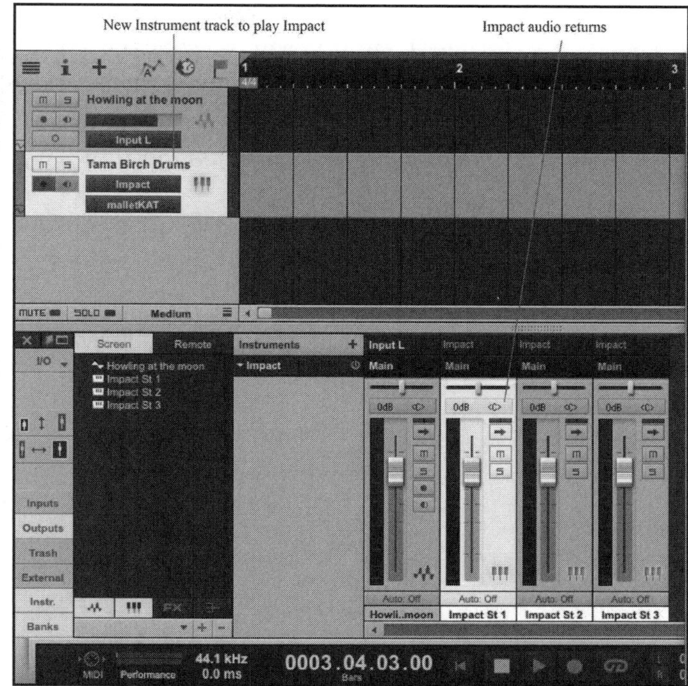

Fig. 4-41: Impact shows up on the Song page as a track of performance data and Instrument return channels in the mixer for the audio. Note that Instrument returns have no Record Enable or Monitor buttons, but they do have Instrument icons that open an editor for the Instrument when clicked.

Now we've got some action going on! Let's heat things up more by laying a Latin percussion loop on top of the Impact drum groove.

1. Go to the Browser and click on the Sounds tab.
2. Click on the triangle next to the Studio One Loops Vol 4 folder to display its contents, and you'll see it contains four folders.
3. Click on the triangle next to the Latin Percussion folder to reveal its contents.
4. Click on the triangle next to the 4-4 Patterns folder.

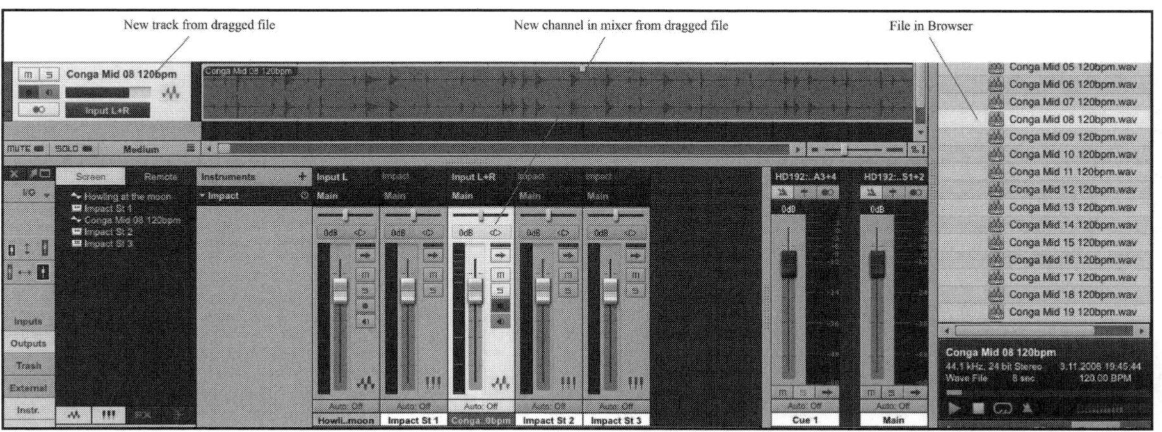

Fig. 4-42: Dragging a loop file from the Browser to the Arrange view creates both a new track and a mixer channel.

5. There's a long list of loops inside the 4-4 Patterns folder, each with the tempo in the name. Drag the loop called "Conga Mid 08 120 bpm" from the Browser, into the Arrange window. Studio One 2 will create a track and mixer channel for it. Make sure to drag the loop to the beginning of your song.
6. Press the Spacebar to play and listen to your beat enhanced with a conga groove!

Virtual instruments rock.

On the Cutting Room Floor: Basic Editing

Editing is the heart of most creative projects. Editing is the process of shaping the tracks you have recorded: changing start or end times, moving pieces around, fixing problems, and much more. Think of yourself as a musical chef preparing a fine dish: first you gather together quality ingredients (record tracks), then you prepare them (edit them), cook them (mix them) and, finally, serve the delicious preparation up (master and deliver them).

Ready to prep your ingredients? Well, let's look at a few of Studio One 2's basic editing features.

LOOKING AT DATA IN THE ARRANGE AND EDIT VIEWS

As you saw in the "Meet Studio One 2" section in chapter 1, there are two views in Studio One 2 in which you will do your editing: the Arrange view and the Edit view. You can adjust how the Song window is divided between the two views by moving the cursor over the dividing line between them and, when the cursor changes to a double-headed arrow, dragging up or down.

While both views can be zoomed in and out, the Edit view is really the place to get in close and do very precise editing, while the Arrange view keeps a larger piece of the song in front of you. These two views serve the same purposes whether you are editing audio or MIDI data.

One crucial area of support for editing is the set of tools available for viewing the material on which you are working in the Arrange and Edit views.

Opening Events and Parts for Editing

Here are the ways to open an Event or Part into the Audio or Music (MIDI) editor:

- Press the F2 key.

- Double-click on a Part or Event in the Arrange view. The appropriate editor will open.
- Click on the Edit button in the lower left of the Arrange view.
- Right-click on the track name in the Track List and choose Edit Track from the contextual drop-down menu that appears.

Detachable Editors

The Edit view and the three processing panels (Audio Bend, Strip Silence, Quantize) can all be popped out of the unified interface and moved around independently.

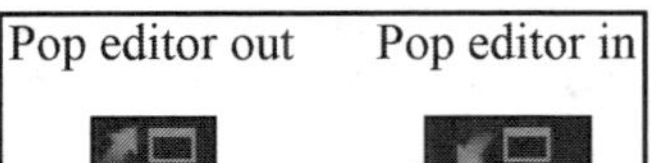

Fig. 5-1: The Detach button is found in the upper right corner of edit windows. The button changes state when the editor is popped out.

- To detach an editor, click on the Detach button in the upper right corner next to the close box. The arrow on the Detach button will now point down and left.
- To reattach an editor to the integrated environment, click on the Detach button (if the arrow is pointing downward).

The Track List

The Track List provides a quick and easy way to manage which tracks are displayed in the Arrange view at any given time.

The Music editor has its own Track List, which is independent of the Arrange view Track List, but serves a similar purpose in multitrack MIDI editing. For more information on the Music editor Track List, see the section "Multitrack MIDI Editing," in this chapter.

- To open the Arrange view Track List, click on the Track List button in the Arrange view toolbar above the track headers.

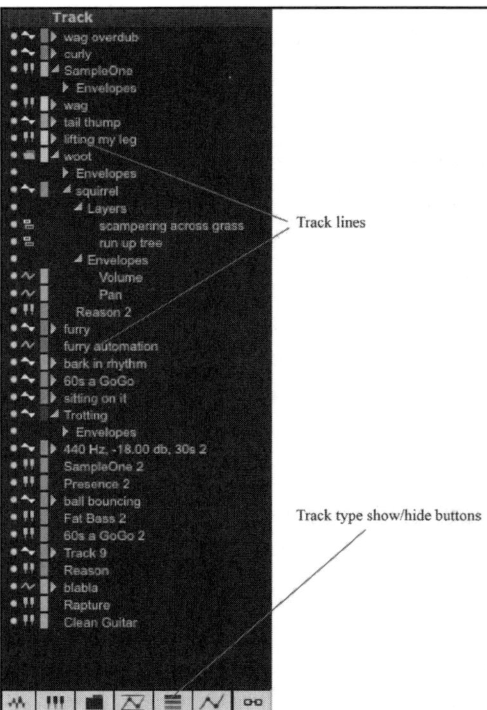

Fig. 5-2: The Arrange view Track List.

The basic layout of the Track List is simple: there is one line for each track in the Song, and, at the bottom of the list, a row of enable/disable buttons for the different track types. Let's take a closer look.

First, notice that the line for each currently selected track is colored blue. If multiple tracks are selected, they will all be colored blue. Note, however, that it is not possible to select multiple tracks in the Track List—you can do this only in the Arrange view. Now let's look at the features in the lines for the tracks.

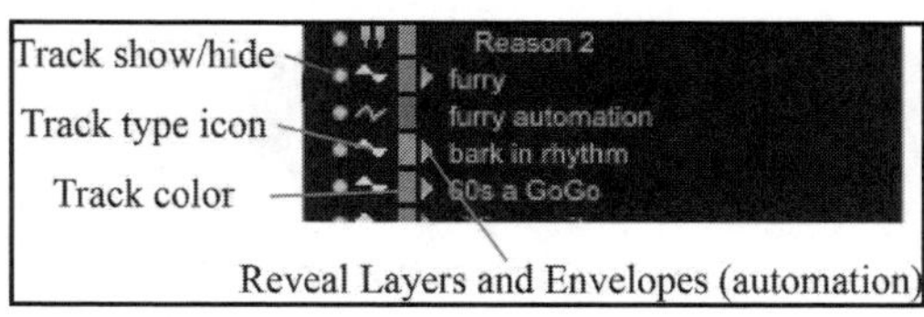

Fig. 5-3: Features of each line in the Track List.

TRACK LINE FEATURES

Fig. 5-4: Showing and hiding tracks from the Track List.

- To hide or show a track in the Arrange view, click on the button (labeled with a dot) on the left end of the line. When a track is visible, the dot is white. When a track is hidden, the dot turns black and the entire line is grayed out.

TIP: Showing or hiding tracks is a display function only; it does not enable or disable playback of the tracks or affect whether the tracks are included in a bounce. However, tracks can be edited only if they are visible. For example, say that a range is selected across two tracks. Now you hide one track and delete the selection. Material will be deleted only from the visible track, even though material was selected on the other track before it was hidden.

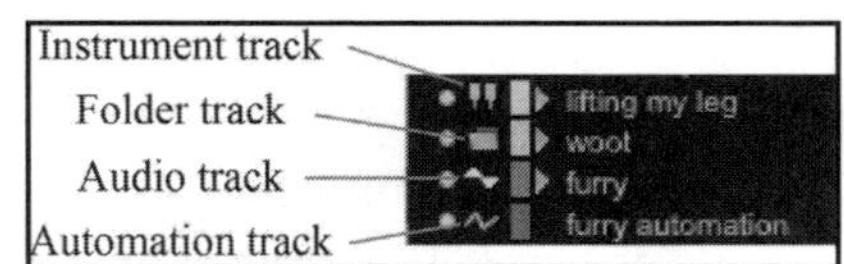

Fig. 5-5: The icon on each Track Line indicates the track's type.

- To the right of the show/hide button is the track type icon, which identifies the track as an Audio, Instrument, Automation, or Folder track.
- To move a track up or down in the Track List, click on the track type icon and drag up or down to place the track in the desired position.
- The color rectangle indicates the color-coding used for the track in the Arrange view. This is for display only; track color cannot be edited from the Track List.
- To display layer or automation lanes in the Arrange view, click on the track name or the disclosure triangle to the right of the color rectangle, then click on the Layers or Envelopes legend or the disclosure triangle next to the legend to display the lanes. The Track contextual menu can also be used to display these lanes. Note that "Envelopes" is the term used in the Track List for automation lanes. Disclosure triangles are present only on tracks that contain automation data or more than one layer, and the Layer or Envelope legends appear only if that kind of data is present on the track. For more information on Track lanes and the Track contextual menu, see the sections on those topics later in this chapter.

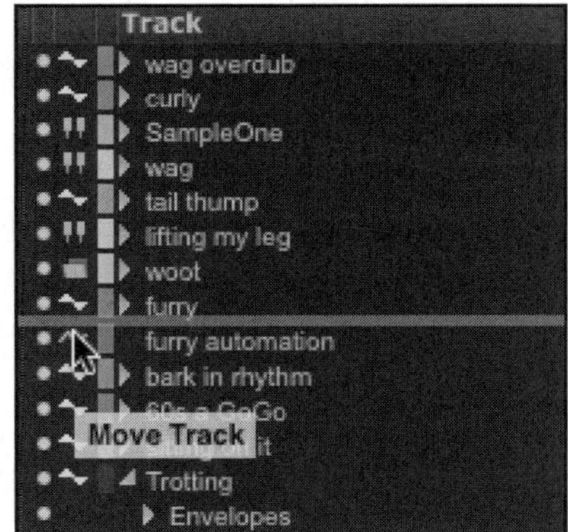

Fig. 5-6: Moving a track in the Track List by dragging its track type icon.

- To hide layer or automation lanes in the Arrange view, click on the appropriate disclosure triangle to collapse the layer or automation parameters list. The Track contextual menu can also hide these lanes, as described below.
- To show or hide an individual layer or automation parameter, click on the show/hide button for the layer or parameter.

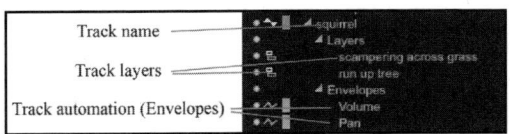

Fig. 5-7: Layers and automation (called "Envelopes") can be shown or hidden in the Arrange view by expanding or collapsing them in the Track List.

TRACK/LANE TYPE
SHOW/HIDE BUTTONS

- To show or hide all tracks or lanes of a given type, click on the button for that type/lane at the bottom of the Track List. The buttons are (from left to right) Audio tracks, Instrument tracks, Folder tracks, Automation tracks, Layers lanes, and Envelopes (automation) lanes.

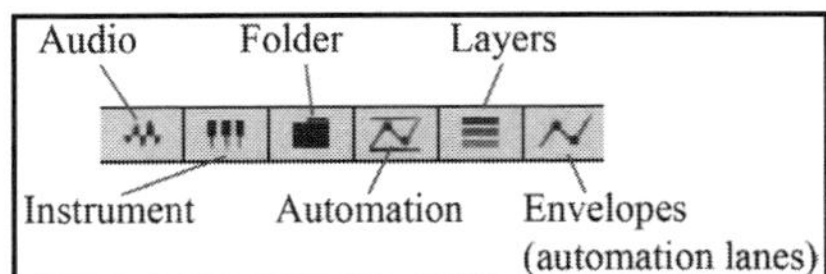

Fig. 5-8: The tracks displayed in the Track List can be filtered by track type using the track type show/hide buttons at the bottom of the Track List.

LINK TRACK
LIST/CONSOLE BUTTON

- To link the Track List to the Mix view (Console), click on the Link Track List/Console button in the lower right corner of the Track List. When this button is enabled, showing or hiding a track in the Track List will cause the associated channel strips in the Mix view to be shown or hidden as well.

Fig. 5-9: When the Link Track List/ Console button is active, hiding tracks causes the corresponding channels in the mixer to be hidden as well.

Track Lanes

When a track contains more than one layer, or one or more automation parameters, multiple layers or parameters can be displayed in lanes below the track. Multiple takes on a track created during loop recording must be unpacked to layers in order to view them in lanes.

Viewing layers in lanes facilitates editing, especially comping. Comping is discussed in chapter 6, "Advanced Editing." Showing and hiding Track lanes are discussed in the section "Track List," above.

Contextual Track Menu

- To open the contextual Track menu, right-click on the track header in the Arrange view, or on the track name in the Track List.

The contextual Track menu offers the list of commands shown below. Most of these commands are also available in the main menu bar.

TIP: Some commands depend on the characteristics of the track that is currently in focus. When only one track is selected, that is obviously the track in focus, but when multiple tracks are selected, the last one selected will be the track in focus. You can see this by looking at the Track inspector and noting for which track information is being displayed. The commands shown in the contextual menu are always determined by the track in focus, but some commands affect only this track, while others affect all selected tracks, which I will note below.

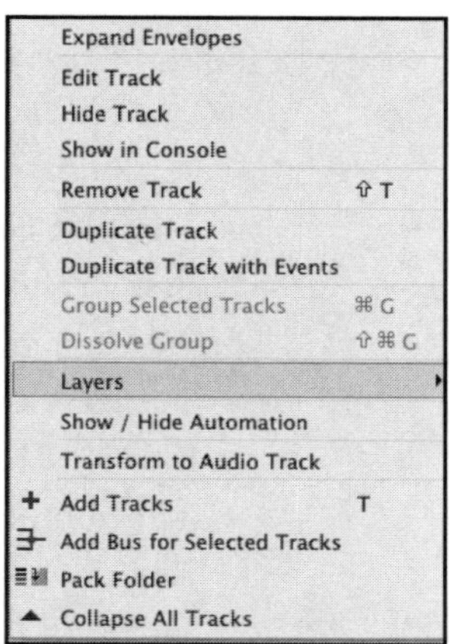

Fig. 5-10: The Instrument track contextual menu. Audio track contextual menus lack the Transform to Audio Track command, but are otherwise the same.

- **Expand Envelopes:** This command will be present only if the track in focus contains automation data. Choosing this command causes the list of automation parameters to drop down in the Track List and Track lanes for each parameter to be shown below the track in the Arrange view. If the Expand Envelopes command is checked in the contextual menu, choosing it will uncheck the command and hide the parameter list in the Track List and the parameter lanes in the Arrange view.
- **Expand Layers:** This command will be present only if the track in focus contains multiple layers. Choosing this command causes the list of layers to drop down in the Track List and Track lanes for each layer to be shown below the track in the Arrange view. Note that the currently active layer will not be shown in the Track List. If the Expand Layers command is checked in the contextual menu, choosing it will uncheck the command and hide the layers list in the Track List and the layer lanes in the Arrange view.
- **Edit Track:** Choosing this command opens the appropriate editor for the track in focus—that is, the Audio editor for an Audio track, the Music editor for an Instrument track.
- **Hide Track:** Choosing this command hides all selected tracks in the Arrange view and grays them out in the Track List. Note that to show hidden tracks you must click on their show/hide buttons in the Track List; the contextual menu does not provide a way to show hidden tracks.
- **Show in Console:** Choosing this command causes the Mix view to be displayed and the channel for the track in focus to be highlighted and expanded to show all panels (Inserts, Sends, Cue mix sends).
- **Remove Track:** Choosing this command deletes the selected track from the Song. When multiple tracks are selected, the command will be called Remove Selected Tracks and will delete all selected tracks from the Song.

- **Duplicate Track:** Choosing this command creates a track with the same settings and name as the original (but with a number appended to the name to differentiate it), but no content (Parts or Events). This command is available only for Audio or Instrument tracks.
- **Duplicate Track with Events:** Choosing this command creates a track with the same content (Parts or Events), settings, and name as the original (but with a number appended to the name to differentiate it). This command is available only for Audio or Instrument tracks.
- **Group Selected Tracks:** Choosing this command creates a new group containing all of the selected tracks. This command is available only when multiple tracks are selected. For more information on groups, see the "Track Groups and Folder Tracks" section later in this chapter.
- **Dissolve Group:** Choosing this command deletes the group indicated in the command name. This command is available only when the track that has been right-clicked is part of a group. For more information on groups, see the "Track Groups and Folder Tracks" section later in this chapter.
- **Layers:** Choosing this command causes a submenu of layer functions to drop down. The submenu contains commands to Add a new layer, or Duplicate, Rename, or Remove the currently active layer. Remember that the currently active layer is not shown in the Track List, so if you choose Rename, for example, the name you see in the Rename dialog box will not be visible in the Track List, nor will the new name you give it. This command is available only for Audio or Instrument tracks.
- **Show/Hide Automation:** Choosing this command toggles the track header in the Arrange view between the standard display and the automation display. It has no effect on the Track List or any lanes being displayed. This command is not available for automation tracks.
- **Transform to Audio Track/Instrument Track/Rendered Audio/Real-time Audio:** This command invokes the freeze function appropriate to the type of track that is in focus. For more on freezing (transforming) Instrument tracks, see chapter 4, "Virtual Instruments and MIDI." For more on freezing Audio tracks, see the chapter "Mixing,"in *Power Tools for Studio One 2*, vol. 2.
- **Add Tracks:** Choosing this command brings up the standard Add Tracks dialog box. This action is entirely independent of and has no effect on selected tracks.
- **Add Bus for Selected Tracks:** Choosing this command when one or more Audio tracks are selected creates a new bus and reassigns the outputs of the channels corresponding to the selected tracks to the new bus. In some cases, this also works with selected Instrument tracks.
- **Pack Folder:** Choosing this command creates a new Folder track and places all selected tracks in it.

- **Collapse All Tracks:** Choosing this command causes all tracks in the Track List with dropped-down automation (Envelopes) or layer lists to collapse. This also means that all lanes in the Arrange view become hidden.

Zooming

Studio One 2 has a variety of ways to zoom the display in, out, or to some specific view. Most of the zoom features listed below are also available in the submenu under View > Zoom.

The range of the zoom functions goes out as far as the time range of the Song as defined in Preferences > Song Setup > General (that is, from Song Start to Song End), and in all the way to the sample level.

TIP: The Arrange and Edit views have separate zoom levels. Generally, the same commands apply to both, and the view affected will be the one that is active at the time. If you are not sure which view is currently active, simply click in a view to activate it before executing zoom commands.

Zoom In	E
Zoom Out	W
Zoom In Vertical	⇧E
Zoom Out Vertical	⇧W
Zoom to Loop	⇧L
Zoom to Selection	⇧S
Zoom to Selection Horizontally	⌥S
Zoom Full	⌥Z
Undo Zoom	⌥W
Redo Zoom	⌥E
Toggle Zoom	Z
Store Zoom State	⇧Z
Restore Zoom State	

Fig. 5-11: The View>Zoom submenu offers a host of options for zooming in and out.

ZOOMING IN AND OUT

HORIZONTAL VIEW ZOOMING

To zoom in or out horizontally in the Arrange or Edit views, use any of the following methods:

- Drag the horizontal zoom bar in the lower right corner of the view until the desired zoom level is reached.
- Press the W key to zoom in and the E key to zoom out.
- Place the cursor over the timeline ruler and drag down or up to zoom in or out.
- Place the cursor over the timeline ruler and use the scroll wheel on your mouse to zoom in or out.
- Choose View > Zoom > Zoom In or View > Zoom > Zoom Out from the main menu bar.

Fig. 5-12: The Horizontal Zoom slider provides an alternative to key shortcuts for zooming.

VERTICAL TRACK WAVEFORM DISPLAY ZOOMING

The size of the waveform in an Audio track can be zoomed independently of the track size itself in either of these ways:

- Place the cursor over the Data Zoom button in the lower right corner of the Arrange or Edit view and drag the pop-up fader up to increase the waveform size, or down to decrease it.

- To size the waveform in the Audio editor, click in the amplitude scale on the left side of the editor display and drag left or right to make the waveform smaller or larger, respectively.

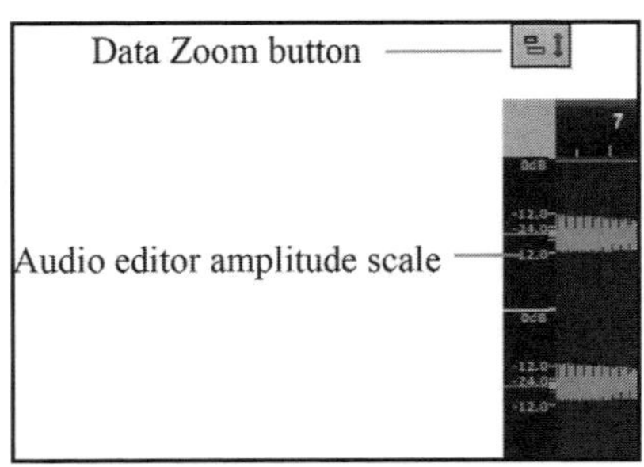

Fig. 5-13: The Data Zoom button changes the size of the waveform display, but does not change vertical track size.

VERTICAL TRACK SIZE ZOOMING

The vertical size of the tracks in the Arrange view can be varied continuously or by steps using one of these methods:

- Click in the Track Size field and choose a size from the drop-down menu that appears.
- Press Shift + E to make the tracks larger or Shift + W to make them smaller. The steps used by this method to change track size are smaller than those in the menu selections mentioned in the previous step.
- Click on the icon to the right of the Track Size field and drag up or down to increase or decrease the track size continuously.
- Place the cursor over the timeline ruler, hold down the Cmd key, and use the scroll wheel on your mouse to increase or decrease the track size continuously.
- Choose View > Zoom > Zoom In Vertical or View > Zoom > Zoom Out Vertical from the main menu bar.

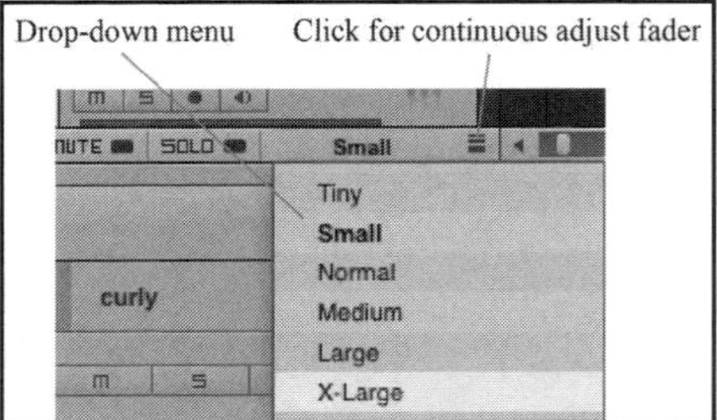

Fig. 5-14: The Track Size controls grow or shrink the vertical size of the track. While the waveform size will grow or shrink with the track size, the proportion of the waveform within the track is unchanged.

The Audio editor allows zooming and a choice between calibrating the vertical scale in decibels or a percentage.

- To zoom in or out vertically in the Audio editor, click in the vertical scale and drag right or left to zoom.
- To change the units in which the vertical scale is calibrated, right-click (Ctrl-click on Mac) in the vertical scale and choose dB or Percent from the contextual menu that drops down.

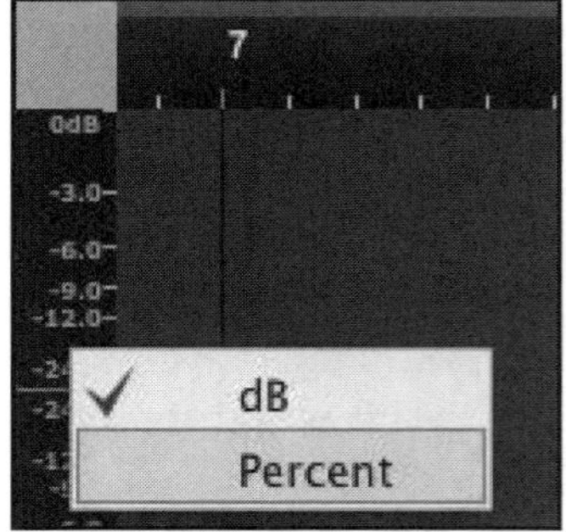

Fig. 5-15: The vertical scale in the Audio Editor can be set to read either in dB or as a percentage of full-scale.

ZOOMING TO A TARGET

Often, it is desirable to jump to a zoom level convenient to the material on which you are working. Studio One 2 provides several excellent tools for this.

- **Zoom to Loop:** If you have defined a loop, you can zoom the Arrange view horizontally to fit the loop by pressing Shift + L or choosing View > Zoom > Zoom to Loop from the main menu bar.
- **Zoom to Selection:** Making a selection and zooming to it is a common editing technique. Pressing Shift + S or choosing View > Zoom > Zoom to Selection from the main menu bar will zoom to the selection both horizontally (the time range) and vertically (the tracks on which a selection has been made). Vertical zooming will include all tracks that have selections, whether or not they are contiguous. For example, if you make a selection on tracks 1 and 2 and then add material from track 4 to that selection, zooming to the selection will show tracks 1 through 4, even though there is no selection on track 3, in order to include all of the tracks that do have selections.
- **Zoom to Selection Horizontally:** Pressing Option + S (Alt + S in Windows) or choosing View > Zoom > Zoom to Selection Horizontally from the main menu bar zooms to the selected time range, but will not zoom vertically—that is, it will not change the number of tracks being viewed.
- **Zoom Full:** Pressing Option + Z (Alt + Z in Windows) or choosing View > Zoom > Zoom Full from the main menu bar will zoom all the way out horizontally—that is, to the time range of the Song. (Of course, if you are zoomed out further than all the time used in the Song, Zoom Full will zoom in.) Since it does not zoom vertically, it is possible for there to appear to be "blank space" at the beginning or the end of the Song when there is material on tracks that are unseen. For instance, if you are zoomed in vertically so that you are seeing only tracks 1 and 2, but there is material on track 3 that extends beyond the material on tracks 1 and 2, it will look as though there is empty space at the end of the Song. Scrolling down will show that the zoom includes the time used on track 3.
- **Fit Timeline to Contents:** Right-click (or Ctrl-click on Mac) in the Arrange view timeline and choose Fit Timeline to Contents from the contextual menu that drops down to zoom horizontally until the end time of the last item in the Song fits onscreen. Note that this may be less than the entire time contained in the Song, which is used by Zoom Full.

TOGGLING BETWEEN ZOOM LEVELS

It is common when editing to jump back and forth between two zoom levels, usually one zoomed fairly far out and one zoomed in more closely. Studio One 2 provides two ways to do this.

TIP: These commands operate independently for the Arrange and Edit views. You can store a zoom level in the Arrange view and toggle between that and the current zoom level, then activate the Edit view, store a zoom level, and toggle back and forth between the stored zoom and the current one in that view. When you activate the Arrange view again, it will still toggle between the zoom level stored in it and the last zoom level used in that view. This makes it easy to do microlevel work in the Edit view and macrolevel work in the Arrange view, yet still have zoom toggling available at both levels.

UNDO/REDO ZOOM

When you zoom, Studio One 2 remembers the last zoom setting. You can flip back and forth between these two with the Undo Zoom and Redo Zoom commands. For example, if you wanted to go back and forth between being zoomed fairly far in to do detail work and seeing the big picture, you could zoom in until you can see the detail you need and then Zoom Full. Now, Undo Zoom will return you to your detailed view, and Redo Zoom will take you back out to the entire Song. Flipping back and forth between the two is easy, especially since the shortcuts are modified versions of the standard zoom in/out key shortcuts.

- Press Option + W (Alt + W in Windows) or choose View > Zoom > Undo Zoom from the main menu bar to Undo Zoom (return to the previous zoom level).
- Press Option + E (Alt + E in Windows) or choose View > Zoom > Redo Zoom from the main menu bar to Redo Zoom (return to the current zoom level).

TOGGLE ZOOM

Toggle Zoom is similar to Undo/Redo Zoom, but slightly more configurable. Instead of jumping to the previous zoom level, as Undo Zoom does, Toggle Zoom jumps to a stored zoom level. Executing Toggle Zoom again jumps back to the zoom level you had before jumping to the stored level.

Many editing tasks are facilitated by jumping between a zoomed in and zoomed out view, but the degree to which one needs to zoom in varies with the type of edit. For instance, if you are comping vocals, you may need to be zoomed in far enough to select individual words; but if you are flying rhythm or background vocal parts around in an arrangement, you may need to zoom in only as far as a section of the song, such as a whole verse.

This suggests that one good way to use Toggle Zoom is to set up a zoomed-in view for detail work just as you are starting a particular edit or series of similar edits. When you move on to a different sort of edit, store a new zoomed-in view and you're instantly ready to keep rocking. To use Toggle Zoom, do the following:

1. Use the zoom commands or tools to find the zoom level you wish to store.
2. Press Shift + Z or choose View > Zoom > Store Zoom State from the main menu bar to store the zoom state.

3. Use the zoom commands or tools to find the alternate zoom level for your edit.
4. Press Z or choose View > Zoom > Toggle Zoom from the main menu bar for Toggle Zoom to flip to the stored zoom level. Press Z again to toggle back.

RESTORE ZOOM STATE

Restore Zoom State returns you to the zoom level and location that were current when you opened the Song (for Arrange view) or editor (for Edit view).

- To restore the original zoom state of the Arrange view or Edit view, be sure that the view you wish to restore is the currently active view and choose View > Zoom > Restore Zoom State from the main menu bar.

Inspectors

The Arrange and Edit views have inspectors that show important information about the content in the tracks. The inspectors are not simply for display, however; they also provide access to some very powerful features of Studio One 2.

ARRANGE VIEW INSPECTORS

To reveal the Inspector panel, do the following:

- Click on the i button to the left of the timeline just above the track headers, or press the F4 key to reveal the Inspector panel. The button will turn blue and the Inspector panel will appear.

There are three panes in the Inspector panel, but often only one is fully visible.

1. To adjust visibility of the Inspector panes, move the cursor over the divider between two panes. The cursor will change to a double-headed arrow.
2. Drag the arrow up to reveal the lower pane, or down to reveal more of the upper pane.

The upper pane shows the inspector for a selected track, the middle pane is the Channel Strip, and the lower pane shows the Inspector for a selected Audio Event or Instrument Part on a track.

- To show the Inspector pane for a track, click in the track's header to select it. When a track is selected, its header will be a light gray color.
- To show the Inspector pane for an Audio Event or Instrument Part in a track, click on the Event or Part. The upper pane will show the inspector for the track, while the lower pane will show the inspector for the selected Event or Part.
- If an Event or Part is selected and then the header for a different track is clicked to select it, the upper pane will show the inspector for the track while the lower pane will show the inspector for the selected Event or Part.

AUDIO TRACK INSPECTOR

The Audio Track inspector is divided into three sections.

The top section contains a number of features important to editing.

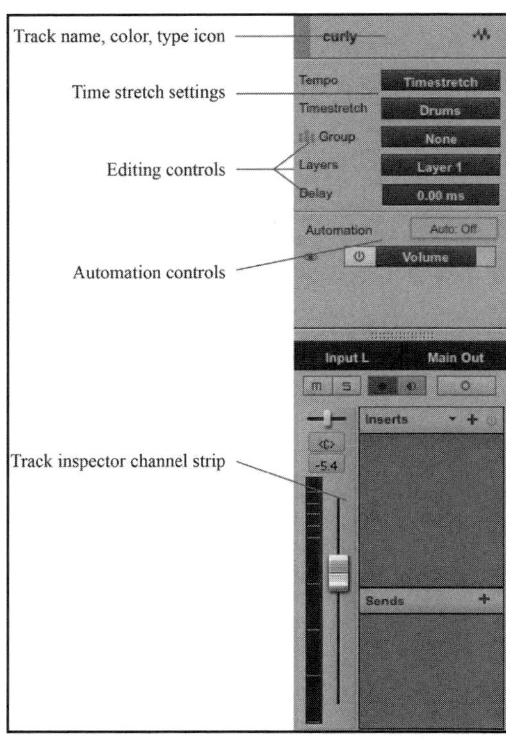

Fig. 5-16: The Audio Track inspector pane.

- **Tempo:** Rather than actually dealing with tempo, the drop-down menu in this field selects the time-stretch mode that will be used for the track. However, a tempo must be set for an audio file before time-stretching can be performed on it. More information on this is in chapter 6, "Advanced Editing."
- **Timestretch:** This field describes the nature of the material in the track for time-stretching purposes. The time-stretching algorithm is optimized for the type of material based on this setting. You can find more information on this in chapter 6, "Advanced Editing."
- **Edit Group:** If any edit groups have been created, they will appear in a drop-down menu in this field and can be selected to add the track to a group, change the track's group, or remove it from all groups. More information about this is in the section "Track Groups and Folder Tracks," below.

Fig. 5-17: The Timestretch menu lets you select the time-stretching algorithm that is most appropriate for the material on the track.

- **Layers:** The drop-down menu in this field manages layers on the track. For more information on this feature, see the "Using Layers" section in chapter 3, "Go! Recording with Studio One 2." More information on techniques using layers can be found in chapter 6, "Advanced Editing."
- **Delay:** Each track can have up to 100 ms of fixed delay time added to it by entering a value in this field. Probably more useful, however, is the fact that negative values of up to –100 ms can be entered in this field to compensate for latency that already exists

on the track. This might be used to compensate for lateness in a performance that was recorded with latency in the monitoring, or it might be to align in time multiple microphones that were used on a source.

The middle section controls the display of automation information.

- **Automation Mode:** When an automatable parameter is selected in the Show field, this field contains a drop-down menu with automation mode choices. More information about automation modes is found in the chapter "Automation," in *Power Tools for Studio One 2*, vol. 2.
- **Show:** The drop-down menu in this field selects the data that will be displayed in the track. The default setting is Events, but Volume and Pan are always available choices in the menu. The contents of the menu can be managed using the Add/Remove command at the bottom of the menu. More information about automation parameters is found in the chapter "Automation," in *Power Tools for Studio One 2*, vol. 2.

Fig. 5-18: The Track inspector Automation Show menu allows you to select any parameter that has been automated on the track. Selecting a parameter from this menu switches the track to Automation mode and shows the selected parameter.

The bottom section is the channel strip described in the next section.

TRACK INSPECTOR CHANNEL STRIP

The Track Inspector channel strip makes it easy to modify mix parameters for the mixer channel corresponding to the currently selected track, even when the Mix view is not visible, and regardless of whether the track or its corresponding channel was selected.

As part of the Track inspector, the channel strip is visible only when the inspector itself is visible. The facilities of the channel strip exactly duplicate those of the mixer channel strip, although the appearance is slightly different. The facilities are listed below, along with very brief descriptions of their functions. For

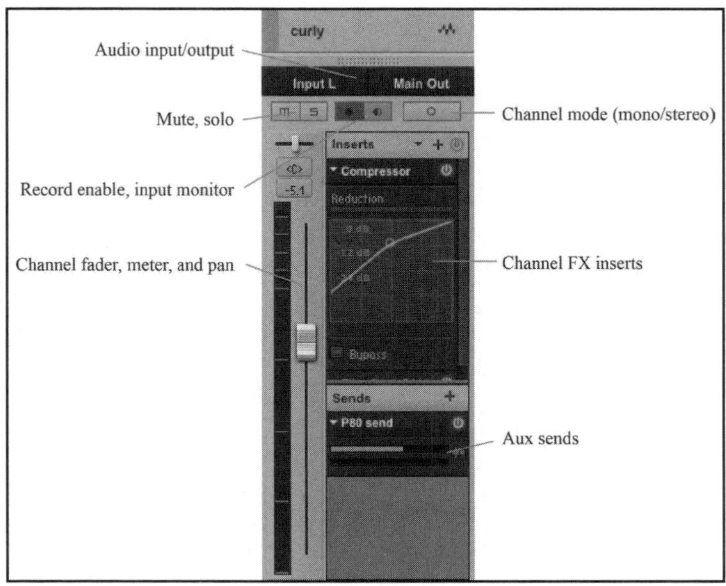

Fig. 5-19: The Track inspector channel strip, shown here for an Audio track.

more information on channel strip facilities, see the chapter "Mixing," in *Power Tools for Studio One 2*, vol. 2.

- **Fader:** Sets channel level. The fader value is displayed just above the fader.
- **Mute:** Mutes channel output.
- **Solo:** Solos channel.
- **Inserts:** Allows adding and configuring plug-ins used directly in the signal path.
- **Sends:** Allows the channel to be assigned to aux sends and effects sidechains.
- **Pan:** Sets channel left/right panning.
- **Level Meter:** Displays channel signal level.
- **Channel Mode (mono/stereo) button:** Toggles channel between mono and stereo playback.
- **Record Enable button:** Arms track for recording.
- **Input Monitor button:** Selects track to monitor input instead of track playback.

AUDIO EVENT INSPECTOR

The Audio Event inspector is tucked at the bottom of the Inspector pane; in fact, it often is collapsed and not visible upon opening the Edit view.

- To make the Audio Event inspector visible, move the cursor over the pane divider until it turns into a double-headed arrow with a line in between, and then drag upward until the Audio Event inspector can be seen.

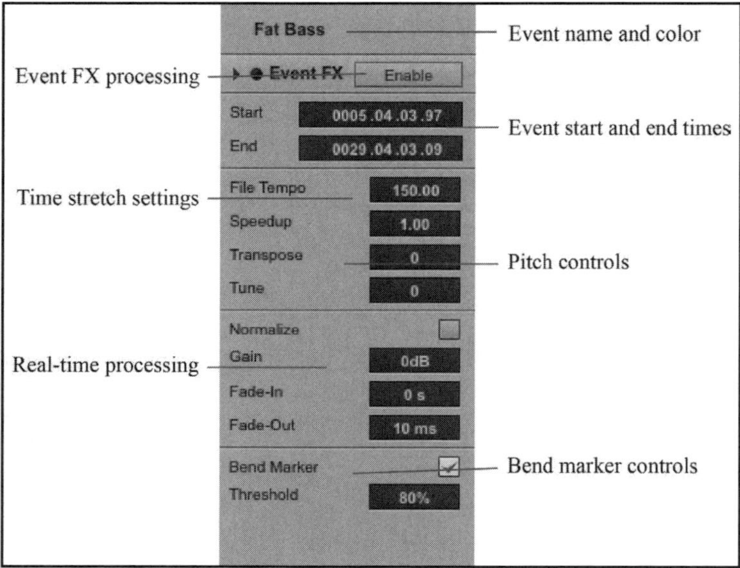

Fig. 5-20: The Audio Event inspector.

Once visible, at least one Event must be selected before the Audio Event inspector displays any information. If multiple Events are selected, the information shown will be for the Event in focus (the last one selected). In this case, some features will affect all selected Events, while others impact only the Event currently in focus.

One of Studio One 2's most powerful features is hidden in the Audio Event inspector, namely Event FX. Event FX facilities are discussed in the chapter "Mixing," in *Power Tools for Studio One 2*, vol. 2.

The Audio Event inspector is divided into six areas, counting Event FX. At the top of the Audio Event inspector is the name of the Event in focus, whose information is being displayed.

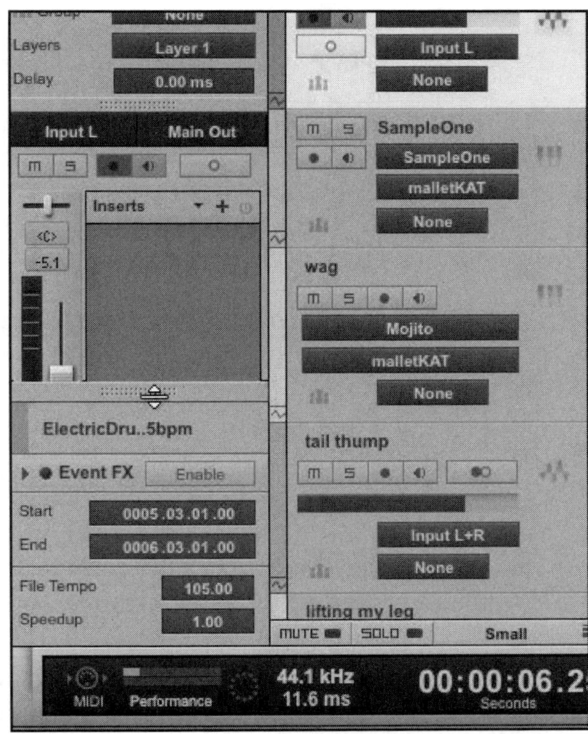

Fig. 5-21: The Audio Event inspector may need to be exposed by dragging up on the divider at its top before it can be seen and used.

Color-Coding Events

To the right of the Event name is the Event color rectangle. The default color for the Event is that of the track on which it resides, but it is possible to assign a separate color to each Event individually. There are numerous uses for color-coding Events. For instance, you might break a musical performance into Events of different passages and then color-code them according to the quality of the performance of each passage: green is excellent, brown is fair, red is poor.

- To color-code an Event from the Audio Event inspector, click on the color bar to the left of the Event name and choose a color from the drop-down color palette that appears.

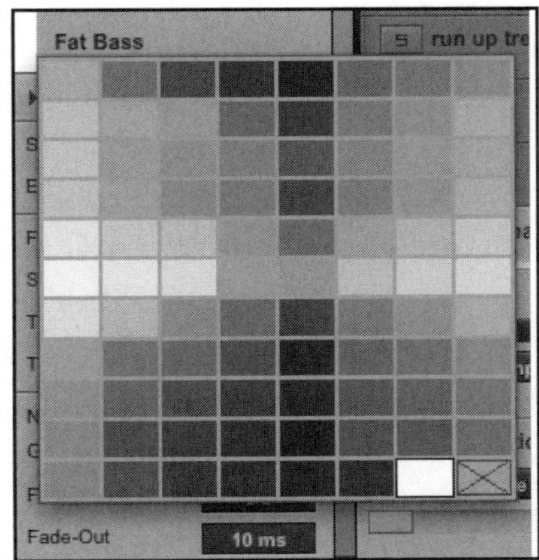

Fig. 5-22: Each Audio Event can be assigned its own color, which can be handy for marking Events that need work, for example.

Event Start and End Times

These parameters affect only the Event in focus, even when multiple Events are selected.

- **Start:** Shows the start time for the Event. To edit the value, click in the portion of the value you wish to edit to make it active and use any of these three methods: drag up or down, use the Up and Down Arrows to increment or decrement the value, or simply type in the desired value.

- **End:** Shows the end time for the Event. To edit the value, click in the portion of the value you wish to edit to make it active and use any of these three methods: drag up or down, use the Up and Down Arrows to increment or decrement the value, or simply type in the desired value.

TIP: When the start time of an Event is changed, the end time is changed by the same amount, maintaining the duration of the Event. However, when the end time of an Event is changed, the start time stays the same, so the duration of the Event is modified.

Nondestructive Processing

The lower three areas of the Audio Event inspector set a number of nondestructive processing options. The fact that these options are nondestructive is very powerful, because it means they can be undone or changed at any time. Any of these features can be applied to any number of selected Events at once, regardless of whether they are on the same track or in the same edit group.

- **File Tempo:** Audio file tempo is used in conjunction with time-stretching. If the selected Event is an imported loop, the tempo may well already be encoded in the file, in which case the tempo value will appear in this field. If the tempo is known but not encoded, click in the field, enter the tempo value, and press the Enter key. More about audio file tempos can be found in the Editing Audio section of chapter 6, "Advanced Editing."
- **Speedup:** This is a time-stretching function that does not use tempo. More about time-stretching can be found in the section "Editing Audio" in chapter 6, "Advanced Editing."
- **Transpose:** This provides real-time, nondestructive transposing of audio in semitones without changing the duration. Enter a value between –24 and +24 (+/–2 octaves) in the field to transpose the audio in the Event. When one or more Events are transposed using this feature, a small symbol appears in the lower left corner of the Event(s) to indicate that it has been transposed.
- **Tune:** Think of Transpose as coarse pitch change and Tune as fine pitch change in cents (hundredths of a semitone). Enter a value between –100 and +100 (+/–1 semitone) in the field to tune the audio in the Event. When one or more Events are tuned using this feature, a small symbol appears in the lower left corner of the Event(s) to indicate that it has been tuned.
- **Normalize:** This checkbox provides real-time, nondestructive peak normalization to 100%. That means that the highest level in the Event is amplified to full scale and all other audio is scaled by the same factor. This just makes the Event level as high as it can be without clipping. Checking the box normalizes the selected Event. The waveform display in the Event(s) will reflect the normalization.

- **Gain:** This field is linked to an Event's gain handle in the Arrange view; when either control is used, the other reflects the change. Both the Gain field and the gain handle can change the gain of an Event over a range of +24 dB to –40 dB. The Gain field can be used either by moving the cursor over the field and dragging up or down to the desired gain, or clicking in the field and simply typing in the desired gain amount.

TIP: In terms of signal flow, the Gain field follows the Normalize checkbox, so if Normalize is checked, the Gain field adds to or subtracts from the normalized Event. Thus, there are few reasons to use both features together, since adding gain to an Event after checking the Normalize box will produce clipping, and subtracting gain defeats the purpose of normalizing. Also note that the Gain field shows only the Event volume, not the combined level of the Event volume and any automation that may be in the track.

- **Fade-In:** Adds a fade-in of the specified duration to all selected Events. This provides an easy way of adding fades to all of your edits ("top and tail," as it is called) by selecting all the Events in a track—or even in the entire Song—and editing the Fade-In and Fade-Out fields. The Fade-In field can be used either by moving the cursor over the field and dragging up or down to the desired fade duration, or clicking in the field and simply typing in the desired fade duration. The shortest duration available is 1 ms, but there is no practical limit to the longest fade you can specify. This field can display durations in either seconds or milliseconds, so be careful to pay attention to both the units and the value.
- **Fade-Out:** Adds a fade-out of the specified value to all selected Events. The Fade-Out field can be used either by moving the cursor over the field and dragging up or down to the desired fade duration, or clicking in the field and simply typing in the desired fade duration. The shortest duration available is 1 ms, but there is no practical limit to the longest fade you can specify. This field can display durations in either seconds or milliseconds, so be careful to pay attention to both the units and the value.
- **Bend Marker box:** This box duplicates and is linked to the Show/Hide Bend Marker box in the Audio Bend panel. Changing this box in either place also changes it in the other. For more information on using this box and Audio Bend markers, see the Audio Bend Panel section of chapter 6, "Advanced Editing."
- **Threshold field:** This box duplicates and is linked to the Threshold bar in the Audio Bend panel. Changing value in either place also changes it in the other. The Threshold field can be used either by moving the cursor over the field and dragging up or down to the desired threshold value, or clicking in the field and simply typing in the desired percentage value. For more information on using this field and Audio Bend markers, see the "Audio Bend Panel" section of chapter 6, "Advanced Editing."

INSTRUMENT TRACK INSPECTOR

The Instrument Track inspector is divided into four sections.

Since Instrument tracks play performance data and not audio, the top section of the Instrument Track inspector does not correspond to any mixer channel features in the way that the Audio Track inspector does. Controls in the inspector affect only the data in the Instrument track. However, the channel strip at the bottom of the inspector accesses the mixer channel through which the VI's audio output is passing.

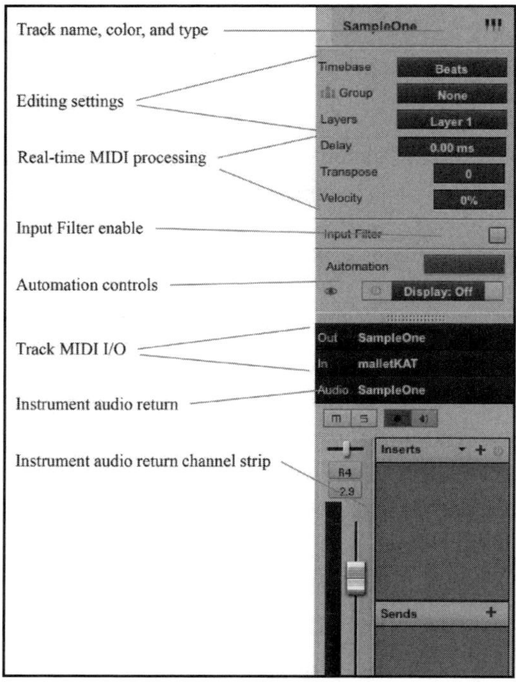

Fig. 5-23: The Instrument Track inspector.

The name of the selected track appears at the top of the pane.

- **Instrument Editor button:** If the track is playing a virtual instrument, clicking on the keyboard icon to the right of the instrument name at the top of the pane opens the instrument for editing.

Modify and Manipulate

The middle section contains a number of settings for modifying and manipulating data in the track.

- **Timebase:** This field determines whether notes in the track move in time when the tempo is changed. When set to Beats, notes are referenced to bars and beats locations. Thus notes move in time when tempo is changed, in order to maintain their locations relative to bars and beats.
- When set to Seconds, notes are referenced to time, not musical structure, so changing the tempo does not move notes.
- **Edit Group:** If any edit groups have been created, they will appear in a drop-down menu in this field and can be selected to add the track to a group, change the track's group, or remove it from all groups. More information about this is in the section "Track Groups and Folder Tracks," below.
- **Layers:** The drop-down menu in this field manages layers on the track. For more information on this feature, see the section "Using Layers" in chapter 3, "Go! Recording with Studio One 2." More information on techniques using layers can be found in chapter 6, "Advanced Editing."

- **Delay:** Each track can have up to 100 ms of fixed delay time added to it or subtracted from it by entering a value in this field. Negative values can be used to compensate for latency that already exists on the track. This might be due to slow response on the part of an instrument, or it may be to compensate for a slow attack on the instrument sound being used for the track. In the latter case, an alternate means of compensating for a slow attack is to slide the parts on the track earlier.
- **Track Transpose:** This field provides real-time, nondestructive transposition of the note data on the track. It does NOT transpose audio—thus, if there are several sounds mapped across the keyboard on an instrument, transposing the data might result in your hearing a different sound rather than a transposed version of the sound you were hearing.
- **Velocity:** This field provides real-time, nondestructive scaling of the note velocity data on the track.

Program Change

When an Instrument track is assigned to play an external device, you will find a Program section in the Track inspector located just above the Input Filter section. This section allows you to manually send a MIDI Program Change message to the External Device. Do the following to send a MIDI Program Change message to an external device:

1. Click in the Bank field and enter the desired bank number.
2. Click in the Prog field and enter the desired program number within the bank.
3. Press the Return key to confirm entry of the values, and the program change will be sent to the external device.

TIP: On some synthesizers, the first program in a bank is program number 1, while in others it is program number 0. It is very easy to determine which scheme a device uses: just send a program change and compare the program number on the device with the value in the Prog field.

Input Filter

Each track can be set to record only notes falling within specified pitch and velocity ranges.

- **To enable the Input Filter:** Check the Input Filter box in the Instrument Track inspector. The pitch and velocity filter fields will drop down.
- **To set the pitch range:** Click in the Lo Key or Hi Key field and type in the desired pitch value or play the pitch on a MIDI controller.
- **To set the velocity range:** Click in the Lo Vel or Hi Vel field and type in the desired velocity value or play a note on a MIDI controller.

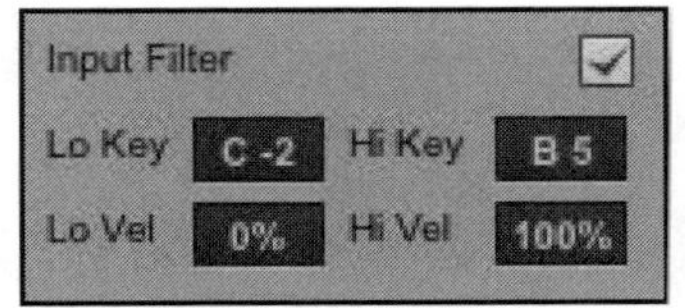

Fig. 5-24: The Input Filter area of the Instrument Track inspector lets you limit both the pitch and velocity ranges to which the track will respond.

Automation Editing

The automation editing features are available only for Instrument tracks playing virtual instruments. These parameters will not appear on Instrument tracks playing external devices.

- **Automation Mode:** When an automatable parameter is selected in the Show field, this field contains a drop-down menu with automation mode choices. More information about automation modes is found in the chapter "Automation," in *Power Tools for Studio One 2*, vol. 2.
- **Show:** The drop-down menu in this field selects the data that will be displayed in the track. The contents of the menu can be managed using the Add/Remove command at the bottom of the menu. More information about automation parameters is found in the chapter "Automation," in *Power Tools for Studio One 2*, vol. 2.

INSTRUMENT PART INSPECTOR

Below the Instrument Track inspector is the Instrument Part inspector. The four parameters in this pane affect only the selected Part in the current track.

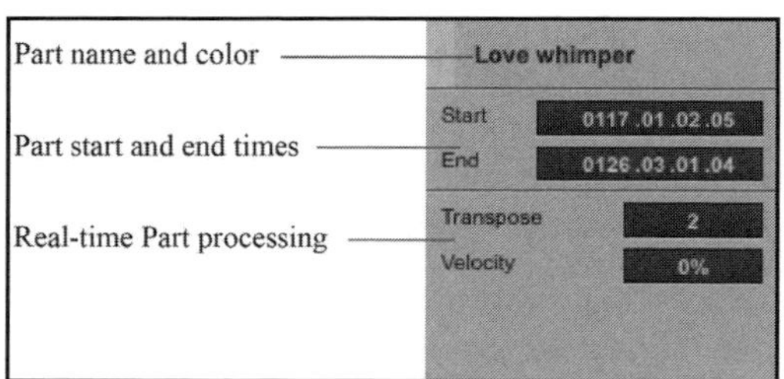

Fig. 5-25: The Instrument Part inspector.

- **Start:** Shows the start time for the selected Part in bars, beats, 1/16ths of a beat, and hundredths of a 1/16th. (For more explanation about this somewhat unusual format, see the section "It's About Time Base" in chapter 1, "On Your Mark.") Each portion of this value (bars, beats, subdivision, hundredths) is separately editable. To edit the value, click in the portion of the value you wish to edit to make it active, and use any of these three methods: drag up or down, use the Up and Down Arrows to increment or decrement the value, or simply type in the desired value.
- **End:** Shows the end time for the selected Part. To edit the value, click in the portion of the value you wish to edit to make it active and use any of these three methods: drag up or down, use the Up and Down Arrows to increment or decrement the value, or simply type in the desired value.

TIP: When the start time of a Part is changed, the end time is changed by the same amount, maintaining the duration of the Part. However, when the end time of a Part is changed, the start time stays the same, so the duration of the Part is modified.

- **Transpose:** This setting is a nondestructive, real-time transposition of the pitches in the selected Part only. It is heard, but not shown graphically—that is, the pitches displayed in Edit view are not changed. The transposition set here is added to the track transposition setting.

- **Velocity:** This setting imposes real-time velocity scaling of all notes in the Part over a range of +100/–101 percent. To figure the result of a negative percentage, subtract it from 100 percent and then scale the existing velocity value. So, when this setting is –45, existing velocity values are scaled by 100–45 = 55 percent.
- Velocity scaling from this parameter is heard, but not reflected graphically—that is, no change is made to the velocity of the notes as seen in the Edit view. To scale the velocity of notes in the Part, either drag up or down over the Velocity field to scale up or down, or double-click in the field and type in the desired percentage value. (Don't forget to type a minus sign to scale down!) Press Enter or Return to complete the entry.

FOLDER TRACK INSPECTOR

When a Folder track is selected and the Inspector pane is visible, the Folder Track inspector is displayed. The Folder Track inspector is very simple and almost exclusively for display. It shows the name of the folder, the track color, and a list of tracks in the folder. The only editable aspect is the track color.

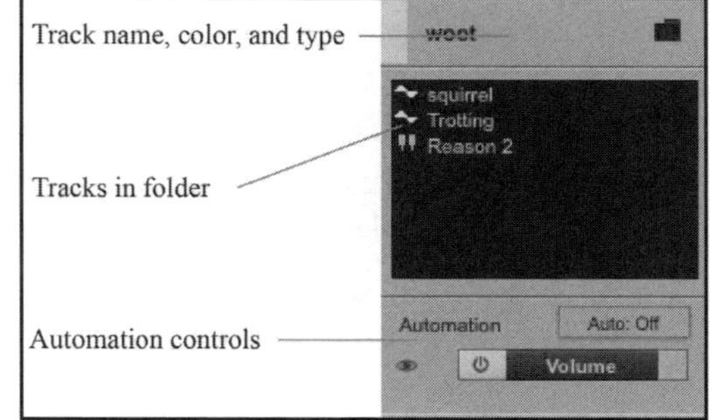

Fig. 5-26: The Folder Track inspector.

EDIT VIEW INSPECTORS

Studio One 2 has a dizzying array of inspectors, a number of which relate to the Audio and Music editors.

AUDIO PART INSPECTOR

Like an Instrument Part, which is a collection of individual notes that is treated as a single entity, an Audio Part is a collection of individual Events that is treated as a single entity. As with Instrument Parts, the Events in an Audio Part can be quantized and otherwise treated individually. For more information on Audio Parts, see the section "Editing Audio," in chapter 6, "Advanced Editing."

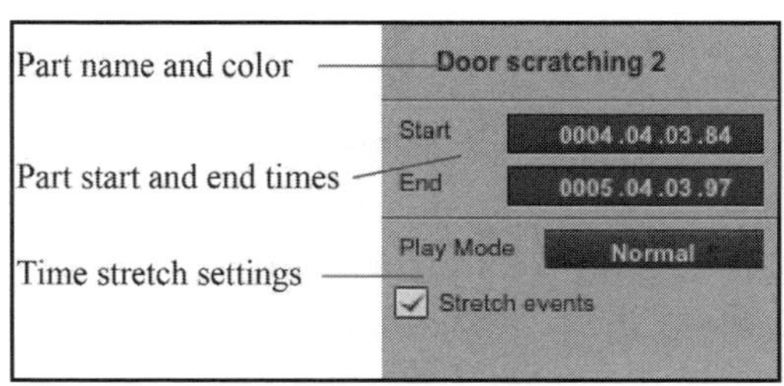

Fig. 5-27: The Audio Part inspector.

The Audio Part inspector contains only four settings. The first two, Start and End, are quite straightforward. The last two, Play Mode and Stretch Events, are used when quantizing, and they are discussed in chapter 6, "Advanced Editing."

- **Start:** Shows the start time for the selected Audio Part. To edit the value, click in the portion of the value you wish to edit to make it active, and use any of these three methods: drag up or down, use the Up and Down Arrows to increment or decrement the value, or simply type in the desired value.

- **End:** Shows the end time for the selected Audio Part. To edit the value, click in the portion of the value you wish to edit to make it active, and use any of these three methods: drag up or down, use the Up and Down Arrows to increment or decrement the value, or simply type in the desired value.

TIP: When the start time of an Audio Part is changed, the end time is changed by the same amount, maintaining the duration of the Part. However, when the end time of an Audio Part is changed, the start time stays the same, so the duration of the Part is modified.

MUSIC EDITOR INSPECTOR

The Music Editor inspector places a small set of features, most of which are also available elsewhere, in a convenient location to facilitate work in the Music editor.

- **Link Track Selection:** Located in the Edit view toolbar just above the track name in the Music Editor, this button, when selected, links the Arrange and Edit views so that they are always displaying the same track.
- **Track List Show/Hide:** Sitting next to the Link Track Selection button, the Track List Show/Hide reveals or hides the Music Editor Track List, which is separate from the Arrange view Track List and is used instead to control multitrack MIDI editing.

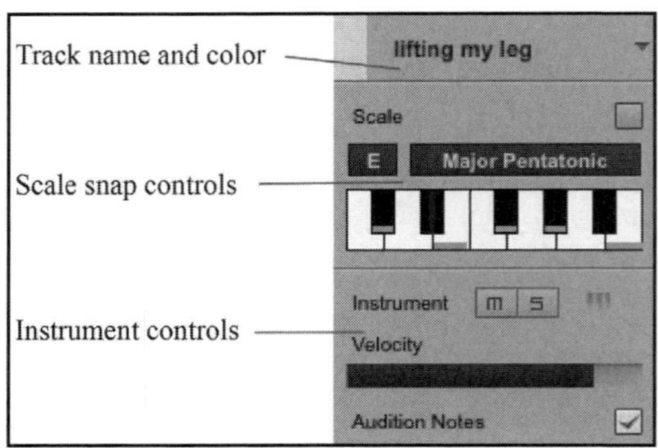

Fig. 5-28: The Music Editor inspector.

- **Track Name:** Double-click in this field to edit the name of the track.
- **Track Display select:** To change the track currently being displayed, click-and-hold on the arrow to the right of the track name and choose the desired track to view from the list that drops down.
- **Scale Snap area:** Pitch quantization can be used to make notes adhere to a specified scale. For more information on Scale Snap, see the section “Quantizing Pitches with Scale Snap,” in chapter 6, “Advanced Editing.”
- **Mute:** This button duplicates and is linked to the Mute buttons on the Instrument track in the Arrange view and the corresponding channel in the Mix view. Clicking on this button changes its state in all three places.
- **Solo:** This button duplicates and is linked to the Solo buttons on the Instrument track in the Arrange view and the corresponding channel in the Mix view. Clicking on this button changes its state in all three places.

- **Instrument Editor button:** This button opens the Instrument editor for the instrument to which the track's output is assigned.
- **Velocity bar:** To set the velocity value for all selected notes, click in the bar at the desired location or drag the bar to the desired value. When you drag, a pop-up tool tip shows the velocity value as a percentage of full scale, not a MIDI value of 0–127. If no notes are selected, the Velocity bar has no effect.
- **Audition Notes box:** When this box is checked, clicking on any note in the Music editor will cause the note to sound. Most people prefer to keep this box checked to make it easy to hear notes as they are edited.

NOTE INSPECTOR

- **Start:** Shows the start time for the selected note. To edit the value, click in the portion (bars, beats, beat subdivision, hundredths) of the value you wish to edit to make it active and use any of these three methods: drag up or down, use the Up and Down Arrows to increment or decrement the value, or simply type in the desired value.
- **End:** Shows the end time for the selected note. To edit the value, click in the portion of the value you wish to edit to make it active and use any of these three methods: drag up or down, use the Up and Down Arrows to increment or decrement the value, or simply type in the desired value.

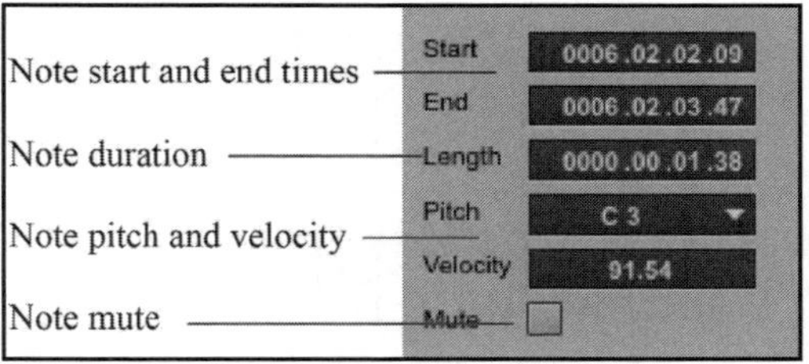

Fig. 5-29: The Note inspector.

TIP: When the start time of a note is changed, the end time is changed by the same amount, maintaining the duration of the note. However, when the end time of a note is changed, the start time stays the same, so the duration of the note is modified.

- **Length:** This field shows the duration of the selected note. Editing it produces the exact same result as editing the note's end time—it just provides a different way of viewing the information. If multiple notes are selected, they will all be set to the same duration when this field is edited. To edit the value, click in the portion of the value you wish to edit to make it active and use any of these three methods: drag up or down, use the Up and Down Arrows to increment or decrement the value, or simply type in the desired value.
- **Pitch:** Shows the pitch of the selected note. To transpose the pitch of the note, either click on the triangle next to the pitch name and choose the desired note from the drop-down menu that appears, or click on the pitch name to make it active and type in the desired pitch. If the pitches are named (as is often the case with drum instruments), you can type in the note's text name. If multiple notes are selected, the note in focus

(the last one selected) will be transposed as shown, while the other selected notes will not be moved to the same pitch, but transposed by the same interval applied to the note in focus. If a note at D3 is in focus and another at E3 is also selected, transposing to G3 will result in the other selected note being transposed to A3.

- **Velocity:** This field is identical to the Velocity bar in the Music Editor inspector: it sets the velocity value of all selected notes to the indicated value. To change the velocity value of all selected notes, either place the cursor over the field and drag up or down to the desired value, or click in the field to make it active and enter the desired value as a percentage of full scale.
- **Note Mute:** When checked, this box mutes all selected notes.

Pitches in the Music Editor

The Music editor can display notes keyboard-style (pitches with note names) or drum machine–style (pitches named for the instrument sounds they play). When displaying pitches drum machine–style, note pitches can be renamed as desired.

- To display notes keyboard-style, click on the button with the keyboard icon located just below the Arrow tool button in the Edit view. A keyboard will appear in the Pitch Audition area just below the button.

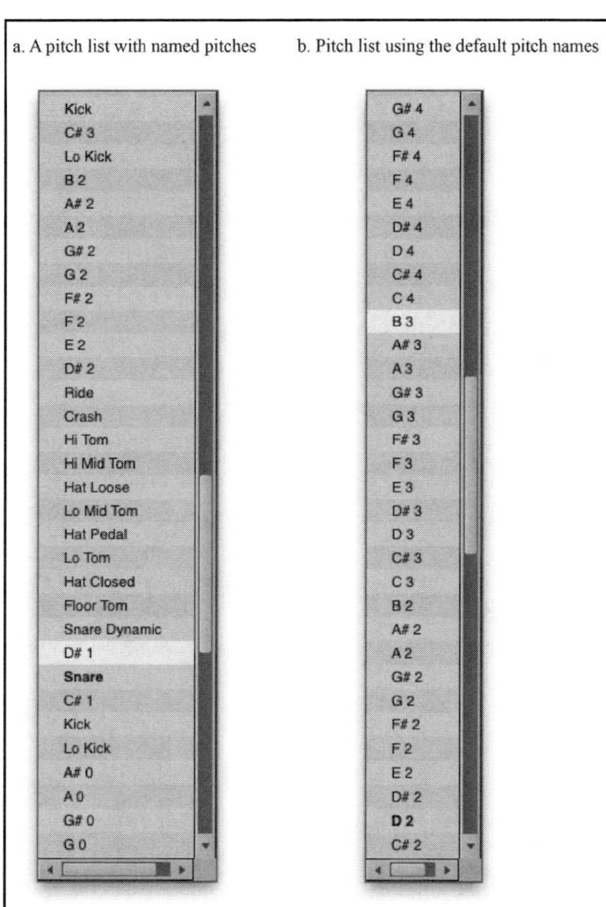

Fig. 5-30: If pitches have been named, the names will appear in the Note inspector Pitch drop-down menu. If not, then the menu will use the default: normal pitch/octave naming.

- To display notes in drum machine–style, click on the button with the drum icon located just below the Arrow tool button in the Edit view. The Pitch Audition area just below the button will show the text names for any pitches that have them.

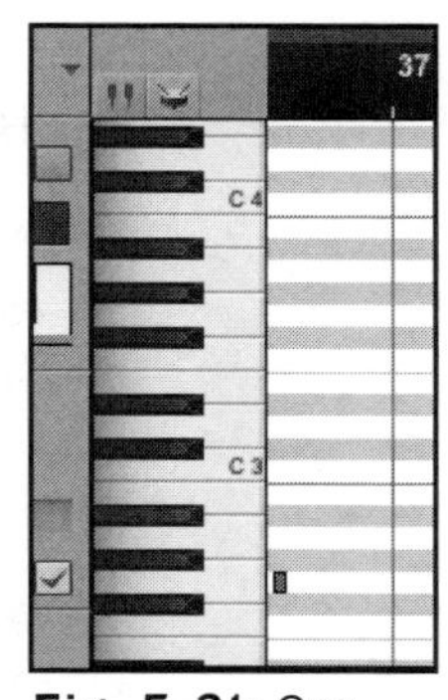

Fig. 5-31: One way to view pitches in the Music Editor is as notes on a keyboard. This is the view you will generally use for everything except drums.

EDITING PITCH NAMES FOR DRUM MACHINE–STYLE DISPLAY

When using drum machine–style display for pitches in the Music editor, you can create, store, and recall custom sets of pitch names.

- To edit pitch names when displaying notes drum machine–style, click on the Edit Pitch Names button (with the tuning fork icon) just below the Paint tool button to open the Edit Pitch Names dialog box. The dialog box shows three columns: Note Number, Pitch, and Name. Only the Name column is editable.
- To edit a pitch name, click in the Name column of the row for the pitch you wish to name and enter the desired name. When you have named all of the pitches as you want, click on the OK button to close the dialog box.
- To store a set of pitch names you have created, click on the Store Preset button, name the set as desired in the Store Preset dialog box that appears, and click on OK to store it. The set will be stored as a .pitchlist file at the location specified in Preferences > Options > Locations > User Data > User Data Location. Inside the specified location, the list will be stored as Presets > User Presets > Pitch Names > (custom set name).pitchlist. Once stored, the set is added to the Browse Presets menu.

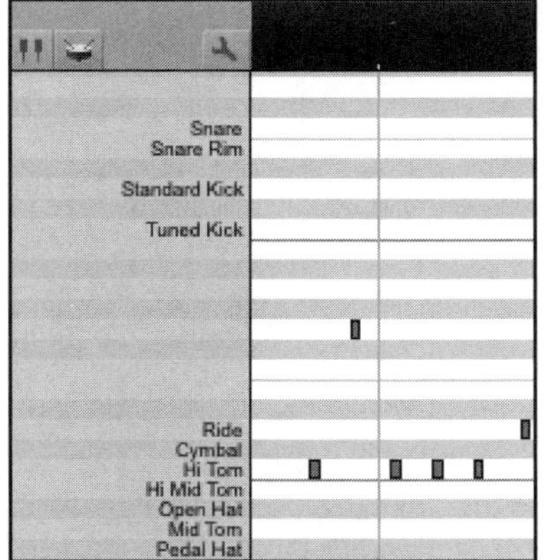

Fig. 5-32: Drums are usually mapped with one sound per note. Studio One 2 allows you to give each pitch the name of the sound it plays. Many drum presets will have these names already entered.

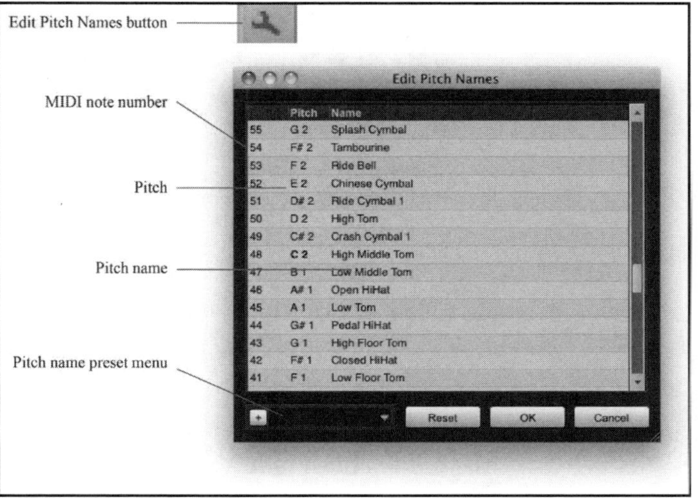

Fig. 5-33: The Edit Pitch Names dialog lets you apply whatever name you want to each pitch. Lists of pitch names can be saved and loaded.

- To recall a stored set of pitch list names, click in the Browse Presets field and choose the desired set of names from the menu that drops down.
- To restore the pitch names to the default set, click on the Reset button.

MULTITRACK MIDI EDITING

The Music editor can display and edit multiple Instrument tracks at the same time. The key to selection of Instrument tracks for display and/or editing is the Music Editor Track List.

The Music editor will display the data in any and all Instrument tracks that are set to Show in the Music Editor Track List. A track's data is editable as well as displayed if it is edit-enabled in the Music Editor Track List. Tracks also can be set to show for reference but not be edit-enabled. Notes default to the color set to the track, which makes it easier to understand the multitrack data as it is viewed.

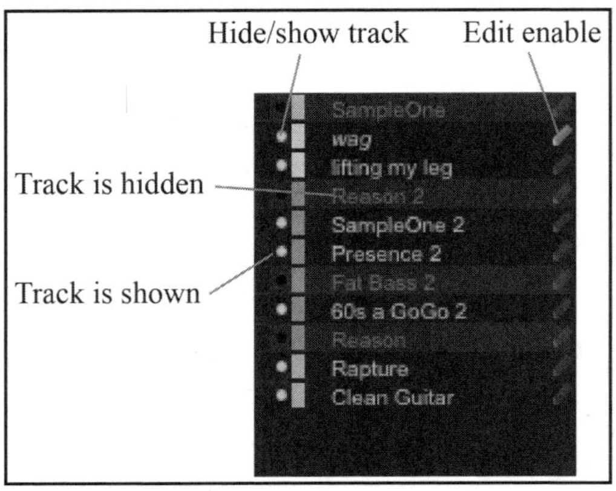

Fig. 5-34: The Music Editor has its own Track List, which controls which tracks are available for multitrack MIDI editing.

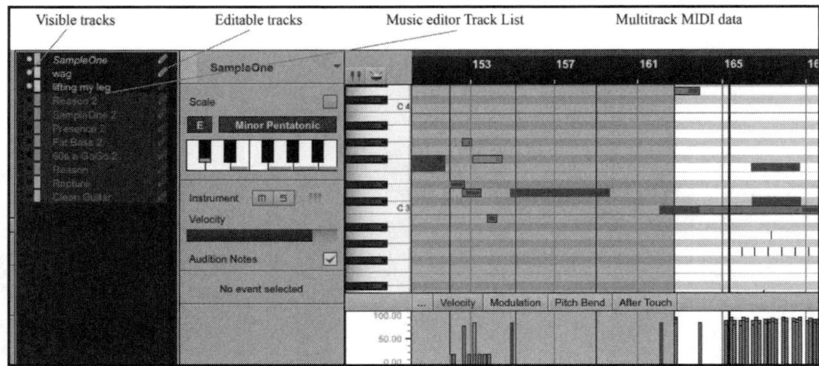

Fig. 5-35: The Music Editor allows you to view and edit several channels easily. Tracks can be made visible and edit-enabled in the Music Editor Track List.

- To hide or show a track in the Music editor, click on the button (which has a dot on it) on the left end of the Instrument line. When the dot is white, the track is visible. When a track is hidden, the dot turns black and the entire line is grayed out.
- To edit-enable a track in the Music editor, click on the X on the right end of the Instrument line in the Music Editor Track List, or Shift-click on a Part in that track in the Arrange view. When the X is white, the track is editable. When editing of a track is disabled, the X turns black. Hiding a track from view also disables editing of it.

THE DEVICE (PLUG-IN AND INSTRUMENT) EDITOR HEADER

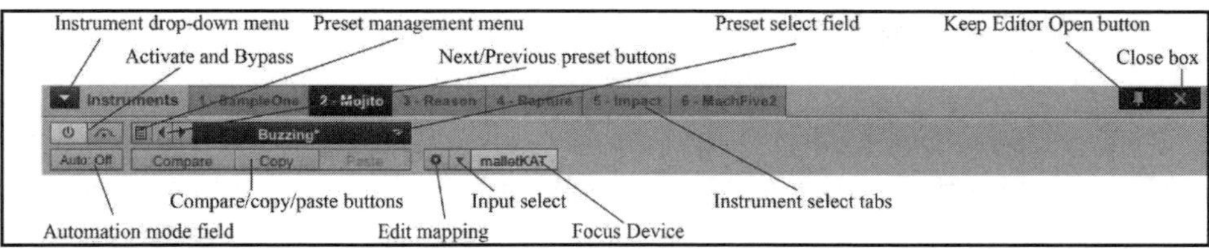

Fig. 5-36: The Instrument editor header is packed with controls for managing presets and control of VIs and plug-ins.

All plug-in and Instrument editor windows share the same header features. Studio One 2 refers to plug-ins and VIs collectively as "devices," a sensible terminology we will adopt here.

- **Keep Editor Open:** By default, only one Instrument editor window is open at a time; opening another closes the first. The same restriction applies to plug-in editor windows. (It is possible to have an Instrument and a plug-in editor window open simultaneously.) When the Keep Editor Open button is enabled in an editor window, that window will not be closed when another is opened. Editor windows cannot be put into the background in Studio One 2, so unless you have a lot of monitor space or don't mind shuffling windows around a lot, this feature should be used sparingly.
- **Close box:** Clicking in this box closes the editor window.

Opening an Editor for a Different Device

DEVICE SELECT TABS

- There is a tab for each instrument currently in use. To change the editor window to a different device, click on the tab for the device you wish to edit.

DEVICE SELECT MENU

The Device Select menu lets you change to editing a different device, but also contains a few utility functions.

- To drop down the Device Select menu, click on the arrow in the upper left corner of the editor. For Instrument editors, this menu will list all Instruments currently in the Song, while for plug-in editors it will list all plug-ins currently used on the channel in the Mix view.
- To change the editor window to a different device, choose it from the Device Select menu.

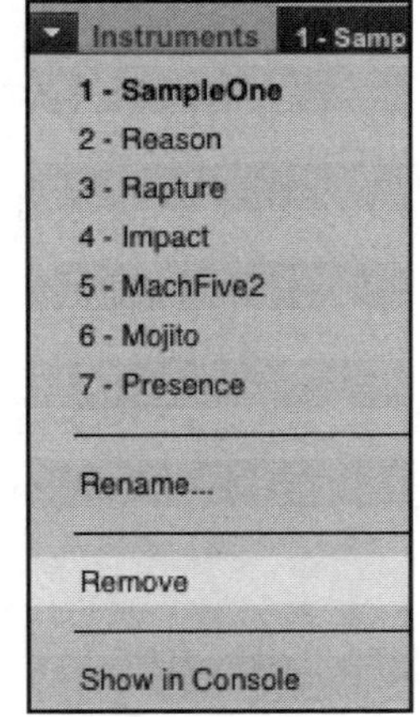

Fig. 5-37: The Instrument menu lets you select a device to edit or manage.

- **Rename:** Choosing this command allows editing of the name of the device currently being edited.
- **Remove:** Choosing this command removes the device currently being edited from the Song, but does not otherwise affect the Instrument track. Removing a device is not undoable!
- **Show in Console:** Choosing this command causes the Mix view to be displayed and the channel for the track in focus to be highlighted and expanded to show all panels (Inserts, Sends, Cue mix sends).

Activating and Bypassing Devices

The Device Editor header contains two adjacent buttons with similar functions, but they differ in a very important way. The Activate button actually controls loading and unloading of the device's computer code, while the Bypass button simply kicks the device in and out of the signal path. What's the difference to you? Plenty.

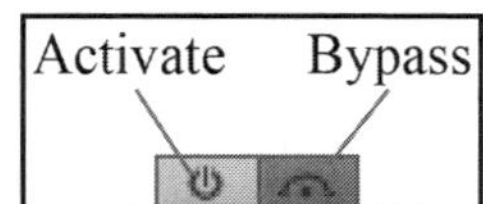

Fig. 5-38: The Activate and Bypass buttons in the Device editor header. The device shown here is activated, but bypassed.

If a device has been deactivated, the code must be reloaded when it is reactivated. This can take a second or two, causing an interruption in the audio. Also, the Activate button is not automatable. Use the Activate button when you won't need the device for a while and won't need it to come back immediately, but want to free up the resources it consumes.

The Bypass button, on the other hand, does not free up resources, but it allows the device to be freely put into or taken out of the signal path with no delay, either manually or under control of automation. Generally, you will want to use the Bypass button more often than the Activate button.

- To activate or deactivate a device, click on the Activate button. When the button is blue, the device is active.
- To bypass a device, click on the Bypass button. When the button is red, the device is bypassed.

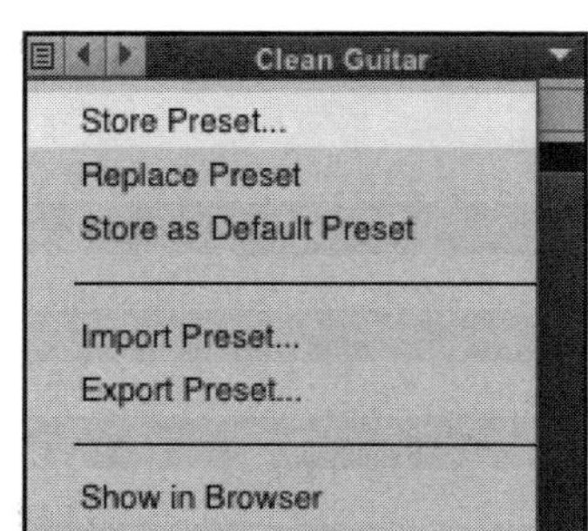

Fig. 5-39: The Preset Management menu lets you load, save, and find presets.

Preset Access

Most plug-ins and VIs offer a great many parameters. The only way to deal with this efficiently is to use presets. Studio One 2 recognizes the following preset formats:

- **.preset:** PreSonus's proprietary format, used by the native plug-ins and VIs included with Studio One 2.
- **.fxb:** A VST preset bank format created by Steinberg (authors and of the VST and VSTi plug-in formats), this type of file contains a set of presets that are loaded as a bank.

- **.fxp:** A VST preset format, also created by Steinberg, this type of file stores a single preset. This is useful for saving versions during development of a custom preset.
- **.aupreset:** A Mac-only format for Audio Units plug-ins.

The .aupreset format is widely (though not universally) used by Audio Units devices. The .fxb and .fxp formats, however, do not have quite the same penetration among VST devices.

Many devices (notably Waves plug-ins) use proprietary formats that Studio One 2 cannot recognize. Those presets will not show up in Studio One 2's preset access system, and you will need to save and load presets from the preset access system you will find in the device itself. Even when a third-party device uses a format that Studio One 2 recognizes, it is often prudent to use the device's preset access system to ensure the smoothest operation. One or two quick tests will usually reveal how well the device works with Studio One 2's preset access facilities.

LOADING PRESETS

You can load a preset using any of the following methods:

- To choose a preset from the Preset Select menu in the header, click in the Preset Select field and choose the desired preset from the menu that drops down. The Preset Select menu supports folder structures. Click on a folder in the menu to open it, then choose the desired preset from the submenu that drops down.
- To step backward through the presets in the Preset Select menu, press Option (Alt in Windows) + Page Up or click on the Previous Preset arrow.
- To step forward through the presets in the Preset Select menu, press Option (Alt in Windows) + Page Down or click on the Next Preset arrow.
- To import a preset to the Preset Select menu, click on the menu icon in the header to drop down the Preset Management menu, choose Import Preset, navigate to the folder containing the desired preset and choose the preset. The preset will be imported into the Preset Select menu and loaded into the device. Only presets in recognized formats can be imported.
- Use the preset access system in a third-party plug-in or VI user interface.
- Drag a preset to an existing track using the same instrument, and it will replace the instrument with another instance of the instrument with the preset loaded.
- If an instrument's editor is open, double-clicking on a preset name in the Browser or simply pressing the Return key while it is selected will load it.

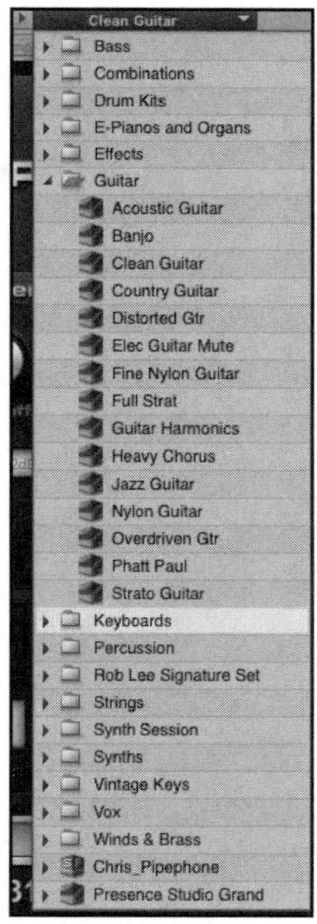

Fig. 5-40: The Preset Select menu in the Instrument editor header shows the presets available for the instrument.

SAVING AND EXPORTING PRESETS

When you have created a preset that you want to preserve, you can do so using any of the following Preset Management menu commands:

- **Store Preset:** This command stores the preset in PreSonus's .preset format to the chosen location with the name entered into the Save Preset dialog box and adds it to the Preset menu.
- **Replace Preset:** This command overwrites the currently loaded preset in its existing location using the same name and the current parameter settings.
- **Export VST Effect Bank:** This command, available only for VST devices, creates a new .fxb file containing only one preset with the current settings and the name entered in the Save As dialog box that appears. The preset will not appear in the Preset Select menu.
- **Export VST Effect Preset:** This command, available only for VST devices, creates a new .fxp file using the current settings and the name entered in the Save As dialog box that appears. The preset will not appear in the Preset Select menu.
- **Export AudioUnit Preset:** This command, available only for Audio Unit devices, creates a new .aupreset file using the current settings and the name entered in the Save As dialog box that appears. The preset will not appear in the Preset Select menu.
- **Export Preset:** This command creates a preset in PreSonus's .preset format and saves it to the chosen location with the name entered into the Export Preset dialog box, but does not add it to the Preset menu.
- Use the preset access system in the device instead of any of the Preset Management menu commands.

FINDING PRESETS

Studio One 2 gives you two ways to find a preset:

- To find a preset in Studio One 2's Browser, choose Show in Browser from the Preset Management menu in the editor header. The Effects tab of the Browser will open along with the preset selected in it.
- To find a preset in your computer's file system, locate the preset in Studio One 2's Browser (using Show in Browser, if necessary), right-click on it, and choose Show in Finder (Explorer in Windows) from the contextual drop-down menu that appears.

It can be very useful to use these two methods back-to-back, so that you first locate the preset in the Browser and then in the computer's file system.

RENAMING PRESETS

- To rename a preset, right-click on it in Studio One 2's Browser and choose Rename Preset from the contextual menu that drops down.

DELETING PRESETS

You can delete a preset using either of the following methods:

- Select the preset in the Browser, then press the Delete key or right-click on it and choose Delete from the contextual drop-down menu that appears.
- Show the preset in the computer's file system and delete it there.

SETTING THE DEFAULT PRESET

Each device has a default preset that is loaded when the device is first added. The default preset can be set to anything you like.

- To set the current preset as the default preset, choose Store as Default Preset from the Preset Management menu.

Comparing and Moving Settings

The header offers a simple A/B comparison feature, plus the ability to copy and paste settings.

- The Compare button automatically becomes active as soon as any edit is made to the last preset loaded. Click on the Compare button to toggle between the edited version (button is gray) and the original preset (button is blue).

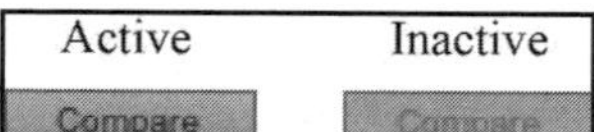

Fig. 5-41: The states of the Compare button.

To copy the current settings to the clipboard, click on the Copy button at any time.

To paste settings from the clipboard, open a different copy of the same instrument or plug-in from which you copied settings and click on the Paste button.

Automation and Parameter Control

Studio One 2 allows real-time control of device parameters using hardware controllers or automation. Much of this control can be accessed from the Device Editor header.

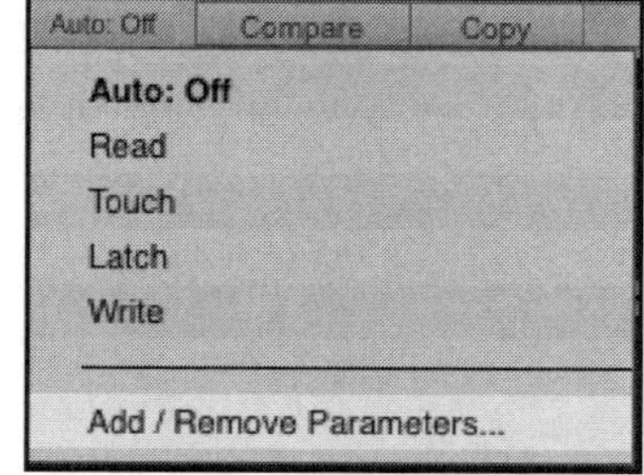

Fig. 5-42: The Automation mode menu not only chooses the automation mode for the track, but also lets you determine which parameters can be automated.

- The Automation Mode field drops down a menu that lets you select an automation mode, as well as add or remove parameters for automation. These capabilities are duplicated in the track header. For more information on automating device parameters, see the chapter "Automation" in *Power Tools for Studio One 2*, vol. 2.
- When enabled, the Edit Mapping button opens a Control Link display below the editor header for VIs, or a Device Controller Map for external devices. For more information on Control Link, see the section "Using Hardware Controllers with Studio One 2: Control Link" in chapter 4, "Virtual Instruments and MIDI."

- To select a hardware controller for real-time control of the device, click on the arrow next to the Edit Mapping button to drop down the Controller Select menu and choose the desired controller from the menu that appears.
- To enable or disable the currently selected controller, click on the Focus Device button. When the button is colored yellow, the controller is enabled, which limits the scope of a control linkage to the current parameter of the VI or plug-in being edited. For more on Focus mapping, see the section "Using Hardware Controllers with Studio One 2: Control Link" in chapter 4, "Virtual Instruments and MIDI." Note that when the controller is disabled, the Control Link display will still respond to controller changes, but the value of any parameter mapped to that controller will not be altered.

Enabling and Disabling Instrument Audio Outputs

When a VI offers multiple audio outputs, the CH button will be seen to the right of the Preset Select menu. The menu dropped down by this menu allows you to enable or disable these outputs as desired. This option is available only in the Instrument header.

To enable or disable one or more audio outputs for a VI:

1. Click on the CH button in the Instrument editor header.
2. In the drop-down menu that appears, check the box for the output(s) you want to enable or uncheck the output(s) you want to disable. If necessary, use the scrollbar on the right of the list to see all of the available outputs.

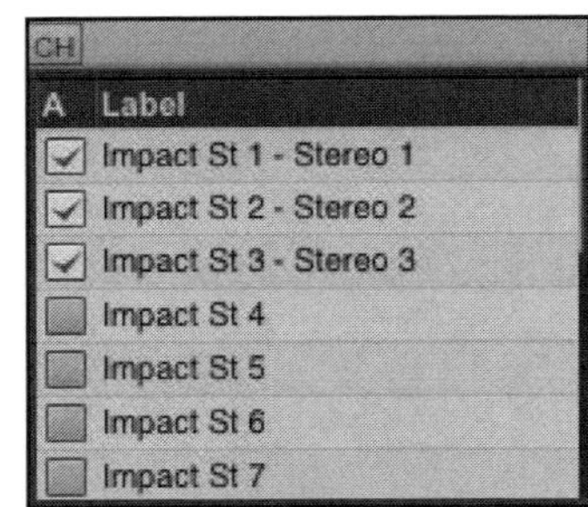

Fig. 5-43: Though it has the same "CH" label as the Instrument track MIDI channel drop-down, the channel drop-down in the Instrument header instead selects which audio output of a multichannel instrument should get used.

ARRANGE VIEW INFO PANEL

The Arrange View Info panel (called "Info View" in Studio One 2) provides a handy reference to the possible actions available given the currently selected tool and the cursor location. It also tells you the keystroke to use to execute each action.

For example, with the Arrow tool selected, let's say we move the cursor over the middle of an Event on an Audio track in the Arrange view. The Info panel tells us that the Arrow tool is active, and holding down the Shift key and clicking will toggle between selecting and deselecting that Event, while holding the Shift key and double-clicking will select all Events on the track.

Fig. 5-44: The Info panel showing options for the arrow cursor hovering over an Audio Event.

What's more, as soon as we hold down the Shift key, every option involving it becomes highlighted in white. Now we move the cursor to the left edge of that Event and we see there is now the option to resize the Event.

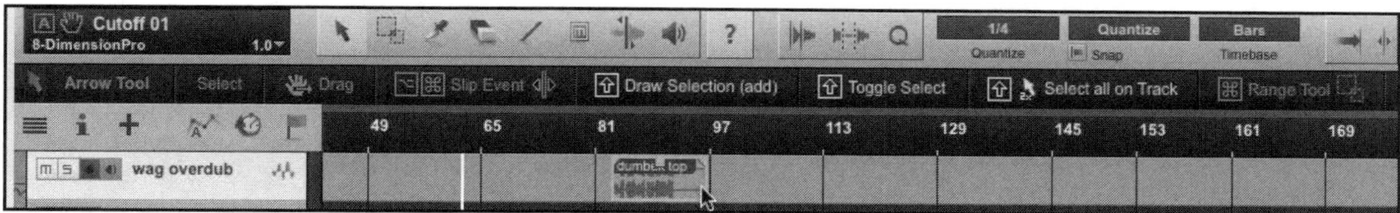

Fig. 5-45: With the Shift key held down, the Info panel shows click actions available in the current context.

- To open the Info panel, choose Views > Additional Views > Info View from the main menu bar or click on the "?" button in the Arrange view toolbar.

Fig. 5-46: This button in the Arrange view toolbar makes the Info view visible.

CONTEXTUAL MENUS

Contextual menus provide fast access to commands that are appropriate to the work you are doing at a given moment. As a result, you are likely to use them often, even though the commands found in contextual menus are also available elsewhere, generally somewhere in the main menu bar. Right-clicking on an object (or Ctrl-clicking on it on Mac) brings up its contextual menu. Since I explain contextual menu commands in the places in this book that refer to their individual functions, here I mostly will give references to where full explanations of the commands can be found. This section does not cover every contextual menu in Studio One 2, but it hits the biggies. (No information on the contextual Track menu is included here because it is discussed in the section "Contextual Track Menu," earlier in this chapter.

Item Contextual Menus

These are the menus you will see if you right-click on an Audio Event or Instrument Part. I will walk you through each section of these menus.

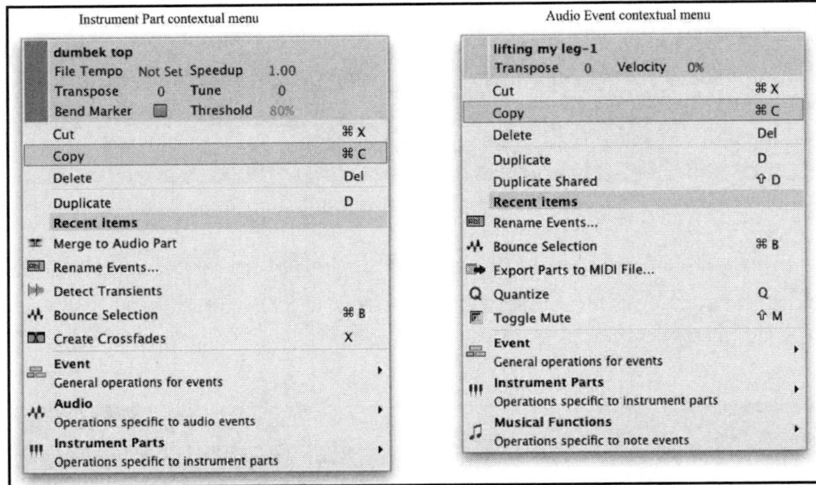

Fig. 5-47: The Instrument Part and Audio Event contextual menus.

ITEM INFO HEADER

When an Instrument Part or Audio Event is right-clicked in the Arrange view, an info header sits at the very top of the contextual menu that appears. This header, like the rest of the menu, allows fast access to parameters for modifying the data in the item.

Choosing a command in a contextual menu causes the menu to close, but editing an info header parameter does not.

- To close a contextual menu after editing an info header parameter, click anywhere outside the menu.

INSTRUMENT PART HEADER

Right-clicking on an Instrument Part presents access in the header to four parameters, all found in the Instrument Part inspector, as described in the "Inspectors" section earlier in this chapter:

lifting my leg-1
Transpose 0 Velocity 0%

Fig. 5-48: The header of the Instrument Part contextual menu has some basic editing functions.

- Part name
- Part color
- Transpose
- Velocity

AUDIO EVENT HEADER

Right-clicking on an Audio Event presents access in the header to a number of parameters, all found in the Audio Event inspector, as described in the "Inspectors" section earlier in this chapter:

sit/stay
File Tempo 150.00 Speedup 1.00
Transpose 0 Tune 0
Bend Marker Threshold 0%

Fig. 5-49: The header of the Audio Event contextual menu collects several significant parameters into one quickly accessible area.

- Event name
- Event color
- File Tempo
- Speedup
- Transpose
- Tune
- Bend Marker
- Threshold

CUT/COPY/DELETE/DUPLICATE

Discussion of these standard operations can be found in the "Editing Operations" section of this chapter.

RECENT ITEMS

The Recent Items area shows the last five commands that were executed, providing easy access for executing any of them again.

EVENT SUBMENU

The Event submenu shows up as part of an item contextual menu when an Audio Event or Instrument Part is right-clicked. The commands that appear at any given time depend on the context, of course. References to full explanations of the commands are given below.

- **Rename Events:** See the section "Editing Operations," in this chapter.
- **Send to Back:** See the section "Editing Audio" in chapter 6, "Advanced Editing."
- **Send to Front:** See the section "Editing Audio" in chapter 6, "Advanced Editing."
- **Mute Events:** See the section "Editing Operations," in this chapter.
- **Toggle Mute:** See the section "Editing Operations," in this chapter.
- **Unmute Events:** See the section "Editing Operations," in this chapter.
- **Bounce Selection:** See the section "Editing Applications" in chapter 6, "Advanced Editing" (brief) or the chapter "Mixing" in *Power Tools for Studio One 2*, vol. 2.
- **Merge Events:** See the section "Segmenting (Advanced Dividing)" in chapter 6, "Advanced Editing."
- **Split at Grid:** See the section "Editing Operations," in this chapter.
- **Quantize (Quantize, Quantize 50%, Quantize on Track, Restore Timing):** See the section "Quantizing" in chapter 6, "Advanced Editing."

AUDIO SUBMENU

Below are the commands in the Audio submenu by groups in the menu, and references to full discussions of them.

AUDIO PROCESSING

- **Normalize Audio:** See the section "Inspectors," in this chapter.
- **Reverse Audio:** See the section "Reversing Audio" in chapter 6, "Advanced Editing."
- **Strip Silence:** See the section "Segmenting (Advanced Dividing)" in chapter 6, "Advanced Editing."
- **Edit with Melodyne:** See the section "Transposing and Tuning Events" in chapter 6, "Advanced Editing."

VOLUME ENVELOPE

- **Create Autofades:** See the section "Fades" in chapter 6, "Advanced Editing."
- **Create Crossfades:** See the section "Fades" in chapter 6, "Advanced Editing."
- **Decrease Volume:** See the section "Event Volume" in chapter 6, "Advanced Editing."
- **Increase Volume:** See the section "Event Volume" in chapter 6, "Advanced Editing."

AUDIO BEND

- **Detect Transients:** See the section "Segmenting (Advanced Dividing)" in chapter 6, "Advanced Editing."
- **Remove Bend Markers:** See the section "Segmenting (Advanced Dividing)" in chapter 6, "Advanced Editing."
- **Split at Bend Markers:** See the section "Segmenting (Advanced Dividing)" in chapter 6, "Advanced Editing."

AUDIO PARTS

- **Merge to Audio Part:** See the section "Segmenting (Advanced Dividing)" in chapter 6, "Advanced Editing."

OTHER

- **Select in Pool:** Selects in The Pool all Events currently selected in the Arrange view.
- **Send to new SampleOne:** Creates a new instantiation of SampleOne and loads the selected Event.

INSTRUMENT PARTS SUBMENU

- **Insert Instrument Part:** See the section "Adding Notes and Parts," in this chapter.
- **Explode Pitches to Tracks:** See the section "Explode Pitches to Tracks," in this chapter.
- **Export Musicloop:** See the section "Musicloop and Audioloop File Formats" in chapter 3, "Go! Recording with Studio One 2."
- **Export Parts as MIDI File:** See the section "Exporting Parts as a MIDI File" in chapter 4, "Virtual Instruments and MIDI."

- **Remove Part Automation:** See the chapter "Automation" in *Power Tools for Studio One 2*, vol. 2.
- **Separate Shared Copies:** See the section "Cut/Copy/Paste," in this chapter.

MUSICAL FUNCTIONS

- **Length:** See the section "Advanced MIDI Editing," in this chapter.
- **Stretch:** See the section "Advanced MIDI Editing," in this chapter.
- **Transpose:** See the section "Transposing MIDI," in this chapter.
- **Velocity:** See the section "Advanced MIDI Editing," in this chapter.
- **Mute Events:** See the section "Editing Operations," in this chapter.
- **Toggle Mute:** See the section "Editing Operations," in this chapter.
- **Unmute Events:** See the section "Editing Operations," in this chapter.
- **Quantize:** See the section "Quantizing" in chapter 6, "Advanced Editing."
- **Quantize 50%:** See the section "Quantizing" in chapter 6, "Advanced Editing."
- **Freeze Quantize:** See the section "Quantizing" in chapter 6, "Advanced Editing."
- **Quantize End:** See the section "Quantizing" in chapter 6, "Advanced Editing."
- **Humanize:** See the section "Quantizing" in chapter 6, "Advanced Editing."
- **Humanize Less:** See the section "Quantizing" in chapter 6, "Advanced Editing."
- **Restore Timing:** See the section "Quantizing" in chapter 6, "Advanced Editing."
- **Restore Velocity:** See the section "Advanced MIDI Editing," in this chapter.
- **Delete Double Notes:** See the section "More Useful Selection Tricks," in this chapter.
- **Delete Short Notes:** See the section "More Useful Selection Tricks," in this chapter.
- **Merge Events:** See the section "Segmenting (Advanced Dividing)" in chapter 6, "Advanced Editing."
- **Split At Grid:** See the section "Dividing," in this chapter.

UNDO AND SESSION HISTORY

Studio One 2 has unlimited undo, as well as, of course, single step undo/redo. It also offers a Versions command that allows you to store many complete versions of the same Song all in one document.

Single Undo

- To undo the last action, press Cmd + Z (Ctrl + Z) or choose Edit > Undo <last command> from the main menu bar. Executing this command repeatedly steps you back in time through the Undo History.

- To redo the last action undone, press Cmd + Y (Ctrl + Y) or choose Edit > Redo <last command> from the main menu bar. Executing this command repeatedly steps you forward in time through the Undo History.

Undo History

Studio One 2 includes an Undo History dialog box for unlimited undo.

TIP: Note that the history is maintained for as long as the document is open, but is cleared when the document is closed.

There are two tabs in the Undo History dialog box: Actions and Trash Bin. Unsurprisingly, the Actions bin is where most of the action takes place, and contains the history of actions that have been executed. Actions are listed from earliest to most recent. Each line in the history displays the following:

- A line number
- A timestamp showing when the action was executed
- A description of the action
- The object of the action

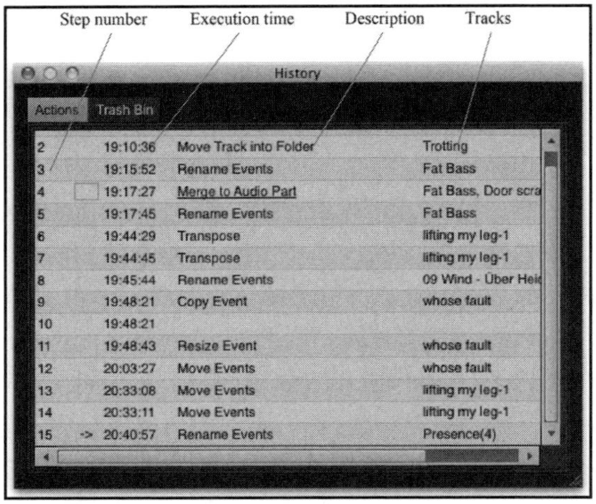

Fig. 5-50: The Undo History enables you to go back in time and undo as many steps of what you've done as you wish.

When you choose to roll back to an earlier point in the Undo History, all steps between where you were and the point in the history to which you roll back are undone; it is not possible to selectively undo steps. Further, once you roll back to an earlier step and then execute any action, all of the actions that before had followed your roll-back point are permanently removed from the history. That is to say, the history does not branch. Once you go back and then do something, you cannot return to where you started before rolling back.

When a file is closed and the history lost, there is no longer a convenient way to do a step-by-step undo of actions executed before the file was closed, but the Versions command can be used to save snapshots of the state of the Song at a point in time. For more information see the section "The Versions Command," below.

- To access the Undo History, choose View > History from the main menu bar. The Undo History dialog box will appear.

- To roll back to any previous point in the Undo History, simply click on the step to which you wish to return. All steps after where you click will become grayed out, and a horizontal blue line will indicate the present time.
- To completely clear the Undo History, choose Edit > Delete Undo History from the main menu bar. A confirmation dialog box will come up. Once you clear the history, it is gone forever.

The Versions Command

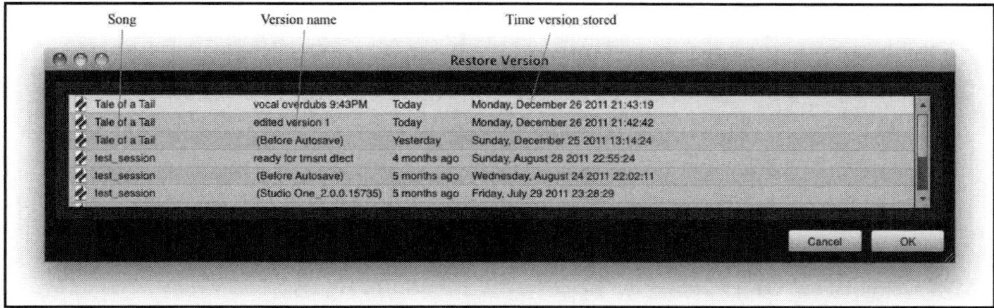

Fig. 5-51: The Versions feature lets you save snapshots of the Song at a point in time. The Restore Versions dialog allows you to return to any of these snapshots.

The Versions command is an invaluable tool in editing—a real lifesaver. What it does is simply capture the entire state of the Song at the time you save the version. You can restore any version at any time, so if you do some work and realize you got off on the wrong track, or accidentally delete some work, you can go back to the last version you saved (or an earlier one, if you wish). In other DAWs that don't have a feature like this, you must save multiple session documents in order to have session snapshots. This can become a real session management hassle. It is much more elegant to have all of the snapshots stored in one session document.

To get the most out of the Versions command, you must save versions often enough and name them methodically. If you work intensely for two hours without saving a version and then somehow mess up your Song, going back to the last saved version will lose everything you did in those two hours. If, on the other hand, you save a version every half hour, or whenever you complete some difficult or intensive task, then you are at a much lower level of risk. A good guideline is that you should save a version as soon as you've done enough work that you would be annoyed or set back by losing it.

If the names you're using are not adequate to tell you the differences between versions, then even if you've saved often you won't be able to figure out which version to return to when the need arises. The Versions dialog box will allow you to enter many characters for the version name, but it allows you to see only about 24 characters, so it is best to keep your names compact.

There are any number of good naming schemes you can use. Of course, it is good to have some descriptive text ("gtr solo comp"), but it is wise to save a number of characters for a version designation, such as "v3.1" or the date and time: "18Jun11 5PM." Although half of your available characters might get used this way, it tremendously improves the effectiveness of saving versions to be able to pinpoint them precisely.

- To save a version of your Song, press Option (Alt in Windows) + Shift + Cmd + S or choose File > Save New Version from the main menu bar. When the Save New Version dialog box appears, type in a name and click on "OK" to save it.
- To restore a saved version of your Song, choose File > Restore Version from the main menu bar. When the Restore Version dialog box appears, either double-click on the version you want to restore, or click on it to select it and then click on the "OK" button to restore it. A confirmation dialog box asking if you want to save your Song before restoring will appear. Clicking on "No" will cause all changes since the last time you saved or saved a version to be lost.

TIP: Saving a version immediately before restoring a version makes it easy to effectively undo your version restore, if you need to. This can be particularly effective when you are restoring to an old version to grab some specific data from the older version that you want to bring into your latest version. To do this, simply save a version, restore the older version, copy the data you need, restore the newest version, and paste it where you want it.

TOOLS, TOOLS, TOOLS

Since there are many kinds of editing tasks, there is a large selection of editing tools in Studio One 2. However, the bulk of your editing is likely to be covered by a relatively small set of features.

There are four basic tools that get used in both the Arrange and Edit views, and two that are available only in the Arrange view. Although they perform the same functions in either view (with a few exceptions that I will note), they are selected independently in each view. I will introduce them here and give you an idea of what they are used for. Details on each of these uses will be given in the sections covering each application.

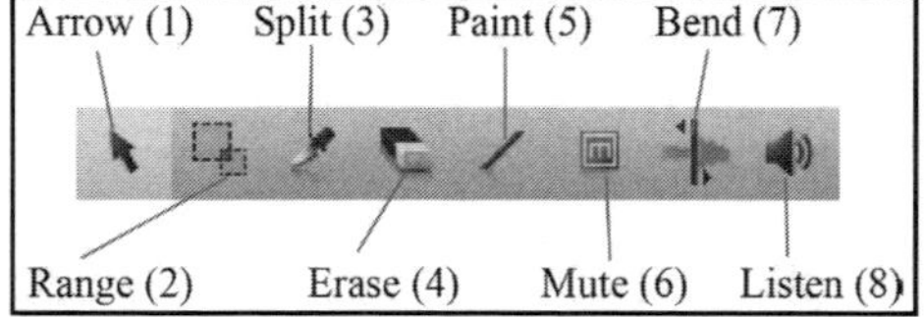

Fig. 5-52: The Arrange view toolbar. In parentheses are the key shortcuts for each of the tools.

Note that the actions of editing tools can be affected by other features. For example, if Snap is enabled, then your selection will increase or decrease by steps of the duration shown in the Quantize Value field. This is very useful for precisely selecting musical sections, like exactly four bars or one chorus of the Song. You can read more about Snap below. Another example is Edit Groups: edits performed on any track in an Edit Group will also be performed on all other tracks in the group. Edit Groups are discussed further in the section "Track Groups and Folder Tracks," below.

Plainly, it is important when editing to be aware when these modes are active.

Arrow Tool

The Arrow tool is used in the Arrange and Edit views for a number of tasks, including selecting Audio Events, Instrument Parts, and notes; moving selected Events, Parts, and notes; sizing Events, Parts, and notes; and editing automation.

To choose the Arrow tool,

Fig. 5-53: The arrow tool cursor.

1. Be sure that you have the desired view (Arrange or Edit) active. If you are not sure, click in the area around the toolbar in the desired view to make the view active.
2. Use any of the following methods to choose the Arrow tool: press the 1 key (on the QWERTY keyboard, not the number pad), right-click in the main area under the timeline in the Arrange or Edit view and choose Arrow Tool from the contextual menu that drops down, or click on the Arrow tool icon in the view's toolbar.

Range Tool

The Range tool is available in the Arrange and Edit views. When the Range tool is active, you can drag across the time period and tracks you want to select. As you drag, a pop-up tool tip shows you the start and end of the range, and, in parentheses, its duration.

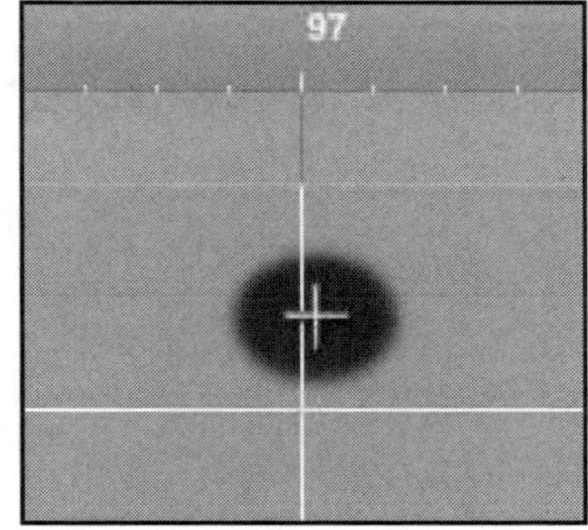

Fig. 5-54: The range tool cursor.

The Range tool allows you to make a selection within an Audio Event or Instrument Part, or select a time range across several tracks without selecting entire Events or Parts. As with the Arrow tool, holding down the Shift key will let you add to a selection. You can increase or decrease a selection's duration, or add another area in another part of the song to the selection.

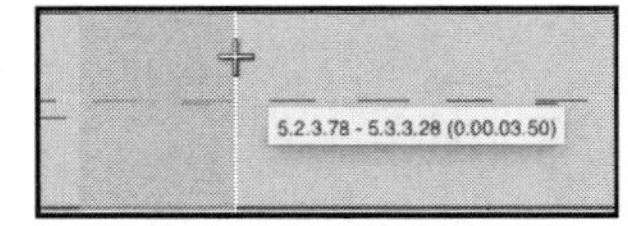

Fig. 5-55: A selection can be made across both time and tracks by dragging with the range tool. Note the tool tip pop-up that displays exact values for the selection.

Since the Range tool is so much more limited in function than the Arrow tool, it is very common to make a selection with the Range tool and then use the Arrow tool to move it.

To choose the Range tool, do the following:

1. Be sure the Arrange view is active. If you are not sure, click in the area around the toolbar in the Arrange view to make the view active.
2. Use any of the following methods to choose the Range tool: press the 2 key (on the QWERTY keyboard, not the number pad), right-click in the main area under the

timeline in the Arrange view and choose Range Tool from the contextual menu that drops down, or click on the Range tool icon in the Arrange view toolbar.

Split Tool

The Split tool is available only in the Arrange view. Clicking on an Event with the Split tool divides the Event into two Events at the location where it is clicked. If multiple Events are selected, only the one that is clicked will be split.

To choose the Split tool, do the following:

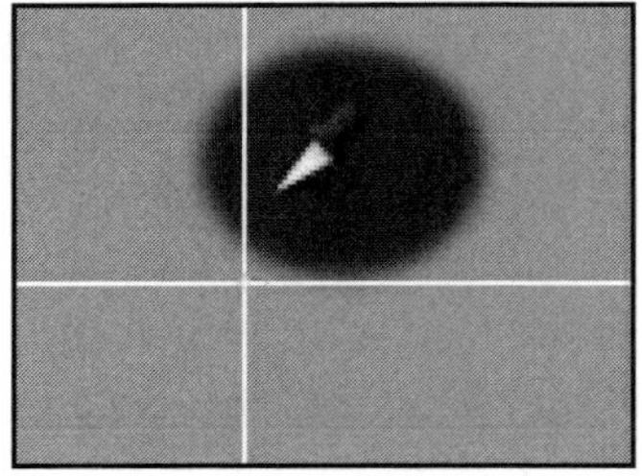

Fig. 5-56: The split tool cursor.

1. Be sure that the Arrange view is active. If you are not sure, click in the area around the toolbar in the Arrange view to make the view active.
2. Use any of the following methods to choose the Split tool: press the 3 key (on the QWERTY keyboard, not the number pad) with the Arrange view active or the 2 key with the Edit view active, right-click in the main area under the timeline in the Arrange or Edit view and choose Split Tool from the contextual menu that drops down, or click on the Split tool icon in the view's toolbar.

Eraser Tool

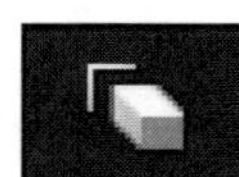

Fig. 5-57: The eraser tool.

The Eraser tool is used in the Arrange and Edit views to delete Events, Parts, or notes. Clicking on or dragging over an Event, Part, or note will delete it regardless of the current selection. Clicking on a selected object will delete all currently selected objects. When looking at Instrument track note data in the Edit view, clicking or dragging affects individual notes, not entire Parts.

The Eraser tool icon is kind of large, which sometimes makes it difficult to use. You may need to zoom in sometimes to be sure you are accurately clicking where you mean to be.

To choose the Eraser tool, do the following:

1. Be sure that the desired view (Arrange or Edit) is active. If you are not sure, click in the area around the toolbar in the desired view to make the view active.
2. Use any of the following methods to choose the Eraser tool: press the 4 key (on the QWERTY keyboard, not the number pad), right-click in the main area under the timeline in the Arrange or Edit view and choose Eraser Tool from the contextual menu that drops down, or click on the Eraser tool icon in the view's toolbar to choose the Eraser tool.

Paint Tool

Fig. 5-58: The paint tool cursor.

The Paint (Pencil) tool is used to insert notes or automation data in the Edit view, or empty Instrument Parts in the Arrange view. Its operation varies with the context. The tool button has a drop-down menu that offers a choice of curve types for drawing automation data. These curves are discussed in the chapter "Automation" in *Power Tools for Studio One 2*, vol. 2.

To choose the Paint tool, do the following:

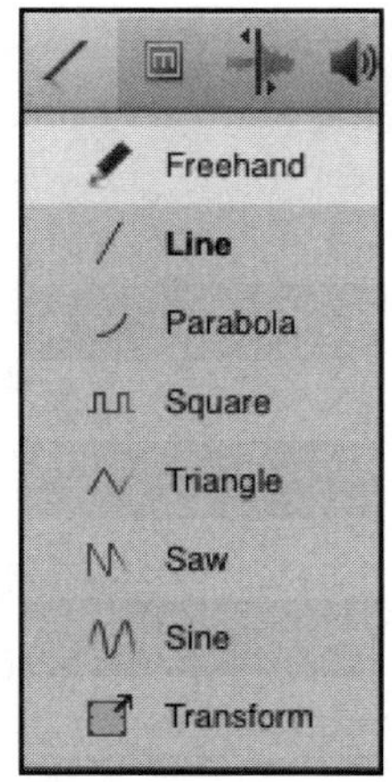

Fig. 5-59: Selecting a paint tool curve makes it very quick to create sophisticated automation moves.

1. Be sure that the desired view (Arrange or Edit) is active. If you are not sure, click in the area around the toolbar in the desired view to make the view active.
2. Use any of the following methods to choose the Paint tool: Press the 5 key (on the QWERTY keyboard, not the number pad) in the Arrange view or the 3 key in the Edit view, right-click in the main area under the timeline in the Arrange or Edit view and choose Paint Tool from the contextual menu that drops down, or click on the Paint tool icon in the view's toolbar to choose the Paint tool.
3. To drop down the submenu of Paint tool curves, select the Paint tool, then click once on it to drop down the curves submenu.

Mute Tool

The Mute tool is used to mute and unmute Events or Parts in the Arrange view, or notes in the Music Editor. The Mute tool icon is kind of large, which sometimes makes it difficult to use. You may need to zoom in sometimes to be sure that you are accurately clicking where you mean to be.

Fig. 5-60: The mute tool cursor

To choose the Mute tool, do the following:

1. Be sure that the desired view (Arrange or Edit) is active. If you are not sure, click in the area around the toolbar in the desired view to make the view active.
2. Use any of the following methods to choose the Mute tool: Press the 6 key (on the QWERTY keyboard, not the number pad) in the Arrange view or the 5 key in the Edit view, right-click in the main area under the timeline in the Arrange or Edit view and choose Mute Tool from the contextual menu that drops down, or click on the Mute tool icon in the view's toolbar to choose the Mute tool.

Listen Tool

The Listen tool enables you to audition an individual Event or Part. The Listen tool works identically in both the Arrange and Edit views.

Fig. 5-61: The listen tool cursor.

- Use any of the following methods to choose the Listen tool: Press the 8 key (on the QWERTY keyboard, not the number pad) in the Arrange view or the 6 key in the Edit view, right-click in the main area under the timeline in the Arrange or Edit view and choose Listen Tool from the contextual menu that drops down, or click on the Listen tool icon in the view's toolbar to choose the Listen tool.

- To solo a track and play from a specific location, select the Listen tool and click-and-hold at the desired location in the track you want to hear. Playback will start from that location and continue (with the track soloed) until the mouse button is released.
- To loop playback of an Event or Part in context, select the Listen tool and Shift-click on the Event or Part. The locators will get set to the Event or Part start and end times, looping will be enabled, and playback will begin. All play-enabled tracks will play as the Event or Part loops, making it easy to make level or device parameter adjustments in context. Press the Spacebar to stop playback.

Bend Tool

The Bend tool inserts and edits Audio Bend markers. For more information on Audio Bend markers and using the Bend tool, see chapter 6, "Advanced Editing."

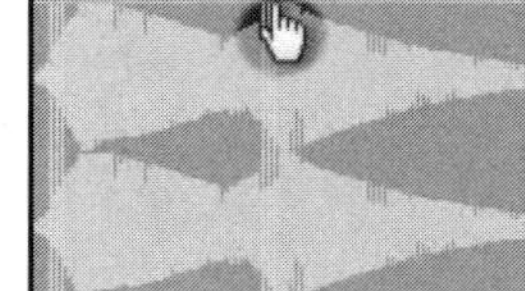

Fig. 5-62: The Audio Bend tool cursor.

- Use any of the following methods to choose the Bend tool: Press the 7 key (on the QWERTY keyboard, not the number pad) in the Arrange view, right-click in the main area under the timeline in the Arrange and choose Bend Tool from the contextual menu that drops down, or click on the Bend tool icon in the Arrange view toolbar to choose the Bend tool.

Accessing a Secondary Tool with the Cmd (Ctrl) Key

In the Arrange and Edit views, holding the Cmd (Ctrl in Windows) key temporarily changes the active tool. This can speed many processes. Imagine that you have selected the Range tool in the Arrange view, selected part of an Event, and hit the Delete button to delete the selected area. If you then hold down the Cmd (Ctrl in Windows) key, making the Arrow tool temporarily active, you easily can move one or the other of the Events created by the deletion.

- If the Arrow tool is currently selected, holding down the Cmd (Ctrl) key will invoke the Range tool.
- If any other tool is currently selected, holding down the Cmd (Ctrl) key will invoke the Arrow tool.

SELECTING

Most editing operations are performed on selected data. Naturally, that makes selection methods very important. Studio One 2's selection methods are easy and straightforward. The most important selection tools are the Arrow tool and the Range tool.

Selecting Tracks

- To select a track, click on its header in the Arrange view.
- To select the track above or below the currently selected one, use the Up and Down Arrow key.
- To select multiple contiguous tracks, click on the track on one end, then Shift-click on the track on the other end.
- To select noncontiguous tracks or add a noncontiguous track to a selection, Cmd (Ctrl)-click on each track you wish to add.
- With the Arrow tool active, click on any Event or Part in a track to select the track.
- With the Range tool active, drag over any portion of one or more Events and or Parts across some number of tracks to select those tracks.
- To select a track in Edit view, click on the arrow next to the track's name in the Audio or Music editor inspector and select the desired track from the menu that drops down. Note that if the Audio editor is open, only Audio tracks will be shown in the menu, and if the Music editor is open, only Instrument tracks will be shown.

Selecting Events, Parts, and Notes

To select an Audio Event or Instrument Part in the Arrange view, do any of the following:

- Click with the Arrow tool on an Event or Part to select it.
- Drag with the Arrow tool over any number of Events or Parts across any number of tracks. All Events or Parts that fall totally or partially within the selection area are selected.
- To select noncontiguous Events or Parts, or add a noncontiguous item to a selection, Shift-click on each item you wish to add.
- You can also add items to a selection by Shift-dragging with the Arrow tool over the items you wish to add.
- Use the Up and Down Arrows to move the selection area to the next track above or below the currently selected track. The Event or Part on the newly selected track that is closest to the previous selection will become selected.
- Hold down the Shift key and use the Up and Down Arrows to add tracks below or above to the selection.

Selecting Notes in the Music Editor

To select notes in the Music editor, do any of the following:

- Click with the Arrow tool on a note to select it.
- Drag with the Arrow tool over any number of notes. All notes that fall totally or partially within the selection area are selected.

- To select noncontiguous notes, or add a noncontiguous note to a selection, Shift-click on each note you wish to add.
- You can also add notes to a selection by Shift-dragging with the Arrow tool over the notes you wish to add.

Select All

- To select all Events or Parts in all tracks in the Arrange view, press Cmd + A (Ctrl + A in Windows) or choose Edit > Select All from the main menu bar.
- To select all Events or Parts on one or more selected tracks in the Arrange view, select the track or tracks, then press Cmd + Shift + A (Ctrl + Shift + A in Windows) or choose Edit > Select > Select All on Tracks from the main menu bar.
- To select all notes in all Parts on a track in the Edit view, press Cmd + Shift + A (Ctrl + Shift + A in Windows) or choose Edit > Select > Select All on Tracks from the main menu bar.
- To select all notes within one or more selected Parts on a track in the Edit view (Music Editor), select the track or tracks, then press Cmd + A (Ctrl + A) or choose Edit > Select All from the main menu bar.
- To select everything within a loop, Press Option + L (Alt + L in Windows) or choose Edit > Select > Select All in Loop from the main menu bar. In the Arrange view, this selects all Events and Parts that are fully or partially within the loop. In Edit view, this selects all Events or notes that are fully or partially within the loop.
- There is no dedicated method of selecting from the edit point to the beginning or end of a track, so either Shift-click at the beginning or end of the track, or drag from the edit point to the beginning or end of the track.

Deselecting

DESELECT ALL

- The fastest way to deselect all selected items on all tracks is to click somewhere in the Arrange view where there are no Events or Parts.
- Press Cmd + D (Ctrl + D in Windows) or choose Edit > Select > Deselect All from the main menu bar to deselect all selected items on all tracks.
- Press Shift + Cmd + D or choose Edit > Select > Deselect All on Tracks from the main menu bar to deselect all selected items on selected tracks only.

REMOVE ITEMS FROM A SELECTION (DESELECT ONE)

- To deselect individual items from a selected group, Shift-click on the items you wish to deselect.

More Useful Selection Tricks

MAKE A LOOP FROM THE SELECTION

- To set the loop to the current selection, press Shift + P or choose Transport > Loop Selection from the main menu bar.
- To snap the current selection to the grid and set the loop to the new selection, press the P key or choose Transport > Loop Selection Snapped from the main menu bar.

INVERTING THE SELECTION

Inverting the selection simply selects everything that had been unselected, and deselects what was selected. This is very useful when you need to select all but a few Events or Parts in the Song, which is easily accomplished by selecting the Events or Parts you *don't* want selected and then inverting the selection so that everything but those Events or Parts are selected.

- To invert the selection, Press Cmd + I (Ctrl + I in Windows) or choose Edit > Select > Invert Selection from the main menu bar.

DELETE DOUBLE NOTES, DELETE SHORT NOTES

These two functions combine select and delete functions to provide a couple of little utilities for cleaning up problems that often occur when recording MIDI performance information from a musical controller. Without these functions, getting rid of double notes (the result of some sort of bounce or perceived bounce in the controller) and short notes (sometimes the result of accidental or partial strikes, sometimes from controller bounce) can be an ongoing process in which you delete them as you stumble across them. With these two commands, it is easy to select an entire performance as soon as it is completed and execute such cleanup instantly.

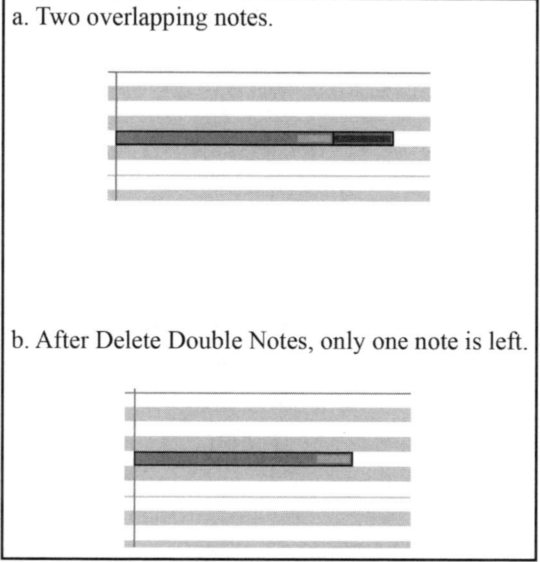

a. Two overlapping notes.
b. After Delete Double Notes, only one note is left.

Fig. 5-63: Delete Double Notes provides a quick way to clean tracks of extra notes that sometimes get generated in MIDI performances. In figure 5-63a, the shorter note is selected, and the gray area behind it is the end of the longer unselected note that is behind it.

DELETE DOUBLE NOTES

Two notes with the same pitch and note-on time are interpreted as double notes. Delete Double Notes fixes this by removing one of the notes.

- To delete double notes, select the notes or range containing the suspect notes in either the Arrange or Music Editor (Edit) views and choose Event > Musical Functions > Delete Double Notes from the main menu bar.

DELETE SHORT NOTES

Delete Short Notes will delete any selected note 50 ticks (that is, 0.0.0.50) or less in duration.

- To delete short notes, select the notes or range containing the suspect notes in either the Arrange or Music Editor (Edit) views and choose Event > Musical Functions > Delete Short Notes from the main menu bar.

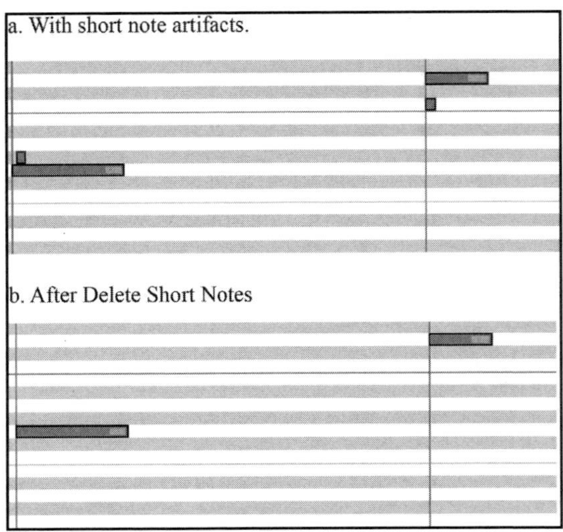

Fig. 5-64: Delete Short Notes removes unwanted note blips caused by bounces and other performance imperfections.

LOCATE SELECTION

Locate Selection moves the play location to the beginning of the selection.

- Press L or choose Transport > Locate Selection from the main menu bar to position the play location at the beginning of the selection.

LOCATE SELECTION END

Locate Selection End moves the play location to the end of the selection. It has no default shortcut, but one can be assigned to it.

- Choose Transport > Locate Selection End from the main menu bar to position the play location at the end of the selection.

INPUT FOLLOWS SELECTION

When recording, it is convenient to be able to choose a track to work on and have its record-enable and input monitoring settings automatically chosen, as well. This is easily accomplished with the Audio Input Follows Selection and Instrument Input Follows Selection commands.

Note that only the last track selected will be made active. If you wish to arm multiple tracks recording or input monitoring, you must record-enable them or set them to monitor input individually. Remember that monitoring input on an Instrument track really means making it the active recipient of performance information from a musical controller, whereas monitoring input on an Audio track allows you to hear the audio at the track's input.

To make a track the active input when it is selected, do the following:

- Choose Options > Audio Input Follows Selection from the main menu bar for Audio tracks.

- Choose Options > Instrument Input Follows Selection from the main menu bar for Instrument tracks.

TRACK SOLO FOLLOWS SELECTION

Equally useful in tracking, editing, and mixing, this setting solos all tracks or channels that are selected. Under these conditions, it is necessary only to click on a track or channel to solo it. This is ideal when going through a song and trying to figure out what's going on with each part. To make soloing follow selection, do the following:

- Choose Options > Solo follows Selection from the main menu bar.

TIP: One or more tracks or channels must be soloed before choosing this command for Solo Follows Selection to be enabled and take effect.

SELECTING USING GROUPS

Grouping is very powerful in editing and mixing because actions performed on one member of the group are performed on all members. See the "Track Groups and Folder Tracks" section below for more information.

ADD BUS FOR SELECTED TRACKS

This command creates a new bus and routes all selected tracks to it. Since the output of the bus can be routed to an interface output, another bus, or an FX channel, this one technique makes various submixing tasks quite quick to configure.

- To add a new bus using a track selection, first select the tracks, then either right-click on one of them in the Arrange view (or a selected channel in the Mix view) and choose Add Bus for Selected Tracks, or choose Track > Add Bus for Selected Tracks from the main menu bar.

SNAP (GRID)

For beat-oriented music, grid snapping is invaluable. If everything revolves around the beat, it is difficult to overstate the utility of being able to select, edit, and bounce using a time grid of definable resolution. In Studio One 2, the action of the grid is determined by the Snap Type, the Snap Reference, and the Quantize and Timebase settings. The Snap Type and Snap Reference are set in the Snap menu, and the Quantize setting in the field to its left.

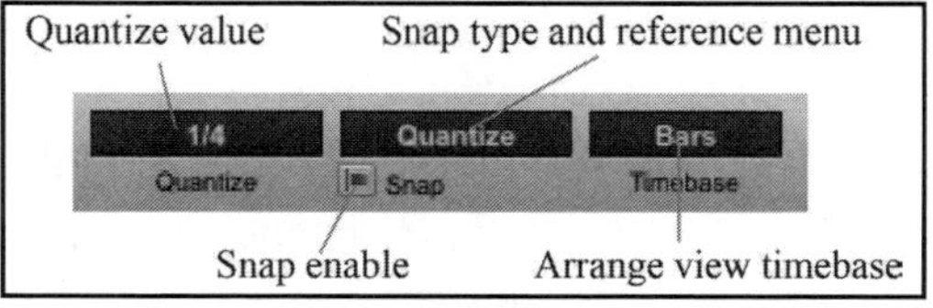

Fig. 5-65: These controls at the top of the Arrange view guide quantization and snap functions and determine the units displayed in the timeline.

Resolution works like this:

- When the Timebase field is set to Bars, the grid resolution is set to the Quantize value.

- When Timebase is set to Seconds, the grid resolution is set to the nearest second.
- When Timebase is set to Frames, grid resolution is at one frame.
- With Timebase set to Timebase on Samples, resolution is one sample.

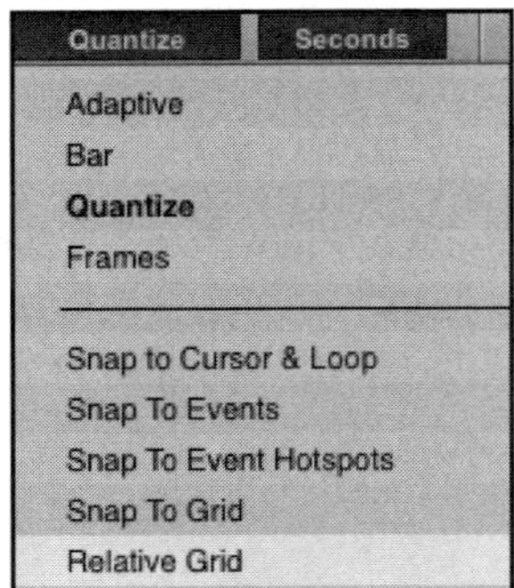

Fig. 5-66: The Snap menu features Snap Type settings in the top half, and Snap Reference settings on the bottom.

(Note that the terms "Snap Type" and "Snap Reference" are not used in Studio One 2. I have used those terms for greater clarity, as the terminology in Studio One 2 is sometimes a tad inconsistent. For instance, the pop-up tool tip for the Snap menu identifies it as the "Snap timebase," but there is a Timebase field right next to it, which sets the units displayed in the timeline ruler and has a tool tip identifying it as the "Timeruler format.")

Studio One 2's snap action is magnetic, not absolute. That is, if you are dragging an item with Snap active, it will "pull" toward the closest grid line or snap destination as the item nears it, but will allow any placement of the item.

In this section, I will discuss the basics of quantization using the Snap feature. More advanced quantization techniques are in the section "Quantizing" in chapter 6, "Advanced Editing."

Snap Type

The Snap Type sets the resolution of the grid. There are four Snap Types.

- **Adaptive:** Adaptive snapping uses the zoom level as a gauge in setting an appropriate grid resolution. The more zoomed in you are, the finer the grid resolution is.
- **Bar:** As one would expect, this snaps to the nearest musical bar line.
- **Quantize:** Quantize uses subdivisions of the value of the Quantize setting. While an Event or Part will "pull" when you drag it close to the Quantize value, it does not enforce strict dragging to that value; it is possible to drag to a subdivision of the Quantize value. Quantize only has an effect on snapping when the time base is set to Bars.
- **Frames:** The grid resolution is set to one frame of SMPTE time. The frame rate is set in Preferences > Song Setup > General > Frame Rate and determines the exact duration of one frame.

Snap Reference

The Snap Reference determines how the grid is applied in snapping. The Snap Reference is set by choosing from the selections in the bottom half of the Snap menu.

SNAP TO CURSOR AND LOOP

The play location and loop start and end points are the snap destinations. This makes it easy to place the cursor in the desired destination and then move an item right to it, and similarly for moving items to the loop boundaries.

SNAP TO EVENTS

Instead of quantizing to a musical value, Snap to Events constructs the grid out of the start and end times of the other items. In the Arrange view, a dragged Event or Part will want to snap to the nearest Event or Part start or end time on any track. This makes it easy to line up Events or Parts.

SNAP TO GRID

When Snap to Grid is active, a moved Event or Part will snap to the nearest grid line at the current resolution.

RELATIVE GRID

When Relative Grid is active, instead of using the Quantize value to form a grid, Quantize value represents the increment by which a dragged Event or Part will move. So, if the grid resolution is set to one quarter-note in 4/4 time, an Event starting at 3:02:02.96 dragged to the left will move to a start time of 3:03:02:96—an offset of one beat. Were Snap to Grid active instead, that same Event would move to 3:02:01:00—the nearest quarter note.

Quantize Value

When the grid is used as the Snap Reference, the Quantize value sets the finest subdivision of the grid. Note that Quantize value can be set only in musical terms. To set it to a time duration instead, set the tempo to a convenient value like 60, 120, or 240 bpm (one, two, or four beats per second), and then subdivide as needed from there to get the desired duration—a tad inconvenient, but workable. For example, setting Quantize value to a 16th note at 300 bpm yields a grid resolution of 50 ms.

There are Quantize Value fields in both the Edit and Arrange views, but these are locked together, so that changing one of them also causes the other to change.

Snap Versus Timebase

The Timebase field sets the basis for snapping as well as the divisions seen in the Arrange or Edit view displays. When Timebase is set to Bars and the Snap Reference is Snap to Grid, items will want to snap to divisions of the Quantize value. When Timebase is set to Seconds, they will snap to the nearest second, and when Timebase is set to Frames, they snap to the nearest frame.

Snap Applications

SELECTING WITH SNAPPING

Snapping is great for ensuring that a selection is made exactly to a musical bar line or beat.

- **Looping:** Make a selection and press P or choose Transport > Loop Selection Snapped from the main menu bar to snap the selection to the grid and loop it.
- **Bouncing:** Before bouncing a mix or selection, set the grid resolution to one bar or some other convenient subdivision, make a selection and press B, right-click on a selected item and choose Event > Bounce Selection from the contextual menu that drops down, or choose Audio > Bounce Selection from the main menu bar to bounce the quantized selection to a file. Alternatively, after making a selection, press P or Shift + P to set the loop to the selection, then choose Song > Export Mixdown from the main menu bar to bounce the audio to files.

EDITING WITH SNAPPING

When using the Split tool, snapping makes it easy to divide items precisely on desired rhythmic or structural subdivisions, such as bar lines, beats, eighth notes, or triplets.

MOVING WITH SNAP

When the Snap box is checked, any of the moving techniques described below will be quantized to the grid resolution. The obvious application for this is to be able to move rhythmic parts around precisely, but another example (assuming a rhythm section that is decently locked to the pulse) could be grabbing an entire verse of lead vocal and moving it from verse to verse or chorus to chorus. Here, snapping is used as a way to preserve all of the slippery timing that good vocalists use.

Snapping is great for grabbing fills or looping sections, as well as when repeating pasting, as described in the "Editing Operations" section below.

TEMPORARILY SUSPENDING SNAPPING

- To temporarily suspend snapping, press and hold the Shift key while dragging one or more items. Do not press Shift before starting to drag.
- Releasing the Shift key before you release the mouse button will cause the items being dragged to snap to the grid line nearest their location at the time the Shift key is released.

EDITING OPERATIONS

Armed with basic knowledge of the editing tools, we will now turn our attention to focusing on common editing tasks and how to accomplish them in Studio One 2. In this section

I will cover the fundamentals; in the next chapter I will look at more advanced editing techniques.

Renaming Items

- To rename an Event or Part, right-click on the Event or Part, choose Event > Rename Events from the contextual drop-down menu that appears, and enter the desired new name.
- To rename all Events or Parts on a track, double-click on the track name, type in a new name for the track, then press Shift + Return. Note that all Events or Parts on the track will be given the exact same name; no number or other distinguishing mark will be appended to the ends of names.

Cut/Copy/Paste

Cut, Copy, and Paste are the usual Cmd (Ctrl) + X, Cmd (Ctrl) + C, Cmd (Ctrl) + V shortcuts. They affect all selected items or range selections. To cut or copy and paste items or ranges, do the following:

- Select the items and/or ranges you wish to cut, copy, or paste using the shortcuts given above, by right-clicking on one of the items and choosing Copy or Cut from the contextual menu that drops down, or by choosing Edit > Copy or Edit > Cut from the main menu bar. Next, position the cursor at the location to which you want to paste, make sure that the appropriate destination track is selected, and press V or choose Edit > Paste from the main menu bar. Since track relationships within the selection are maintained, the selected track will receive the item or range from the top track of the selection, and the other items and/or ranges will be pasted into lower tracks in accordance with their relationship to the item or range in the top track of the selection.

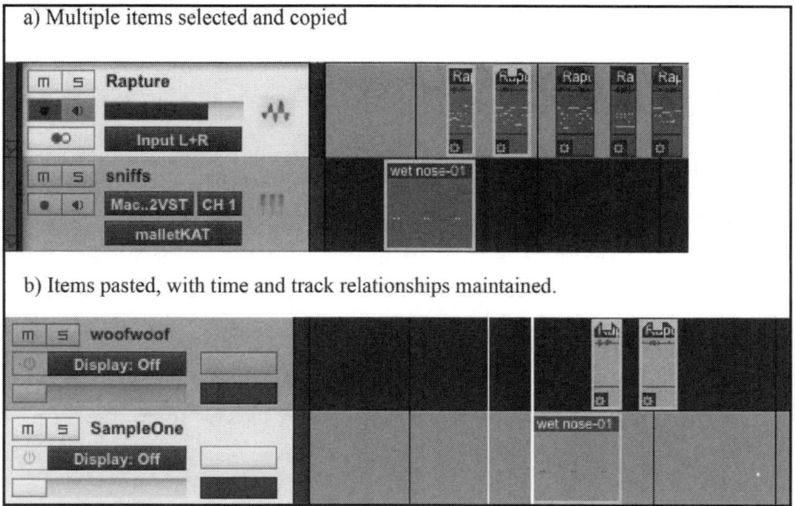

Fig. 5-67: Multiple items are copied and pasted like a single composite entity.

- A selection of notes copied in the Edit view can be pasted into the Arrange view. The result is a new Part containing the selected notes.

DRAG COPY

- To move a copy of one or more selected items to a new location by dragging: Select the items and/or ranges you wish to copy, hold down the Option (Alt) key, and drag to the location where you want the copies to be. Again, remember that time and track relationships are maintained when multiple items or ranges are duplicated.

DUPLICATING ITEMS

Duplicating combines copy-and-paste in a single command. Multiple items can be duplicated simultaneously just as they can be slipped as one item. As with slipping, time and track relationships within the selection are maintained. To duplicate items or ranges, do the following:

- Select the items and/or ranges you wish to duplicate and press D, right-click on a selected item and choose Duplicate from the contextual menu that drops down, or choose Edit > Duplicate from the main menu bar. This will make a copy of the selection and paste it in after the end of the selection. If Snap is not active, the duplicate will be pasted immediately after the end of the selection. If Snap is active, the selection will be pasted as dictated by the Snap settings. If there is existing material in the destination location, the duplicate will be pasted on top of it.
- Select the Part, Parts, and/or ranges you wish to duplicate and choose Edit > Duplicate and Insert from the main menu bar. This does exactly the same thing as Duplicate, except that if there is existing material in the destination location, it will be slipped later in time by the amount of the selection to make room for the duplicate. This is the easiest method for creating stuttering effects, as described in the section "Editing Applications" in chapter 6, "Advanced Editing."

SHARED COPIES OF INSTRUMENT PARTS

When you duplicate an Instrument Part, the duplicate is independent of the original. If you edit the contents of one, the other will be unaffected. However, it is possible to create duplicates that are linked such that editing the contents of any one of them changes all of them identically. These are called "shared copies." If you add or delete notes to a shared copy, the same notes are added or deleted to the others. Note that this applies only to editing the content of a Part, not the Part's attributes; resizing a Part (or any shared copy of it), or changing its location in time or the track it is on will not cause those changes to be performed on shared copies of it.

- To make a shared copy of a selection, select the Part, Parts, and/or ranges within Parts you wish to duplicate and press Shift + D, right-click on a selected item and choose Duplicate Shared from the contextual menu that drops down, or choose Edit > Duplicate Shared from the main menu bar. This does exactly the same thing as Duplicate, except that the duplicate that is made is a shared copy.
- To turn all shared copies of a Part or selection into independent copies, select any of the shared copies, right-click on it, and choose Instrument Parts > Separate Shared Copies from the contextual menu that drops down, or choose Event > Separate Shared Copies from the main menu bar.

Moving Items

SLIPPING

SLIPPING AN ITEM OR RANGE SELECTION BY DRAGGING

An item can be slipped by dragging it to the desired destination time and/or track. A range selection can be dragged as well; doing so "tears it off" from the Part or Event in which it was contained. To slip an item or range selection freely (without snapping), be sure that the Snap box is unchecked or that all Snap References are deselected. If Snap is on, it will affect the dragging as described in the "Snap" section above.

To slip an item or range selection in time and/or between tracks, do the following:

- With the Arrow tool active, select an item you wish to move and drag it to the time and track where you want it.
- With the Range tool active, select a range that you wish to slip. The cursor will turn to an arrow when placed over the selected range, enabling you to drag the selection to the time and track where you want it without having to select the Arrow tool. If you have selected only a portion of an Event or Part, that portion will be separated into a new Event or Part when you drag it, leaving the original Event or Part separated into two, with a gap where the selected range had been.
- If you are dragging beyond the time displayed onscreen, hold down the Spacebar to increase the scrolling speed.

SLIPPING AN ITEM OR RANGE SELECTION USING THE EVENT INSPECTOR

An item (but not a range selection) can be slipped by changing its start time in the Event inspector using any of the following methods:

- With the Arrow tool active, select an item you wish to move and place the cursor over the Start field in the Event inspector. Drag up or down to change the start time, and the item will move with no change to its duration or contents. The item will be moved in increments of the units the cursor is positioned over. That is, if you position the cursor over the Beats area of the Start field, the item will be moved by beats as you drag up or down; if the cursor is positioned over the Bars area, dragging will move the item a whole bar at a time. This makes it easy to move an item with the precision most appropriate to the situation.

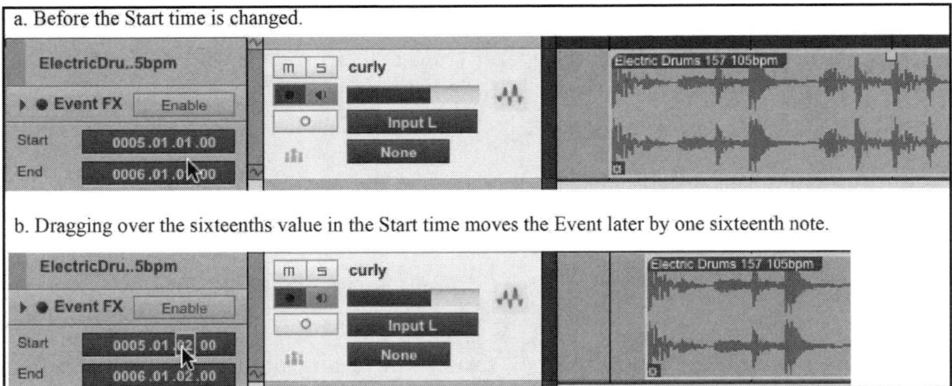

Fig. 5-68: Items can be moved in time by dragging over part of the Start time field in the Event inspector.

- With the Arrow tool active, select the item you wish to move and click in the Start field of the Event inspector. The Up and Down Arrows on the keyboard will then slip the item by increments of the units being changed.
- With the Arrow tool active, select the item you wish to move, click in the Start field of the Event inspector, and type in the value of the start time to which you want to slip the item.
- With the Arrow tool active, select the item you wish to move and cut it to the clipboard. Click in the timeline ruler at the time location where you want the item, make sure that the track into which you want the item pasted is selected, and paste it in.

SLIPPING MULTIPLE ITEMS SIMULTANEOUSLY

- To slip multiple items at the same time, select all of the items you wish to move and use any of the Arrange view methods given above for moving a single item. You cannot use the Event inspector Start field to move multiple items together.
- Once you have selected multiple items, they move as a single unit, retaining their time and track relationships relative to each other. For example, if you select an item starting at bar 4, beat 1, on track 1, and another starting at bar 5, beat 1, on track 3, wherever you move them to, the second item will still end up one bar later than the first item, two tracks away.

- Your selection can mix items and range selections if you switch between using the Arrow tool to select items and the Range tool to select ranges. As always, you must hold down the Shift key when adding to the selection.

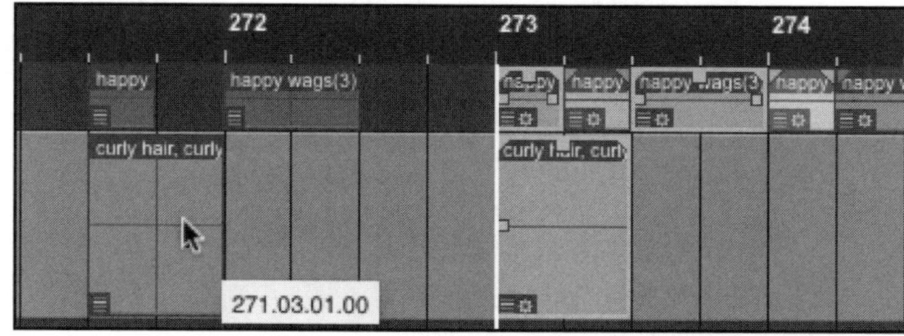

Fig. 5-69: When multiple selected items are dragged, the items retain their time and track relationships. Note the pop-up tool tip showing the start time that will result if the items are dropped at that location.

SLIPPING WITH SNAPPING

When the Snap box is checked, items are "pulled" to the nearest grid line (as specified by the Quantize setting) when dragged close to them; however, Studio One 2's snapping is magnetic, not absolute. The items may jump to a subdivision of the Quantize setting.

- To slip with snapping, check the Snap box, choose a Snap Reference and Snap Type, and, if necessary, set the Quantize value.

NUDGING

When timing is critical, nudging can be a powerful method for finding exactly the right placement for items. To make the process a fluid one, nudging is performed on the computer keyboard. The one important parameter to set is the size of the nudge increment: how far the selected material will move with each key press. In Studio One 2, nudging is most straightforward when using musical divisions, rather than samples, seconds, or frames.

To nudge selected items sooner or later by a musical division, do the following:

1. Be sure that the Timebase field is set to Bars.
2. Set the Quantize setting to the desired nudge duration.
3. Be sure that the Snap box is checked.
4. Set the Snap Type to Quantize.
5. Set the Snap Reference to Snap to Grid.
6. Press Option + Right Arrow (Alt + Right Arrow in Windows) or choose Edit > Nudge > Nudge from the main menu bar, or Option + Left Arrow (Alt + Left Arrow in Windows) or choose Edit > Nudge > Nudge Back from the main menu bar, to nudge the selected items later or sooner (respectively) in time by the Quantize value.
7. Press Option + Cmd + Right Arrow (Ctrl + Alt + Right Arrow in Windows) or choose Edit > Nudge > Nudge Bar from the main menu bar, or Option + Cmd +Left Arrow (Ctrl + Alt + Left Arrow in Windows) or choose Edit > Nudge > Nudge Bar Back from the main menu bar to nudge the selected items later or sooner (respectively) in time by exactly one bar.

- When Timebase is set to Seconds and Quantize value is 1/2.(half-note), the nudge increment is one second. Changing the Quantize value alters the increment proportionally: a Quantize value of 1/4. sets the increment to a half a second, setting Quantize to 1/8 sets the increment to 250 ms, and so forth.

When Timebase is set to Frames, the nudging increment is not regular. Avoid using this.

MOVE TO CURSOR

Although this command is called Move to Cursor, it actually moves selected items to the play location, not to the mouse cursor location.

- To move one or more selected items to the current play location, press Cmd + L (Ctrl + L) or choose Edit > Move to Cursor from the main menu bar. If multiple items are selected, they will be moved as a unit—that is, the start of the earliest item will be moved to the play location, with all other items retaining their relative time relationships.

MOVE TO ORIGIN

This applies only to files in the Broadcast Wave Format (BWF). When chosen, it moves the selected Event to the time given in the file's BWF Origination Time metadata field.

- To move one or more selected Events to their BWF Origination Time, choose Edit > Move to Origin from the main menu bar.

Deleting

DELETING ITEMS

One or more items can be deleted in any of these ways:

- Select the Eraser tool and click on an item to delete it.
- Select the Eraser tool and click on any one of a group of selected items to delete them all.
- Select an item and press the Delete key to delete it.
- Select a group of items and press the Delete key to delete them all.

DELETE TIME

Suppose that you decide you want to remove the bridge after the third chorus altogether. That is easily done with Delete Time, which removes all of the material in the selected area and moves the material after the selection up by the same amount—in effect, deleting the time. It is most valuable when used with the Snap box checked, which makes it equally easy to remove a beat, a bar, or a 16-bar verse. To delete a time range, do the following:

1. Make the Range tool active.
2. Drag over the time range you want to remove to select it. It does not matter how many tracks you drag over.
3. Press Option + Cmd + D (Ctrl + Alt + D in Windows), right-click anywhere in the selected range and choose Delete Time from the contextual menu that drops down, or choose Edit > Delete Time from the main menu bar to delete the time.

DELETE DOUBLE NOTES, SHORT NOTES

Great cleanup utilities. Read more in the section "More Useful Selection Tricks," above.

Sizing Items

"Sizing" refers to adjusting the start and/or end times of Events, Parts, and notes.

SIZING AN ITEM BY DRAGGING

1. Make the Arrow tool active.
2. Move the cursor over the start or end edge of the item you wish to size; the cursor icon will change to an arrowhead and a line. It is not necessary to select the item before sizing it.
3. Drag the edge to size the item as desired. The largest size an Audio Event can be dragged to is the duration of the file on which it is based.

Here are more sizing tricks:

- To size multiple items simultaneously, simply select them all and drag the left or right edge of any of them.
- To set multiple notes in the Music Editor to the same duration, hold down the Cmd (Ctrl) key while dragging. All selected notes will snap to the duration of the note that was clicked on.

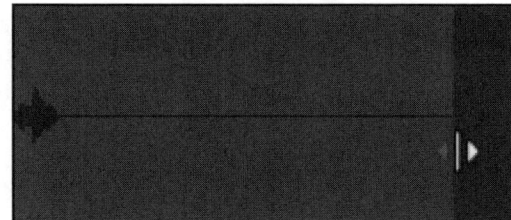

Fig. 5-70: An item can be sized by placing the cursor over its edge and dragging.

- To set the ends of multiple notes to the same location, hold down the Option (Alt) key while sizing. The ends of all selected notes will snap to the location of the end of the note that was clicked.

SIZING AN ITEM WITH THE EVENT INSPECTOR

You can also size items by changing their end times in the Event inspector with any of the methods described in the section "Moving Items," above. Of course, items can also be sized simply by selecting and deleting their beginnings and/or ends.

Dividing

Dividing Events, Parts, and even notes, is a basic capability. Studio One 2 includes a number of methods for this, from simple and obvious to advanced and subtle.

Among the more advanced and subtle methods is Strip Silence, which segments by detecting periods of silence, assuming that they are spaces between important audio occurrences, and deleting the silence to leave the occurrences as separate Events.

Transient Detect and Audio Bend markers take a very different approach, detecting and marking transients in the audio, assuming that they suggest where the bars and beats fall, and deriving a tempo from that so that the audio material can be manipulated in a tempo-based context.

Strip Silence, Transient Detect, and Audio Bend Markers are discussed in the section "Segmenting" in chapter 6, "Advanced Editing." ("Segmenting" is just a fancy word for "dividing," which we use here as a way to distinguish the fancier methods of splitting material up that we want to talk about later from the more basic methods described in this section.)

DELETING TO DIVIDE

The most obvious method, this is also often the quickest way to separate a few takes recorded in one pass.

1. Make the Range tool active.
2. Select a range where you want to divide and press the Delete key, right-click in the range and choose Delete from the drop-down menu that appears, or choose Edit > Delete from the main menu bar.

CUTTING WITH THE SPLIT TOOL

The Split tool makes a division of "zero length," which is useful for very precise splits.

1. Make the Split tool active.
2. Click at the spot where you want the split made.
3. If multiple items are selected, all will get split.

MAKE NEW ITEM FROM SELECTION (SPLIT ITEMS AROUND SELECTION)

You can make a selection into a new item with the Split Range command. The command makes splits at the edges of a selection, creating new items at the selection start and end times. Note that if there are discontiguous ranges selected, new items will be created at the start and end of each range. Splits are made only on tracks on which a selection has been made. So, you could have selected a range on one track and a later discontiguous range that spans three tracks, and end up with splits in all those spots. To make splits at the selection edges:

1. Select the ranges and tracks you want made into new items.
2. Press Option + Cmd + X (Ctrl + Alt + X in Windows), right-click in the range and choose Split Range from the contextual menu that drops down, or choose Edit > Split Range from the main menu bar to make new items out of the selected area(s). A split will be created across all tracks on which the range selection is made.

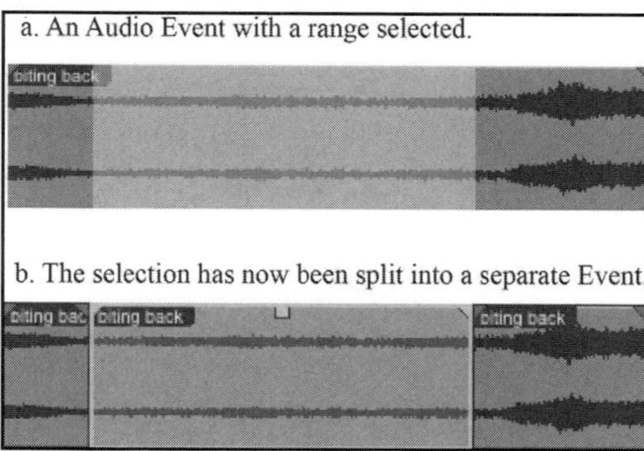

Fig. 5-71: The Split Range command is the way to extract a portion of an Audio Event into its own Event.

SPLIT AT CURSOR

This works the same as the Split tool: a split of "no duration" is created in selected items wherever the play location (not mouse cursor) is when the command is invoked. Items that are not selected are unaffected. To make a split at the play location:

1. Select the items that you want split at the play location.
2. Click in the timeline to place the play location where you want the split to be made.
3. Press Option + X (Alt + X in Windows) or choose Edit > Split at Cursor from the main menu bar to split the selected items at the play location.
4. If no items are selected, this command will create a split at the play location across all tracks.

SPLIT LOOP

The Split Loop command creates splits at the loop start and end points across all tracks, regardless of the selection. If you've found the perfect loop, this is the way to isolate it for easy bouncing and duplicating. To make splits at the loop points, do the following:

1. Set the loop start and end points as desired.
2. Press Cmd + Shift + X (Ctrl + Shift + X in Windows) or choose Edit > Split Loop from the main menu bar to make new items at the loop points.

SPLIT AT GRID LINES

Using the grid, it is easy to create splits at precise divisions like bars, beats, or other specific note values.

- To split selected items at grid lines of the duration set in the Quantize Value field, right-click on any selected item and choose Event > Split at Grid from the contextual drop-down that appears, or choose Event > Musical Functions > Split at Grid from the main menu bar. This is another way of splitting and quantizing a performance using fairly constant note durations, like an eighth-note bass part.

SPLIT AT AUDIO BEND MARKERS

Once transient detection has been used, splits can be created at the Bend markers that were created. This is a vital step in quantizing audio: transient detection marks rhythmic subdivisions, splitting divides the Event into multiple Events, and, finally, those Events can be quantized. The split Events can also be made into Audio Parts for a different approach to quantizing. For more on all of this, see chapter 6, "Advanced Editing."

- To split one or more selected Audio Events at the Audio Bend markers, right-click on any selected Audio Event containing Bend markers and choose Audio > Split at Bend Markers from the contextual drop-down that appears, or choose Audio > Split at Bend Markers from the main menu bar.

Muting

MUTING TRACKS

We have already looked at muting tracks, but just to review:

- Use the Mute buttons in the track header or mini–channel strip inspector.
- Type the M key to toggle the Mute status of a selected track.
- You can also click on the Mute button of a channel in the Mix view and drag across adjacent channels to mute or unmute multiple channels. This is not a simple state toggle. If you mute a track and drag, tracks that are already muted will not be affected, and similarly if you unmute a track and drag. It is, however, a one-shot operation: if you drag across several channels to mute them, moving the mouse back over them while still dragging will not unmute them.

MUTING AND UNMUTING ITEMS

Mute Events or Parts in the Arrange view, and Events or notes in the Edit view using any of these methods:

- With the Mute tool active, click on an item to mute/unmute it.
- Select multiple items, then make the Mute tool active and click on any of them to mute/unmute them all.
- Select one or more items and press Shift + M, right-click on an item and choose Toggle Mute from the contextual menu that drops down, or choose Event > Toggle Mute from the main menu bar to toggle their mute statuses.
- Select one or more notes in the Edit view and click on the Mute button in the Note inspector.

TIP: Studio One 2 does not automatically assign a unique name to each Event created from a file. If you do not rename the Events yourself, all Events created from one file will bear the name of that file. This means that there can be a number of Events in a Song that sound totally different but have the same name.

TRACK GROUPS AND FOLDER TRACKS

About Groups

When tracks are grouped, performing an operation on one of them causes the action to be performed identically and instantaneously on all other tracks in the group. There are oh so many uses for grouping tracks. Here are just a few:

- While tracking, groups are useful with instruments using multiple microphones, like drums or piano. Grouping makes it easy to create new takes for all tracks in the group with one command, or arm them all for recording with a single click.
- In editing it is common to use grouping in much the same way as in tracking: to allow an action to be performed on the entire group with a single gesture. Perhaps you need to make a drum edit and want all of the tracks kept in phase, or you want to create identical fades at the end of multiple guitar overdubs.
- Mixing has probably the most uses for grouping. Whenever there are multiple tracks that are parts of the same function, such as drum groups, background vocals, brass, and so forth, it may be beneficial to group them. It is common for grouped tracks to also be submixed. To be clear on the difference, if you group your drum tracks, you can edit on one track or change its volume, and the other tracks are affected identically. You can then take the outputs of all of those tracks and mix them to a stereo drum submaster channel, which allows you to control the level of the whole drum mix, compress all of the drums together, or otherwise treat the drum tracks as a composite whole.

Groups in Studio One 2

In Arrange view, selections are extended across all tracks in the group, as are operations performed on those selections, whether it be dragging, cutting, deleting, or processing.

In Mix view, grouped channels have their levels, mute, solo, and monitoring statuses locked together. Levels are locked relative to their settings when the channels are grouped, so the relationships between the channel levels are maintained.

- To create a group, select the tracks (or channels) you wish to group, and press Cmd + G (Ctrl + G in Windows), right-click on a selected track/channel and choose Group Selected Tracks from the contextual menu that drops down, or choose Track > Group Selected Tracks from the main menu bar.

- To dissolve a group, click on any track in the group to select the group, then press Shift + Cmd + G (Ctrl + G), right-click on a selected track/channel and choose Dissolve Group <group name> from the contextual menu that drops down, or choose Track > Dissolve Group from the main menu bar.

The need often arises to make a mix adjustment to only one member of a group, maybe a small level tweak to a drum. It is awkward to dissolve a group, make the adjustment, then regroup the tracks. A group can be temporarily suspended so you can make the adjustment, then reinstated.

- To temporarily suspend a group and make a mix adjustment on a single member, hold down the Option (Alt) key while adjusting the fader or clicking on Mute, Solo, Record Enable, or Monitor. When the Option (Alt) key is released, the group is reinstated.

Folder Tracks

Any time you are working with a number of tracks that are related in some way, such as drum tracks or background vocals, it is efficient to be able to treat them collectively. Edit groups provide one set of grouping conveniences, and collecting them into a Folder track provides another set. Here are some reasons to use Folder tracks:

- By naming a Folder track appropriately and collapsing its tracks into it, you can reduce the number of tracks onscreen at once. A mix containing 40 tracks might be put into half a dozen Folder tracks, any of which can be expanded when you want to work on the tracks in that folder.
- Folder tracks provide another way of subgrouping. A Folder track has its own mute and solo functions that are independent of those on the individual tracks it contains, an output setting that causes all the tracks it contains to be assigned to the same bus or output, and access to the output level of the bus or output to which it is assigned.
- A Folder track can act as an Edit Group for all of the tracks it contains.
- Dropping an effect on a Folder track causes that effect to be inserted on the bus or output to which it is assigned.

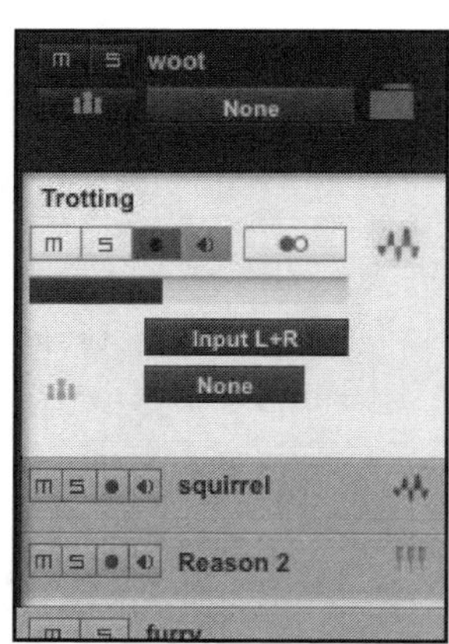

Fig. 5-72: Folder tracks enhance efficiency and make your session neater by collecting a number of related tracks together.

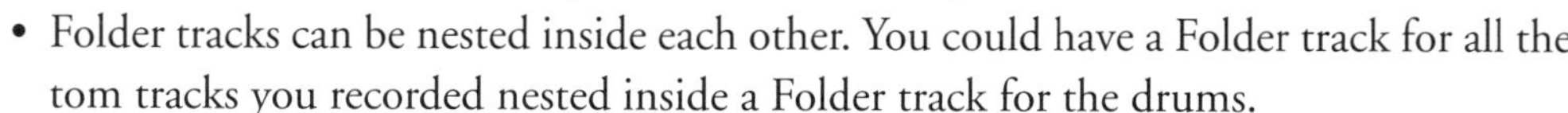

- Folder tracks can be nested inside each other. You could have a Folder track for all the tom tracks you recorded nested inside a Folder track for the drums.

Folder tracks are used only in the Arrange view.

PACKING TRACKS INTO FOLDER TRACKS

There are two ways to create a Folder track and pack it with tracks.

To select tracks and pack them into a Folder track, do the following:

1. Select all of the tracks you want to put into a folder.
2. Right-click (or Ctrl-click on Mac) in the header of any of the selected tracks and choose Pack Folder from the contextual menu that drops down, or choose Track > Pack Folder from the main menu bar. A new Folder track will be created with the selected tracks packed into it.

To make a Folder track and pack tracks into it, do the following:

1. Add a new track by pressing T, right-clicking in any track header and choosing Add Tracks, choosing Track > Add Tracks from the main menu bar, or clicking on the Arrange view Add Tracks button, and set it to be a Folder track.
2. Select one or more tracks that you want to pack into the folder and drop them onto the folder track or its header.

The Folder track will show the contents of the tracks in the Folder track, but this is for display only. Editing must be performed on the individual tracks, as usual. Also for display purposes only is the list in the Folder Track inspector of the tracks contained in the Folder track.

REMOVING TRACKS FROM A TRACK FOLDER

- To remove one or more tracks from a Folder track, select the track and drag it beyond the Folder track and all of the tracks it contains, until the pop-up tool tip changes from Move Track to Move Track Out Of Folder, then drop it.

EXPANDING, COLLAPSING, AND HIDING FOLDER TRACKS

- To expand or collapse the tracks in a Folder track, click on the folder icon in the Folder track header or the Folder track's name in the Track List.
- To hide a Folder track, click on its Show/Hide button in the Track List. The Folder track and all the tracks it contains will be hidden.

FOLDER TRACK AUDIO CONTROLS

- To mute a Folder track, click on the Mute button in the Folder Track header or Folder Track inspector. The Mute buttons for each track in the Folder track will change state along with the Mute button of the Folder track itself.
- To solo a Folder track, click on the Solo button in the Folder Track header or Folder Track inspector. The Solo buttons for each track in the Folder track will change state along with the Solo button of the Folder track itself.

- To use a Folder track as a submix, click in the Output Bus field in the Folder Track header or Track inspector channel strip and choose a bus from the drop-down menu that appears. When a bus has been selected, the controls for that bus channel will appear in the Track inspector channel strip, and a volume bar will appear below the bus name in the Folder Track header.

USING A FOLDER TRACK AS AN EDIT GROUP

- To make an Edit Group out of a Folder track, click on the Group Tracks button in the Folder track's header or the Track inspector channel strip. All tracks contained in the Folder track will now show the name of the Folder track in the Edit Group fields in their track headers, and an edit performed on one track contained in the Folder track will affect all the other tracks as well.

USING A FOLDER TRACK TO ADD AN EFFECT

You can insert an effect on the bus or output to which a Folder track is assigned using either of these methods:

- Drag the effect from the Effects pane of the Browser and drop it on the Folder track or its header, or in the Insert area of the mini–channel strip in the Track inspector.
- Click on the Add Insert button at the top of the mini–channel strip in the Track inspector.

Fig. 5-73: One benefit of putting tracks into a Folder track is that they can become an Edit group simply by clicking this button.

FOLDER TRACK AUTOMATION CONTROLS

Folder tracks can also act as Automation tracks. Any available automation parameter can be controlled from a Folder track, not just parameters that apply to the tracks contained in the Folder track. The automation controls are in the Automation section of the Track inspector. For more information on automation, see the chapter "Automation" in *Power Tools for Studio One 2*, vol. 2.

- To select an automation mode, click in the Automation Mode field and choose the desired mode from the drop-down menu that appears.
- To enable or disable automation in the Folder track Arrange view display, click on the Automation Enable/Disable button in the Automation section of the Track inspector or the Folder Track header.
- To add or remove an automation parameter to the Folder track, click in the Select Parameter field of the Automation section of the Track inspector or the Folder Track header, choose Add/Remove from the drop-down menu that appears, and select the desired parameter.

- To select an automation parameter for editing on a Folder track, click in the Select Parameter field of the Automation section of the Track inspector or the Folder Track header, and choose the desired parameter from the drop-down menu that appears.
- To color-code an automation parameter in a Folder track, click in the Select Parameter Color field of the Automation section of the Track inspector or the Folder Track header, and choose the desired color from the drop-down palette that appears.

Advanced Editing

6

Now that you know your edit tools and essential processes, let's dig deeper and find out what Studio One 2 really has to offer.

IT'S ABOUT TIME

Studio One 2 has many facilities for dealing with time in various ways. Meter and tempo changes can be added, time can be added to or subtracted from a Song, audio can be stretched or compressed to fit the tempo, time can be massaged to fit a groove template, and more.

Overview

What happens when you mess with time in Studio One 2? The answer to that question depends on whether the items concerned are referenced to musical structure (bars and beats) or directly to an absolute time value. For example:

- Notes and Parts will move to different time locations when tempo is changed in order to maintain their positions in the musical structure.
- If the Marker Track time base is set to Bars, tempo changes will move the markers in time to maintain their musical positions. But if it is set to Time, the markers are locked to their time locations, so tempo changes will give the markers different musical positions.

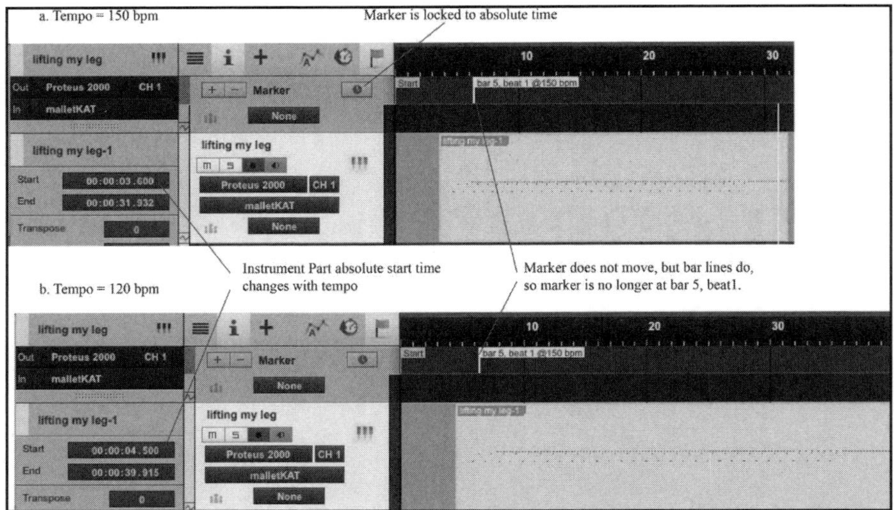

Fig. 6-1: The Part start time in bars is 3.02.01.00 at any tempo because it is referenced to musical location. However In seconds, the Part's start time changes from 00:00:03.600 when the tempo is 150 to 00:00:04.500 when the tempo is 120. The marker is locked to absolute time, so when the tempo is 150 is falls at bar 5, beat 1, but it does not move with tempo, so when the tempo is 120, the marker is at 4.01.04.20

- Inserting a time signature change affects the counter and metronome, but does not move any notes, Parts, or Events in time.

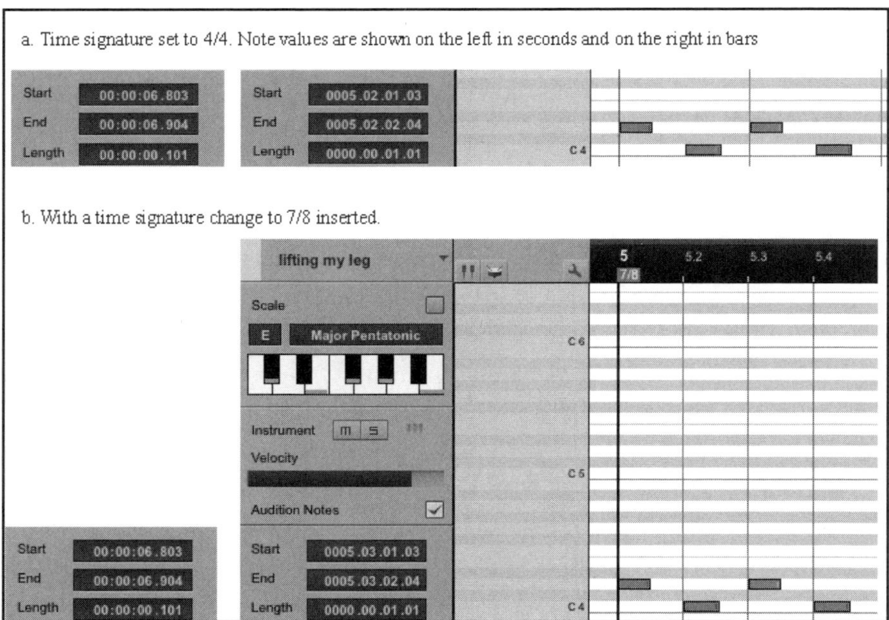

Fig. 6-2: A demonstration that time signature changes do not move notes in time. In figure 6-2a, notes are shown with a 4/4 time signature. In 6-2b, a time signature change to 7/8 has been inserted. The musical location has changed from bar 5 beat 2 to bar 5 beat 3, but the time location is unchanged.

- An Audio track with a file tempo value can be set to respond to tempo changes by moving Events to maintain musical positions, moving Events and altering their duration, or ignoring them altogether.

This chapter will look at each of these features and more.

Tempo Changes

CHANGING TEMPO ON THE FLY

Tempo is easily changed on the fly in the Transport bar using either of the following methods:

Fig. 6-3: The Transport bar Tempo field is the primary place to view and adjust tempo.

- Move the cursor over the Tempo field and drag up or down to increase or decrease the tempo.
- Click in the Tempo field and enter the desired tempo value.

THE TEMPO TRACK

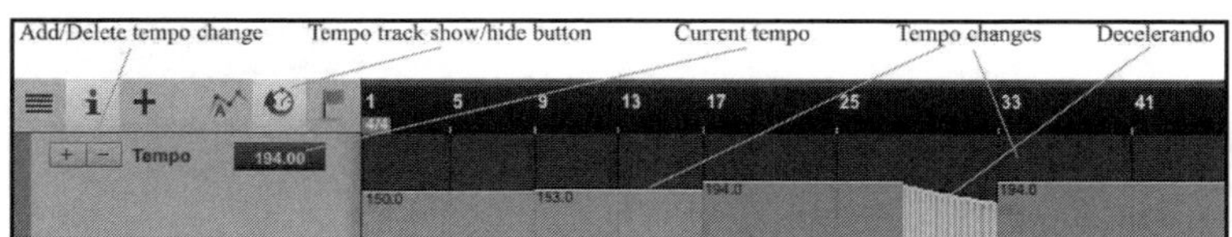

Fig. 6-4: The Tempo track is where tempo changes are defined. Individual tempo changes can be put in, accelerandi and decelerandi can be inserted, and tempo changes can be generated by operations such as Scale Time.

Tempo changes at key points can add life to a song. In Studio One 2, this is accomplished by inserting tempo changes into the Tempo track. Tempo changes are also essential when scoring music to picture. The Tempo track is located between the timeline and the Arrange view tracks.

Fig. 6-5: The Tempo track is opened and closed by the Tempo track button.

- To open the Tempo track, click on the button with the stopwatch icon in the toolbar above the Arrange view track headers.

TO CHANGE TEMPO ON THE FLY

To change tempo on the fly, use any of the methods listed below. Note that these changes are not stored in any way; the tempo stays at the last value to which it was set.

- Move the cursor over the Tempo field in the Transport window and drag up or down to increase or decrease the tempo. When the desired value is reached, click on it to accept it.
- Click on the Tempo field in the Transport window and enter the desired tempo value. Press the Enter or Return key to accept the value.

- Click on the Tempo field in the Tempo track, enter the desired value, and press the Enter or Return key to accept it.

INSERTING TEMPO CHANGES

Tempo changes can be inserted into the Tempo track in several different ways.

INSERTING TEMPO CHANGES WITH THE PAINT TOOL

1. Make the Paint tool active in the Arrange window.
2. Position the cursor in the Tempo track at the location where you want to insert the tempo change.
3. Click to insert the tempo change. The vertical position within the Tempo track at which you click determines the value of the inserted change, but there is no real-time readout of the cursor as you move it vertically, making it very difficult to insert a tempo change at the desired value. The solution is to just insert the tempo change and then edit it.
4. Once the tempo change has been inserted, position the cursor at the top of the tempo change block in the Tempo track. The cursor will change to double-headed arrows with a line in between.
5. Drag up or down to adjust the tempo change to the desired value. As you drag, a small pop-up tool tip will show the value changing in real time.

Fig. 6-6: Editing a tempo change in the Tempo track.

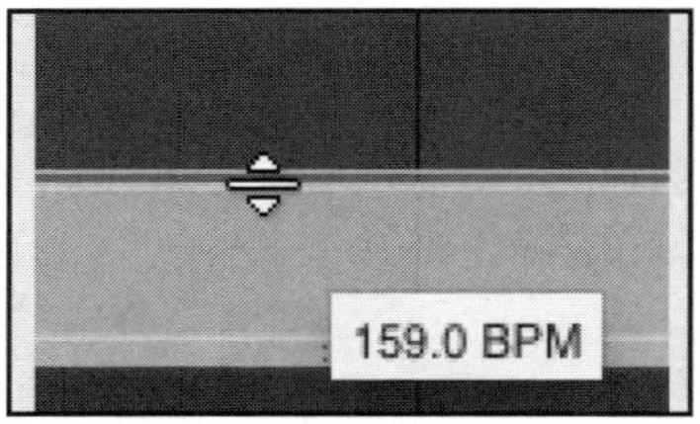

Fig. 6-7: Tempo changes are edited in the Tempo track by dragging with the arrow tool. The tool tip pop-up shows the exact tempo.

INSERTING TEMPO CHANGES WITH THE PLUS/MINUS KEYS

1. Position the cursor in the Tempo track at the location where you want to insert the tempo change.
2. Click on the + (plus) key in the Tempo track header to insert the tempo change. The new tempo will be set to the same value as the existing one.
3. Once the tempo change has been inserted, position the cursor at the top of the tempo change block in the Tempo track. The cursor will change to up/down double-headed arrows with a line in between.
4. Drag up or down to adjust the tempo change to the desired value. As you drag, a small pop-up window will show the value changing in real time.

CREATING A NEW TEMPO CHANGE WITH THE SPLIT TOOL

1. Make the Split tool active in the Arrange view.

2. Position the cursor in the Tempo track at the location where you want to create a new tempo change and click.
3. A new tempo change set to the same value as the existing one will be inserted. Use one of the editing techniques below to set the new tempo change to the desired value.

INSERTING AN ACCELERANDO (SPEEDUP) OR DECELERANDO (SLOWDOWN) WITH OPTION-DRAG

You can insert an accelerando (gradual tempo increase) or decelerando (gradual tempo decrease) instead of a single tempo change.

1. Make the Arrow, Range, Paint, or Mute tool active in the Arrange window.
2. Position the cursor in the Tempo track at the location where you want tempo changes to begin.
3. Hold down the Option (Alt in Windows) key and drag up or down to create an accelerando or decelerando. As you drag, use the real-time display of the cursor position to set the ending tempo.
4. When you release the mouse, the accelerando or decelerando will be inserted as a ramp of tempo changes with a logarithmic curve.
5. Since there is no real-time display of the cursor before you start dragging, it is unlikely that you will be able to start at a specific chosen tempo. However, the tempo changes that are inserted are editable, so you can go back afterward and edit them individually to get the range you want. It's a labor-intensive method, but, at this time, the only choice.

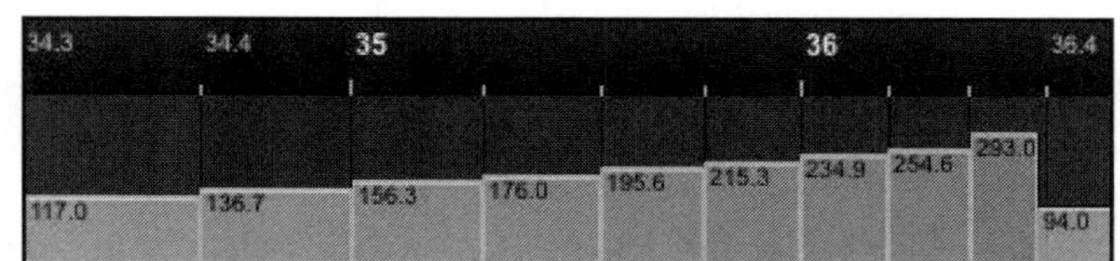

Fig. 6-8: An accelerando or decelerando is created as a series of tempo changes.

MODIFYING TEMPO CHANGES

Both the location and value of tempo changes can be edited in any of several ways, but there are a few things to keep in mind about the impact of tempo changes:

- Tempo changes alter the length of notes in Instrument Parts in order to maintain their musical durations.
- Tempo changes will affect Audio Events only if a file tempo has been defined for the Event in the Edit View inspector.
- If a file tempo has been defined, the setting in the Tempo field of the Track inspector will determine the exact effect of tempo changes on the Event. For more information, see the section "Quantizing," below.

With that in mind, let's take a look at the ways to modify tempo changes.

CHANGING THE VALUES OF TEMPO CHANGES

- To change the value of a tempo change, make the Arrow, Range, Paint, or Mute tool active, and position the cursor at the top of the tempo change block that you want to alter in the Tempo track. The cursor will change to an up/down double-headed arrow with a line in between. Drag up or down to adjust the tempo change to the desired value. As you drag, a small pop-up tool tip will show the value changing in real time.
- To edit the value of multiple tempo changes simultaneously, select the tempo changes you want to change, then drag any one of them up or down. The value of all selected tempo changes will be modified by the same amount.

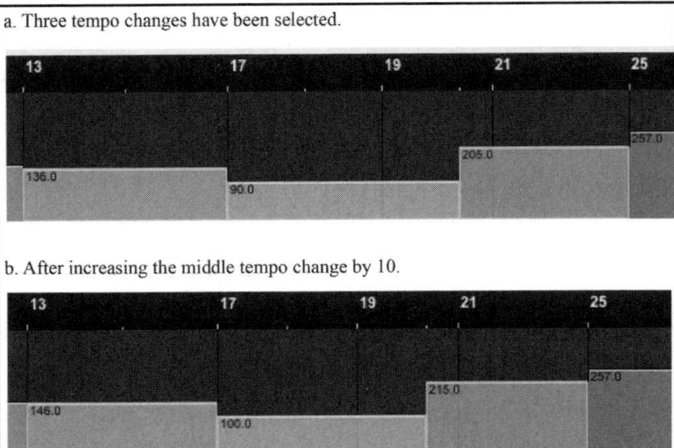

Fig. 6-9: In figure 6-9b, the middle tempo change was increased by 10, also increasing the other two selected tempo changes by the same amount.

CHANGING THE LOCATIONS OF TEMPO CHANGES

To change the location of a tempo change, do the following:

1. Make the Arrow, Range, Paint, or Mute tool active and position the cursor at the left edge of the tempo change that you want to alter in the Tempo track. The cursor will change to a left/right double-headed arrow with a line in between.
2. Drag left or right to make the tempo change earlier or later. As you drag, a small pop-up tool tip will show the location changing in real time.
3. To edit the locations of multiple tempo changes simultaneously, select the tempo changes you want to change, then drag any one of them left or right. The locations of all selected tempo changes will be modified.

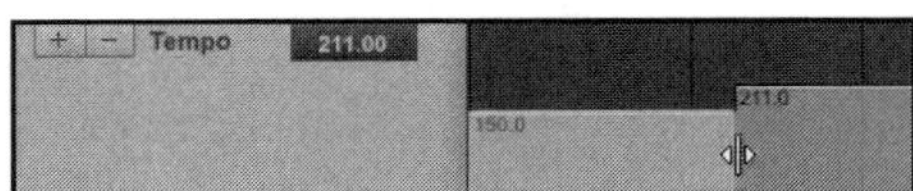

Fig. 6-10: Tempo changes can be dragged left or right to move them in time.

SCALE TIME IN THE TEMPO TRACK

Scale Time is a way of fitting a musical location, such as a particular bar line, to a point in time. Two good applications for this are lining up a downbeat with a specific video frame, and creating a tempo map to follow performance variations. This last is the same idea as a groove map, giving you two different methods to approach the same sort of problem. Scaling time couldn't be easier to do, either: just drag the bar line you want to the time you want.

To scale time, do the following:

Fig. 6-11: The first step in scaling time is making sure the Arrange view time base is set to Bars.

1. If the Tempo track is not open, click on the button with the clock icon in the row of buttons above the track headers to open it.
2. Check that the Timebase field for the Arrange view timeline is set to Bars.
3. Position the cursor in the Tempo track at the bar line you want to place.
4. As you drag, a pop-up tool tip will display telling you the tempo change that will result at the bar line you are dragging if you release the mouse at the current location, the musical location being dragged, and the time at which that musical location will occur if you release the mouse button at the current location.
5. When you reach the desired time, simply release the mouse and the appropriate tempo change will be calculated and inserted.

You could create a tempo map for an entire Song from audio this way if Groove Quantize were not doing the job for some reason, but it could turn out to be a fairly labor-intensive method if you need to go bar by bar.

DELETING TEMPO CHANGES

You can delete tempo changes using any of these methods:

- With the Arrow, Range, or Mute tool active, click on the tempo change that you wish to delete in the Tempo track, then press the Delete key.
- To delete multiple tempo changes, Shift-click with the Arrow, Range, or Mute tool on each of the tempo changes you want to delete, then press the Delete key.
- With the Range tool active, drag over any number of contiguous tempo changes to select them. As long as the cursor touches any part of a tempo change, it will be included in the selection. You can Shift-click to add

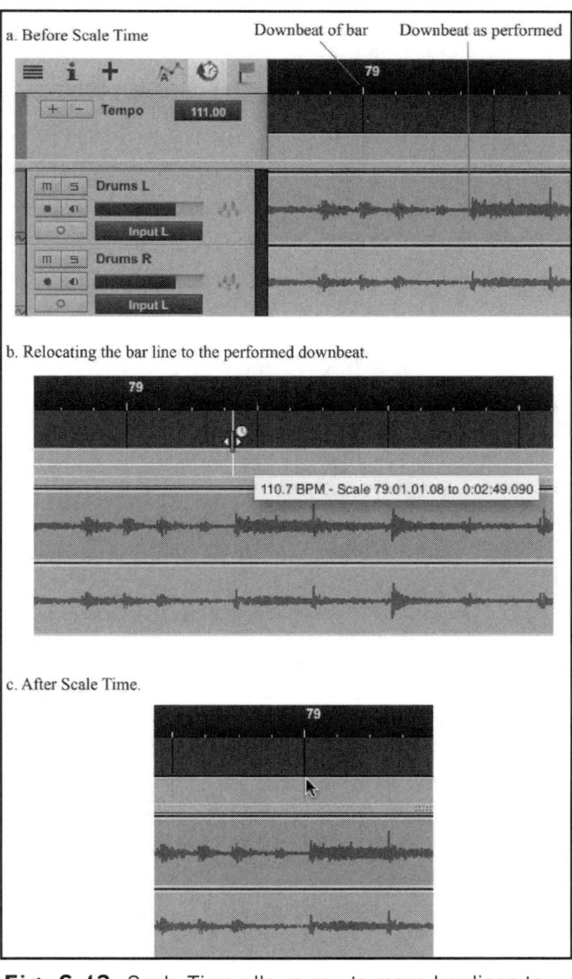

Fig. 6-12: Scale Time allows you to move bar lines to match up with performance variations, simply by dragging the bar line in the Tempo track.

discontiguous tempo changes to the selection. Press the Delete key to delete the selected tempo changes.

- Make the Erase tool active and click on any tempo change to delete it.
- To delete multiple tempo changes, Shift-click with the Arrow, Range, or Mute tool on each of the tempo changes you want to delete, then click on any of them with the Erase tool. Note that clicking on an unselected tempo change will delete only that change, not any of the selected tempo changes.

Time Signature Changes

Time signature changes are inserted on bar lines in the timeline.

INSERTING A TIME SIGNATURE CHANGE IN THE TIMELINE

1. Set Timebase in the Arrange window to Bars.
2. Position the cursor over the location in the timeline where you want to insert the time signature change.
3. Right-click (or Ctrl-click on Mac) in the timeline and choose Insert Timesignature from the drop-down menu that appears. The Insert Timesignature dialog box will open.
4. Enter any number between 1 and 16 in the numerator to indicate the number of beats per bar.
5. Choose the value that will be the pulse from the drop-down menu that appears in the Denominator field.

Fig. 6-13: The Insert Timesignature dialog.

EDITING THE VALUE OF A TIME SIGNATURE CHANGE

1. Double-click on the time signature change you wish to edit in the timeline.
2. Edit the values as desired in the Edit Timesignature dialog box that appears.

CHANGING THE LOCATION OF A TIME SIGNATURE CHANGE

- To relocate a time signature change, simply click on the time signature change you want to relocate and drag it left or right to move it earlier or later.

DELETING A TIME SIGNATURE CHANGE

1. Set Timebase in the Arrange window to Bars.
2. Position the cursor in the timeline over the time signature change you want to delete.
3. Right-click (or Ctrl-click on Mac) in the timeline and choose Remove Timesignature from the drop-down menu that appears.

Tap Tempo

Sometimes it is easier to show Studio One 2 the tempo you want than to enter a tempo value. Tap Tempo is the means for doing this. Tap Tempo enables you to set the tempo of a Song by feel or match it to the tempo of an audio recording, or simply to find the tempo of an audio file so that information can be used elsewhere. To set the tempo of a Song by tapping, do the following:

1. Be sure that the Tempo mode of the currently selected track is set to Don't Follow. If it is set to Follow or Timestretch, Studio One 2 will be trying to move and/or time-stretch Events on the track as you tap.
2. Start playback just before the passage whose tempo you want to use.
3. On each beat, click on the word "Tempo" beneath the Tempo field in the Transport window. After a few taps, the tempo will be calculated and displayed.

Fig. 6-14: Before using Tap Tempo to set the tempo, be sure the Tempo mode of the track is set to Don't Follow.

TAP TEMPO APPLICATIONS

- Set the Song tempo by feel.
- Match the Song tempo to a loop or performance.
- Find the tempo of a particular passage where it changes so that you can insert a tempo change to match it. A complete tempo map of a performance can be built up this way. This is a useful technique in situations where transient detection is not effective.
- Identify the tempo of an audio file for Studio One 2. For more information on using audio file tempos, see the section "Audio File Tempos," below.

Adding and Deleting Time

Adding and deleting time are common arranging techniques. Deleting time causes material after the deleted range's end to be moved forward by the amount of time deleted.

INSERT SILENCE

Time is added by inserting a silence of some duration into the Song and moving all items after the insertion point later by the same amount of time. Only selected tracks are affected when silence is inserted.

a. Make a selection where you want to insert silence.

b. After inserting silence. Note that bottom Event has been broken into two Events.

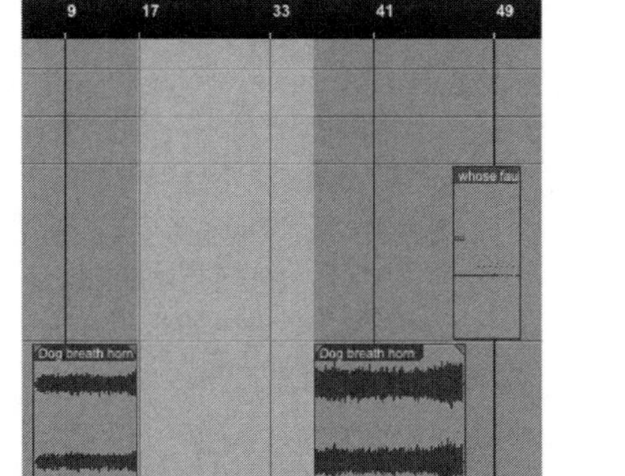

Fig. 6-15: Insert Silence will move Events or break them in two as needed.

- To insert silence into a Song, select a range of time in a Song and press Option + Cmd + I (Ctrl + Alt + I in Windows), right-click in the range and choose Insert Silence from the contextual drop-down menu that appears, or choose Edit > Insert Silence from the main menu bar.

DELETE TIME

Time is deleted by removing material in the selected range and moving all items after the deletion end point earlier by the same amount of time. Only selected tracks are affected when time is deleted.

- To delete time from a Song, select a range of time and press Option + Cmd + D (Ctrl + Alt + D in Windows), right-click in the range and choose Delete Time from the contextual menu that appears, or choose Edit > Delete Time from the main menu bar.

TIP: On the Mac, Option + Cmd + D is used as a shortcut to turn Dock hiding on and off. To disable this and free the combination for use with Studio One 2, open System Preferences > Keyboard > Keyboard Shortcuts > Dashboard & Dock, and uncheck Turn Dock Hiding On/Off.

EDITING AUDIO

Fades

Fades work essentially the same way in the Arrange and Edit views of the Song window. There are some additional fade features in the Project window, which will be discussed in the chapter "Mastering," in *Power Tools for Studio One 2*, vol. 2.

ADDING A FADE-IN OR FADE-OUT

When a fade is added to an Event, the waveform display is adjusted to show the effect of the fade. This is very helpful in setting the duration and shape, and sometimes the waveform display is useful in showing when you have eliminated an artifact you are trying to hide, but you should always let your ears tell you when it sounds right.

- To add a fade-in to an Event, drag the triangular handle in the upper left corner of the Event to the right until the desired fade duration is reached. When the mouse is released, the fade will be inserted.
- To add a fade-out to an Event, drag the triangular handle in the upper right corner of the Event to the left until the desired fade duration is reached. When the mouse is released, the fade will be inserted.
- To add fades-in or fades-out to multiple Events, simply select all of the Events to which you want to add fades and drag the triangular handle at the start (for a fade-in) or end (for a fade-out) on any one of them. Identical fades will be added to all selected events.

As you drag a fade handle, a pop-up tool tip will indicate whether you are adding a fade-in or a fade-out and what its duration will be if the handle is released at the current position. In parentheses, the tool tip will indicate how far the duration has changed from what it was.

Fig. 6-16: Adding a fade-in to an Event. The pop-up tool tip gives the current fade-in time and the change from the original time.

TIP: Because Studio One 2 automatically adds short (10 ms) fades for some editing operations, the change in duration shown in the tool tip may not equal the duration of the fade. When multiple fades are created at once, the tool tip will show the values for the fade whose handle is actually being dragged. Don't be confused!

EDITING THE FADE SHAPE

- To edit the shape of a fade, click on the Event to select it, then drag the square handle sitting on the fade curve up or down. The shape will vary from exponential (when the handle is at the bottom), through linear (when the handle is in the middle), to logarithmic (when the handle is at the top). A pop-up tool tip will identify the shape as you drag.
- To edit the shapes of multiple fades at once, Shift-click to select all of the events, then drag the square handle sitting on the curve of any of the fades up or down. The fade shapes will be varied relative to their starting points. That is, all of the fades will not end up with the same shapes unless they started with the same shapes. Instead, each shape will be moved from its starting position as far "'up" or "down" as the handle gets dragged.

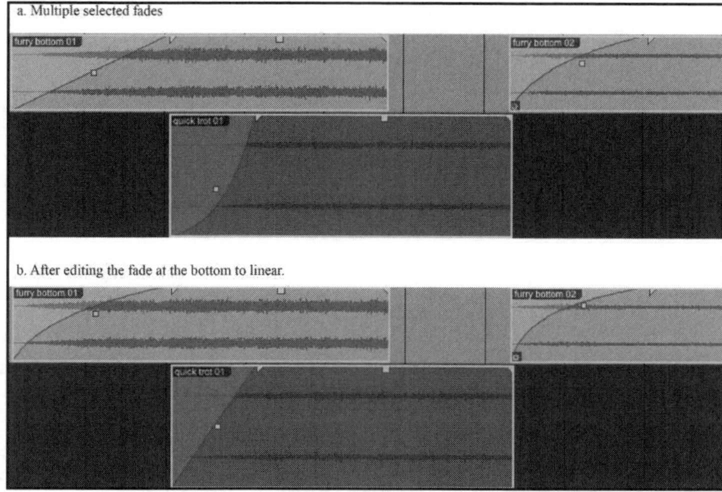

Fig. 6-17: In figure 6-17b, the shape of the fade at the bottom has been edited to linear. The other two fade shapes have been edited by the same amount, but relative to the shapes they started at.

EDITING FADE DURATION

Fade durations may be edited in any of the following ways:

- Click on the Event to select it, then drag the triangular handle at the end (for a fade-in) or start (for a fade-out) of the fade to the left or right to shorten or lengthen it.
- Select the Event containing the fade you want to edit, move the cursor over the Fade-In or Fade-Out field in the Event inspector, and drag up or down to increase or decrease the fade duration.
- Select the Event containing the fade you want to edit, click in the Fade-In or Fade-Out field in the Event inspector, and enter the desired fade duration value.

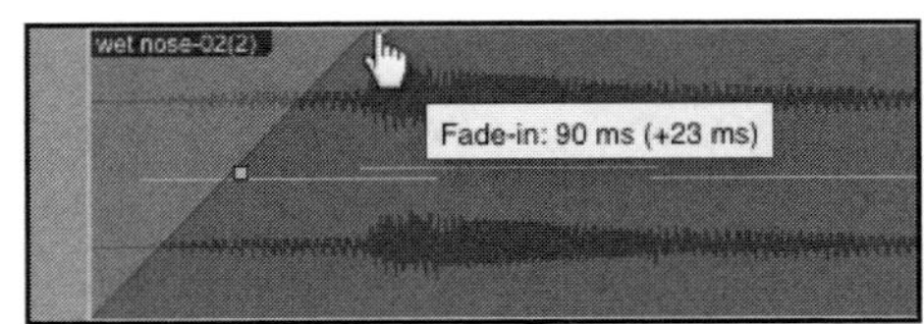

Fig. 6-18: Fade duration can be edited simply by dragging. A pop-up tool tip shows exact fade duration values.

- To edit the duration of multiple fades at once, Shift-click to select all of the Events, then drag the triangular handle at the end (to edit fades-in) or start (to edit fades-out) of any of the fades to the left or right to shorten or lengthen them. The durations of the fades are not all set to the same value. Instead, the duration of each fade is changed from its starting duration by the amount of time the handle is moved.
- To edit the duration of multiple fades at once, setting all fades to the *same* duration, select the Events containing the fades you want to edit, move the cursor over the Fade-In or Fade-Out field in the Event inspector, and drag up or down to increase or decrease the fade duration. All selected fades will snap to the duration you set. Clicking in the Fade-In or Fade-Out field in the Event inspector and entering the desired fade duration value will also set all fades to the specified duration.

FADES AND EVENT SIZING

When the start or end of an Event with a fade is dragged to resize the Event, the fade start and end times are moved together to keep the fade duration constant. When multiple Events with fades are sized, all fades maintain their durations, but are moved in time by the same amount.

AUTOFADES (TOP AND TAIL)

Editing can sometimes create clicks or other artifacts. The common solution to this is to put very short fades in and out on Events, known in some professional circles as "top and tail" fades.

Even with Studio One 2's ability to add fades to multiple Events at once, it turns out to be a number of steps to select the Events, zoom in enough to be able to create a fade-in of very short duration, then do the same for the fades-out. There is an easier way.

To add top and tail fades to one or more Events, do the following:

1. Select the Events to which you want to add top and tail fades.
2. Press Shift + X, right-click on one of the Events and choose Create Autofades from the contextual drop-down menu that appears, or choose Audio > Create Autofades from the main menu bar. Each selected Event will have 10 ms linear fades-in and -out added to them.
3. If you want some other duration or shape, the fades may be edited just like fades that are created manually. You will need to zoom in fairly far to do the editing.

In addition, top and tail fades are created automatically whenever a punch-in or punch-out is performed during recording.

FADES AND VOLUME AUTOMATION

Track volume automation is entirely separate from Event fades, but it can be used to create fades as well. Volume automation is covered in *Power Tools for Studio One 2*, vol. 2, so all I will give you here are two things to keep in mind about how volume automation relates to Event fades:

- Volume automation can be used to create fades-in or fades-out instead of using Event fades, but the waveform display will not be scaled to show the effects of the automation. Also, fades can be slower to create with automation.
- You can use Event fades and volume automation together. When you do, the resulting level is simply the addition of the two at any point in time. If a fade-in is at –16 dB at a location and the volume automation at that location is set to +3 dB, then the track will play at –13 dB at that location. Using volume automation in combination with an Event fade is a good way to get an unusual fade shape when the shape needs to be tailored for a specific situation. If you do this, though, you create a relationship between the two that can be rather complex to keep track of as you make changes, especially since the composite fade shape created when the two are working in tandem is not graphically represented anywhere. This means that all adjustments must be done entirely by ear. It is powerful to use Event fades and volume automation together, but you must remain acutely aware of each thing you do.

CROSSFADES

Any time two Events overlap you will want to use a crossfade. Without a fade-out of the old Event and a complementary fade-in of the new one, clicks and other artifacts can occur. In fact, even with a crossfade there can be artifacts if it is not the right duration and shape for the situation. This is true whether the Events are on the same track or on different ones.

Studio One 2 automatically creates a crossfade whenever you do a punch-in while recording, but for any other situation, you must create crossfades you want yourself.

CROSSFADING OVERLAPPING EVENTS ON THE SAME TRACK

1. Position two Events so that they overlap by the desired duration and in the desired location. The overlap is shown in gray, to make it easily visible. It makes no difference which Event is in front and which in back, but one or the other of the Events must be selected.
2. Press X on the keyboard, right-click on one of the Events and choose Create Crossfade from the contextual drop-down menu that appears, or choose Audio > Create Crossfades from the main menu bar. A linear crossfade will be created in the overlap region (from the beginning of the later Event to the end of the earlier Event).

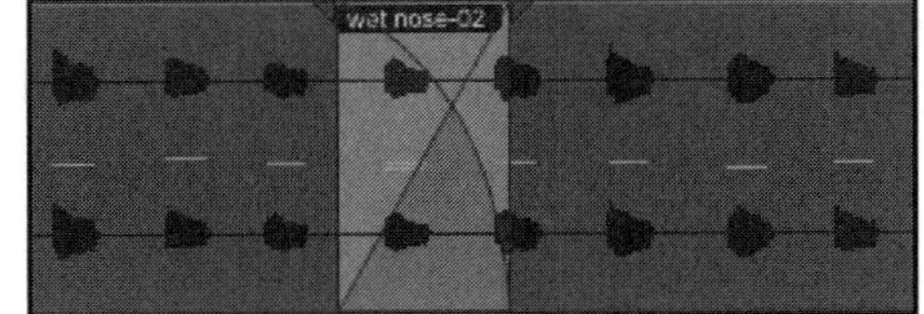

Fig. 6-19: A crossfade created with the X command.

Here are a few more tips on creating crossfades:

- Multiple crossfades can be created at the same time simply by selecting all of the overlapping Events and pressing X on the keyboard, right-clicking on one of the Events and choosing Create Crossfades from the contextual drop-down menu that appears, or choosing Audio > Create Crossfades from the main menu bar. The crossfades are likely to have different durations, since each crossfade is created to the duration of its overlap area.
- If two nonoverlapping Events with fades are moved so that they overlap, as soon as the mouse button is released the two fades will start to behave as a crossfade.

EDITING CROSSFADES

The duration and/or shape of any crossfade can be manually edited after it is created. The fade-in and fade-out will remain locked, so that adjusting either one affects the other identically. If a crossfade is edited to be a shorter duration than the overlap region, it can be slid back and forth in time to place it anywhere in the overlap region.

To shorten the duration of a crossfade, do the following:

1. With the Arrow tool active, move the cursor over either the start or end of the crossfade until the cursor icon becomes an arrowhead with a line.
2. Drag right from the start or left from the end of the crossfade to shorten its duration.

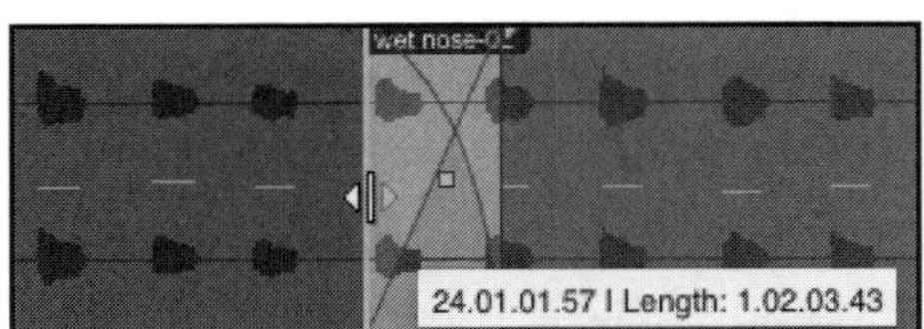

Fig. 6-20: A crossfade can be shortened by dragging its boundary.

To shorten the duration of a crossfade by reducing the amount of overlap, do the following:

- Select either of the overlapping Events and move it so that the Events are further apart in time. As the overlap decreases, the duration of the crossfade will be shortened.
- If you drag far enough that the two Events no longer overlap, each of the Events will have a fade the duration of the original overlap.

To lengthen the duration of a crossfade, do the following:

- Select either Event and drag it toward the other. As the overlap increases, the crossfade will lengthen in duration.

To edit the shape of a crossfade, do the following:

- Drag the square handle sitting on the crossfade curve up or down. The shape will vary from exponential (when the handle is at the bottom), through linear (when the handle is in the middle), to logarithmic (when the handle is at the top). A pop-up tool tip will identify the shape as you drag.

To edit the shape and duration of a crossfade simultaneously, do the following:

- Hold down the Shift key while dragging to edit either fade shape or duration in the Arrange view as described above.

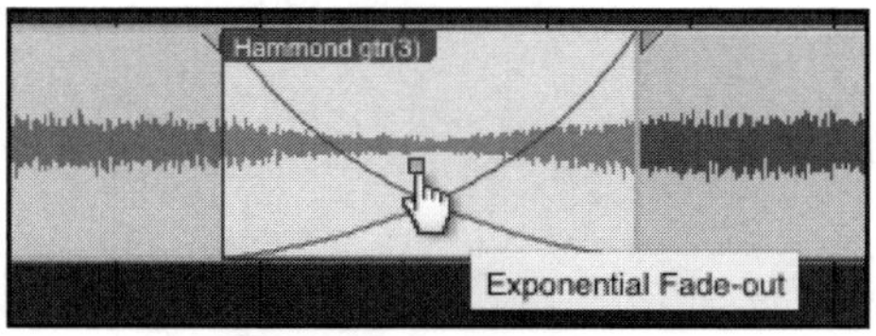

Fig. 6-21: The shape of a crossfade can be varied between linear and exponential by dragging the square handle at the crossfade's center.

ASYMMETRIC CROSSFADES

There are times when it is desirable for the fade-in and fade-out of a crossfade to have different shapes, or even be of different durations. This is called an "asymmetric crossfade." There is no simple way to accomplish asymmetric crossfades in Studio One 2, but it can be done.

To create an asymmetric crossfade, do the following:

1. Create a crossfade as described above.
2. Activate Snap and set the Snap Type to Relative Grid. This will let you move an Event in precise increments of the Quantize Amount without causing it to actually snap to the grid lines. If it is not important to exactly re-create the original time relationship between the two Events, you can skip this step.
3. Note where the overlap starts and then drag one or the other of the Events until they no longer overlap. Separate fades of the duration of the original overlap will be created.
4. Change the shape and/or duration of one or both fades as desired.
5. Drag the Event back to re-create the original overlap.

Event Volume

Just as each Event can have a fade-in and/or fade-out that is "attached" to it, it also has a fixed volume level that sits between the fades. This volume level is independent of mixer channel volume or track volume automation, and, as with fades, Event volume simply adds to mixer channel volume or volume automation. The Event volume always represents the level at which an Event's fade-in ends or fade-out begins. Just as with fades, Event volume can be adjusted graphically in the Arrange view or numerically in the Event inspector. The Event's waveform display, including the fades, adjusts appropriately to reflect the Event volume you have set. Event volume can be set over a range of +24 dB to –40 dB.

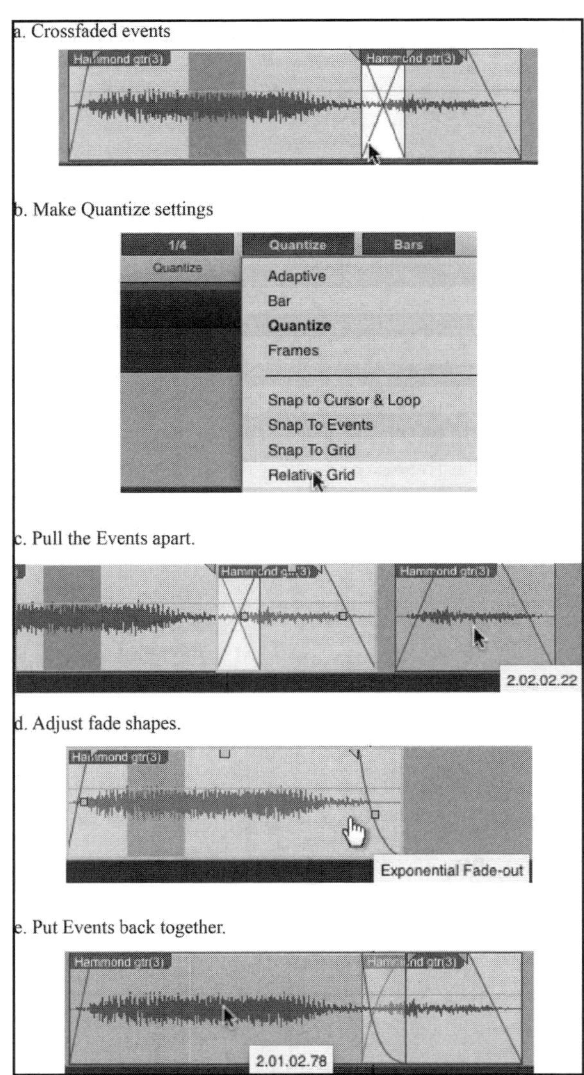

Fig. 6-22: To make an asymmetric crossfade, first make a regular crossfade, then separate the Events, edit the fade shapes, and put them back together.

Event volume may be edited in any of the following ways:

- With the Arrow tool active, click on the Event to select it, position the cursor at the top of the Event anywhere between its fade-in and fade-out (if it has those) until it turns into a pointing hand, and drag the volume up or down to the desired level. As you drag, a pop-up tool tip will show the current Event volume, and, in parentheses, the "Diff," or difference between the current volume and the volume before you started dragging. The tool shows only the Event volume, not the combined level of the Event volume and any automation that may be in the track.

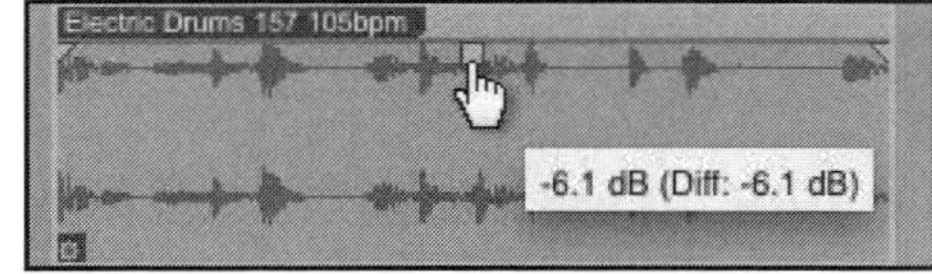

Fig. 6-23: Each Audio Event has its own volume level, which is set by dragging on the volume box. The tool tip pop-up shows the current volume level and the change from the starting value ("Diff").

- Select the Event whose volume you want to edit, move the cursor over the Gain field in the Event inspector, and drag up or down to increase or decrease the volume.
- Select the Event whose volume you want to edit, click in the Gain field in the Event inspector, and enter the desired volume value.
- To edit the volume of multiple Events at once, Shift-click to select all of the Events in the Arrange view, then drag the volume of any of the Events up or down to change it. The volumes of the Events are not all set to the same value. Instead, the volume of each Event is offset from its starting duration by the Diff (the amount the volume is changed by dragging).
- To edit the volume of multiple Events at once and set them all to the *same* value, select the Events whose volumes you want to edit, move the cursor over the Gain field in the Event inspector, and drag up or down to increase or decrease the volume. All selected Events will snap to the volume you set. Clicking in the Gain field in the Event inspector and entering the desired volume value will also set all Events to the specified volume.
- To change the volume of one or more selected Events by +6 dB, press Option + numpad + (plus sign) (Alt + numpad + in Windows), right-click (or Ctrl-click on Mac) on a selected Event and choose Audio > Increase Volume from the contextual drop-down menu that appears, or choose Audio > Increase Volume from the main menu bar.
- To change the volume of one or more selected Events by –6 dB, press Option + numpad – (minus sign) (Alt + numpad – in Windows), right-click on a selected Event and choose Audio > Decrease Volume from the contextual drop-down menu that appears, or choose Audio > Decrease Volume from the main menu bar.

Front/Back Arranging

Items can overlap on a track. When that happens, the track can be thought of as a kind of pile, in which the items are stacked up front to back. In most DAWs, these relationships are called "layers," but Studio One 2 already uses the word "Layers" to indicate what are called "takes" or "playlists" in other DAWs—so to avoid confusion with any other commonly used terms, I will refer to them here as "tiers." It's a little awkward, but unambiguous.

Anyway, the point is that when there are overlapping items, the frontmost tier is the one that will be heard during playback, unless you create a crossfade (as described above) to transition between tiers.

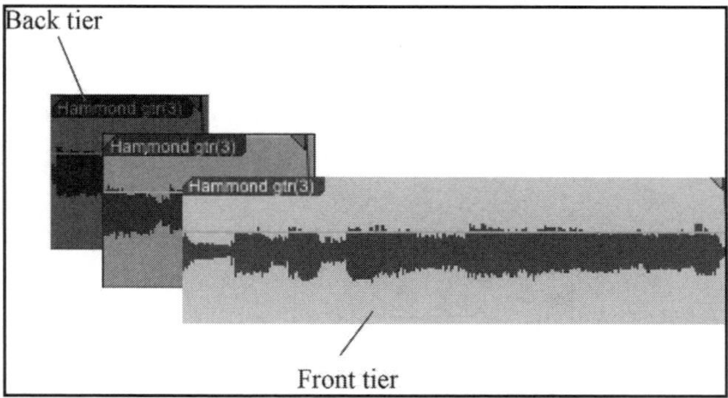

Fig. 6-24: Events on a track can be stacked on top of each other in tiers. Whatever is visible will play, that which is blocked behind another Event will not.

- To make an item the frontmost tier, select it and choose Event > Send to Front from the main menu bar.
- To make an item the back tier, select it and choose Event > Send to Back from the main menu bar.
- To move multiple items to the front or back, select them all and choose Event > Send to Front or Event > Send to Back.

Reversing Audio

Ever since the Beatles, we have all loved backwards sound. (Not that they were the first to do it, but they were the first most of us heard do it!) It's a LOT easier to do now than it was then. Best of all, it's nondestructive: a new file is created for the reversed audio.

- To reverse audio, select one or more Audio Events in the Arrange view and press Cmd + R (Ctrl + R in Windows), right-click on one of them and choose Audio > Reverse Audio from the contextual menu that drops down, or choose Audio > Reverse Audio from the main menu bar. The audio will be reversed. The original files are still available in The Pool.

Transposing and Tuning Events

Studio One 2 does not have an Audio track transpose feature, but it does have transposition and tuning for Audio Events. It also has integrated support for Celemony Melodyne. The Event inspector Transpose and Tune fields were described in the section "Audio Event Inspector" in chapter 5, "On the Cutting Room Floor: Basic Editing."

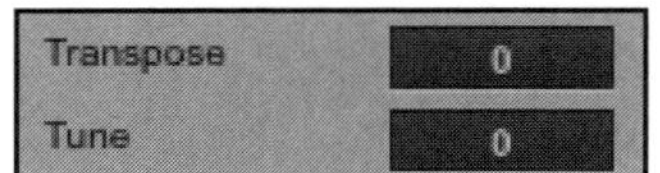

Fig. 6-25: The Transpose and Tune fields in the Event inspector are real-time processes, making them easily undone or modified.

To transpose or tune one or more Audio Events, do the following:

- Select the Event(s) whose pitch you want to change and set the Transpose or Tune field in the Event inspector to the desired value(s). All selected Events will assume those values.
- To transpose an entire track, select all Events on the track and then set the Transpose and Tune fields as desired.
- One other possibility for transposing audio is to put it into SampleOne or another sampler and use the sampler's transposition capabilities. In most cases, this is accomplished through variable playback, which changes the duration at the same time it changes the pitch. For some applications this is desirable, or, at least, acceptable.

MELODYNE SUPPORT

Celemony Melodyne is possibly the industry's most admired pitch correction software because of its impeccable sound quality, intuitive interface, and amazing capabilities. PreSonus and Celemony collaborated to create Audio Random Access (ARA), which allows extremely tight integration of Melodyne into Studio One 2. To support this, a fully licensed version of Melodyne Essential is included with Studio One 2 Pro. (Artist and producer users get 30-day trial versions.) I will talk here about the integration enabled by ARA, while Celemony's documentation is the place to learn how to use Melodyne.

The Melodyne window opens in the Edit view in place of the Audio editor. Of course, the Audio editor is still very much available any time you care to bring it back up.

The first big benefit of the integration of Studio One 2 and Melodyne is the elimination of the real-time analysis Melodyne used to require. Now, double-clicking on one or more Events invokes analysis that finishes in a few seconds. This time savings becomes much more powerful when a number of Events are analyzed at the same time.

Once an Event has been analyzed in Melodyne, it can be displayed in Melodyne, so batch analysis gives you the ability to click around to different Events and have them come up in the Melodyne editor window instantly. This is very useful if, for example, you are tweaking harmony vocals from a live performance where the monitoring wasn't what it should have been.

What's more, an analyzed Event can be simply dragged to an Instrument track to create MIDI data that duplicates the notes played or sung in the Event. This is a seriously easy way to convert audio to MIDI.

Melodyne alterations follow an Event; make some adjustments to an Event in Melodyne, make a copy of the Event, and take a look at the copy. All of the Melodyne alterations have been inherited by the copy.

Many Studio One 2 editing facilities, such as event muting and volume automation, work seamlessly in Melodyne, and Melodyne can do auto time-stretching when the tempo of the Song is changed in Studio One 2.

- To bring one or more Audio Events into Melodyne for analysis and editing, select the Event(s) and press Cmd + M (Ctrl + M), right-click on one of the Events and choose Edit with Melodyne from the contextual menu that drops down, or choose Audio > Edit with Melodyne from the main menu bar. Melodyne will be inserted in the Event FX section, then it will open and analysis will happen automatically. As long as the Event FX have not been rendered (meaning that Melodyne is active), double-clicking on the Event will open the Event in the Melodyne editor.

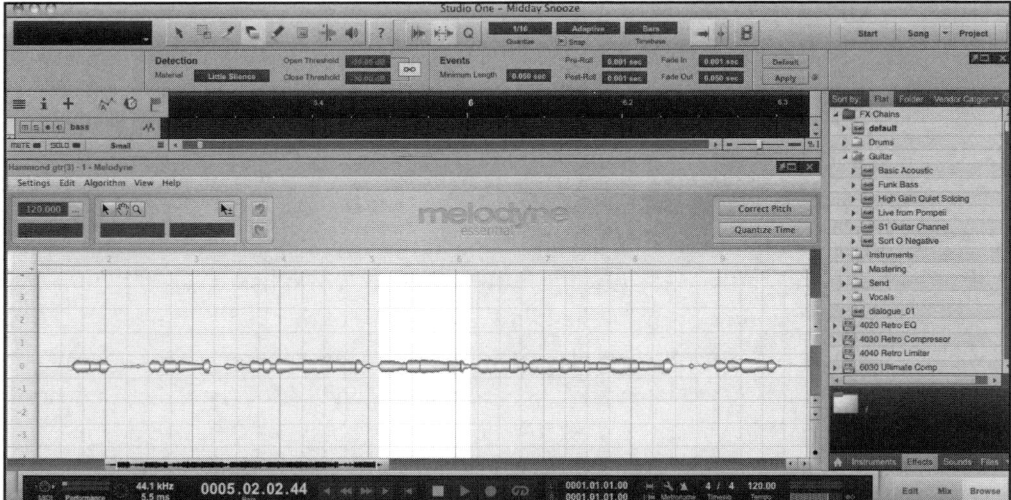

Fig. 6-26: Celemony Melodyne is tightly integrated with Studio One 2.

- To create MIDI data from one or more analyzed Events, select the Events and drag them onto an Instrument track. An Instrument Part containing the notes in the Audio Event will be created.

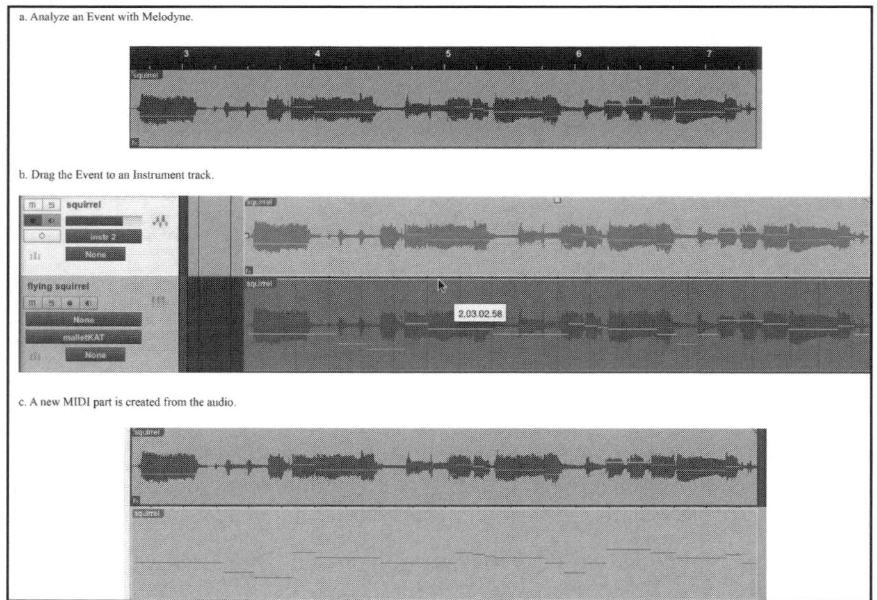

Fig. 6-27: Creating an Instrument Part from an Audio Event with Melodyne requires only analyzing the Event with Melodyne and then dragging it to an Instrument track.

Segmenting (Advanced Dividing)

Sometimes a track can be easily divided using the simple features described in the section "Dividing," in chapter 5, "On the Cutting Room Floor: Basic Editing." However, there are numerous applications in which dividing by hand becomes so labor-intensive as to be impractical. Studio One 2 offers a few sophisticated methods of dividing up audio material. To distinguish these methods from those described in chapter 5, I refer to them as "segmenting" methods, although that's really just a fancy word for "dividing" to indicate that these features are fancy tools for dividing.

STRIP SILENCE

Strip Silence is a powerful segmenting tool, especially useful for separating drum hits, splitting sound effects takes, and separating phrases. It works a bit like a noise gate: the algorithm identifies areas of silence and deletes them, thereby dividing an Event into multiple smaller events. Once segmented, the smaller Events can be used individually, quantized like MIDI data or REX files, and otherwise more flexibly handled.

The key to getting good results with Strip Silence is finding good settings for the detection parameters, for that determines the accuracy with which the algorithm can determine what is a silence between phrases and what is just a pause between notes. The open and close thresholds and the minimum duration time are the critical parameters.

It is important to be realistic about using Strip Silence. While it is capable of excellent results, only under the best circumstances is it possible to find settings that segment material exactly as you want it done. In most cases, it is necessary to settle for settings that get you most of the way there, then do some hand-tweaking to fix what does not come out right.

THE STRIP SILENCE PANEL

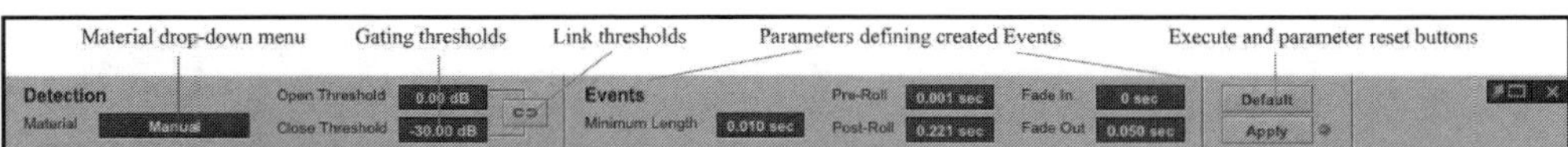

Fig. 6-28: The Strip Silence panel.

The Strip Silence feature is accessed through its own panel. To open the Strip Silence panel, do the following:

- Click on the Strip Silence panel button in the toolbar above the Arrange view at the top of the Song window.

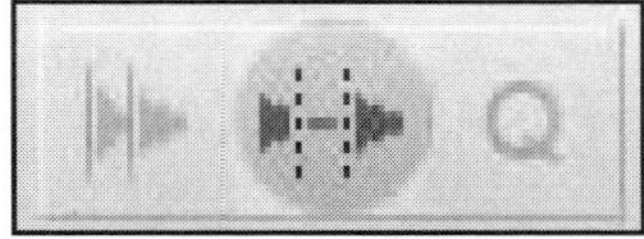

Fig. 6-29: The Strip Silence panel is opened and closed by the Strip Silence button in the Arrange view toolbar.

When the Edit view is open, an identical button appears in the toolbar above the waveform display in the Edit view. The only difference between the two buttons is where the Strip Silence panel appears, which will be below whichever of the buttons is clicked. So, clicking on the Edit view button causes the Strip Silence panel to appear above the waveform display of the Edit view, while clicking on the Arrange view button makes the panel appear above the Arrange view. Regardless of where the panel is showing up, clicking on either button causes it to become hidden.

Executing Strip Silence

- To strip silence from a selected Event, set the Detection and Event parameters described below and click on the Apply button.

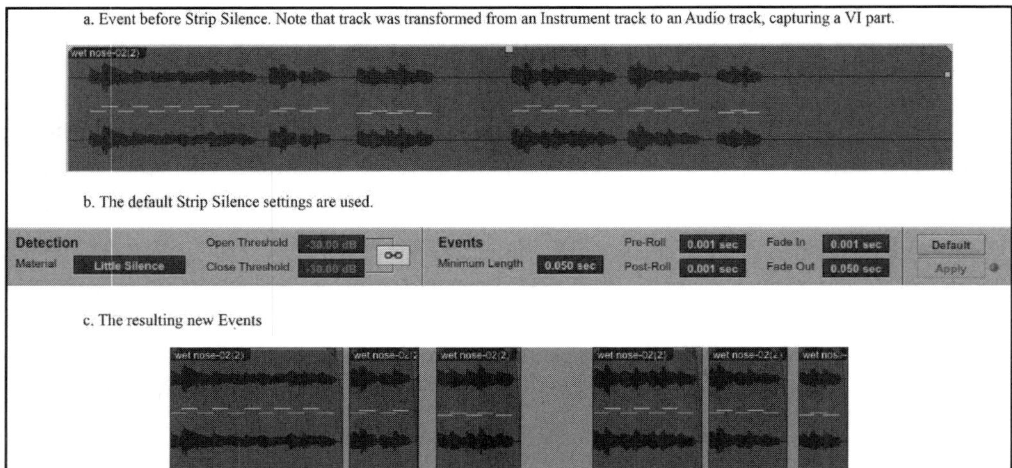

Fig. 6-30: Strip Silence in action. An Instrument track has been transformed into an Audio track, and now we wish to break the phrases into individual Events. The settings shown in (b) are applied to the Event shown in (a), resulting in the multiple new Events in (c).

Detection Parameters

Material

This parameter tells Studio One 2 the general character of the material relative to detecting silence. There are four settings:

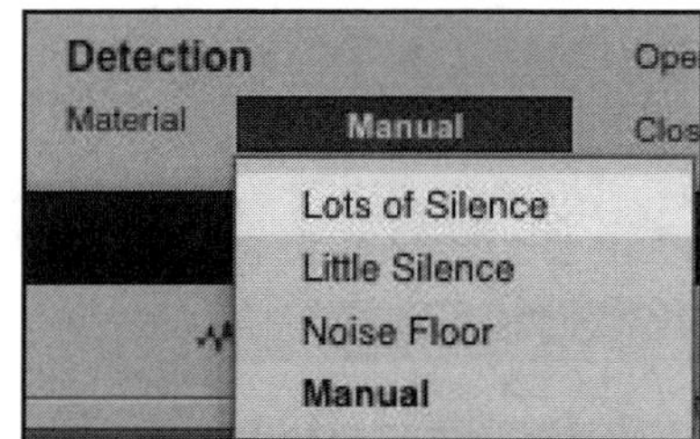

Fig. 6-31: The Strip Silence panel's Material submenu describes how the feature is likely to encounter silence in the material.

- **Little Silence:** This setting is used with tracks that may only have short breaks between notes.
- **Lots of Silence:** This setting is good for tracks in which there is a significant amount of time between notes or phrases. This might be cleanly recorded backbeat snare or background vocals, for instance.
- **Noise Floor:** This setting is useful when there is background noise that prevents the level from ever dropping to silence.

- **Manual:** Manual mode allows you to edit the Open and Close threshold levels, as well as unlink them (they default to being linked), so that they can have different values. This gives much more flexibility in configuring Strip Silence for the exact material you are trying to segment.

TIP: The settings you make in Manual mode are retained if you switch to one of the other modes. Therefore, you can go to Manual mode, unlink the Open and Close thresholds, set them to different values, and then switch back to whichever mode you think will work best.

Open and Close Thresholds

As with a gate, when the signal exceeds the Open threshold it is interpreted as the beginning of a new sound, whereas the Close threshold determines when a sound has ended. Material falling between the Close threshold of a sound and the Open threshold of the next sound is seen as silence and deleted.

Event Parameters

- **Minimum Length:** The signal must stay above the threshold for at least the amount of time indicated as the Minimum Length in order to be split into its own Event. If its level falls below the Close threshold before the Minimum Length has been met, the material is left alone.
- **Pre/Post Roll:** When threshold values have been found that result in the desired segmenting, attacks or decays may sometimes get cut off short. Preroll and postroll are extra amounts of time—"padding," if you will, that is added to the head and tail of each new Event to counter this problem.
- **Fade In/Out:** Segmenting is done with hard edits, which can sound clipped or even produce clicks and other artifacts. Adding a small fade-in and fade-out to each Event can smooth out the results of segmenting.

Restoring Default Settings

- To restore the default values of the Detection and Event parameters, click on the Default button at any time.

TRANSIENT DETECTION AND AUDIO BEND

Transients are short-duration audio episodes. In audio recordings of musical instruments, a transient frequently indicates the attack of a note. In rhythmic music, the ability to detect note attacks is a stepping-stone to figuring out the tempo and to quantizing audio.

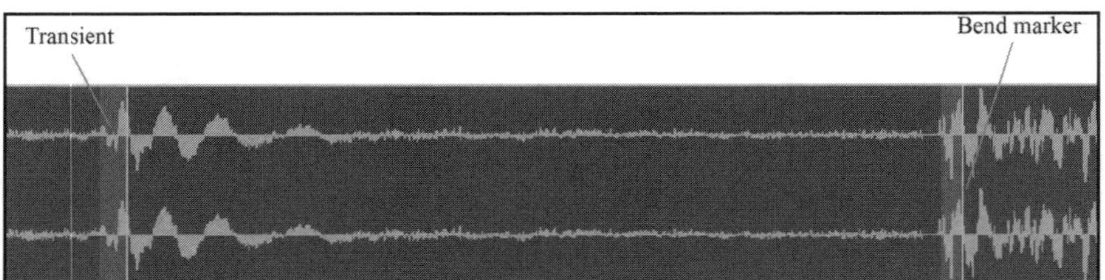

Fig. 6-32: After transient detection, Audio Bend markers are placed, but attack transients are treated separately to preserve their character and impact.

As you have already seen, one way to quantize audio is to segment it into smaller Events and then quantize those Events. Audio Bend markers are also based on the idea of segmenting the audio and then quantizing. However, instead of breaking the audio into separate Events, Bend markers create segments within the Event based on transients it detects in it. The tempo of each segment is then determined.

Once a map of these tempo changes exists, it can be used for audio quantizing, either as the basis for a groove map (where it acts like a grid, to which audio or MIDI can be quantized), or to go the opposite direction and allow the Event to be matched to the grid or an existing groove map. Time-stretching is applied to conform the segments to the grid or groove. That could be used to make a sloppy performance lock to a grid, or to make one performance match up to another, like putting a straight groove into a laid-back shuffle. This last is the essence of groove quantization: fitting the feel of one track to that of a reference track.

After an Event has been analyzed for transients and Bend markers inserted, the markers can be edited, including adding in ones that might have gotten missed by the detection algorithm (transient detection can be tricky stuff).

DETECT TRANSIENTS

- Right-click on the Event in which you want to detect transients and choose Audio > Audio Bend > Detect Transients or choose Audio > Detect Transients from the main menu bar. The detection is entirely automatic from there. When it is done, the coloring of the waveform display changes and Bend markers appear as vertical lines in the waveform.

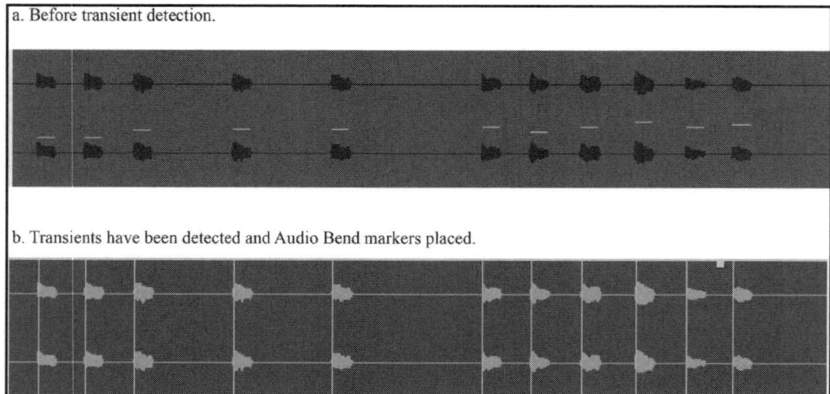

a. Before transient detection.
b. Transients have been detected and Audio Bend markers placed.

Fig. 6-33: Transient detection.

- The only parameter for Transient Detection is Threshold. It defaults to 80% but can be edited by right-clicking on the Event and adjusting the Threshold control in the header of the contextual menu that pops up.
- If the transient detection is missing a lot of transients, try setting the Detection Mode field in the Audio Bend panel to Sensitive. This makes transient detection pay more attention to smaller transients in the signal.

EDITING BEND MARKERS

Bend markers can be edited in a number of ways. Make sure that the tempo mode for the track on which you are working is set to Audio Bend to ensure that the transients themselves don't get time-stretched.

- To hide Bend markers, right-click on the Event and uncheck the Bend Marker box in the header of the contextual menu that drops down, or check the box to show them. You can also click on the Show/Hide Bend Markers button (with the eye icon) in the Bend panel.
- A Bend marker created using Detect Transients will have an extremely small highlighted range at its start that indicates the transient itself. If needed, this range can be edited in the same way as any other range.
- To manually insert a Bend marker, make the Bend tool active and click on an Event in which you want the marker to be placed. Bend markers placed manually will not have the transient range at its start.
- Bend markers can be repositioned simply by dragging them left or right. A small arrowhead at the bottom of the Bend marker points in the direction the marker was moved. When a Bend marker is moved in this way, the material on either side of it is time-stretched. Compressed audio is indicated by green coloring; the intensity of the color indicates how much compression was applied. Stretched audio is colored red, and, as with compressed audio, deeper color indicates more stretching.

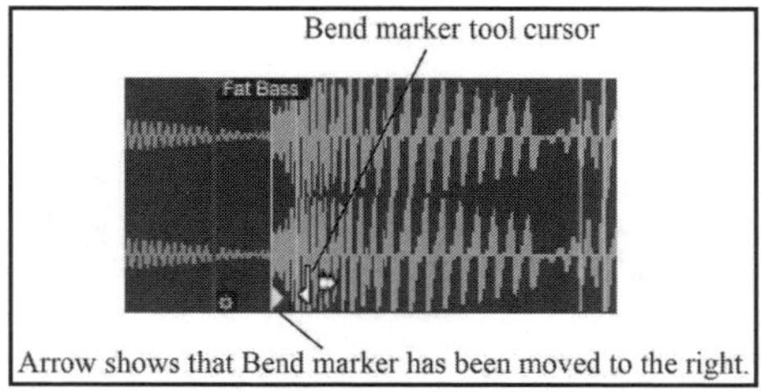
Bend marker tool cursor
Fat Bass
Arrow shows that Bend marker has been moved to the right.

Fig. 6-34: An Audio Bend marker can be moved by dragging it with the Bend marker tool selected.

- If no Bend marker exists to the left or right of one being edited, the start or end of the Event will be used as the other reference point for time-stretching.
- To select multiple Bend markers for editing, Shift-drag over them.
- To undo an edit you have performed on a Bend marker, right-click on the marker and choose Reset Bend Marker from the contextual menu that drops down. You can restore an entire passage to its original timing by selecting multiple Bend markers and then choosing Reset Bend Marker.

REMOVE BEND MARKERS

There are two ways to remove Bend markers:

- With the Bend tool active, double-click on a Bend marker to remove it.
- Select the Event and choose Audio > Remove Bend Markers from the main menu bar. Remove Bend Markers is also available in the contextual menu that drops down when you right-click on an Event.

SPLIT AT BEND MARKERS

Instead of using time-stretching, the option exists to use the Bend markers as the basis for breaking up an Event into multiple smaller Events and quantizing that way.

- To break an Event up using Bend markers, select the Event after the Bend markers have been put in place, right-click (or Ctrl-click on Mac) on the Event, and choose Split at Bend Markers from the contextual menu that drops down, or choose Audio > Split at Bend Markers from the main menu bar.

THE AUDIO BEND PANEL

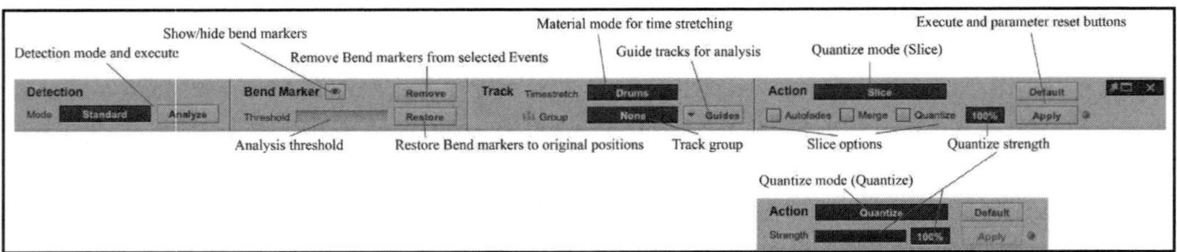

Fig. 6-35: The Audio Bend panel.

The Audio Bend panel collects most of the transient detection and Bend marker functionality in one panel. The Bend panel can be used in and appear above either the Arrange or Edit views. The Bend panel is broken into four areas: Detection, Bend Marker, Track, and Action.

Open the Audio Bend panel using any of these methods:

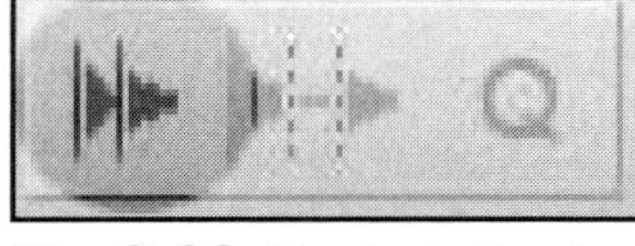

Fig. 6-36: The Audio Bend panel is opened and closed by this button in the Arrange view toolbar.

- Click on the Audio Bend panel button in the toolbar at the top of the Arrange view.
- Click on the Audio Bend panel button in the toolbar at the top of the Edit view.
- Choose View > Additional Views > Audio Bend.

DETECTION AREA

To detect transients using the Bend panel, do the following:

1. Select the Events in which you want to detect transients.
2. Click in the Mode field and choose either Standard or Sensitive. As you might guess, Sensitive uses detection settings that will interpret more audio variations to be transients than the Standard setting does. If you're not happy with the results of using one setting, try the other. The algorithms can't be perfect, so whichever you choose, expect to do some hand tweaking.
3. Click on the Analyze button. Transient detection will be performed, Bend markers will be placed, and the transients themselves will be selected as small ranges, as described above.

BEND MARKER AREA

- To make a Bend marker visible, click on the Show/Hide Bend Marker button (with the eye icon) next to the Bend Marker legend to highlight it. To make it invisible, click to unhighlight it.
- To adjust the Threshold used for analysis and placing Bend markers, click at or drag to the desired value in the Threshold bar. As soon as you change the value, the Bend markers will update to reflect the new value.

Fig. 6-37: When the button with the eye icon is selected, Bend markers are shown; when it is not selected they are hidden.

TIP: You must detect transients before the Threshold bar becomes active. You cannot set the Threshold before the first analysis; it is only for editing the value after the first pass is done.

- To remove all Bend markers, select the Event(s) from which you wish to remove all Bend markers and click on the Remove button.
- To restore Bend markers that have been moved back to their original positions in an Event (that is, to remove time-stretching but leave the Bend markers), select the Event(s) in which you wish to restore all Bend markers and click on the Restore button.

THE ACTION AREA

The Action section looks deceptively simple. In fact, it is quite powerful. This section offers both methods of quantizing audio: cutting it into smaller Events and quantizing those by the Event start times, as one would MIDI notes, or quantizing audio based on its content.

TIP: When quantizing audio, the Bend panel uses the Arrange view Quantize Value to determine the grid lines. There is no Quantize Value setting in the Bend panel itself. If you are using a Groove Template, that will be reflected in the Quantize Value field, and you can open the Quantize panel to see the template in greater detail or modify it.

Studio One 2 quantizes audio based on content by lining up the Bend markers to grid lines, and time-stretching as needed to make it all fit. The assumption in this method is that the Bend markers fall on rhythmic divisions. Under that assumption, Quantize Value clearly becomes critically important to the process. For example, perhaps you have detected the transients in a piano solo that has lots of 16th-note runs. The Quantize Value can't be set any larger than a 16th note to make this work. If Quantize Value is set to 8th notes, the 16th note runs will not be quantized correctly.

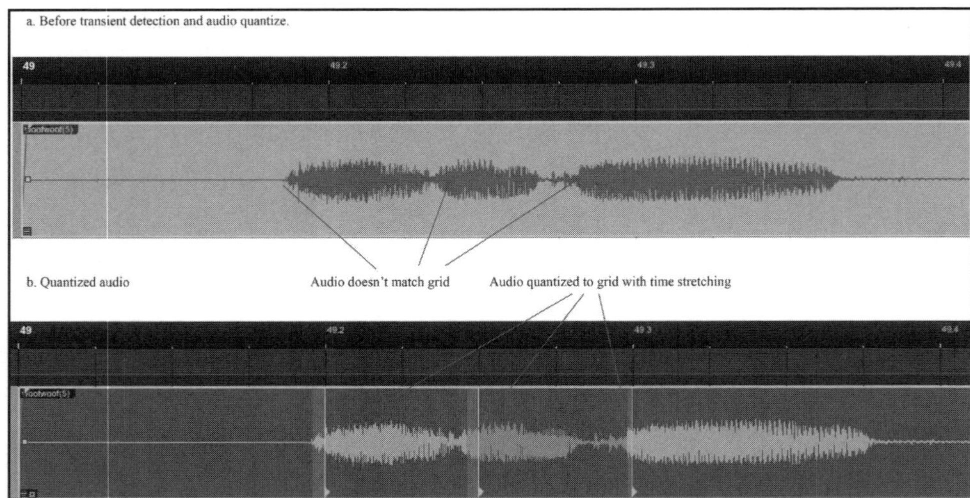

Fig. 6-38: One way of quantizing audio is to have Studio One 2 detect transients, place Bend markers, then time-stretch as needed to fit the Bend markers to the grid.

The Default button unchecks the option boxes in Slice mode and sets Quantize Mode to Quantize.

Quantizing Audio by Content (Quantize Bend Markers to Grid)

1. Select the Event(s) you wish to quantize.
2. Detect transients and edit Bend markers as desired, as described above.
3. If Quantize is not already chosen in the Quantize Mode field, click in the field and choose Quantize. (Note that Quantize is the default value.)
4. Click-and-drag to the desired value in the Quantize Strength bar, or enter a percentage value in the Strength field. The Quantize Strength value determines how intensely an item will be affected by the quantizing engine. When the quantize strength is set to 0%, for instance, the quantize will move the start times of the notes 0% of the way to the closest grid line, which is to say they won't move at all. When set to 50%, the quantize does the same as the Quantize 50% command: it moves the note half of the distance between its original position in time and the nearest grid line. At 100%, notes are hard quantized right to the grid lines.
5. Click on the Apply button to quantize the selected audio, lining Bend markers up to grid lines as defined by the Arrange view Quantize Value. The indicator next to the Apply button will turn blue to indicate that the audio has been quantized.

Dividing Audio Events and Quantizing

Performances with short sounds, like drums and percussion, often quantize better as individual Events rather than time-stretched segments of an Event. The Bend panel lets you use transient detection as the basis for dividing each selected Event into multiple Events, which can then be quantized. Options include adding top and tail autofades on each new Event, and merging the new Events into an Audio Part.

Here's how to divide an Event into smaller Events and quantize them:

1. Select the Event(s) you wish to quantize.
2. Detect transients and edit Bend markers as desired, as described above.
3. Choose Slice from the drop-down menu that appears in the Quantize Type field.
4. If you want to add short fades at the head and tail of each new Event, check the Autofades box.
5. Check the Merge box if you want the new Events to be merged into an Audio Part.
6. Check the Quantize box and enter a value in the Quantize Strength field if you want the new Events quantized to the grid (or Groove Template). Note that this is the same Quantize Strength field as in Quantize mode.
7. Click on the Apply button to slice the Event(s) into a number of smaller Events based on Bend markers using the indicated options. The indicator next to the Apply button will turn blue to indicate that the audio has been quantized.

TRACK AREA

The Track area has settings that affect both analysis (the Group and Guides fields) and time-stretching (the Timestretch field). The Timestretch and Group fields are the same ones found in the Track inspector, and those settings for the selected track can be adjusted in either place.

The Timestretch Setting

The Timestretch setting selects the best time-stretching algorithm for the source material. To set the Timestretch mode, click in the Timestretch field and select from the choices in the menu that drops down. For information on the four modes, see the section "Time Stretch Material Modes," in this chapter.

The Group Field

- The Group field is the same one seen in the Track inspector; settings can be changed either place. To change the group an Event is in, click in the field and choose from the groups listed there, or choose none.
- To rename a group from the Group field, click in the field, choose Rename Group from the menu that drops down, and enter the new name.

Guide Tracks

There are many advantages to collecting a number of tracks that are related in some way into a group. However, analyzing groups of tracks complicates our process, and frequently is not necessary. For example, the snare or maybe the hi-hat and kick tracks might be adequate for analysis. Studio One 2 enables you to pick and choose which tracks in a group will be included in the analysis. To choose the tracks in a group that will be used in transient analysis, do the following:

1. Click in the Guides field and a small panel will drop down showing all tracks within the group.
2. To exclude a track from the analysis, uncheck the box next to it.
3. When you have configured the tracks as desired, click on the Guides button again or anywhere else outside the panel to close it.

MERGING EVENTS AND AUDIO PARTS

Once audio has been segmented, it can be useful to assemble the segments into an Audio Part. Here are a few of the many ways to segment audio in preparation for merging them into an Audio Part:

- Manually select ranges in between the audio you want and delete them.
- Use the Strip Silence feature.
- Use transient detection and the Slice feature in the Audio Bend panel.

Just as an Instrument Part contains a number of individual notes, an Audio Part is just a container: in the Arrange view it looks like a regular Audio Event, but in Edit view the segments can still be accessed and manipulated separately. This is an idea similar to a REX file, as we shall soon see. Once merged, you can segment it with Detect Transients and be able to time-stretch it—unless, of course, you already used Detect Transients to do the segmenting in the first place, in which case you can just merge and quantize.

To merge several Events into an Audio Part, do the following:

- Select the Events on a track that you wish to merge and press the G key, right-click on one of the Events and choose Event > Merge Events or Audio > Merge to Audio Part from the contextual drop-down menu that appears, or choose Event > Merge Events from the main menu bar.
- If you select discontinuous events (that is, there are one or more unselected events somewhere between the first and last selected ones), the resulting merged Event will include only the selected Events. The merged Event will be the front tier, the unselected Events in the back.

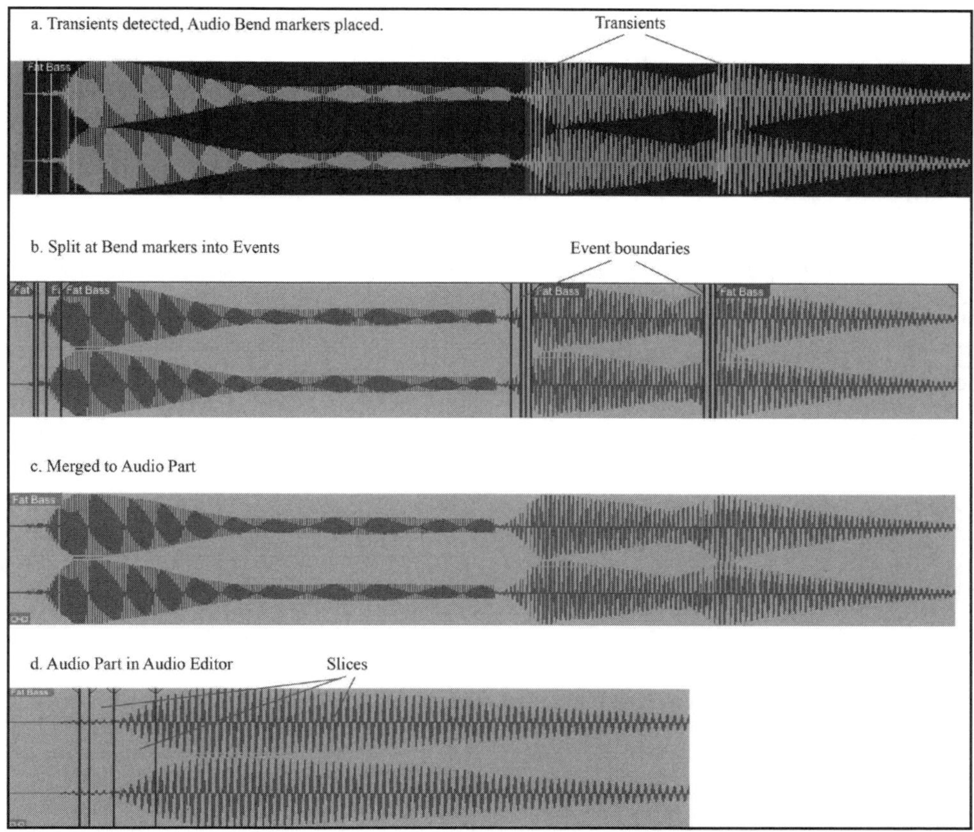

Fig. 6-39: An Audio Part is a collection of Events created by detecting transients and then using the resulting Bend markers to break the original Event into multiple Events. The Events are then merged into an Audio Part, though they can still be edited individually in the Audio Editor.

- To dissolve an Audio Part, right-click on the Audio Part and choose Audio > Dissolve Audio Part from the drop-down contextual menu that appears, or choose Audio > Dissolve Audio Part from the main menu bar.

AUDIO PARTS AND REX FILES

Audio Parts follow essentially the same concept as REX files, so it's no surprise that Studio One 2 makes it easy to go back and forth between the two.

- To make a REX file from an Audio Part, simply drag it to your computer's file system (Finder on Mac, Explorer in Windows) and a REX2 file will be created.
- When a REX file is brought into Studio One 2, it will look like an Audio Part containing slices that can be individually edited and time-stretched.

Time-Stretching (Compression/Expansion) and Quantizing Audio

MIDI data has traditionally held an advantage over audio in the greater ease with which it can be manipulated, especially in terms of changing pitch and time. But audio processing has advanced a long way in the past few years, and this is no longer as true as it used to be. While it is still more complicated to treat time in audio as flexibly as with MIDI data, it is now much more possible, and Studio One 2 provides a full set of time compression and expansion facilities.

There are two basic approaches to manipulating time with audio files, which can be used individually or in combination:

- Chop the audio into small “slices” and manipulate those. A slice might be a single drum or bass note, or it could be an entire riff. The preceding section “Segmenting” discusses Studio One 2’s chopping features. Once audio has been segmented, the individual pieces can be manipulated much as MIDI notes can. This is the basis of the REX file format, of which Studio One 2 makes good use. Most of the tools described in the section “Quantizing MIDI” below can be applied to segmented audio as well.
- Use processing algorithms to stretch or compact a piece of audio to fit a desired amount of time or a particular musical tempo. This is primarily what is discussed in this section.

TIME-STRETCH MATERIAL MODES

Time-stretching audio changes the duration of an Event without changing its pitch. This is a powerful capability with a number of applications. Here are just a few examples:

- Fitting rhythmic phrases in an audio file to a different tempo than that at which it was originally recorded.
- Modifying the phrasing of a musical line. For instance, if several singers did not cut off the last notes of their harmony at the same time, it is possible to time-stretch the errant notes to match the rest.
- Modify the rhythmic timing of two parts that are not quite locked.

Time-stretching requires very sophisticated algorithms, and the best results are obtained when the algorithm is optimized for the kind of material being stretched. While many kinds of material don’t fit cozily into a standard description, some applications (such as time-stretching drums or lead/single-line instruments like vocals) are so common that optimized time-stretching modes are supplied for them. However, experimenting to find the mode that produces the best results with the material you are time-stretching is a good practice. Once a mode has been selected for a track, that mode will be used for any time-stretching performed on the track or its contents.

The four time stretch-material modes in Studio One 2 are the following:

- **Drums:** Use for percussive material, especially unpitched instruments.
- **Sound:** A generic catchall for sounds that don't fit into any of the other categories. Choral instruments, sound effects, and sections of instruments (such as string or brass sections) are good examples of what this mode might work for.
- **Solo:** Single-line instruments, such as vocals, brass, woodwind, single-line guitar leads.
- **Audio Bend:** Use with audio that has been segmented using transient detection and contains Audio Bend markers, as described above.

To choose a time-stretch material mode, do the following:

1. Select the track or track group that you want to time-stretch.
2. Click in the Timestretch field of the Track inspector and choose the desired time-stretch material mode.

AUDIO FILE TEMPOS

Time-stretching is ideal for beat-oriented production because it lets loops and other material be tempo-matched to existing elements. (Groove templates do the opposite: they enable existing elements to be tempo-matched to a piece of audio.) However, Studio One 2 can't match two tempos unless it can compare them, meaning that the tempos for the Song and for the audio material you are trying to integrate both must be known.

The Song tempo is always known, but determining the tempo of audio material can be more challenging than figuring it out from MIDI data. Loops often include tempo information, which makes life easy, and Studio One 2 always encodes the current Song tempo in any audio track recorded directly into Studio One 2.

If the tempo value is not stored in the file, either you must tell Studio One 2 the audio file tempo, or it has to figure out the audio tempo itself, which still requires that it get at least a few clues. To tell Studio One 2 the tempo, you can enter the tempo value in the Event inspector File Tempo field, or use Tap Tempo. Manual time-stretching can also result in a file tempo value; see the "Manual Time-Stretching" section below for more details.

For Studio One 2 to figure out the tempo itself, the first clue you can give it is to feed it audio for analysis that is rhythmic in nature, with a fairly steady tempo. Small tempo variations such as those produced by any human playing an instrument can be followed, but music that is very rubato (time is extremely loose) or that changes tempo repeatedly is more challenging for a tempo-tracking algorithm.

The next clue is transients in the audio. The tempos of bass and drum tracks are going to be easier to follow than a bagpipe track because they have better defined attacks, which are easier to detect. The algorithm looks at those attacks, infers a pattern from them, and tries to extract the tempo from that pattern.

The process, then, is for Studio One 2 to detect the transients in the audio, make an educated guess as to the tempo, and mark the transients, creating a map of bars and beats that can be then used for time-stretching.

TELLING STUDIO ONE 2 THE TEMPO OF AN AUDIO FILE

If you know the tempo of a piece of audio, you can simply enter it in the Event inspector. This might happen because you have a loop that does not store the tempo information in a way that Studio One 2 can read, or maybe doesn't store the tempo in the file at all, but does have the tempo printed in the documentation. Alternatively, you can tap the tempo out for Studio One 2 or define the file tempo using the Time Stretch tool.

You can enter an audio file tempo using any of these methods:

- Select the Event for which you wish to set a file tempo, click in the File Tempo field in the Event inspector, and enter the audio file tempo value.
- Select multiple Events for which you wish to set a file tempo, click in the File Tempo field in the Event inspector, and enter the audio file tempo value. All selected Events will be set to the file tempo you enter.

Fig. 6-40: The File Tempo field in the Event inspector is key to auto time-stretching.

- Select the track in which you are time-stretching and check that the Tempo field in the Track inspector is set to Timestretch. With the Arrow tool selected, move the cursor over the end of the Event you wish to time-stretch, hold down the Option and Cmd keys until you see a cursor with a metronome icon next to the regular line and arrowhead, and drag until the Event fits the amount of time in which you want it to play. Release the mouse button when the Event is at the desired length and a tempo is assigned to the audio file. Further important details about this can be found in the section "Manual Time-Stretching," below.
- If you use manual time-stretching on the Event, it will assume that the starting tempo before you time-stretch is the same as that of the Song. When you finish time-stretching, the tempo value will appear in the File Tempo field. This generally is not the best way to get the file tempo, but it may sometimes be helpful.
- Listen to the audio file and use Tap Tempo as described in the Tap Tempo section above. Once you find the tempo, enter it into the File Tempo field.

MANUAL TIME-STRETCHING

Manual time-stretching of Events can be very useful for fitting an Event of a specified duration in bars and beats into the same duration at a different tempo, fitting an Event into a specified duration in seconds, or for when you are trying to stretch a sound not by tempo, but by feel.

There are two techniques for manual time-stretching, the difference between them being whether an audio file tempo is calculated and inserted into the file. This is significant because once an audio file tempo exists, all Events based on that audio file will be affected by tempo changes. When you do not want Events based on the same audio file to be linked in this way, you will want to use the time-stretching method that employs only Speedup factor and does not involve tempo. Manual time-stretching can be performed in either the Arrange view or the Edit view.

To manually time-stretch an Event without generating an audio file tempo, do the following:

1. With the Arrow tool active, select the Event you wish to time-stretch.
2. Position the cursor over the end of the Event and hold down the Option (Alt in Windows) key. The time-stretch cursor (a clock next to the usual sizing cursor of an arrowhead and line) will appear.
3. If you want to size the Event exactly to the grid (that is, fit it to a precise musical or absolute time duration), be sure that Snap is active and that the desired Quantize Value setting is displayed in the Arrange view toolbar.
4. Drag while holding down Option (Alt in Windows) to size the Event. As you drag, a pop-up tool tip will show you the duration of the Event in seconds and the Speedup factor that will be applied if you release the mouse button at the current location.
5. Release the mouse button when the Event is at the desired location.

To manually time-stretch an Event and generate an audio file tempo, do the following:

1. With the Arrow tool active, select the Event you wish to time-stretch.
2. Check that the Tempo field in the Track inspector is set to Timestretch.
3. Position the cursor over the end of the Event and hold down the Option + Cmd (Alt + Ctrl in Windows). The cursor will change to a metronome icon next to the usual sizing cursor of an arrowhead and line.
4. If you want to size the Event exactly to the grid (that is, fit it to a precise musical or absolute time duration), be sure that Snap is active and that the desired Quantize Value setting is displayed in the Arrange view toolbar.
5. Drag while holding down Option + Cmd (Alt + Ctrl in Windows) to size the Event. As you drag, a pop-up tool tip will show you the duration of the Event in seconds and the tempo that will be assigned to the audio file if you release the mouse button at the current location.
6. Release the mouse button when the Event is at the desired duration.

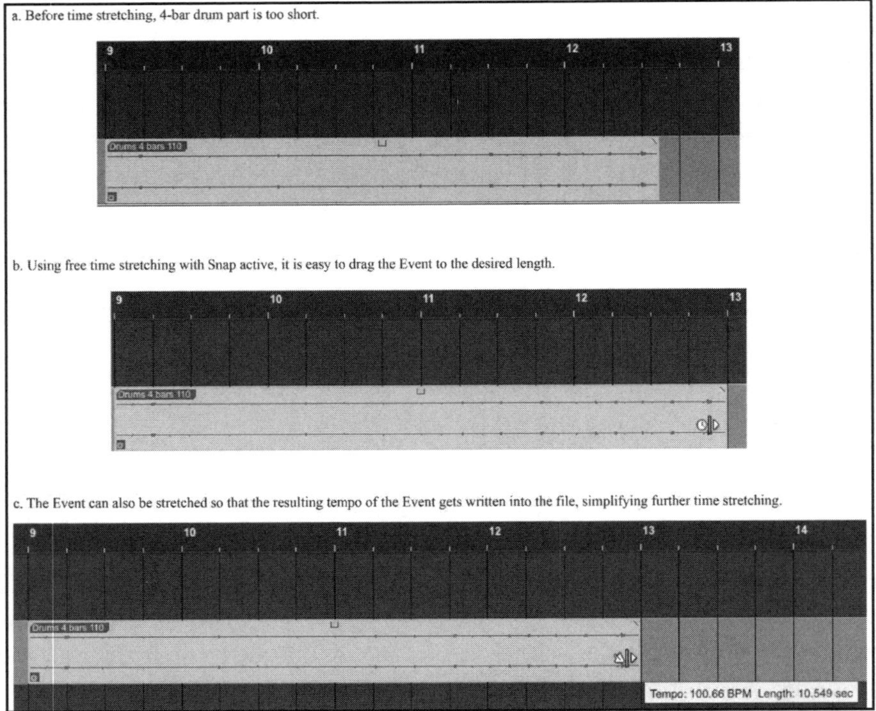

a. Before time stretching, 4-bar drum part is too short.
b. Using free time stretching with Snap active, it is easy to drag the Event to the desired length.
c. The Event can also be stretched so that the resulting tempo of the Event gets written into the file, simplifying further time stretching.
Tempo: 100.66 BPM Length: 10.549 sec

Fig. 6-41: Manual time stretching can be handy for fitting a phrase of an intended length in a file with no audio tempo to the desired length in the song. In figure 6-41b, free time stretching is used by holding down the Option (Alt) key, while in 6-41c, invoked by holding down Option+cmd (Alt+ctrl), a tempo gets written into the file as well.

Here are a few more things you should know about manual time-stretching:

- If Snap is on, dragging will be quantized to the increments displayed in the Arrange view Quantize Value field.
- You can select and time-stretch multiple Events at the same time, but the tool tip will show you correct information only for the Event you are actually dragging. The other Event(s) will have their start or end points dragged to the same location.
- Manual time-stretching affects the entire audio file. If there are several Events based on this file, all will be affected.
- Another method of time-stretching an Event without affecting the rest of the file it is based on is to select the Event you wish to time-stretch, position the cursor over the Speedup field in the Event inspector, and drag up or down to make the Event longer or shorter.

Fig. 6-42: Dragging over the Speedup field allows you to manually time stretch an Event without affecting the rest of the file it comes from.

If you are fitting an Event into the same duration at a different tempo, it can be most effective not to rely on the length of the Event itself, but instead to reference notes within it to their proper locations. For example, say you are fitting a two-bar Caribbean percussion groove recorded at 120 bpm into two bars at a Song tempo of 107 bpm. You might go about it like this:

1. Make sure that the Event is trimmed so that it starts right on bar 1, beat 1, with no extra time before the downbeat.
2. Place the Event so that it starts exactly on the proper downbeat. Activating Snap will make this easy.
3. Look at the waveform display in the Event as you listen to it and try to spot a distinctive beat near the end. Perhaps you can spot a hit that falls on the downbeat of bar 2. Even better if you can also spot a hit that follows the first hit by an eighth note; that will give you two references.

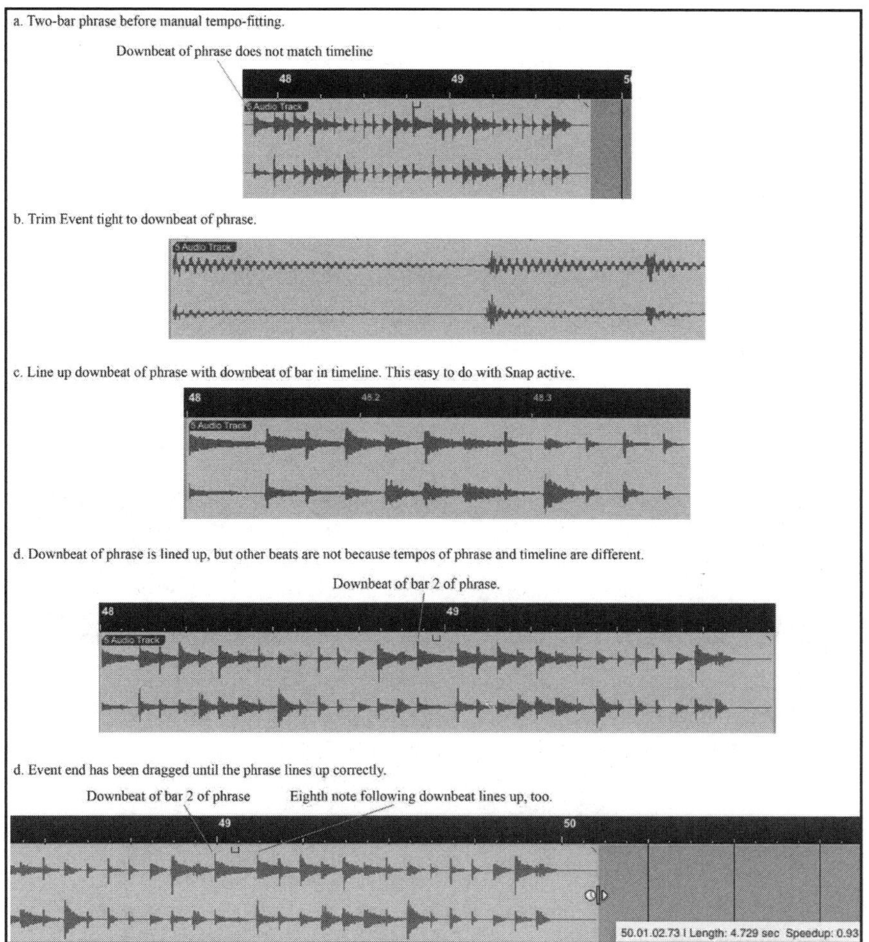

Fig. 6-43: Sometimes the best way to match recorded material to the Song is by manual tempo-fitting, in which you trim and place the audio, then stretch it to line up reference points in the audio with the timeline.

4. Position the cursor over the end of the event and hold down Option + Cmd (Alt + Ctrl in Windows). The metronome time-stretch cursor will appear.
5. Drag the end point of the Event to the right until the hit at the downbeat of bar 2 in the Event lines up with the downbeat of bar 2 in the timeline. As a double-check, look to make sure that the following hit point you find falls on the offbeat of beat 1. If both hits line up right, you're there.
6. Release the mouse button. Your Event has now been time-stretched to fit 100 bpm and a value has been set in the File Tempo field.

The same visual reference approach works when applying Speedup instead of time-stretching.

AUTO TIME STRETCHING

AUDIO TRACK TEMPO MODE

Once the File Tempo is known, you can use Auto Time Stretching. The Audio Track tempo mode and Timestretch material mode are the crucial parameters that determine how Auto Time Stretching will work. The Timestretch material mode was described above. There are three tempo modes:

- **Don't Follow:** Time-stretching is not performed automatically nor are Events moved when the tempo changes.
- **Follow:** When the tempo is changed, Events are moved in time to maintain their musical positions (the bars and beats locations). No time-stretching is performed.
- **Timestretch:** When the tempo is changed, Events are moved in time to maintain their musical positions (that is, the bars and beats location), and time-stretching is applied to keep the Events in tempo.

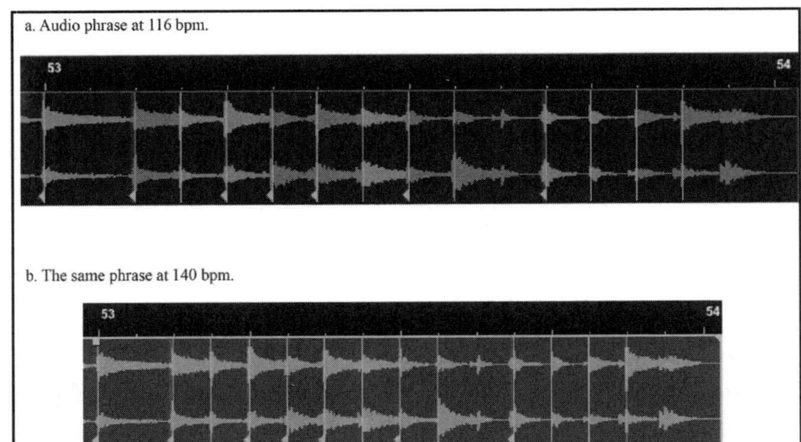

Fig. 6-44: Auto time stretching adjusts Events containing Bend markers whenever the tempo changes. Figure 6-44a shows an audio phrase at its original tempo of 116 bpm, where the beats in the phrase all line up perfectly with the timeline. In figure 6-44b, the same phrase is shown after the tempo has been increased to 140 bpm. The beats still line up perfectly.

DEFAULT AUDIO TRACK TEMPO MODE

New audio tracks are automatically set to Follow as the default track tempo mode. However, it is possible to change the default tempo mode to Timestretch in the following way:

- Open Preferences > Song Setup > General and check the box marked Stretch Audio Files to Song Tempo.
- Stretch Audio Files to Song Tempo is also available in the New Song dialog box, so it can be selected at the time you create the Song.

AUDIO PART INSPECTOR PLAYBACK OPTIONS

PLAY MODE

Quantizing Events in an Audio Part can result in overlapping Events, especially if time-stretching is not used. Play Mode defines how playback is handled in this situation.

- **Normal:** The Event playing is always the one in front.
- **Overlaps:** Overlapping Events are mixed in real time, so the earlier Event finishes playing; no Event gets cut off.
- **Slices:** This mode is designed for REX and Audioloop files, which are collections of slices. Overlaps are not played, but short, real-time crossfades are generated between overlapping slices for smooth transitions. Each slice plays only once.

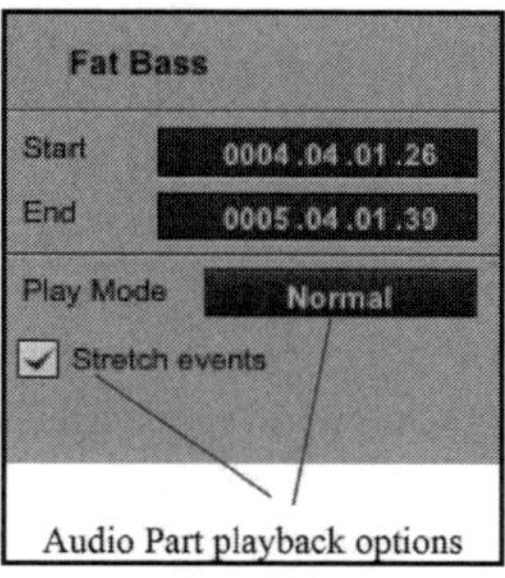

Fig. 6-45: While the Audio Part inspector looks simple, the playback options are important to auto time stretching.

STRETCH EVENTS BOX

When checked, the Stretch Events box causes each Event in an Audio Part or slice in a REX or Audioloop file to be time-stretched as needed from the audio file tempo to fit the Song tempo, rather than the Event or Part being time-stretched as a whole.

QUANTIZING AUDIO

Now that we have discussed Audio Bend markers, transient detection, and time-stretching (whew!), quantizing audio is easy. We already talked some about quantizing audio in section "The Action Area" above, but the Quantize command described in the section "Quantizing," below, is a simple method of combining all of that into a single keystroke. Selecting an Event and choosing the Quantize command triggers transient detection, inserting Bend markers, moving them to the grid and time-stretching as needed, and indicating how they've been moved.

Can't get much easier.

- To quantize a selected Audio Event, press Q.

TIME-STRETCH CACHE

Time-stretch caching shifts some of the burden of time-stretching from the processor in your computer to your hard disk. For each file that requires time-stretching, a cache file will be created on your hard disk. Clearly, this can consume more hard disk space, and it incurs greater hard disk access demands, as well. However, the processor no longer needs to perform time-stretching in real time.

By default, time-stretch caching is turned on, but if you notice performance problems (as might happen with a Song having a high track count, for example), you can try deactivating it.

- To deactivate time-stretch caching, go to Preferences > Options > Advanced > Audio Engine and uncheck Use cache for time-stretched audio files.

EDITING MIDI

Studio One 2's MIDI editing capabilities are extensive. Automation using MIDI program changes, continuous controllers, and VI parameters are discussed in the chapter "Automation" in *Power Tools for Studio One 2*, vol. 2.

Adding Notes and Parts

ADDING PARTS

Instrument Parts are added in the Arrange view. There are three ways to add a new, empty Part:

- With the Paint tool active, position the cursor in the track where you want to create a Part and drag from where you want the Part to start to where you want it to end. If Snap is active, start and end points will be quantized according to the Snap and Quantize settings.
- Set the left and right locators to the times where you want the Part to begin and end, then press Cmd + P (Ctrl + P in Windows) or choose Event > Insert Instrument Part from the main menu bar.

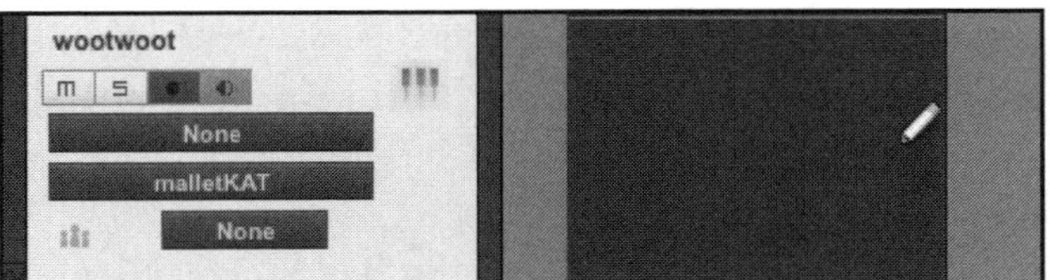

Fig. 6-46: New, empty Instrument Parts can be added with the pencil tool.

- With the Arrow tool active, double-click in any area of the track where there is not already a Part. A new, empty Part exactly one bar in duration will be created starting at the nearest bar line to the left of the point clicked.

ADDING NOTES

Notes are added in the Edit view. Since notes must reside in Parts and Parts cannot be created in the Edit view, you add notes by opening a Part in the Arrange view for editing in the Edit view. The Part that is opened could be an existing Part or a new, empty one you create using one of the methods given above. Notes are added to a Part in Edit view by drawing them with the Paint tool in the following way:

- With the Paint tool active, position the cursor at the time and pitch where you want to create a note. Use the onscreen keyboard along the left side of the Edit view and the stripes in the Part representing notes to identify the pitch that the cursor is positioned over. As you move the cursor up and down, the current note is slightly highlighted on the keyboard. Once the cursor is positioned at the start point, drag to the right to create the note.
- If Snap is active, the note's start and end points will be quantized according to the Snap and Quantize settings.
- If Snap is not active, holding down the Shift key while dragging will snap the end point of the note to the nearest quantization value on the grid.
- If Scale Snap is engaged, only the pitches in the selected scale will be highlighted, and notes can be created only at one of those pitches.
- If you drag up or down while creating a note by dragging, it changes the velocity of the note.

Fig. 6-47: Creating new notes with the paint tool.

Notes can also be added with standard editing techniques such as the following:

- Copy and paste
- Option-drag (on Mac)
- Duplicate

AUDITIONING NOTES IN THE EDIT VIEW

It is often desirable to be able to hear what a note sounds like, especially when trying different sounds on an instrument. There are two ways that this can be done in the Edit view:

- Clicking on a note on the keyboard on the left of the Edit view will play that note on the instrument to which the track is assigned.
- To play a note in the track, check the Audition Notes box in the Edit View inspector, then click on any note to play it.

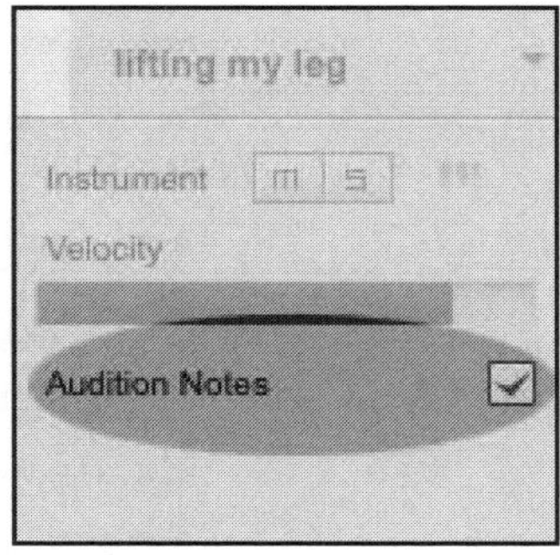

Fig. 6-48: To hear a note in the Music Editor sounded when it is clicked, be sure the Audition Notes box is checked.

Deleting Notes and Parts

Deleting notes and parts is easy using either of these methods:

- With the Eraser tool active, click on the Part you want to delete in the Arrange view or the note you want to delete in the Edit view.

- Select the Part(s) you want to delete in the Arrange view or the note(s) you want to delete in the Edit view and press the Delete key, right-click on the Part or note and choose Delete from the contextual menu that drops down, or choose Edit > Delete from the main menu bar.

Transposing MIDI

Studio One 2 has quite a few tools for transposition at every level: track, Part, and note. It also offers scale snapping, which quantizes pitches to a chosen scale.

TIP: Keep in mind that, with Studio One 2's multitrack MIDI editing, your transpositions may affect multiple tracks, depending on the method you use and the tracks that are visible. Stay alert to the context or you may get some disconcerting results!

THE TRANSPOSE DIALOG BOX

The Transpose dialog box can be used with selected notes in a Part in the Edit view, or on entire Parts in the Arrange view, though it offers few advantages over transposing a Part using the Transpose field in the Event inspector. However, transposition executed using the Transpose dialog box is reflected visually in the Edit view, which moves the notes to their new pitches, while the Transpose field in the Event inspector does not.

To transpose notes or Parts using the Transpose dialog box, do the following:

1. Select the note(s) in the Edit view or Part(s) in the Arrange view that you want to transpose.
2. Right-click (Ctrl-click on Mac) on a note or Part and choose Transpose from the contextual drop-down menu that appears, or choose Event > Musical Functions > Transpose from the main menu bar. The Transpose dialog box will appear.

- To transpose the selection by one or two octaves, simply click on one of the preset buttons in the Add/Subtract area in the top half of the dialog box.
- To transpose the selection by some other number of semitones, drag the slider in the Add/Subtract area until the desired transposition is displayed, or simply click in the Transposition Amount field and enter the desired transposition value.
- To set all notes in the selection to a single pitch, drag the slider in the Set All To area until the desired pitch is displayed, or simply click in the Set All To field and enter the desired note to which the selection should be transposed.
- After setting the desired transposition, click on OK to execute the transposition.

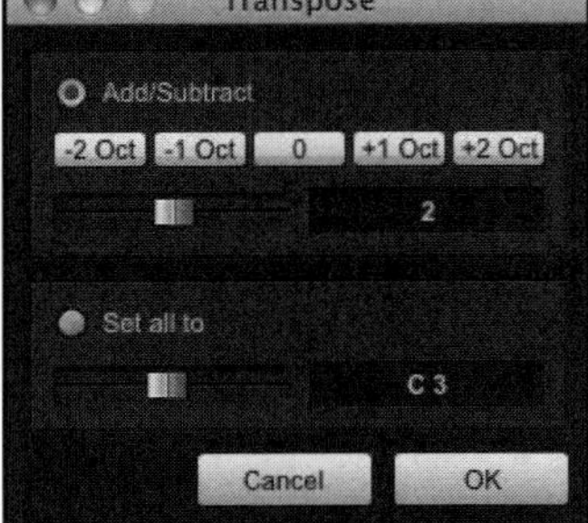

Fig. 6-49: The Transpose dialog changes the selected note data, as opposed to the Instrument Track inspector Transpose field, which performs transposition on the fly.

TRANSPOSING INSTRUMENT TRACKS

Instrument tracks are transposed using the Transpose field in the Track inspector. This transposes the entire track in semitone steps, over a range of +/–64 semitones, which is about 10.5 octaves. Since the transposition amount is always shown in the display, it is very easy to undo track transposition without resorting to the undo history. Note that transposition created in the Track inspector is not reflected graphically. To transpose tracks, use either of these methods:

- Select the track you want to transpose, then position the cursor over the Transpose field in the Track inspector and drag up or down to the desired transposition amount.
- Click in the Transpose field in the Track inspector and enter the value of the desired transposition amount.

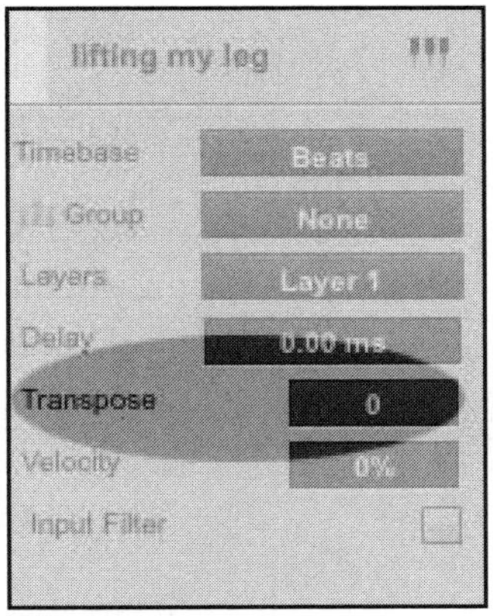

Fig. 6-50: The Track inspector Transpose field performs in real time and does not change the appearance of notes in the Music editor.

TRANSPOSING PARTS

I have already described how to transpose Parts using the Transpose dialog box, but Parts can be transposed using the Transpose field in the Event inspector in the same fashion as tracks are transposed using the Transpose field in the Track inspector, with the one difference that multiple Parts can be selected and transposed at once. As with track transposition, Part transposition achieved in the Event inspector is not reflected graphically. To transpose Parts, use either of these methods:

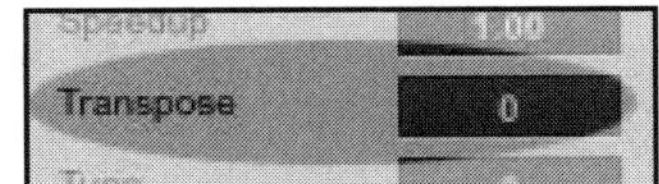

Fig. 6-51: Audio Events can be transposed in the Event inspector.

- Select the Part(s) you want to transpose. If multiple Parts are selected, it makes no difference which part is displayed in the Event inspector. Position the cursor over the Transpose field in the Event inspector and drag up or down to the desired transposition amount. All selected Parts will be set to the same transposition amount.
- Click in the Transpose field in the Track inspector and enter the value of the desired transposition amount. All selected Parts will be set to the same transposition amount.

TRANSPOSING NOTES

One or more selected notes can be transposed in these three different ways:

1. Using the Transpose dialog box as described above.
2. Using the Pitch field in the Note inspector immediately to the left of the Edit view.
3. Dragging the selection up or down in the Edit view to the desired pitch.

I have already discussed how to use the Transpose dialog box.

TRANSPOSING NOTES USING THE NOTE INSPECTOR PITCH FIELD

There are two methods of transposing notes with the Note Inspector Pitch field. One is to scroll to the desired transposition:

1. Select the note you want to transpose. The Pitch field will display the pitch of the note.
2. Click on the arrow next to the Pitch field and use the scrollbar or your mouse scroll wheel to find the pitch to which you want to transpose the note in the drop-down menu that appears.
3. Click on the pitch in the drop-down menu to select it.

The other is direct entry: Simply click in the Pitch field and enter the name of the pitch to which you want to transpose the note.

You can select and transpose multiple notes at once. The first note selected will be the one displayed in the Pitch field, and all other notes will be transposed by the transposition interval indicated for that note. For example, if the first note selected is D# 3 and you change the Pitch field to, say, F3, then all selected notes will be transposed by two semitones (a major second interval).

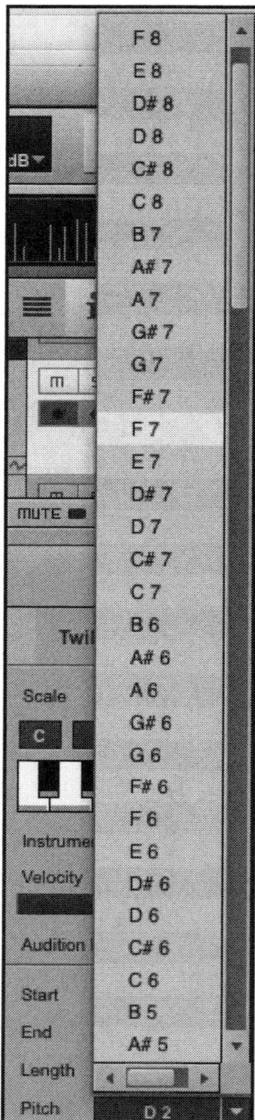

Fig. 6-52: Individual notes can be transposed by bringing up the pitch list from the Note inspector Pitch field and scrolling to the desired pitch.

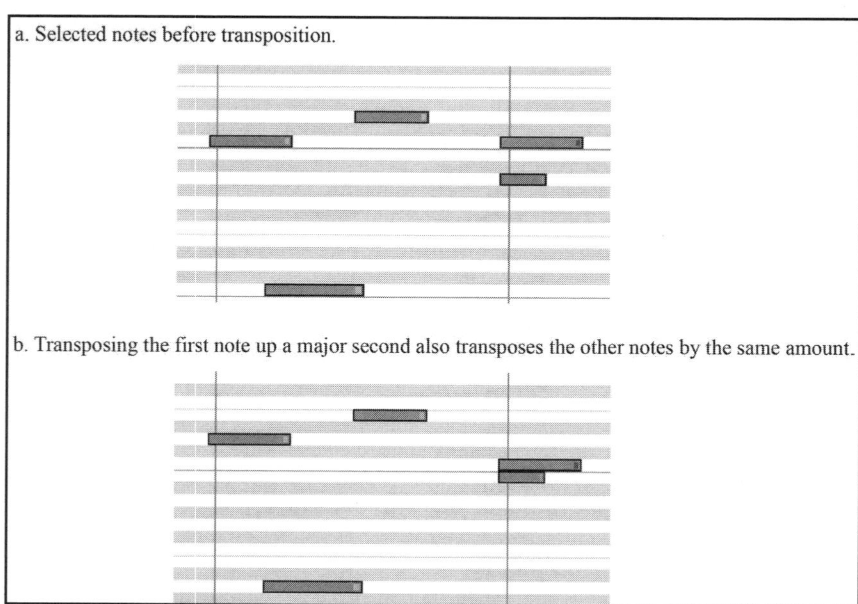

a. Selected notes before transposition.
b. Transposing the first note up a major second also transposes the other notes by the same amount.

Fig. 6-53: Transposing multiple notes together.

TRANSPOSING NOTES BY DRAGGING

Transposing notes by dragging is quite straightforward:

1. Select the note(s) you wish to transpose.
2. Grab any of the selected notes and drag them to the desired new pitch. All other notes will be transposed by the same amount.

Notes dragged vertically are "sticky" in time—that is, they try to maintain their start times. If you want to change a note's location in time as you drag, hold down the Shift key while dragging to defeat the stickiness.

QUANTIZING PITCHES WITH SCALE SNAP

When people speak of quantization, they generally mean quantization in time—that is, quantizing to a rhythmic grid, as provided by Studio One 2's Snap function. But Studio One 2 also allows snapping of note pitches to a particular scale when transposing by dragging. To transpose with scale snapping, do the following:

1. Click in the Root Note field above the minikeyboard in the Track inspector and choose the desired root note for the scale from the drop-down menu that appears.
2. Click in the Scale Type field above the minikeyboard in the Track inspector and choose the desired scale type from the drop-down menu that appears. (Don't be confused by the pop-up tool tip that says "Snap Value.") The minikeyboard will highlight the notes in the selected scale so you can see how pitches will be quantized.
3. Check the Enable box to the right of the "Scale" label in the Track inspector.
4. Select and drag notes as described above to transpose them. Only notes in the selected scale and root will be allowed as destinations.

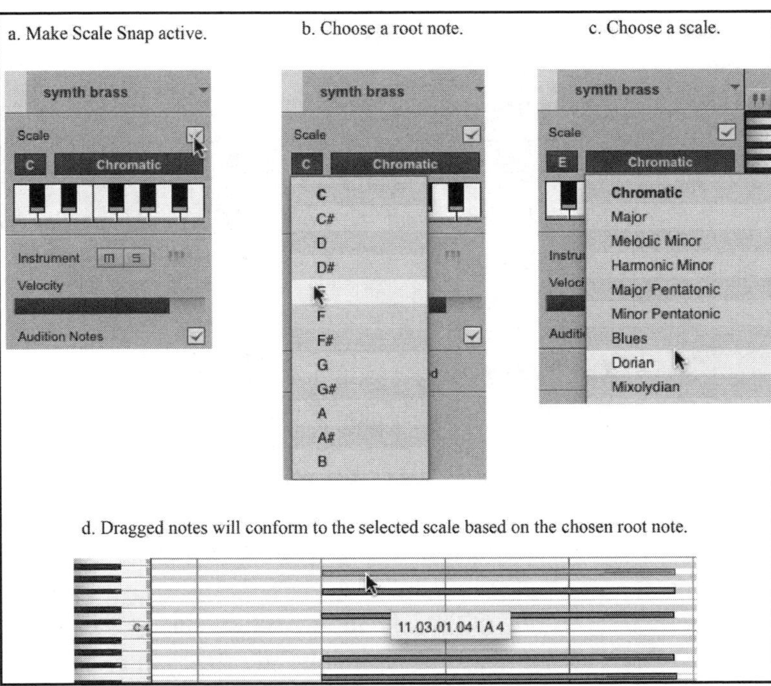

Fig. 6-54: Scale Snap forces transposed notes to conform to a specific scale and root note.

Explode Pitches to Tracks

There are some situations in which it is helpful to take pitches on one track and separate each pitch onto its own track. One example would be a drum loop for which you might want to assign the notes for different drums to sounds produced by different virtual instruments (VIs) or different presets. Another would be if you wanted the notes of chords recorded from a keyboard performance to be sounded by different instruments. Explode Pitches to Tracks does exactly this for Parts selected in the Arrange view: each pitch played in the selected Part(s) is given its own track. To explode pitches from one track to a track per pitch, do the following:

1. Select the Part(s) you want to explode in the Arrange view. If you are selecting multiple Parts, they do not all need to be on the same track.
2. Choose Event > Explode Pitches to Tracks from the main menu bar. A track will be created for each pitch played and the notes of that pitch moved to the new track.

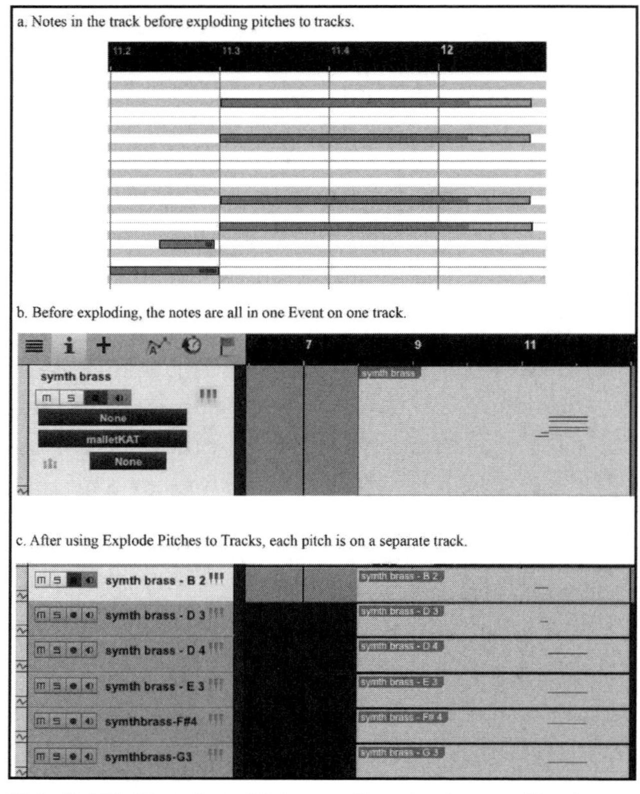

Fig. 6-55: Explode to Pitches splits notes from an Event so that each note has its own track.

Velocity

Note velocity is displayed in three places:

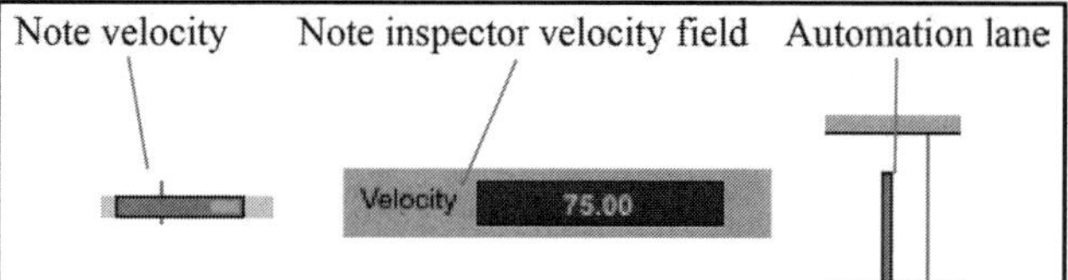

Fig. 6-56: Note velocity is displayed in three places in Studio One 2.

- In Edit view, each note is displayed with two colors. The color in the left section of the note indicates the velocity. When a note is selected, for instance, the left section is a darker orange and the right section a lighter orange. If the darker orange completely fills the note, the velocity value is at its maximum (100), while if it fills only half of the note, the velocity value is half of the maximum (50).

- When velocity is displayed in the Part Automation lane at the bottom of the Edit view, the velocity value is shown as a vertical bar whose height indicates the proportion of the maximum value.
- When a note is selected, its velocity is displayed in the Velocity field of the Note inspector.

Velocity values for notes can be edited in any of these ways:

EDITING VELOCITY IN THE EDIT VIEW

Velocity can be edited in the Edit view it two ways:

- Dragging up or down while drawing a note with the Paint tool will change the velocity of the new note.
- With the Paint tool active, select one or more notes in the Edit view, hold down the Shift key, and drag up or down. The same amount will be added to the existing velocity values of all selected notes.

EDITING VELOCITY IN THE NOTE INSPECTOR

There are two editable Note Velocity fields in the Edit view: a bar graph in between the Instrument Mute and Solo buttons and the Audition Notes checkbox in the Instrument inspector, and a text field between the Mute button and Pitch field in the Note inspector. Note that editing velocity with the bar graph will always cause the value in the text field to be updated, but editing in the text field does not update the bar graph.

You can edit note velocity in any of the following ways:

- Select the note whose velocity you wish to edit, position the cursor over the Velocity field in the Note inspector, and drag up or down to the desired velocity value.
- Click in the Velocity field in the Note inspector and enter the desired velocity value.
- Select the note whose velocity you wish to edit, position the cursor over the Velocity bar graph in the Instrument inspector, and drag left or right to the desired velocity value.
- Click anywhere in the Velocity bar graph in the Instrument inspector to make the velocity jump to the value represented at that position.

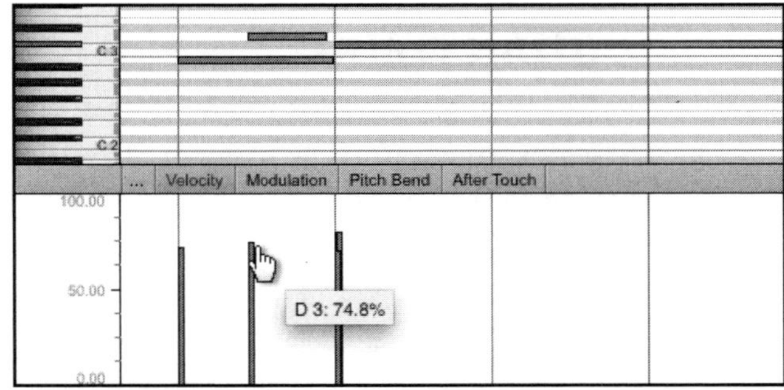

Fig. 6-57: Velocity can be edited in the Part Automation lane simply by selecting the notes whose velocity you want to edit and then dragging the velocity bars.

EDITING VELOCITY IN A PART AUTOMATION LANE

- With the Arrow tool active, select one or more notes in the Edit view, then drag the vertical velocity bar for any of the notes in the Part Automation lane up or down. The same amount will be added to the existing values of all selected notes.

As with any other controller, velocity values can be automated using the Paint tool in the Part Automation lane of the Edit view. This will be covered in the discussion of Automation in the chapter "Automation," in *Power Tools for Studio One 2*, vol. 2.

THE VELOCITY DIALOG BOX

The Velocity dialog box provides several different ways to edit note velocity values. It can be applied to selected notes in the Edit view or Parts in the Arrange view. To edit velocity with the Velocity dialog box, do the following:

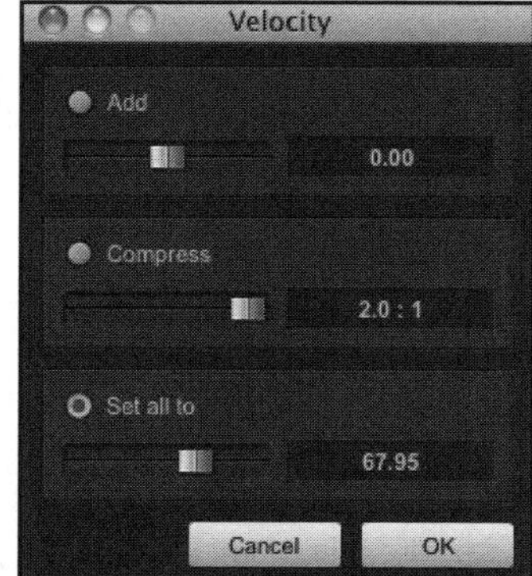

Fig. 6-58: The Velocity dialog provides three different ways of modifying velocity values of selected notes or Parts.

1. Select the notes in the Edit view or Parts in the Arrange view whose velocity you wish to edit.
2. Right-click on any note or Part and choose Velocity from the contextual pop-up menu that appears or choose Event > Musical Functions > Velocity from the main menu bar. The Velocity dialog box will then appear.
3. To add a fixed amount to the velocity of each note, drag the slider in the Add section until the desired value to add is displayed, or click in the Add field and enter the desired value to add. Note that values can use up to two decimal places for fine control.

RESTORE VELOCITY

- To return notes to the velocity values originally recorded for them, select the note(s) in the Edit view, right-click on any of them, and choose Musical Functions > Restore Velocity from the contextual menu that drops down, or Event > Musical Functions > Restore Velocity from the main menu.

QUANTIZING

Quantizing note start times is one of the most common operations performed on performance data. The basics of quantizing were covered in the section "Snap" in chapter 5, "On the Cutting Room Floor: Basic Editing." In Studio One 2, the Arrange and Edit views each have settings that are independent of each other, with the exception of Quantize Value, which is locked between the two views so that changing it in one view causes it to be changed to the same value in the other.

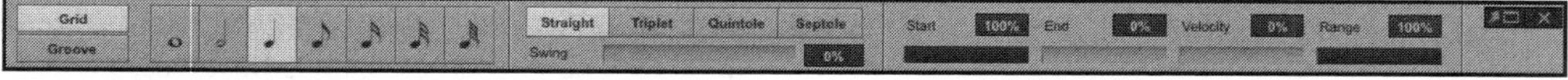

Fig. 6-59: The Quantize panel.

The Quantize panel is new in Studio One 2 and offers a considerable number of new features, including groove quantization. It also incorporates a number of existing quantization features, including the Quantize Value field, Quantize End command, and Quantize 50% command. Many people will find the Quantize panel sufficient for most or all of their quantizing needs.

For more information on quantizing audio, see the section "Time-Stretching (Compression/Expansion) and Quantizing Audio," earlier in this chapter.

Input Quantize

Input Quantize can be used to quantize input from a MIDI performance controller as it is recorded. For more information see the section "Recording on Instrument Tracks" in chapter 4, "Virtual Instruments and MIDI."

Edit View Auto Quantize

In the Edit view there is an Auto button below the Quantize Value field, although it is not labeled as such. When active, this button causes selected notes to be quantized to the Quantize Value when a value is chosen from the drop-down menu.

To quantize using Edit view Auto Quantize, do the following:

1. Select the note(s) you wish to quantize.
2. Be sure that the Auto button below the Quantize Value field is active. If it is, it will be colored blue rather than gray.
3. Click in the Quantize Value field and choose the desired value from the drop-down menu that appears. You must do this step even if the desired value is already displayed. The notes will be quantized to the grid using the selected value. It is not necessary for the Snap box to be checked for this to work.

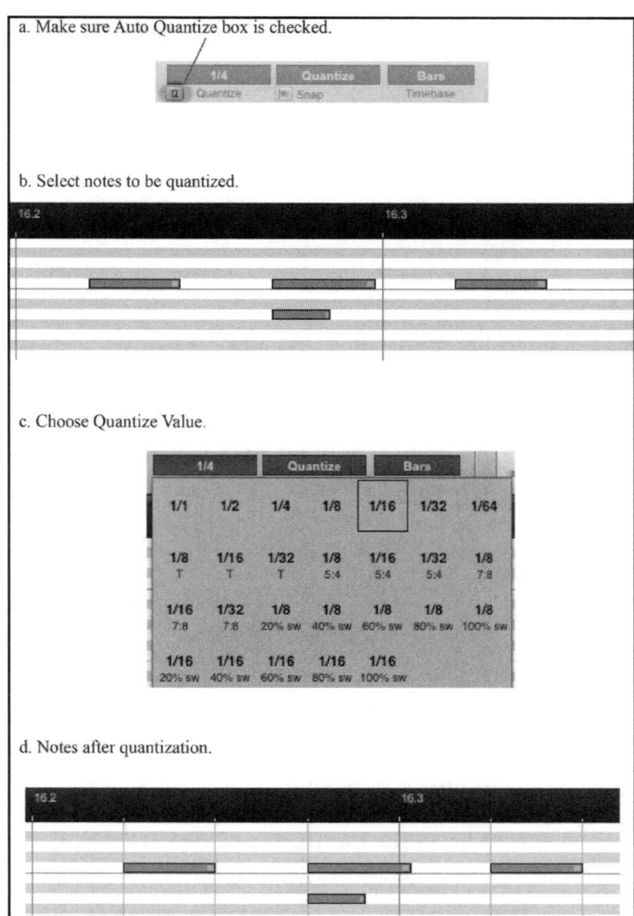

Fig. 6-60: The Edit view Auto Quantize feature is a very fast way to quantize a handful of notes.

Quantize Submenu

The Event > Quantize submenu contains four different commands for quantizing. Most of these commands can be used on selected Parts and Events in the Arrange window (see the section "Quantizing Audio," below, for more information on quantization and Audio Events) or on selected notes in the Edit view.

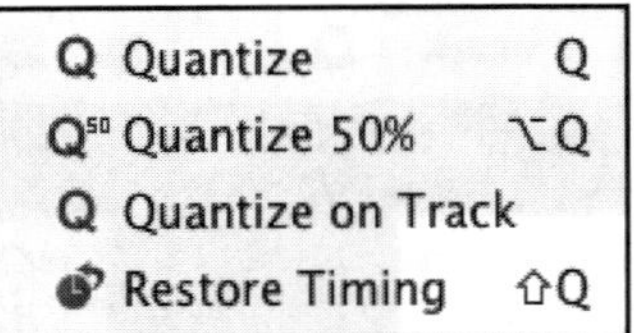

Fig. 6-61: The Quantize submenu offers four different quantizing options.

QUANTIZE COMMAND

The Event > Quantize > Quantize command can be invoked from either the Arrange or Edit view to provide basic, "hard" quantization using the Quantize Value set in the view. Used in the Arrange view, the Quantize command quantizes the notes contained in the selected Parts. To quantize the placement of the Parts themselves (quantizing where the Part starts but not affecting the relationships between the notes in it) use the Quantize on Track command. To perform hard quantization using the Quantize command, do the following:

1. Select the note(s) in the Edit view or Part(s) in the Arrange view that you wish to quantize.
2. Set the Quantize Value to the desired grid resolution.
3. Press the Q key, right-click on a note and choose Event > Quantize in the contextual drop-down menu that appears, or choose Event > Quantize > Quantize from the main menu. The Quantize command also appears in the Action menu in the Edit view.

QUANTIZE 50% COMMAND

The Quantize 50% command is identical to the Quantize command in every way except that instead of moving notes to the nearest grid line, it moves them half the distance from their original positions to the grid line. This is intended to produce a less rigid and mechanical sound. Its operation is exactly as described for the Quantize command above.

QUANTIZE ON TRACK

If the Quantize command is used in the Arrange window, it quantizes the notes within the selected Parts. But what if you need to quantize the start times of the Parts themselves without changing the timing inside it? That's exactly what the Quantize on Track command does. Quantize on Track works the same for Audio Events as it does for Instrument Parts, making it very useful for quantizing drum tracks. To quantize Parts and/or Events on tracks, do the following:

1. Select the Parts and/or Events you wish to quantize. The selection can include both Parts and Events across any number of tracks.
2. Set the Quantize Value to the desired resolution.

3. Choose Event > Quantize > Quantize on Track or right-click on any selected Part or Event and choose Quantize on Track from the contextual menu that drops down. The Parts and Events will be quantized as specified.

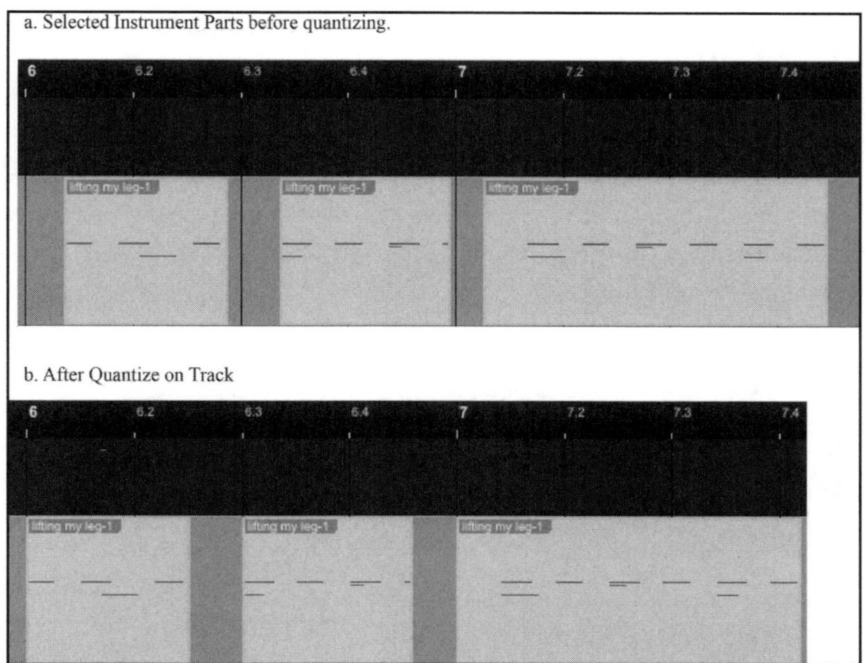

a. Selected Instrument Parts before quantizing.
b. After Quantize on Track

Fig. 6-62: Quantize on Track quantizes entire Parts in the Arrange view without affecting the internal relationships of the contents of the Parts.

RESTORE TIMING

The Restore Timing command allows you to undo quantization and set the note start point back to its original value. Note, however, that it can accomplish this only if you have not moved the note in any way since it was quantized. In this sense, it works similarly to the way a typical, single-level undo does, except that it undoes only quantization operations.

To restore the timing of quantized notes, do the following:

Select the item(s) for which you wish to restore timing and press Shift + Q, right-click on the note and choose Event > Restore Timing from the contextual menu that drops down, or choose Event > Quantize > Restore Timing from the main menu bar. The Restore Timing command is found in the Action menu near the top of the Music Editor (Edit view). If no timing changes have been performed on the note since it was quantized, it will be restored to its original start point.

In the Edit view, Restore Timing operates on a note-by-note basis. This means that it will work when used on individual notes that may have been quantized as part of a selection of multiple notes, as well as working on a selection of multiple notes that were quantized individually.

Quantize End

Most quantizing applications call for quantizing the note start times. The Quantize End command enables quantizing the note end time. One big difference between this and the usual quantization of start times is that start time quantization moves the end time by the same amount by which the start time is moved, thus maintaining the duration of the note. End time quantization, by contrast, maintains the start time and just changes the end time, thereby changing the note duration.

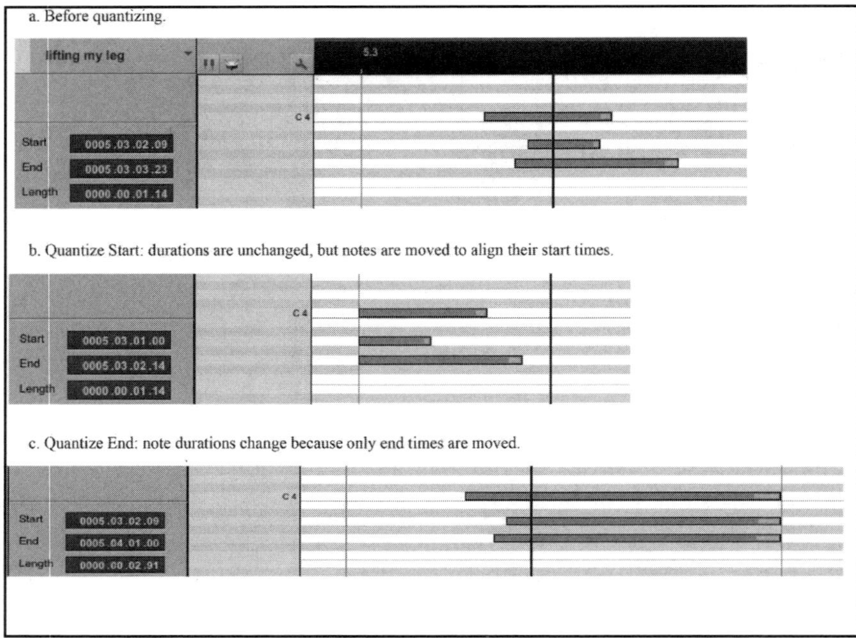

Fig. 6-63: Quantizing the start of a note moves the note but does not change its duration, however, quantizing the end of a note does alter its length.

To quantize note end times, do the following:

1. Set the Quantize Value to the desired resolution.
2. Choose Event > Musical Functions > Quantize End. The Quantize End command is also found in Edit > Action or the contextual menu that appears when you right-click on the note. The end points of each selected item will be quantized to the grid line nearest it.

Freeze Quantize

Freeze Quantize simply makes quantization that has been performed undoable.

To freeze quantization, do the following:

- Select the items for which you wish to make quantization permanent and choose Event > Musical Functions > Freeze Quantize from the main menu bar. The Freeze Quantize command is also found in the Edit view Action menu or the contextual menu that appears when you right-click on the note.

Humanize

Hard quantizing entirely eliminates timing variations. For some kinds of music this is fine, but for others it produces a mechanical precision that can lack feel. To counter this problem, various features have been introduced to maintain or introduce some amount of timing variation, in order to retain more of the feeling of human imperfection that is often the source of expressiveness. Each of these features is useful in different situations. One example is the Quantize 50% command, which is useful when there is too much variation in a performance and it is desirable to reduce the timing slop without eliminating it.

Humanizing is a term invented to describe a complementary approach, in which very small, pseudo-random variations are introduced to add more feeling to a passage that may be quantized too strictly. Studio One 2 has two commands for humanizing: Humanize and Humanize Less. Humanize Less is intended to create smaller variations than Humanize, but, since the effects of both commands are random, the actual difference between them in use is variable; sometimes the variations they produce are indistinguishable. In Studio One 2, there are no parameters you can adjust to influence the variations that are introduced. This means that obtaining the best results sometimes means repeated attempts: humanize, listen, undo, humanize again, iterating until you get a version that sounds good.

Another thing to keep in mind is that, since the variations introduced are random, repeatedly applying one of these commands to the same note or group of notes does not necessarily increase the variations in timing. In fact, it can sometimes result in a note returning to a grid line. Humanizing is applied to each selected note separately, so the most effective use of these commands is on groups of notes, whether by applying humanizing to one or more selected Parts in the Arrange view or to multiple notes in the Edit view.

To humanize note timing, do the following:

- Select one or more items in the Arrange or Edit views and choose Event > Musical Functions > Humanize or Event > Musical Functions > Humanize Less from the main menu bar. The Humanize and Humanize Less commands are also found in the Edit view Action menu and the contextual menu that appears when you right-click on the note.

Quantize Panel

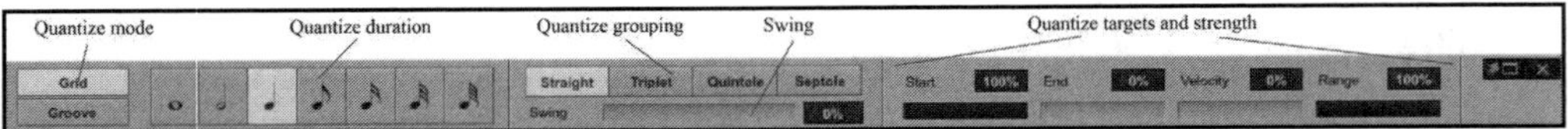

Fig. 6-64: The Quantize panel.

The Quantize panel consolidates a great many of the quantization parameters. Many quantizing applications will require only the Quantize panel to configure the quantization and the Quantize command to execute it.

Open the Quantize panel using any of these methods:

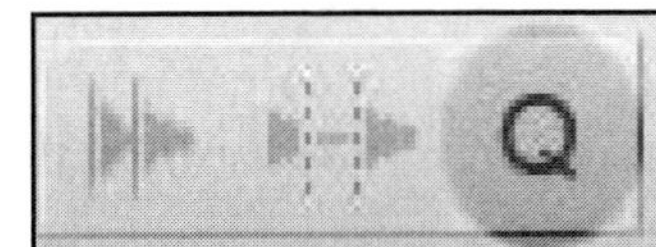

Fig. 6-65: The Quantize panel is opened and closed by this button in the Arrange view toolbar.

- Click on the Quantize panel button in the toolbar at the top of the Arrange view.
- Click on the Quantize panel button in the toolbar at the top of the Edit view.
- Choose View > Additional Views > Quantize from the main menu bar.

QUANTIZE MODE

The Quantize panel can operate in two modes: Grid (traditional quantization) and Groove (groove template quantization). The mode is selected by two buttons on the left of the Quantize panel.

The Duration, Grouping, and Swing parameters described in the rest of this section apply only to Grid mode; Quantize Targets are used in both Grid and Groove modes. See below for further information on Groove Quantize.

- To choose a quantize mode, click on either the Grid or Groove button on the left side of the Quantize panel.

QUANTIZE DURATION

In Grid mode, this array of buttons selects the basic note duration for the grid. This field and the Quantize Grouping field combined provide an expanded version of the functionality of the Quantize Value field. Its operation is completely simple and obvious.

- To select a quantize duration, click on the button for the desired note duration for the grid.

QUANTIZE GROUPING

Note groupings other than the standard two subdivisions per note value (for example, two eighth notes in a quarter, two sixteenth notes in an eighth note) are often referred to as "tuplets." Tuplets are usually described in terms of the number of notes in the tuplet for a given duration of standard grouping. For example, eighth-note triplets are three notes in the duration of a quarter note, which is more often divided into two eighth notes. This could be expressed as the ratio 3:2. Since sixteenth notes are grouped four to a quarter note, there are six sixteenth-note triplets, which could also be accurately described as 3:2, or as 6:4, which is the same thing. The Quantize Grouping area makes certain kinds of tuplets available.

Here are the available settings:

- **Straight:** This is a standard subdivision into two notes per larger note duration.
- **Triplet:** This quantizes to a 3:2 ratio.
- **Quintile:** More commonly known as "quintuplets," this quantizes to a 5:4 ratio.
- **Septole:** Also called "septuplets," this quantizes seven notes into the duration usually occupied by eight.
- To select a quantize grouping, click on the appropriate button in the Quantize panel.

SWING

Swing is a quantizing function intended to add a user-definable amount of "swing" to a rhythm. The classic jazz definition of swing is a rhythmic distortion in which eighth notes on the offbeat are played late, as though they were triplets rather than eighth notes. Of course, there are many variations in swing feel—hence a variable parameter is the best.

Studio One 2's Swing is a bit different than those you may have seen in other DAWs. Swing is usually given as a percentage of the distance between beats (alternate grid lines, actually, but most commonly we use swing for eighth notes). Using this scheme, if Quantize Value was set to 1/8th, a swing value of 50 percent would be a regular eighth note, and a classic swing eighth would be 67 percent (two-thirds of the way between beats, which fall on alternate grid lines).

In Studio One 2, instead of being the percentage of distance between alternate grid lines, it is the percentage of distance between adjacent grid lines. With Quantize Value set to 1/8th, a Swing value of 0 is a straight eighth, and a Swing value of 67 means 67 percent of the distance from a straight eighth to the next beat. A classic swing eighth would require a Swing value of 33 percent.

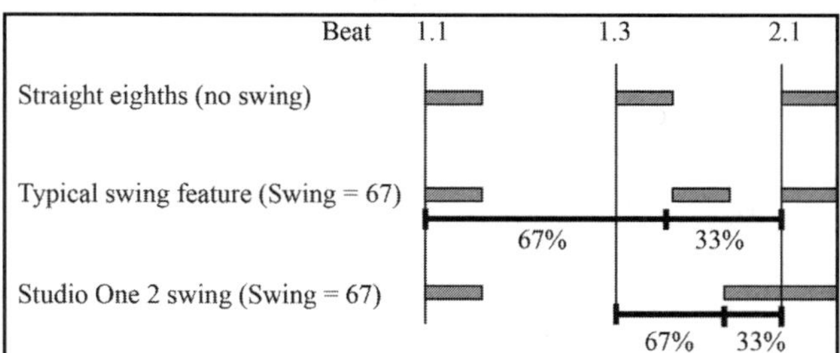

Fig. 6-66: Swing in Studio One 2 works somewhat differently than in many other DAWs.

- To set the Swing value, click on or drag to the desired value in the Swing bar, or click in the Swing field and enter a value.

QUANTIZE TARGETS

The Quantize targets are the attributes affected by quantizing. The Start, End, and Velocity quantize strength fields determine how strongly an item will be affected by the quantizer. When the quantize strength for Start is set to 0%, for instance, the quantizer will move the start times of the notes 0% of the way to the closest grid line, which is to say that they won't move at all. When set to 50%, the quantizer does the same as the Quantize 50% command: it moves the note half of the distance between its original position in time and the nearest grid line. At 100%, notes are hard quantized right to the grid lines. The quantize targets are the following:

- **Start:** This is the note start time. Start moves the note in time.
- **End:** This is the note end time. End changes the duration of the note.
- **Velocity:** This is the note velocity.
- **Range:** This is the distance from a grid line that will be affected by quantizing. Notes falling within the range will be quantized, and those outside the range will be unaffected. There is no visual indication of Range, so trial and error is usually required.

You can set the quantize strength for a target using any of the following methods:

- Click in the quantize strength field for the target and enter the desired value.
- Select the note(s) you wish to quantize, position the cursor over the target's quantize strength bar graph, and drag left or right to the desired value.
- Click anywhere in the bar graph for the target to make the value jump to the value represented at that position.

QUANTIZE PRESETS

The Quantize presets make it a snap (if you'll pardon the pun) to compare up to five different quantization setups. When you get a quantization pattern that interests you, store it in one of the memories (A through E) and then recall it during playback with a single click. Need more presets? You can store them in a drop-down menu just below the buttons. It's not just a comparison tool—it's a compositional aid!

- To store the current quantization settings in a preset button memory, hold down Option + Cmd (Alt + Ctrl in Windows) and click on the button.
- To recall a quantization preset, click on one of the memory buttons.
- To store the current quantization settings in the preset menu, click on the + (plus) key just below the A button, and name the preset when the name dialog box comes up.
- To recall a preset from the preset menu, click on the arrow in the preset menu field and choose one of the presets in the drop-down menu that appears.

Groove Templates

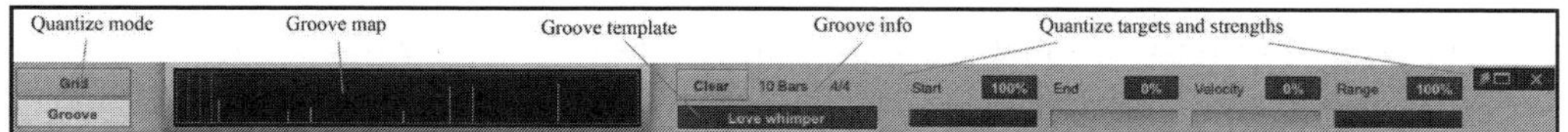

Fig. 6-67: The Quantize panel's Groove mode lets you make audio follow a MIDI groove or vice versa, plus a number of other very powerful capabilities for working with rhythmic feel.

Groove templates are an extremely powerful means of manipulating feel. Originally, groove quantization became popular as a way to take the feel of a real musician, like a great drummer, and apply it to rigidly quantized MIDI parts. However, the concept itself is broad and simple (though actually executing groove quantization is rather more of a trick), so it can be used to apply just about any feel to performances recorded or created with a different feel: it can make things more on top of the beat, turn a rocker into a soft shuffle, and so forth.

Groove templates are quantization grids extracted from input material. This means that the grid is based on the timing and dynamic variations that give the performance a feel. A Groove Template captures timing information as tempo changes, and dynamic changes as velocity values.

In Studio One 2, the input material can be audio or MIDI. Once a groove template has been constructed, it can be stored as a preset and pulled from the browser or Groove Preset menu at any time. Since creating, storing, and recalling groove templates requires nothing more than a single drag-and-drop operation, groove quantization can be very fast to use, allowing you to try lots of grooves on for size, or get to a particular groove you know is right quickly.

Groove quantization is accessed as the alternative to Grid mode in the Quantization panel. When you select Groove mode, the left half of the panel changes, but the Quantize Targets and Presets sections remain the same. These settings can be used in conjunction with the Groove Template, if desired.

The first step in making a good Groove Template, naturally, is to hear a great groove in the audio or MIDI performances before you start.

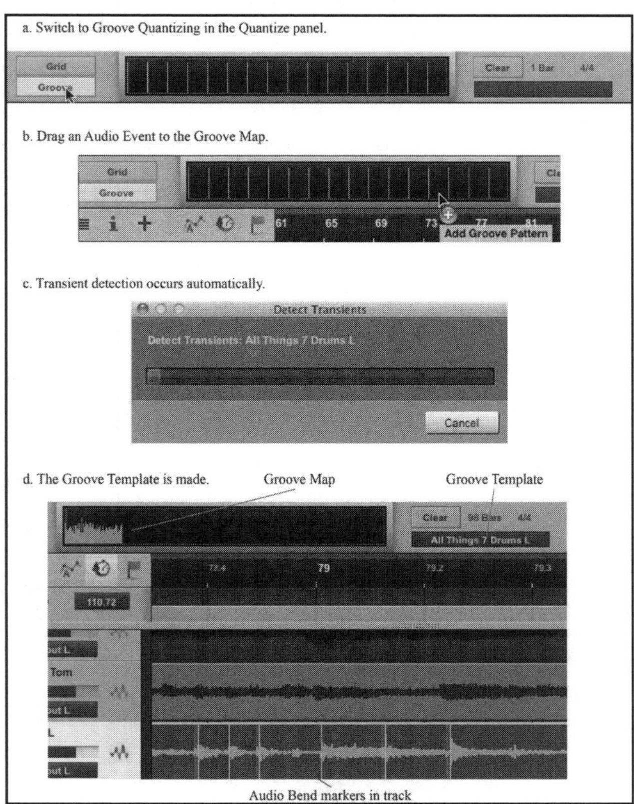

Fig. 6-68: Making a Groove Template requires only putting the Quantize panel into Groove Quantize mode and dragging audio (or MIDI) to the Groove Map area of the panel.

- To access Groove Quantization, open the Quantize panel and click on the Groove button on the left to put the panel into Groove mode.
- To create a Groove Template, select the notes in the Edit view or Part in the Arrange view from which you want to extract a groove, and, with the Arrow tool active, drag the selection to the Groove Map in the panel. If it is audio, transients will be automatically detected. The Groove Template will be displayed in the Groove Map. To the right of the Groove Map the panel will show the detected time signature and groove duration in bars. These are not editable.
- To rename a Groove Template, click in the Groove Name field to the right of the Groove Map, and enter the desired name.
- To store a Groove Template, drag from the Groove Map to the Files tab of the Browser. Although you can drag it to any location in the file system (such as a folder of presets used for a specific project), a recommended location is Studio One 2 > Presets > User Presets > Quantize Settings.
- To load a Groove Template, drag it from the Browser to the Groove Map or choose it from the Groove Preset menu.
- To add a new Part based on a Groove Map, drag from the Groove Map to an empty range on an Instrument track, or an empty spot in the Arrange view. A new Part or a new Instrument track containing a new Part will be created. The Part will contain notes from the Groove Map, set to the pitch of C3.
- To create a new pattern in an Instrument track that is based on an audio groove (MIDI follows audio), create a Groove Map from the audio, and use the Paint tool to draw in notes wherever you want them. Since the Groove Map is now the grid, the new notes will be locked to the audio.

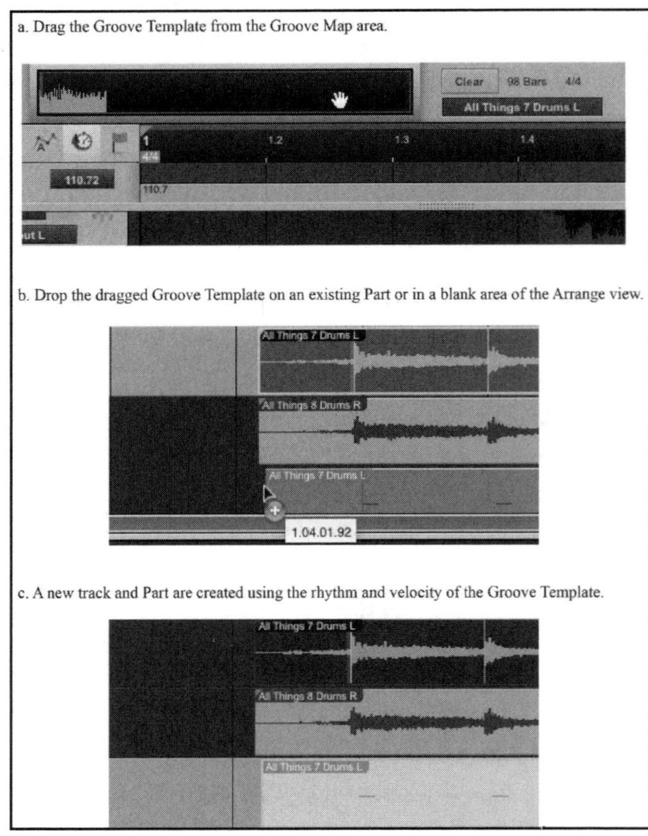
a. Drag the Groove Template from the Groove Map area.
Clear
98 Bars
4/4
All Things 7 Drums L
110.72
b. Drop the dragged Groove Template on an existing Part or in a blank area of the Arrange view.
All Things 7 Drums L
All Things 8 Drums R
All Things 7 Drums L
1.04.01.92
c. A new track and Part are created using the rhythm and velocity of the Groove Template.
All Things 7 Drums L
All Things 8 Drums R
All Things 7 Drums L

Fig. 6-69: Deriving a new Instrument Part from a Groove Template is done by dragging the Template to the Arrange view.

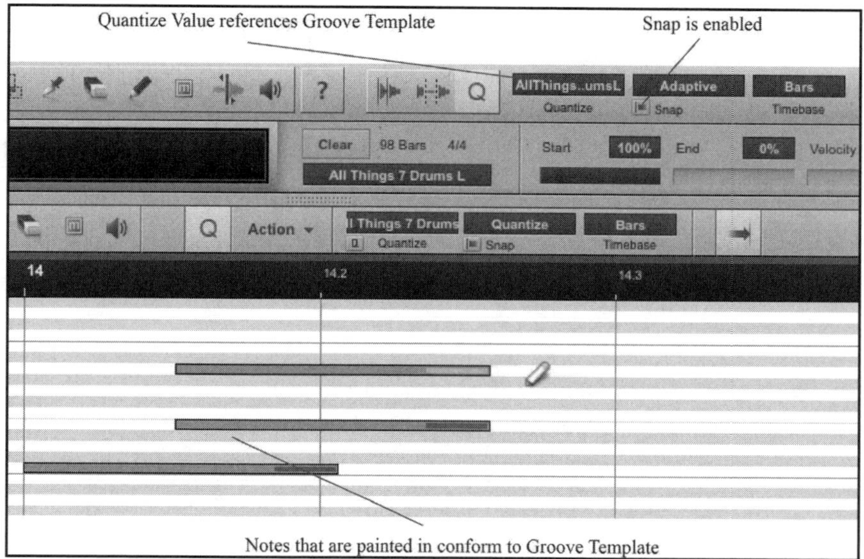

Fig. 6-70: When using a Groove Template, the grid is referenced to it. Therefore, notes you paint in or items you quantize are snapping to the Groove Template.

- To clear the Groove Map, click on the Clear button immediately to its right.
- To delete a Groove Template from the Browser, just select it and press the Delete key.

ADVANCED MIDI EDITING

Studio One 2 has a number of options for advanced MIDI editing, most of them found, appropriately enough, in the Preferences dialog box.

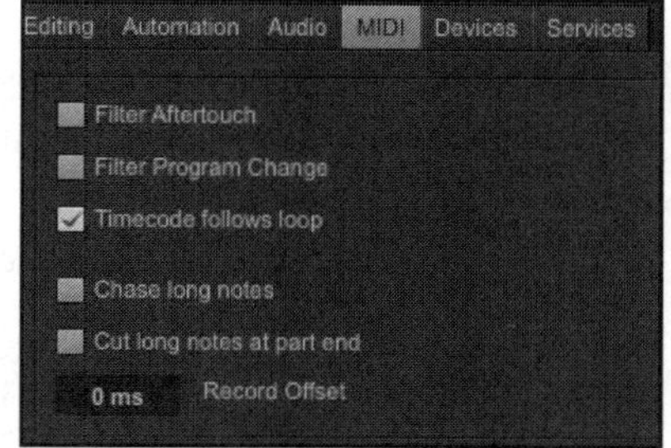

Fig. 6-71: Advanced MIDI options are located under the MIDI tab of Preferences>Options>Advanced.

Preferences Dialog Box Advanced MIDI Options

The following options are found in Preferences > Options > Advanced > MIDI:

FILTER AFTERTOUCH

Check this box to filter MIDI channel pressure (mono aftertouch) and polyphonic pressure (poly aftertouch) from incoming controller data.

FILTER PROGRAM CHANGE

Check this box to filter MIDI program change messages from incoming controller data.

TIMECODE FOLLOWS LOOP

This setting determines how Studio One 2 acts when sending timecode from Studio One 2 to external devices equipped to sync to it while looping. The timecode can jump back when the loop does (Timecode Follows Loop is checked), or continue to be generated linearly (Timecode Follows Loop is unchecked), ignoring that the Song has actually looped back in time. By default, Timecode Follows Loop is active.

- To change how timecode addresses are transmitted when looping, open Preferences > Options > Advanced > MIDI and check or uncheck the Timecode Follows Loop box.

CHASE LONG NOTES

When this box is checked, if playback is started in the middle of a note, Studio One 2 will play the note as though it started from where playback starts. If it is not checked, then the first note to begin after playback is started will be the first played.

CUT LONG NOTES AT PART END

It can happen that an Instrument Part ends before some of the notes it contains—for example, if the end of a Part is shortened after a musical passage has been recorded. When the Cut Long Notes at Part End box is checked, notes extending beyond the Part boundary are cut off when the Part ends. By default, this box is unchecked, so that long notes continue to play even after the Part ends.

RECORD OFFSET

This field compensates for MIDI interfaces that do not accurately report the amount of latency they introduce by subtracting up to 100 ms from recorded MIDI data. This is not merely a monitoring delay, but a delay that is in the data, as can easily be seen by viewing an Instrument track recorded with a Record Offset in Edit view.

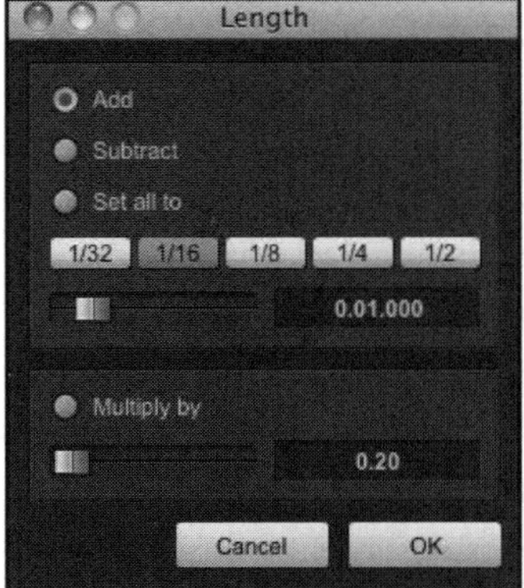

Fig. 6-72: The Length dialog modifies the duration of selected notes or Parts.

Length

The Length dialog box provides tools for altering the duration of notes selected in the Edit view or in Parts in the Arrange view. Duration values can be added to, subtracted from, multiplied by a specified factor, or simply all set to a selected value. The placement of notes is not affected—only the duration is changed; that is, the note end is moved, not the start.

To change the length of selected notes in the Edit view or notes in selected Parts in the Arrange view, do any of the following:

- Right-click on a note or Part and choose Musical Functions > Length from the contextual drop-down menu that appears or Choose Event > Musical Functions > Length from the main menu bar. The Length dialog box will appear.
- To add or subtract to the duration of the selected notes, click on the Add or Subtract radio button and choose a value to add or subtract, as described below.
- To change the duration of the selection by a common note duration, simply click on one of the five preset buttons displayed below the Set All To radio button. The value will be shown in the Duration Change field.
- To change the duration of the selection by some other value, drag or click on the Duration Change slider below the preset buttons until the desired value is displayed, or simply click in the Duration Change field and enter the desired duration.
- To set all notes in the selection to a single duration, click on the Set All To radio button and drag or click on the Duration Change slider until the desired duration is displayed, or simply click in the Duration Change field and enter the desired duration.
- To multiply all notes in the selection by a single duration, click on the Multiply By radio button and drag or click on the Multiplication Factor slider just below it until the desired duration is displayed, or simply click in the Multiplication Factor field and enter the desired factor by which durations in the selection should be multiplied. The factor can be set to values between 0.2 and 5.0.
- After setting the desired duration change, click on OK to execute the Length modification.

Stretch

The Stretch command is essentially time-stretching for MIDI. Like the Length command, Stretch scales note durations, but it is different than Length in that it scales the time range in which the notes occur as well. A four-bar phrase can be scaled into a two-bar phrase in which the tempo is twice as fast and the note durations all half as long, or, going the other way, into an eight-bar phrase at half the tempo and doubled note durations.

Fig. 6-73: Like the Length dialog, the Stretch dialog modifies note durations, but it changes the time period over which the notes occur, as well.

Stretch essentially scales a selection of notes so that note durations and the spaces between are all scaled.

TIP: Stretch does *not* change Part durations. If you stretch a range without sufficient duration in the Part, some notes may disappear from view. However, they are there in the Part and simply need to be revealed by dragging the end point of the Part to increase its duration. Alternatively, you can lengthen the Part before stretching it.

To stretch a selected range of notes in the Edit view or selected Parts in the Arrange view, do the following:

1. Right-click on a note or Part and choose Musical Functions > Stretch from the contextual drop-down menu that appears or Choose Event > Musical Functions > Stretch. The Stretch dialog box will appear.
2. To double or halve the selected range or Part, click on the Double Tempo or Half Tempo radio button.
3. To stretch the selected range or Part by some other factor, click on the Free radio button and drag or click on the Multiplication Factor slider just below it until the desired factor is displayed, or simply click in the Multiplication Factor field and enter the desired factor by which the selection should be stretched. The factor can be set to values between 0.2 and 5.0.
4. Multiple ranges or Parts can be selected and stretched, but keep in mind that Part durations are unaffected, which may produce confusing results when multiple items are stretched at once.
5. When the desired stretch settings are in place, click on OK to execute the Stretch operation.

EDITING APPLICATIONS

Here are just a few examples of common editing tasks and how they are accomplished in Studio One 2.

Comping

The word "comping" is short for "compositing," and it refers to the process of piecing together a passage from multiple performances. There are other methods of piecing together a performance, as well, such as punching in, but comping has the benefit of allowing the performer to do a complete pass of the passage, which can be important for flow and rhythm.

In Studio One 2, comping is most easily done by taking the best parts from multiple takes on a track. However, there is more flexibility in using layers rather than takes for the same process. Of course, you can take pieces of a passage from another part of the Song, or even from an entirely different Song, if you like. The basic process of comping is given below:

1. Create takes or layers containing the record passes through the material.
2. Audition the takes/layers to find the best version of each piece of the performance.
3. Assemble the selected pieces into a single layer.
4. Bounce the assembled layer into a single audio file.

COMPING FROM TAKES

Creating a comp from bits and pieces of different takes is quick and easy.

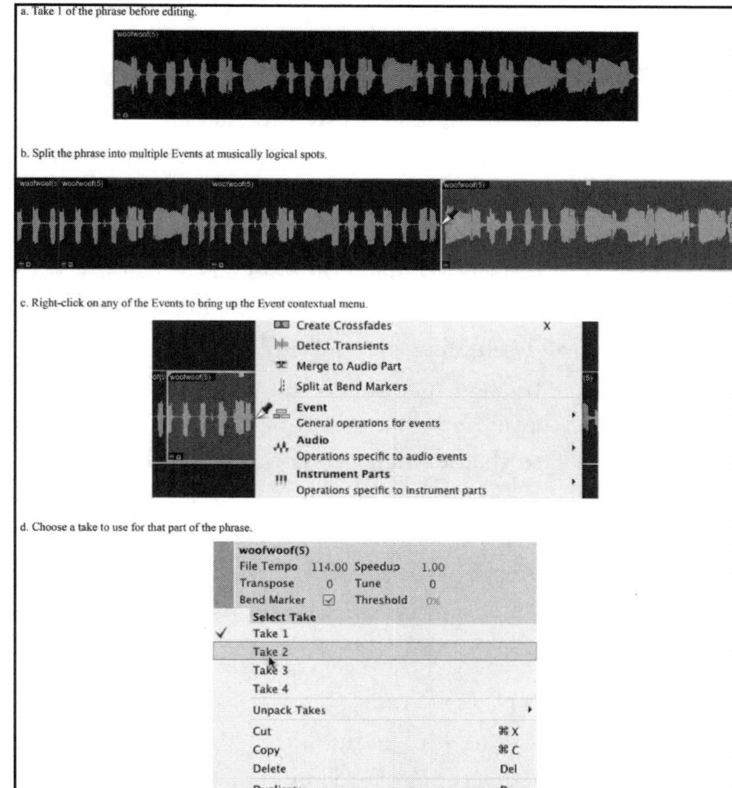

Fig. 6-74: A comp can be created from takes very simply. First cut the original phrase into multiple Events. Then, go through the phrase one Event at a time, selecting and auditioning the takes to find the best take for that part of the phrase. You can also set Studio One 2 for loop playback and then change takes for an Event each time through so you can audition the takes in the context of the entire phrase.

1. Create takes by loop recording.
2. Make splices wherever you want to edit between takes. All takes are affected by these splices, which will create new Audio Events on each take.
3. Audition each Event to find the best version by right-clicking on the Event in the track, selecting a take from contextual drop-down menu that appears, and listening to it.
4. After auditioning the takes, go back and select the take that you like the best.
5. Repeat this process for each Audio Event. When you finish the last Event, your comp is done!
6. To bounce the assembled pieces to a single file, select all of the pieces and press Cmd + B, right-click on any of the selected pieces and choose Event > Bounce Selection from the contextual menu that drops down, or choose Event > Bounce Selection from the main menu bar to bounce the selection to a new file.

COMPING FROM LAYERS

CREATING LAYERS FOR COMPING

Here are four different methods of creating layers that you can use for comping.

The section "Loop Recording" in chapter 3, "Go! Recording with Studio One 2," discussed how you could set up a loop and record, creating a new take on each pass through the loop. To comp from these takes requires converting them into layers.

- To convert takes into layers, right-click on the Event containing the takes and choose Unpack Takes > Unpack Takes To Existing Layers or Unpack Takes > Unpack Takes

To New Layers from the contextual drop-down menu that appears. For more about unpacking takes, see the section "Loop Recording," in chapter 3, "Go! Recording with Studio One 2."

- To record each pass of a loop recording directly into a new layer instead of a take, choose Options > Record Takes to Layers from the main menu bar.
- To record multiple passes into layers without looping, before each recording pass, right-click in the track header in the Arrange view and choose Layers > Add Layer from the contextual menu that drops down, click in the Layers field of the Track inspector and choose Add Layer from the menu that drops down, or choose Track > Layers > Add Layer from the main menu bar.
- Assembling pieces from different sections of the Song or from other Songs is the trickiest method. To do this, you must find a piece you want, copy it, create a new layer in the track in which you are creating your comp, expand all layers on the track so that alternate versions are visible, paste the piece in roughly where it should go, zoom way in, and slip the piece around in time until its waveform lines up as closely as possible with another version. You will need to do the final timing tweak by ear by looping the section and slipping or nudging the pasted piece while listening until it sounds right. As I said, this is the trickiest method, but it does work very well in most cases.

AUDITIONING LAYERS

You will need to audition the different layers to find the best versions of each piece. There are two ways to do this:

- With all layers for the track expanded, click on the Solo button in the Layer header and play. Note that the Layer Solo button is independent of the Track Solo button, so you can solo the layer and play it with the track in isolation (soloed) or in context.
- Choose the Listen tool in the Arrange view, click on the mouse where you want to start auditioning, and hold the mouse button down for as long as you want to audition. Note that this will solo the track as well as the layer.

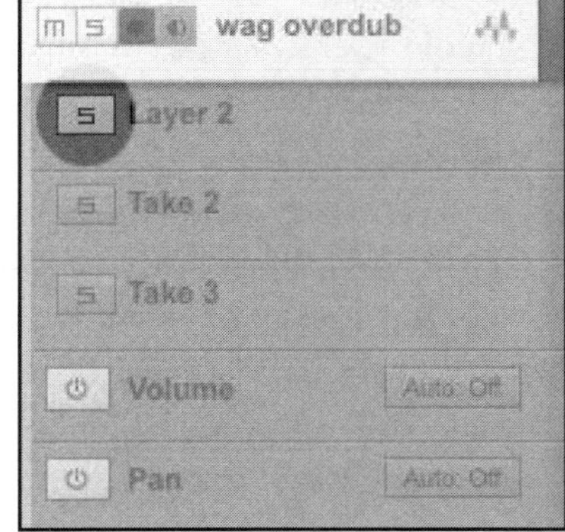

Fig. 6-75: Each Layer on a track has its own solo button, which is separate from the track solo function.

ASSEMBLING SELECTED PIECES INTO A COMP LAYER

1. When moved over an expanded layer, the Arrow tool becomes the Range tool. Use this to select the piece of a layer you want in the comp.

2. Press V, right-click (Ctrl-click on Mac) on the range (the cursor is once again an arrow when placed over the range) and choose Copy Ranges to Track from the contextual menu that drops down, or choose Event > Copy Ranges to Track from the main menu bar to copy the range to the active layer in the track. The range will be copied to the same time as on its original layer.
3. Repeat for each piece of each layer that you want to use in the comp.

BOUNCING TO A FILE

Although it is convenient to bounce the assembled pieces to a single file, it is not necessary. One alternative technique would be to merge the assembled ranges into an Audio Part, which can be quantized or processed with Event FX. For more about bouncing and freezing audio, see the chapter "Mixing" in *Power Tools for Studio One 2*, vol. 2.

- To bounce the assembled pieces to a single file, select all of the pieces and press Cmd + B, right-click (or Ctrl-click on Mac) on any of the selected pieces and choose Event > Bounce Selection from the contextual menu that drops down, or choose Event > Bounce Selection from the main menu bar to bounce the selection to a new file.

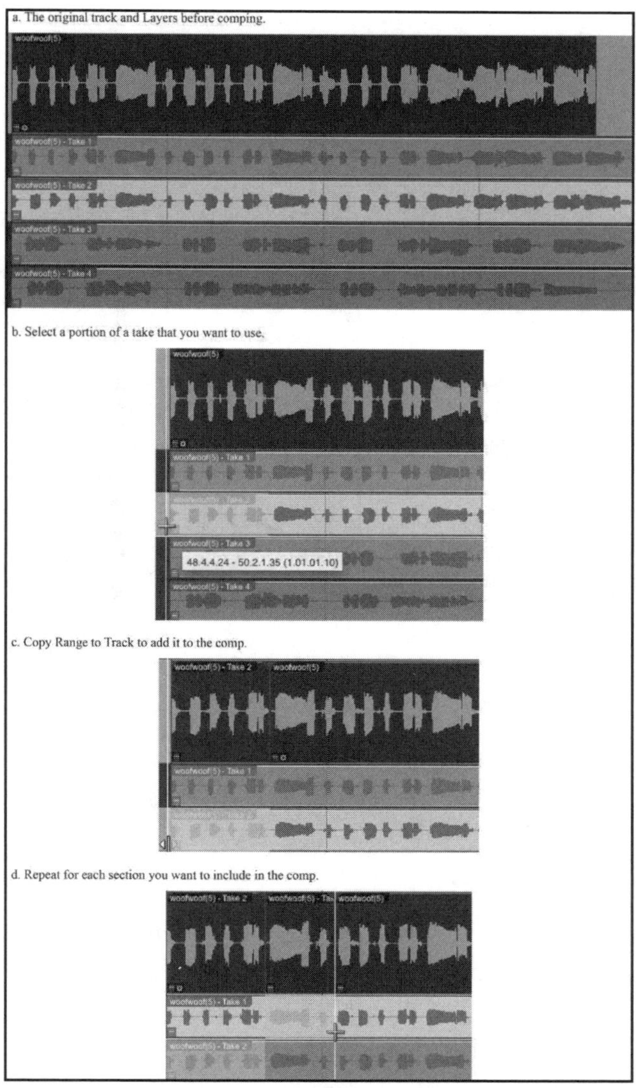

Fig. 6-76: Comps can be created from Layers. Just select the portion of the take you want to use and use the Copy Range to Track command.

Repeat Paste and Stutter Effects

Studio One 2's Edit > Duplicate command provides repeat-paste functionality. This is the core technique for stutter effects, as well as copying loops.

REPEAT PASTE

- To paste copies of a group of selected Events, Parts, or notes end to end, press the D key or choose Edit > Duplicate from the main menu bar. The copy will be pasted in starting exactly at the end of selected group. Press the D key as many times as necessary to make the desired number of copies.

- To paste copies of a group of selected Events, Parts, or notes that start at grid lines, be sure that Snap is enabled and the Quantize setting is at the desired resolution, then press the D key or choose Edit > Duplicate from the main menu bar. The copy will be pasted in starting exactly at the beginning of the next appropriate grid line.

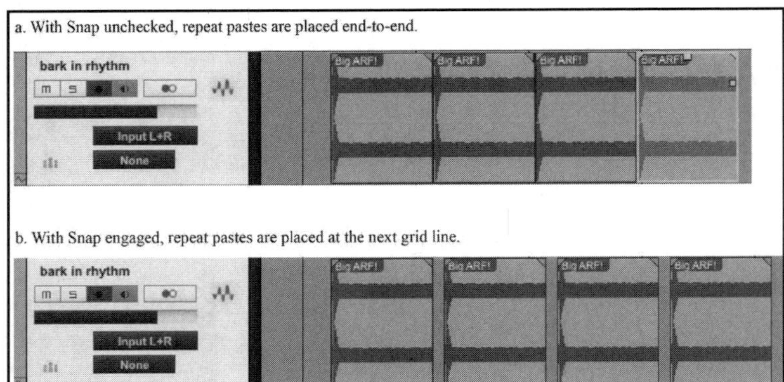

Fig. 6-77: The behavior of the Duplicate (repeat paste) command depends on whether or not Snap is engaged.

STUTTER EFFECTS

The key to creating stutter effects in Studio One 2 is the Duplicate command. There are a variety of techniques you can use, depending on the particular effect you are after. Here's one example:

1. Check the Snap box so that selections adhere to the grid.
2. Set Quantize to 1/32nd.
3. Select the entire sound to which you want to add a stutter and drag it down to move it onto a new track.
4. Now select the portion of the sound that you want to stutter. In this case, that is the first 1/32nd note of the sound.
5. Uncheck the Snap box. (You may not need to do this if you know your selection is exactly the length of the Quantize setting.)
6. Press Option + D or choose Edit > Duplicate and Insert from the main menu bar. A new Event containing the stutter section is created at the original Event's start point, and the original Event is slid later by the same amount.
7. Repeat the duplicating process however many times are needed for the stutter effect you want. In this example, you want one beat of stuttering, so you duplicate and insert a total of eight times.

8. In this example, you are done at this point because you want the original to occur at a later time than it was played.

If you had wanted the sound to remain at its original time, you could have selected all of the stutter Events and the original and dragged them all one beat earlier. (With Snap on, this is easy.) You also could select all of the Events and merge them into an Audio Part.

It's easy to see how flexible Studio One 2 can be!

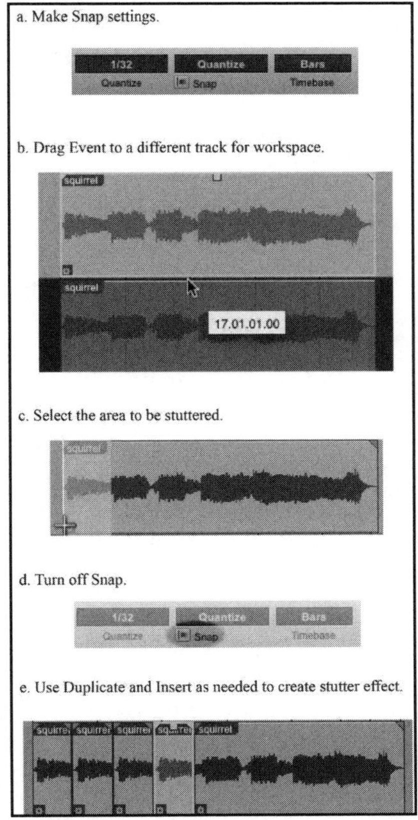

Fig. 6-78: One fast way of achieving the ever-popular stuttering effect uses Snap and Duplicate and Insert (repeat paste).

Editing Drums

Editing drum tracks is a common task, but there are a number of different kinds of edits people need to do. Here are three just to get you started:

USING EDIT GROUPS IN DRUM EDITING

Typical multitrack recording scenarios involve using anywhere from three to eight microphones on drums; some situations call for twice that many. If the mics are well placed, phase cancellations resulting from mixing them will be minimal, and this is how you want things to stay when you edit. The challenge, then, is to edit all of the drum tracks together to keep them phase-coherent.

Studio One 2 provides an easy solution, which is to group the drum tracks.

1. Assuming that all of the drum tracks are adjacent in the Arrange view, click in the header for the top track to select it, then Shift-click on the header for the bottom track. All of the drum tracks should now be selected.
2. Press Cmd + G, right-click in any of the track headers and choose Group Selected Tracks from the contextual menu that drops down, or choose Track > Group Selected Tracks from the main menu to group the tracks. Now, any edit you perform on one track will be performed identically on all of the rest. Edits are entirely phase-coherent.

In Studio One 2, an edit group also acts as a mix group, so when we move one drum channel fader, for example, they all will move together. This can be very handy most of the time (although controlling the overall level of the group is more flexibly done by routing all of the channels to an aux channel), but what if you need to tweak the level of only one channel?

- To temporarily suspend an edit group and adjust a single group member separately, hold down the Option key while executing the edit or mix operation.

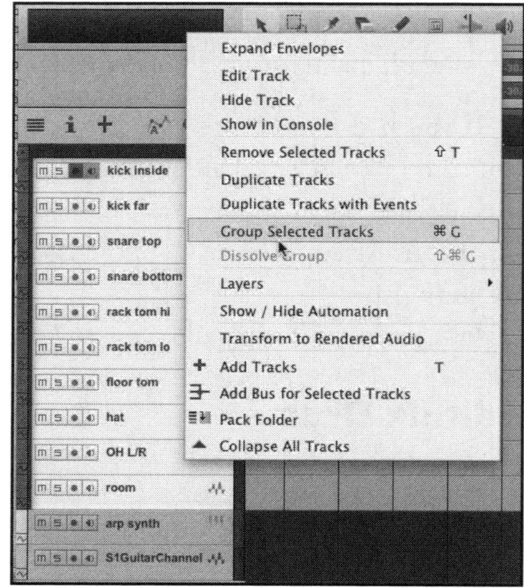

Fig. 6-79: Grouping drum tracks.

DRUM REPLACEMENT

Studio One 2's ease in extracting groove timing from audio and converting audio into MIDI notes make drum replacement amazingly fast.

1. Set up Impact or another VI on an Instrument track and choose the drum sounds you want.
2. If the Quantize panel is not visible, click on the Quantize panel button in the Arrange view toolbar or choose View > Additional Views > Quantize from the main menu bar to open it.
3. Click on the Groove button in the Quantize panel to bring up the Groove Quantize display.
4. Select the Audio Events in the track for the drum you want to replace.
5. Drag the selected Events to the Groove Map in the Quantize panel. This will initiate transient detection on the audio and generate a Groove Template from it.
6. Drag the Groove Template to the Instrument track with Impact or another drum replacement sound source. This will generate a new Part with MIDI notes for each drum hit.
7. Select the first Event in the original drum track.
8. Press L or choose Locate Selection from the main menu bar to move the play location to the beginning of the first Event.
9. Select the newly created Part on the Instrument track.
10. Press Cmd + L or choose Edit > Move to Cursor from the main menu bar. The Part will move to the time at which the first Event starts. The two are now synchronized.
11. Transpose the pitches in the Part to play the sound you want.

12. Repeat this process for each drum you want to replace.

The result of this process will be that each replacement drum will be on its own track. This makes it convenient if you need to do further editing. If you are using the replacement drum in combination with the original, you may want to consider grouping the Audio and Instrument tracks for each drum. Another option is transforming the Instrument tracks into Audio tracks. (Of course, these, too, can be grouped with the original Audio tracks.)

Finally, remember that this method works equally well if the original tracks are Instrument tracks and not Audio tracks, as would be the case if the drummer used electronic, instead of acoustic, drums to record. You can even create a groove template from a single Instrument track containing an entire drum performance, but things could get messy when you get to the last step of transposition.

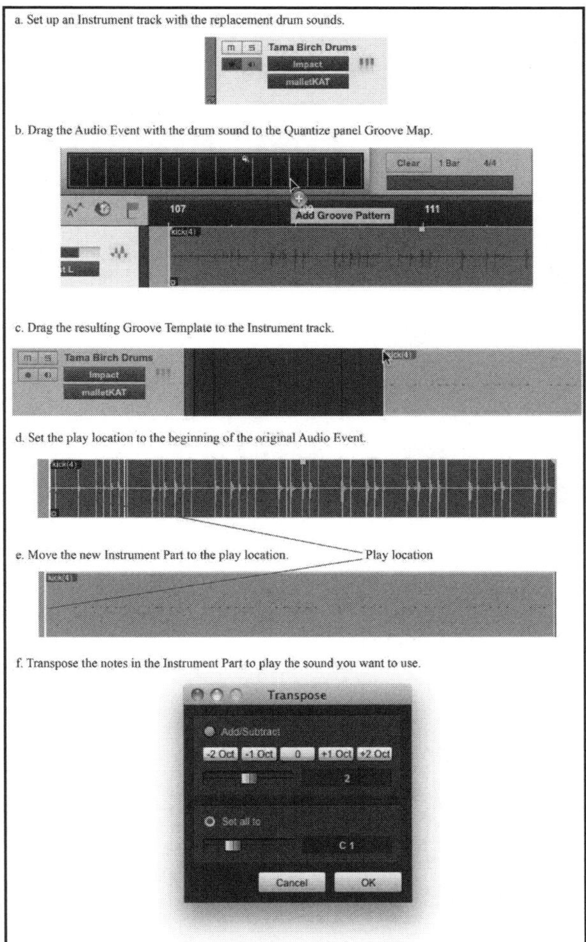

Fig. 6-80: Drum replacement in just a few easy steps: Make a Groove Template from the original audio, then drag it to the Instrument track with the replacement sounds. Synchronize the new Instrument Part with the audio, then transpose it to the proper note for the sound you want. Repeat for each drum you want to replace.

QUANTIZING DRUMS

In a program as powerful as Studio One 2, there is almost always more than one way to skin a cat (though I always thought that a nasty expression). Here are a few methods of quantizing recordings of drum tracks:

- Use the Strip Silence feature to separate the hits into individual Events. Once they are separated, you can use the standard quantization features as described in the section "Quantizing," in this chapter.
- Use the Detect Transients and Slice features instead of Strip Silence, and then use standard quantization features.
- Use the Detect Transients feature and then quantize the Bend markers to the grid, so that the drum hits are time-stretched as needed to fit.

- Create a Groove Template from another track (such as bass), then use any of the previous three methods of segmenting and quantizing to match the drum track to the Groove Template.

Appendix A
Advanced Options

Here is a list of the options available under Preferences > Options > Advanced. Most of these are described in the *Studio One 2 Reference Manual.* If you don't know what these are, you can mess yourself up pretty badly, so be careful, but there are some very useful features here. An asterisk (*) next to an entry indicates that it is selected by default.

EDITING

Tools

- Enable crosshair cursor for tools*
- Locate when clicked in empty space*

Event Appearance

- Don't show event names
- Draw events translucent (grid shines through)
- Smooth edges of automation envelopes

AUTOMATION

- Automation follows events*
- Disable events under automation envelopes*
- Automatically add envelopes for all touched parameters
- Default envelopes for new Audio tracks: Volume*, Pan*, Mute*

AUDIO

- Play overlapping events
- Use non-buffered audio file access
- Use cache for timestretched audio files*

- Record tempo information to audio files*
- Use dithering for audio devices and audio file export*
- Use realtime processing to update mastering files
- Stop playback when opening options*
- Release audio device in background
- Process audio in safe mode (higher latency)*

MIDI

- Filter Aftertouch
- Filter Program Change
- Timecode follows loop*
- Chase long notes
- Cut long notes at part end
- Record Offset

DEVICES

- Device Editor follows Channel Selection*
- Audio Track Monitoring follows Record*
- Instrument Track Monitoring follows Record*
- Fader Mode: Touch*/Jump

SERVICES

- ARA Plug-in Support
- AudioUnit Plug-in Support
- CD-Burning support
- CoreAudio Support
- CoreMIDI Support
- PreSonus Hardware Support
- External Device Support
- QuickTime Video Support
- ReWire Support
- VST 3 Plug-in Support
- VST 2.4 Plug-in Support

Appendix B Video Extras

Included with your *Power Tools for Studio One 2* book is a DVD with nearly an hour of video training on topics taken straight out of the book. While I tried to write as clearly as I could, seeing is almost always a faster way to grasp features. Here's what you'll find in these videos:

- Song Page Tour: As the name suggests, this is a fairly comprehensive tour of the page of Studio One 2 where you will do the most work.
- Drag and Drop: Drag-and-drop functionality is in Studio One 2's DNA, and is one of the program's best workflow features. I show you a nice selection of ways that drag-and-drop can make your session go faster and smoother.
- Session Organization: Studio One 2 has plenty of tools for imposing order in your Song documents. Session organization may not be sexy, but it has everything to do with hassle-to-fun ratio when you work.
- Comping: Studio One 2 features like layers and takes are set up to make comping a master take from several record passes (one of the fundamental editing processes) nearly effortless.
- Smart Transposition (Scale Snap): Pick a scale and root and transpose melodies and chords. I show you the ups and downs of transposing to a tonality.
- Fades: There is no editing task you will do more often than creating and editing fades. Here's the scoop on how Studio One 2 handles top and tail fades, crossfades, and much more.
- The Tempo Track: Studio One 2 has many features for making your Song follow tempo changes. In this video, I show you how to create the tempo changes you need.
- Tips for Drum Production with Studio One 2: Most of us record drums, and it's a lot of work. This video shows you how to use Studio One 2's features to tame the drum recording beast, whether you are using samples or live drums.
- Quantizing Audio: Studio One 2 has multiple ways to make audio follow tempo changes, and this video will show them to you.

- Macros: Studio One 2's Macro feature was in development when this book was written, but was released as these videos were being produced, so I'm giving you a sneak peek at one of Studio One 2's most powerful aids to workflow before I write it up in detail for an Updates chapter in *Power Tools for Studio One 2,* volume 2.

Index

ABOUT THE AUTHOR

Larry the O is. Perhaps you are looking more for what he has been. At his best he has been an audio and music maven, and, at worst, a blowhard. Either way, he has managed to perpetrate his silliness far and wide through the audio and music industries for more than 30 years as performer and recording artist, sound engineer, audio director, producer, composer, sound designer, dialog editor, magazine writer, marketing communications manager, product manager, music editor, bench technician, coffee boy, free ride to the mall, and college teacher. He has worked on albums, television, film, video games, magazines, books, websites, industrial sound design, and other things he can hardly remember. Yes, it's been tiring at times.

The O has worked for otherwise well-respected companies such as Lexicon (in its early days), LucasArts, Meyer Sound Laboratories, Electronic Arts, and the late, lamented Russian Hill Recording in San Francisco. Perhaps his most significant and unique contribution has been to provide the only voices ever heard from The Blockheads in any of the *Gumby* cartoons.

Larry the O runs his music and audio services business, Toys in the Attic, out of Vallejo, California—a pop, sip, and DUI away from the San Francisco Bay Area Wine Country. Most of his work is done in his Studio Faire La Nouba, where computers regularly befuddle him just to prove who's boss.

POWER TOOLS SERIES

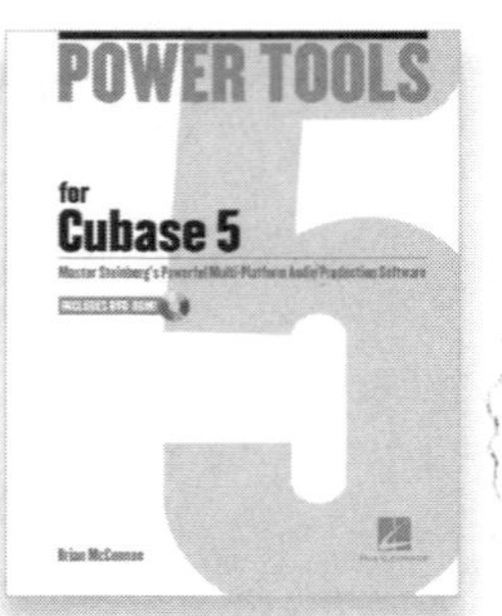

POWER TOOLS FOR STUDIO ONE 2

by Larry the O DVD ROM

Power Tools for Studio One 2 shows the reader how to get around Studio One and perform recording, editing, mixing, and mastering. From the simplicity of drag-and-drop to the integration of mixing and mastering, Studio One is a fast, powerful, and fun way to make music.

Book/DVD-ROM Pack
978-1-4584-0226-4 .... $39.99

POWER TOOLS FOR LOGIC PRO 9

by Rick Silva DVD ROM

Power Tools for Logic Pro 9 unlocks Logic's immense capabilities to help you achieve amazing results for your audio and music productions with techniques you won't find in beginner-level books or videos. Rick Silva teaches powerful ways to use both Studio and Express, giving you easy-to-understand strategies for using the complex production tools built into Logic.

Book/DVD-ROM Pack
978-1-4234-4345-2 .... $39.99

POWER TOOLS FOR PRO TOOLS 10

by Glenn Lorbecki DVD ROM

Instructor, certified *Pro Tools* trainer, and award-winning producer/engineer Glenn Lorbecki will walk you through the best ways to get the most of out of Pro Tools 10. See and experience the new features incorporated in this powerful software offering, all the way from the new ways it handles data, memory, and gain functions to some seemingly small updates that make a huge difference in your productivity.

Book/DVD-ROM
978-1-4584-0035-2 .... $39.99

POWER TOOLS FOR REASON 6

by Andrew Eisele DVD ROM

Power Tools for Reason 6 is a comprehensive book that provides a quick-start tutorial that not only gets you up and running quickly, but also delves into advanced sequencing and mixing techniques. With the advent of Reason 6, it is now possible to record, mix, and produce music at a professional level. With an unbelievable array of tools, you'll find everything necessary to complete your projects from start to finish.

Book/DVD-ROM Pack
978-1-4584-0227-1 .... $39.99

POWER TOOLS FOR CUBASE 5

by Brian McConnon DVD ROM

The author channels his 15 years of working daily with Cubase into this ultimate guide to the most productive tips, tricks, and shortcuts for making great music with Cubase 5. Covers VariAudio and Pitch Correct, Groove Agent One and Beat Designer, and LoopMash—with expert tips from top artists, producers, and engineers.

Book/DVD-ROM Pack
978-1-4234-7453-1 .... $39.99

www.halleonardbooks.com

Prices, content, and availability subject to change without notice.

0512